The Jesus
Mysteries

The Jesus Mysteries

Was the "Original Jesus" a Pagan God?

TIMOTHY FREKE AND PETER GANDY

Harmony Books
New York

With special thanks to Ellen Freke, our editor Lizzie Hutchins, our agent Susan Mears and to Michelle Pilley and all at Thorsons.

Copyright © 1999 by Tim Freke and Peter Gandy

The extracts from R.J. Hoffmann, *Celsus on the True Doctrine*,
are reproduced by kind permission of Oxford University Press.

Published by Harmony Books, New York, New York.
Member of the Crown Publishing Group.

Random House, Inc. New York, Toronto, London, Sydney, Auckland

www.randomhouse.com

Harmony Books is a registered trademark and the Harmony Books
colophon is a trademark of Random House, Inc.
Originally published in Great Britain by HarperCollins Publishers, Ltd., in 1999.
Published by Harmony Books in 2000.

Printed in the United States of America

Library of Congress Cataloging-in-Publication Data
Freke, Timothy, 1959–
The Jesus mysteries : was the "original Jesus" a pagan god? /
Timothy Freke and Peter Gandy.
p. cm
Includes bibliographical references (p.   ) and index.
1. Christianity and other religions—Greek.   2. Jesus Christ—Historicity.
3. Mysteries, Religious.   4. Greece—Religion.   I. Gandy, Peter.   II. Title.
BR128.G8 F69   2000
232.9—dc21   99-088179

ISBN 0-609-60581-X

10 9 8 7 6 5 4 3 2

This book is dedicated
to the Christ
in you.

Contents

1

The Unthinkable
Thought

Jesus said, "It is to those who are worthy of my Mysteries that I tell my Mysteries." [1]

The Gospel of Thomas

On the site where the Vatican now stands there once stood a Pagan temple. Here Pagan priests observed sacred ceremonies, which early Christians found so disturbing that they tried to erase all evidence of them ever having been practiced. What were these shocking Pagan rites? Gruesome sacrifices or obscene orgies perhaps? This is what we have been led to believe. But the truth is far stranger than this fiction.

Where today the gathered faithful revere their Lord Jesus Christ, the ancients worshiped another godman who, like Jesus, had been miraculously born on December 25 before three shepherds. In this ancient sanctuary Pagan congregations once glorified a Pagan redeemer who, like Jesus, was said to have ascended to heaven and to have promised to come again at the end of time to judge the quick and the dead. On the same spot where the Pope celebrates the Catholic mass, Pagan priests also celebrated a symbolic meal of bread and wine in memory of their savior who, just like Jesus, had declared:

> He who will not eat of my body and drink of my blood, so that he will be made one with me and I with him, the same shall not know salvation. [2]

When we began to uncover such extraordinary similarities between the story of Jesus and Pagan myth we were stunned. We had been brought up in a culture which portrays Paganism and Christianity as entirely antagonistic religious perspectives. How could such astonishing resemblances be explained? We were intrigued and began to search farther. The more we looked, the more resemblances we found. To account for the wealth of evidence we were unearthing we felt compelled to completely review our understanding of the relationship between Paganism and Christianity, to question beliefs that we previously regarded as unquestionable and to imagine possibilities that at first seemed impossible. Some readers will find our conclusions shocking and others heretical, but for us they are merely the simplest and most obvious way of accounting for the evidence we have amassed.

We have become convinced that the story of Jesus is not the biography of a historical Messiah, but a myth based on perennial Pagan stories. Christianity was not a new and unique revelation but actually a Jewish adaptation of the ancient Pagan Mystery religion. This is what we have called *The Jesus Mysteries Thesis*. It may sound far-fetched at first, just as it did initially to us. There is, after all, a great deal of unsubstantiated nonsense written about the "real" Jesus, so any revolutionary theory should be approached with a healthy dose of skepticism. But although this book makes extraordinary claims, it is not just entertaining fantasy or sensational speculation. It is firmly based upon the available historical sources and the latest scholarly research. While we hope to have made it accessible to the general reader, we have also included copious notes giving sources, references, and greater detail for those who wish to analyze our arguments more thoroughly.

Although still radical and challenging today, many of the ideas we explore are actually far from new. As long ago as the Renaissance, mystics and scholars saw the origins of Christianity in the ancient Egyptian religion. Visionary scholars at the turn of the nineteenth century also made comparable conjectures to our own. In recent decades, modern academics have repeatedly pointed toward the possibilities we consider. Yet few have dared to boldly state the obvious conclusions that we have drawn. Why? Because to do so is taboo.

For 2,000 years the West has been dominated by the idea that Christianity is sacred and unique while Paganism is primitive and the work of the Devil. To even consider that they could be parts of the same tradition has been simply unthinkable. Therefore, although the true origins of Christianity have been obvious all along, few have been able to see them, because to do so requires a radical break with the conditioning of our culture. Our contribution has been to dare to think the unthinkable and to present our conclusions in a popular book rather than some dry academic tome. This is certainly not the last word on this complex subject, but we hope it may be a significant call for a complete reappraisal of the origins of Christianity.

THE PAGAN MYSTERIES

In Greek tragedies the chorus reveals the fate of the protagonists before the play begins. Sometimes it is easier to understand the journey if one is already aware of the destination and the terrain to be covered. Before diving deeper into detail, therefore, we would like to retrace our process of discovery and so provide a brief overview of the book.

We had shared an obsession with world mysticism all our lives which recently had led us to explore spirituality in the ancient world. Popular understanding inevitably lags a long way behind the cutting edge of scholarly research and, like most people, we initially had an inaccurate and outdated view of Paganism. We had been taught to imagine a primitive superstition, which indulged in idol worship and bloody sacrifice, and dry philosophers wearing togas stumbling blindly toward what we today call *science.* We were familiar with various Greek myths, which showed the partisan and capricious nature of the Olympian gods and goddesses. All in all, Paganism seemed primitive and fundamentally alien. After many years of study, however, our understanding has been transformed.

Pagan spirituality was actually the sophisticated product of a highly developed culture. The state religions, such as the Greek worship of the Olympian gods, were little more than outer pomp and ceremony. The real spirituality of the people expressed itself through the vibrant and mystical "Mystery religions." At first underground and heretical movements, these Mysteries spread and flourished throughout the ancient Mediterranean, inspiring the greatest minds of the Pagan world, who regarded them as the very source of civilization.

Each Mystery tradition had exoteric Outer Mysteries, consisting of myths, which were common knowledge, and rituals, which were open to anyone who wanted to participate. There were also esoteric Inner Mysteries, which were a sacred secret known only to those who had undergone a powerful process of initiation. Initiates of the Inner Mysteries had the mystical meaning of the rituals and myths of the Outer Mysteries revealed to them, a process that brought about personal transformation and spiritual enlightenment.

The philosophers of the ancient world were the spiritual masters of the Inner Mysteries. They were mystics and miracle-workers, more comparable to Hindu gurus than dusty academics. The great Greek philosopher Pythagoras, for example, is remembered today for his mathematical theorem, but few people picture him as he actually was—a flamboyant sage, who was believed to be able to miraculously still the winds and raise the dead.

At the heart of the Mysteries were myths concerning a dying and resurrecting godman, who was known by many different names. In Egypt he was Osiris, in Greece Dionysus, in Asia Minor Attis, in Syria Adonis, in Italy Bacchus, in Persia Mithras. Fundamentally all these godmen are the same mythical being. As was the practice from as early as the third century BCE,[3,4] in this book we will use the combined name *Osiris-Dionysus* to denote his universal and composite nature, and his particular names when referring to a specific Mystery tradition.

From the fifth century BCE philosophers such as Xenophanes and Empedocles had ridiculed taking the stories of the gods and goddesses literally. They viewed them as allegories of human spiritual experience. The myths of Osiris-Dionysus should not be understood as just intriguing tales, therefore, but as a symbolic language, which encodes the mystical teachings of the Inner Mysteries. Because of this, although the details were developed and adapted over time by different cultures, the myth of Osiris-Dionysus has remained essentially the same.

The various myths of the different godmen of the Mysteries share what the great mythologist Joseph Campbell called "the same anatomy." Just as every human is physically unique yet it is possible to talk of the general anatomy of the human body, so with these different myths it is possible to see both their uniqueness and fundamental sameness. A helpful comparison may be the relationship between Shakespeare's *Romeo and Juliet* and Bernstein's *West Side Story*. One is a sixteenth-century English tragedy about wealthy Italian families, while the other is a twentieth-century American musical about street gangs. On the face of it they look very different, yet they are essentially the same story. Similarly, the tales told about the godmen of the Pagan Mysteries are essentially the same, although they take different forms.

The more we studied the various versions of the myth of Osiris-Dionysus, the more it became obvious that the story of Jesus had all the characteristics of this perennial tale. Event by event, we found we were able to construct Jesus' supposed biography from mythic motifs previously relating to Osiris-Dionysus:

- ❖ Osiris-Dionysus is God made flesh, the savior and "Son of God."
- ❖ His father is God and his mother is a mortal virgin.
- ❖ He is born in a cave or humble cowshed on December 25 before three shepherds.
- ❖ He offers his followers the chance to be born again through the rites of baptism.
- ❖ He miraculously turns water into wine at a marriage ceremony.
- ❖ He rides triumphantly into town on a donkey while people wave palm leaves to honor him.
- ❖ He dies at Eastertime as a sacrifice for the sins of the world.
- ❖ After his death he descends to hell, then on the third day he rises from the dead and ascends to heaven in glory.
- ❖ His followers await his return as the judge during the Last Days.
- ❖ His death and resurrection are celebrated by a ritual meal of bread and wine, which symbolize his body and blood.

These are just some of the motifs shared between the tales of Osiris-Dionysus and the biography of Jesus. Why are these remarkable similarities not common knowledge? Because, as we were to discover later, the early Roman Church did everything in its power to prevent us perceiving them. It systematically destroyed Pagan sacred literature in a brutal program of eradicating the Mysteries—a task it performed so completely that today Paganism is regarded as a "dead" religion.

Although surprising to us now, to writers of the first few centuries CE these similarities between the new Christian religion and the ancient Mysteries were extremely obvious. Pagan critics of Christianity, such as the satirist Celsus, complained that this recent religion was nothing more than a pale reflection of their own ancient teachings. Early "Church fathers," such as Justin Martyr, Tertullian, and Irenaeus, were understandably disturbed and resorted to the desperate claim that these similarities were the result of *diabolical mimicry*. Using one of the most absurd arguments ever advanced, they accused the Devil of "plagiarism by anticipation," of deviously copying the true story of Jesus before it had actually happened in an attempt to mislead the gullible! These Church fathers struck us as no less devious than the Devil they hoped to incriminate.

Other Christian commentators have claimed that the myths of the Mysteries were like "pre-echoes" of the literal coming of Jesus, somewhat like premonitions or prophecies. This is a more generous version of the diabolical mimicry theory, but seemed no less ridiculous to us. There was nothing other than cultural prejudice to make us see the Jesus story as the literal culmination of its many mythical precursors. Viewed impartially, it appeared to be just another version of the same basic story.

The obvious explanation is that as early Christianity became the dominant power in the previously Pagan world, popular motifs from Pagan mythology became grafted onto the biography of Jesus. This is a possibility that is even put forward by many Christian theologians. The virgin birth, for example, is often regarded as an extraneous later addition that should not be understood literally. Such motifs were "borrowed" from Paganism in the same way that Pagan festivals were adopted as Christian saints' days. This theory is common among those who go looking for the "real" Jesus hidden under the weight of accumulated mythological debris.

Attractive as it appears at first, to us this explanation seemed inadequate. We had collated such a comprehensive body of similarities that there remained hardly any significant elements in the biography of Jesus that we did not find prefigured by the Mysteries. On top of this, we discovered that even Jesus' teachings were not original, but had been anticipated by the Pagan sages! If there was a "real" Jesus somewhere underneath all this, we would have to acknowledge that we could know absolutely nothing about him, for all that remained for us was later Pagan accretions! Such a position seemed absurd. Surely there was a more elegant solution to this conundrum?

THE GNOSTICS

While we were puzzling over these discoveries, we began to question the received picture of the early Church and have a look at the evidence for ourselves. We discovered that far from being the united congregation of saints and martyrs that traditional history would have us believe, the early Christian community was actually made up of a whole spectrum of different groups. These can be broadly categorized into two different schools. On the one hand there were those we will call *Literalists*, because what defines them is that they take the Jesus story as a literal account of historical events. It was this school of Christianity that was adopted by the Roman Empire in the fourth century CE, becoming Roman Catholicism and all its subsequent offshoots. On the other hand, however, there were also radically different Christians known as *Gnostics*.[5]

These forgotten Christians were later persecuted out of existence by the Literalist Roman Church with such thoroughness that until recently we knew little about them except through the writings of their detractors. Only a handful of original Gnostic texts survived, none of which were published before the nineteenth century. This situation changed dramatically, however, with a remarkable discovery in 1945 when an Arab peasant stumbled upon a whole library of Gnostic gospels hidden in a cave near Nag Hammadi in Egypt. This gave scholars access to many texts which were in wide circulation among early Christians, but which were deliberately excluded from the canon of the New Testament—gospels attributed to Thomas and Philip, texts recording the acts of Peter and the 12 disciples, apocalypses attributed to Paul and James, and so on.

It seemed to us extraordinary that a whole library of early Christian documents could be discovered, containing what purport to be the teachings of Christ and his disciples, and yet so few modern followers of Jesus should even know of their existence. Why hasn't every Christian rushed out to read these newly discovered words of the Master? What keeps them confined to the small number of gospels selected for inclusion in the New Testament? It seems that even though 2,000 years have passed since the Gnostics were purged, during which time the Roman Church has split into Protestantism and thousands of other alternative groups, the Gnostics are still not regarded as a legitimate voice of Christianity.

Those who do explore the Gnostic gospels discover a form of Christianity quite alien to the religion with which they are familiar. We found ourselves studying strange esoteric tracts with titles such as *Hypostasis of the Archons* and *The Thought of Norea*. It felt as if we were in an episode of *Star Trek*— and in a way we were. The Gnostics truly were "psychonauts" who boldly explored the final frontiers of inner space, searching for the origins and meaning of life. These people were mystics and creative free-thinkers. It was obvious to us why they were so hated by the bishops of the Literalist Church hierarchy.

To Literalists, the Gnostics were dangerous heretics. In volumes of anti-Gnostic works—an unintentional testimony to the power and influence of Gnosticism within early Christianity—they painted them as Christians who had "gone native." They claimed they had become contaminated by the Paganism that surrounded them and had abandoned the purity of the true faith. The Gnostics, on the other hand, saw themselves as the authentic Christian tradition and the orthodox bishops as an "imitation church."[6] They claimed to know the secret Inner Mysteries of Christianity, which the Literalists did not possess.

As we explored the beliefs and practices of the Gnostics we became convinced that the Literalists had at least been right about one thing: the Gnostics were little different from Pagans. Like the philosophers of the Pagan Mysteries, they believed in reincarnation, honored the goddess Sophia, and were immersed in the mystical Greek philosophy of Plato. *Gnostics* means "Knowers," a name they acquired because, like the initiates of the Pagan Mysteries, they believed that their secret teachings had the power to impart *Gnosis*—direct experiential "Knowledge of God." Just as the goal of a Pagan initiate was to become a god, so for the Gnostics the goal of the Christian initiate was to become a Christ.

What particularly struck us was that the Gnostics were not concerned with the historical Jesus. They viewed the Jesus story in the same way that the Pagan philosophers viewed the myths of Osiris-Dionysus—as an allegory that encoded secret mystical teachings. This insight crystallized for us a remarkable possibility. Perhaps the explanation for the similarities between Pagan myths and the biography of Jesus had been staring us in the face the whole time, but we had been so caught up with traditional ways of thinking that we had been unable to see it.

THE JESUS MYSTERIES THESIS

The traditional version of history bequeathed to us by the authorities of the Roman Church is that Christianity developed from the teachings of a Jewish Messiah and that Gnosticism was a later deviation. What would happen, we wondered, if the picture were reversed and Gnosticism viewed as the authentic Christianity, just as the Gnostics themselves claimed? Could it be that orthodox Christianity was a later deviation from Gnosticism and that Gnosticism was a synthesis of Judaism and the Pagan Mystery religion? This was the beginning of the Jesus Mysteries Thesis.

Boldly stated, the picture that emerged for us was as follows. We knew that most ancient Mediterranean cultures had adopted the ancient Mysteries, adapting them to their own national tastes and creating their own version of the myth of the dying and resurrecting godman. Perhaps some of the Jews had, likewise, adopted the Pagan Mysteries and created their own version of the Mysteries, which we now know as Gnosticism. Perhaps initiates of the Jewish Mysteries had adapted the potent symbolism of the Osiris-Dionysus myths into a myth of their own, the hero of which was the Jewish dying and resurrecting godman Jesus.

If this was so, then the Jesus story was not a biography at all but a consciously crafted vehicle for encoded spiritual teachings created by Jewish Gnostics. As in the Pagan Mysteries, initiation into the Inner Mysteries would reveal the myth's allegorical meaning. Perhaps those uninitiated into the Inner Mysteries had mistakenly come to regard the Jesus myth as historical fact and in this way Literalist Christianity had been created. Perhaps the Inner Mysteries of Christianity, which the Gnostics taught but which the Literalists denied existed, revealed that the Jesus story was not a factual account of God's one and only visit to planet Earth, but a mystical teaching story designed to help each one of us become a Christ.

The Jesus story does have all the hallmarks of a myth, so could it be that that is exactly what it is? After all, no one has read the newly discovered Gnostic gospels and taken their fantastic stories as literally true; they are readily seen as myths. It is only familiarity and cultural prejudice that prevent us from seeing the New Testament gospels in the same light. If those gospels had also been lost to us and only recently discovered, who would read these tales for the first time and believe they were historical accounts of a man born of a virgin, who had walked on water and returned from the dead? Why should we consider the stories of Osiris, Dionysus, Adonis, Attis, Mithras, and the other Pagan Mystery saviors as fables, yet come across essentially the same story told in a Jewish context and believe it to be the biography of a carpenter from Bethlehem?

We had both been raised as Christians and were surprised to find that, despite years of open-minded spiritual exploration, it still felt somehow dangerous to even dare think such thoughts. Early indoctrination reaches very deep. We were in effect saying that Jesus was a Pagan god and that Christianity was a heretical product of Paganism! It seemed outrageous. Yet this theory explained the similarities between the stories of Osiris-Dionysus and Jesus Christ in a simple and elegant way. They are parts of one developing mythos.

The Jesus Mysteries Thesis answered many puzzling questions, yet it also opened up new dilemmas. Isn't there indisputable historical evidence for the existence of Jesus the man? And how could Gnosticism be the original Christianity when St. Paul, the earliest Christian we know about, is so vociferously anti-Gnostic? And is it really credible that such an insular and anti-Pagan people as the Jews could have adopted the Pagan Mysteries? And how could it have happened that a consciously created myth came to be believed as history? And if Gnosticism represents genuine Christianity, why was it Literalist Christianity that came to dominate the world as the most influential religion of all time? All of these difficult questions would have to be satisfactorily answered before we could wholeheartedly accept such a radical theory as the Jesus Mysteries Thesis.

THE GREAT COVER-UP

Our new account of the origins of Christianity only seemed improbable because it contradicted the received view. As we pushed farther with our research, the traditional picture began to unravel completely all around us. We found ourselves embroiled in a world of schism and power struggles, of forged documents and false identities, of letters that had been edited and added to, and of the wholesale destruction of historical evidence. We focused forensically on the few facts we could be confident of, as if we were detectives on the verge of cracking a sensational "whodunit," or perhaps more accurately as if we were uncovering an ancient and unacknowledged miscarriage of justice. For, time and again, when we critically examined what genuine evidence remained, we found that the history of Christianity bequeathed to us by the Roman Church was a gross distortion of the truth. Actually the evidence completely endorsed the Jesus Mysteries Thesis. It was becoming increasingly obvious that we had been deliberately deceived, that the Gnostics were indeed the original Christians, and that their anarchic mysticism had been hijacked by an authoritarian institution which had created from it a dogmatic religion—and then brutally enforced the greatest cover-up in history.

One of the major players in this cover-up operation was a character called Eusebius who, at the beginning of the fourth century, compiled from legends, fabrications, and his own imagination the only early history of Christianity that still exists today. All subsequent histories have been forced to base themselves on Eusebius' dubious claims, because there has been little other information to draw on. All those with a different perspective on Christianity were branded as heretics and eradicated. In this way falsehoods compiled in the fourth century have come down to us as established facts.

Eusebius was employed by the Roman Emperor Constantine, who made Christianity the state religion of the Empire and gave Literalist Christianity the power it needed to begin the final eradication of Paganism and Gnosticism. Constantine wanted "one God, one religion" to consolidate his claim of "one Empire, one Emperor." He oversaw the creation of the Nicene creed—the article of faith repeated in churches to this day—and Christians who refused to assent to this creed were banished from the Empire or otherwise silenced.

This "Christian" Emperor then returned home from Nicaea and had his wife suffocated and his son murdered. He deliberately remained unbaptized until his deathbed so that he could continue his atrocities and still receive forgiveness of sins and a guaranteed place in heaven by being baptized at the last moment. Although he had his "spin doctor" Eusebius compose a suitably obsequious biography for him, he was actually a monster—just like many Roman Emperors before him. Is it really at all surprising that a "history" of the origins of Christianity created by an employee in the service of a Roman tyrant should turn out to be a pack of lies?

Elaine Pagels, one of the foremost academic authorities on early Christianity, writes:

> It is the winners who write history—their way. No wonder, then, that the traditional accounts of the origins of Christianity first defined the terms (naming themselves "orthodox" and their opponents "heretics"); then they proceeded to demonstrate—at least to their own satisfaction—that their triumph was historically inevitable, or, in religious terms, "guided by the Holy Spirit." But the discoveries [of the Gnostic gospels] at Nag Hammadi reopen fundamental questions.[7]

History is indeed written by the victors. The creation of an appropriate history has always been part of the arsenal of political manipulation. The

Roman Church created a history of the triumph of Literalist Christianity in much the same partisan way that, two millennia later, Hollywood created tales of "cowboys and Indians" to relate "how the West was won" not "how the West was lost." History is not simply related, it is created. Ideally, the motivation is to explain historical evidence and come to an accurate understanding of how the present has been created by the past. All too often, however, it is simply to glorify and justify the status quo. Such histories conceal as much as they reveal.

To dare to question a received history is not easy. It is difficult to believe that something that you have been told is true from childhood could actually be a product of falsification and fantasy. It must have been hard for those Russians brought up on tales of kindly "Uncle Joe" Stalin to accept that he was actually responsible for the deaths of millions. It must have strained credibility when those opposing his regime claimed that he had in fact murdered many of the heroes of the Russian revolution. It must have seemed ridiculous when they asserted that he had even had the images of his rivals removed from photographs and completely fabricated historical events. Yet all these things are true.

It is easy to believe that something *must* be true because everyone else believes it. But the truth often only comes to light by daring to question the unquestionable, by doubting notions which are so commonly believed that they are taken for granted. The Jesus Mysteries Thesis is the product of such an openness of mind. When it first occurred to us, it seemed absurd and impossible. Now it seems obvious and ordinary. The Vatican was constructed upon the site of an ancient Pagan sanctuary because the new is always built upon the old. In the same way Christianity itself has as its foundations the Pagan spirituality that preceded it. What is more plausible than to posit the gradual evolution of spiritual ideas, with Christianity emerging from the ancient Pagan Mysteries in a seamless historical continuum? It is only because the conventional history has been so widely believed for so long that this idea could be seen as heretical and shocking.

RECOVERING MYSTICAL CHRISTIANITY

As the final pieces of the puzzle were falling into place, we came across a small picture tucked away in the appendices of an old academic book. It was a drawing of a third-century CE amulet. We have used it as the cover of this book. It shows a crucified figure which most people would immediately recognize as Jesus. Yet the Greek words name the figure Orpheus Bacchus, one of the pseudonyms of Osiris-Dionysus. To the author of the book in which we found the picture, this amulet was an anomaly. Who could it have possibly belonged to? Was it a crucified Pagan deity or some sort of Gnostic synthesis of Paganism and Christianity? Either way it was deeply puzzling. For us, however, this amulet was perfectly understandable. It was an unexpected confirmation of the Jesus Mysteries Thesis. The image could be that of either Jesus or Osiris-Dionysus. To the initiated, these were both names for essentially the same figure.

The "chance" discovery of this amulet made us feel as though the universe itself was encouraging us to make our findings public. In different ways the Jesus Mysteries Thesis has been proposed by mystics and scholars for centuries, but has always ended up being ignored. It now felt like an idea whose moment had come. We did, however, have misgivings about writing this book. We knew that it would inevitably upset certain Christians, something that we had no desire to do. Certainly it has been hard to be constantly surrounded by lies and injustices without experiencing a certain amount of outrage at the negative misrepresentation of the Gnostics, and to have become aware of the great riches of Pagan culture without feeling grief that they were so wantonly destroyed. Yet we do not have some sort of anti-Christian agenda. Far from it.

Those who have read our other works will know that our interest is not in further division, but in acknowledging the unity that lies at the heart of all spiritual traditions—and this present book is no exception. Early Literalist Christians mistakenly believed that the Jesus story was different from other stories of Osiris-Dionysus because Jesus alone had been a historical rather than a mythical figure. This has left Christians feeling that their faith is in opposition to all others, which it is not. We hope that by understanding its true origins in the ongoing evolution of a universal human spirituality, Christianity may be able to free itself from this self-imposed isolation.

While the Jesus Mysteries Thesis clearly rewrites history, we do not see it as undermining the Christian faith, but as suggesting that Christianity is in fact richer than we previously imagined. The Jesus story is a perennial myth with the power to impart the saving Gnosis, which can transform each one of us into a Christ, not merely a history of events that happened to someone else 2,000 years ago. Belief in the Jesus story was originally the first step in

Christian spirituality—the Outer Mysteries. Its significance was to be explained by an enlightened teacher when the seeker was spiritually ripe. These Inner Mysteries imparted a mystical Knowledge of God beyond mere belief in dogmas. Although many inspired Christian mystics throughout history have intuitively seen through to this deeper symbolic level of understanding, as a culture we have inherited only the Outer Mysteries of Christianity. We have kept the form, but lost the inner meaning. Our hope is that this book can play some small part in reclaiming the true mystical Christian inheritance.

The Pagan Mysteries

Blest is the happy man
Who knows the Mysteries the gods ordain,
And sanctifies his life,
Joins soul with soul in mystic unity,
And, by due ritual made pure,
Enters the ecstasy of mountain solitudes;
Who observes the mystic rites
Made lawful by the Great Mother;
Who crowns his head with ivy,
And shakes his wand in worship of Dionysus.[1]

Euripides

Paganism is a "dead" religion—or more accurately an "exterminated" religion. It did not simply fade away into oblivion. It was actively suppressed and annihilated, its temples and shrines desecrated and demolished, and its great sacred books thrown onto bonfires. No living lineage has been left to explain its ancient beliefs. So, the Pagan worldview has to be reconstructed from the archaeological evidence and texts that have survived, like some giant metaphysical jigsaw puzzle.

Pagan was originally a derogatory term meaning country-dweller, used by Christians to imply that the spirituality of the ancients was some primitive rural superstition. But this is not true. Paganism was the spirituality which inspired the unequaled magnificence of the Giza pyramids, the exquisite architecture of the Parthenon, the legendary sculptures of Phideas, the powerful plays of Euripides and Sophocles, and the sublime philosophy of Socrates and Plato.

Pagan civilization built vast libraries to house hundreds of thousands of works of literary and scientific genius. Its natural philosophers speculated that human beings had evolved from animals.[2] Its astronomers knew the Earth was a sphere,[3] which, along with the planets, revolves around the sun.[4] They had even estimated its circumference to within one degree of accuracy.[5] The ancient Pagan world sustained a population not matched again in Europe until the eighteenth century.[6] In Greece, Pagan culture gave birth to the concepts of democracy, rational philosophy, public libraries, theater, and the Olympic Games, creating a blueprint for our modern world. What was the spirituality that inspired these momentous cultural achievements?

Most people associate Paganism with either rustic witchcraft or the myths of the gods of Olympus as recorded by Hesiod and Homer. Pagan spirituality did indeed embrace both. The country people practiced their traditional shamanic nature worship to maintain the fertility of the land and the city authorities propped up formal state religions, such as the worship of the Olympian gods, to maintain the power of the status quo.

It was, however, a third, more mystical, expression of the Pagan spirit that inspired the great minds of the ancient world. The thinkers, artists, and innovators of antiquity were initiates of various religions known as Mysteries. These remarkable men and women held the Mysteries to be the heart and soul of their culture. The Greek historian Zosimos writes that without the Mysteries "life for the Greeks would be unlivable" for "the sacred Mysteries hold the whole human race together."[7] The eminent Roman statesman Cicero enthuses:

> These Mysteries have brought us from rustic savagery to a cultivated and refined civilization. The rites of the Mysteries are called "initiations" and in truth we have learned from them the first principles of life. We have gained the understanding not only to live happily but also to die with better hope.[8]

Unlike the traditional rituals of the official state religions, which were designed to aid social cohesion, the Mysteries were an individualistic form of spirituality, which offered mystical visions and personal enlightenment.[9] Initiates underwent a secret process of initiation, which profoundly transformed their state of consciousness. The poet Pindar reveals that an initiate into the Mysteries "knows the end of life and its God-given beginning."[10] Lucius Apuleius, a poet-philosopher, writes of his experience of initiation as a spiritual rebirth, which he celebrated as his birthday, an experience for which he felt a "debt of gratitude" that he "could never hope to repay."[11] Plato, the most influential philosopher of all time, relates:

> We beheld the beatific visions and were initiated into the Mystery which may be truly called blessed, celebrated by us in a state of innocence. We beheld calm, happy, simple, eternal visions, resplendent in pure light.[12]

The great Pagan philosophers were the enlightened masters of the Mysteries. Although they are often portrayed today as dry academic intellectuals, they were actually enigmatic gurus. Empedocles, like his master Pythagoras, was a charismatic miracle-worker.[13] Socrates was an eccentric mystic prone to being suddenly overcome by states of rapture during which his friends would discover him staring off into space for hours.[14] Heraclitus was asked by the citizens of Ephesus to become a lawmaker, but turned the offer down so that he could continue playing with the children in the temple.[15] Anaxagoras shocked ordinary citizens by completely abandoning his farm to fully devote his life to "the higher philosophy."[16] Diogenes owned nothing and lived in a jar at the entrance of a temple.[17] The inspired playwright Euripides wrote his greatest tragedies during solitary retreats in an isolated cave.[18]

All of these idiosyncratic sages were steeped in the mysticism of the Mysteries, which they expressed in their philosophy. Olympiodorus, a follower of Plato, tells us that his master paraphrased the Mysteries everywhere.[19] The works of Heraclitus were renowned even in ancient times for being obscure and impenetrable, yet Diogenes explains that they are crystal clear to an initiate of the Mysteries. Of studying Heraclitus he writes:

> It is a hard road to follow, filled with darkness and gloom; but if an initiate leads you on the way, it becomes brighter than the radiance of the sun.[20]

At the heart of Pagan philosophy is an understanding that all things are One. The Mysteries aimed at awakening within the initiate a sublime experience of this Oneness. Sallustius declares: "Every initiation aims at uniting us with the World and with the Deity."[21] Plotinus describes the initiate transcending his limited sense of himself as a separate ego and experiencing mystical union with God:

> As if borne away, or possessed by a god, he attains to solitude in untroubled stillness, nowhere deflected in his being and unbusied with self, utterly at rest and become very rest. He does not converse with a statue or image but with Godhead itself. And this is no object of vision, but another mode of seeing, a detachment from self, a simplification and surrender of self, a yearning for contact, and a stillness and meditation directed towards transformation. Whoever sees himself in this way has attained likeness to God; let him abandon himself and find the end of his journeying.[22]

No wonder the initiate Sopatros poetically mused, "I came out of the Mystery Hall feeling like a stranger to myself."[23]

THE SACRED SPECTACLE AT ELEUSIS

What were these ancient Mysteries that could inspire such reverent awe and heartfelt appreciation? The Mystery religion was practiced for thousands of years, during which time it spread throughout the ancient world, taking on many different forms. Some were frenzied and others meditative. Some involved bloody animal sacrifice, while others were presided over by strict vegetarians. At certain moments in history the Mysteries were openly practiced by whole populations and were endorsed, or at least tolerated, by the state. At other times they were a small-scale and secretive affair, for fear of persecution by unsympathetic authorities. Central to all of these forms of the Mysteries, however, was the myth of a dying and resurrecting godman.

The Greek Mysteries celebrated at Eleusis in honor of the Great Mother goddess and the godman Dionysus were the most famous of all the Mystery cults. The sanctuary of Eleusis was finally destroyed by bands of fanatical Christian monks in 396 CE, but up until this tragic act of vandalism the Mysteries had been celebrated there for over eleven centuries.[24] At the height of their popularity people were coming from all over the then known world to be initiated: men and women, rich and poor, slaves and emperors[25]—even a Brahmin priest from India.[26]

Each year some 30,000 Athenian citizens embarked on a 30-kilometer barefoot pilgrimage to the sacred site of Eleusis on the coast to celebrate the autumn Mysteries of Dionysus.[27] For days they would have been preparing for this important religious event by fasting, offering sacrifices, and undergoing ritual purification. As those about to be initiated danced along the "Sacred Way" to Eleusis, accompanied by the frenzied beat of cymbals and tambourines, they were accosted by masked men who abused and insulted them, while others beat them with sticks.[28] At the head of the procession was carried the statue of Dionysus himself, leading them ever onward. After ritual naked bathing in the sea and other purification ceremonies the crowd reached the great doors of the Telesterion, a huge initiation hall. Only the chosen few who were already initiated or about to be initiated into the secret Mysteries could enter here.

What awesome ceremony was held behind these closed doors that touched the great philosophers, artists, statesmen, and scientists of the ancient world so deeply? All initiates were sworn to secrecy and held the Mysteries so sacred that they kept this oath.[29] From large numbers of hints and clues, however, we know that they witnessed a sublime theatrical spectacle. They were awed by sounds and dazzled by lights. They were bathed in the blaze of a huge fire and trembled to the nerve-shattering reverberations of a mighty gong. The Hierophant, the high priest of the Mysteries, was quite literally a showman who orchestrated a terrifyingly transformative dramatic reenactment of sacred myth. He himself was dressed as the central character—the godman Dionysus.[30]

A modern scholar writes:

A Mystery Religion was thus a divine drama which portrayed before the wondering eyes of the privileged observers the story of the struggles, sufferings, and victory of a patron deity, the travail of nature in which life ultimately triumphs over death, and joy is born of pain. The whole ritual of the Mysteries aimed especially at quickening the emotional life. No means of exciting the emotions was neglected in the passion-play, either by way of inducing careful predispositions or of supplying external stimulus. Tense mental anticipations heightened by a period of abstinence, hushed silences, imposing processions and elaborate pageantry, music loud and violent or soft and enthralling, delirious dances, the drinking of spirituous liquors, physical macerations, alternations of dense darkness and dazzling light, the sight of gorgeous ceremonial vestments, the handling of holy emblems, autosuggestion and the promptings of the Hierophant—these and many secrets of emotional exaltation were in vogue.[31]

This dramatization of the myth of Dionysus is the origin of tragedy and theater.[32] But the initiates were not a passive audience. They were participants who shared in the passion of the godman whose death and rebirth symbolically represented the death and spiritual rebirth of each one of them. As a modern authority explains:

> Dionysus was the god of the most blessed ecstasy and the most enraptured love. But he was also the persecuted god, the suffering and dying god, and all whom he loved, all who attended him, had to share his tragic fate.[33]

By witnessing the awesome tragedy of Dionysus, the initiates at Eleusis shared in his suffering, death and resurrection, and so experienced a spiritual purification known as "catharsis."[34]

The Mysteries did not offer religious dogmas to simply be believed, but a myth to be entered into. Initiation was not about learning something, but about experiencing an altered state of awareness. Plutarch, a Pagan high priest, confesses that those who had been initiated could produce no proof of the beliefs that they acquired. Aristotle maintains, "It is not necessary for the initiated to learn anything, but to receive impressions and to be put in a certain frame of mind."[35] The philosopher Proclus talks of the Mysteries as evoking a "sympathy of the soul with the ritual in a way that is unintelligible to us and divine, so that some of the initiates are stricken with panic, being filled with divine awe; others assimilate themselves to the holy symbols, leave their own identity, become at home with the gods, and experience divine possession."[36]

Why did the myth enacted by the Mysteries have such a profound effect?

ENCODED SECRET TEACHINGS

In antiquity the word *mythos* did not mean something "untrue," as it does for us today. Superficially a myth was an entertaining story, but to the initiated it was a sacred code that contained profound spiritual teachings.[37] Plato comments, "It looks as if those also who established rites of initiation for us were no fools, but that there is a hidden meaning in their teachings."[38] He explains that it is "those who have given their lives to true philosophy" who will grasp the "hidden meaning" encoded in the Mystery myths, and so become completely identified with the godman in an experience of mystical enlightenment.[39]

The ancient philosophers were not so foolish as to believe that the Mystery myths were literally true, but wise enough to recognize that they were an easy introduction to the profound mystical philosophy at the heart of the Mysteries. Sallustius writes:

> To wish to teach all men the truth of the gods causes the foolish to despise, because they cannot learn, and the good to be slothful, whereas to conceal the truth by myths prevents the former from despising philosophy and compels the latter to study it.[40]

It was the role of the priests and philosophers of the Mysteries to decode the hidden depths of spiritual meaning contained within the Mystery myths. Heliodorus, a priest of the Mysteries, explains:

> Philosophers and theologians do not disclose the meanings embedded in these stories to laymen but simply give them preliminary instruction in the form of a myth. But those who have reached the higher grades of the Mysteries they initiate into clear knowledge in the privacy of the holy shrine, in the light cast by the blazing torch of truth.[41]

The Mysteries were divided into various levels of initiation, which led an initiate step by step through ever deepening levels of understanding. The number of levels of initiation varied in different Mystery traditions, but essentially the initiate was led from the Outer Mysteries, in which the myths were understood superficially as religious stories, to the Inner Mysteries, in which the myths were revealed as spiritual allegories. First the initiate was ritually purified. Then they were taught the secret teachings on a one-to-one basis.[42] The highest stage was when the initiate understood the true meaning of the teachings and finally experienced what Theon of Smyrna calls "friendship and interior communion with God."

THE INTERNATIONAL MYSTERIES

The Mysteries dominated the Pagan world. No other deity is represented on the monuments of ancient Greece and Italy as much as Dionysus, godman of the Eleusinian Mysteries.[43] He is a deity with many names: Iacchos, Bassareus, Bromios, Euios, Sabazius, Zagreus, Yhyoneus, Lenaios, Eleuthereus, and so the list goes on.[44] But these are just some of his Greek names! The godman is an omnipresent mythic figure throughout the ancient Mediterranean, known in different ways by many cultures.

Five centuries before the birth of Christ, the Greek historian Herodotus, known as "the father of history," discovered this when he traveled to Egypt. On the shores of a sacred lake in the Nile delta he witnessed an enormous festival, held every year, in which the Egyptians performed a dramatic spectacle before "tens of thousands of men and women," representing the death and resurrection of Osiris. Herodotus was an initiate into the Greek Mysteries and recognized that what he calls "the Passion of Osiris" was the very same drama that initiates saw enacted before them at Eleusis as the Passion of Dionysus.[45] The Egyptian myth of Osiris is the primal myth of the Mystery godman and reaches back to prehistory. His story is so ancient that it can be found in pyramid texts written over 4,500 years ago![46]

In traveling to Egypt Herodotus was following in the footsteps of another great Greek. Before 670 BCE, Egypt had been a closed country, in the manner of Tibet or Japan more recently, but in this year she opened her borders and one of the first Greeks who traveled there in search of ancient wisdom was Pythagoras.[47] History remembers Pythagoras as the first "scientist" of the Western world, but although it is true that he brought back many mathematical theories to Greece from Egypt, to his contemporaries he would have seemed anything but scientific in the modern sense.

A wandering charismatic sage dressed in white robes and crowned with a gold coronet, Pythagoras was part scientist, part priest, and part magician.[48] He spent twenty-two years in the temples of Egypt, becoming an initiate of the ancient Egyptian Mysteries.[49] On returning to Greece he began to preach the wisdom he had learned, performing miracles, raising the dead, and giving oracles.

Inspired by Pythagoras, his disciples created a Greek Mystery religion modeled on the Egyptian Mysteries. They took the indigenous wine god Dionysus, who was a minor deity all but ignored by Hesiod and Homer, and transformed him into a Greek version of the mighty Egyptian Osiris, godman of the Mysteries. This initiated a religious and cultural revolution that was to transform Athens into the center of the civilized world.[50]

The followers of Pythagoras were models of virtue and learning, regarded as puritans by their neighbors. Strict vegetarians, they preached nonviolence toward all living things and shunned the temple cults that practiced the sacrifice of animals. This made it impossible for them to participate in the traditional Olympian religion of Athens. Forced to live on the fringes of acceptability, they often organized themselves into communities that shared all possessions in common, leaving them free to devote themselves to their mystical studies of mathematics, music, astronomy, and philosophy.[51] Nevertheless, the Mystery religion spread quickly among the ordinary people and within a few generations the Egyptian Mysteries of Osiris, now the Mysteries of Dionysus, inspired the glory of Classical Athens.

In the same way that Osiris was synthesized by the Greeks with their indigenous god Dionysus to create the Greek Mysteries, other Mediterranean cultures that adopted the Mystery religion also transformed one of their indigenous deities into the dying and resurrecting Mystery godman. So, the deity who was known as Osiris in Egypt and became Dionysus in Greece was called Attis in Asia Minor, Adonis in Syria, Bacchus in Italy, Mithras in Persia, and so on. His forms were many, but essentially he was the same perennial figure, whose collective identity was referred to as Osiris-Dionysus.[52]

Because the ancients recognized that all the various Mystery godmen were essentially the same mythic being, elements from different myths and rites were continually combined and recombined to create new forms of the Mysteries. In Alexandria, for example, a charismatic sage called Timotheus consciously fused Osiris and Dionysus to produce a new deity for the city called Serapis.[53] He also gave an elaborate account of the myth of the Mystery godman Attis. Lucius Apuleius received his initiation into the Egyptian Mysteries from a high priest named after the Persian godman Mithras. Coins were minted with Dionysus represented on one side and Mithras on the other.[54]

One modern authority tells us that "possessed by the knowledge of his own secret rites," the initiate of the Mysteries "found no difficulty in conforming to any religion in vogue."[55]

Like the Christian religion, which superseded it, the Mysteries reached across national boundaries, offering a spirituality that was relevant to all human beings, regardless of their racial origins or social status. Even as early as the fifth-century BCE philosophers such as Diogenes and Socrates called themselves "cosmopolitans"—"citizens of the cosmos"—rather than of any particular country or culture, which is testimony to the international nature of the Mysteries.[56]

One modern scholar, commenting on the merging and combining of different mystery traditions, writes:

> This went a long way towards weaning the minds of men from the idea of separate gods from the different nations, and towards teaching them that all national and local deities were but different forms of one great Power. But for the rise of Christianity and other religions, there can be little doubt but that the whole of the Graeco-Roman deities would continually have merged into Dionysus.[57]

OSIRIS-DIONYSUS AND JESUS CHRIST

Osiris-Dionysus had such universal appeal because he was seen as an Everyman figure who symbolically represented each initiate. Through understanding the allegorical myth of the Mystery godman, initiates could become aware that, like Osiris-Dionysus, they were also "God made flesh." They too were immortal Spirit trapped within a physical body. Through sharing in the death of Osiris-Dionysus initiates symbolically "died" to their lower earthly nature. Through sharing in his resurrection they were spiritually reborn and experienced their eternal and divine essence. This was the profound mystical teaching that the myth of Osiris-Dionysus encoded for those initiated into the Inner Mysteries, the truth of which initiates directly experienced for themselves.

Writing of the Egyptian Mystery godman Osiris, Sir Wallis Budge, who was keeper of antiquities in the British Museum, explains:

The Egyptians of every period in which they are known to us believed that Osiris was of divine origin, that he suffered death and mutilation at the hands of the power of evil, that after great struggle with these powers he rose again, that he became henceforth the king of the underworld and judge of the dead, and that because he had conquered death the righteous might also conquer death.[58]

He represented to men the idea of a man who was both God and man, and he typified to the Egyptians in all ages the being who by reason of his sufferings and death as a man could sympathize with them in their own sickness and death. The idea of his human personality also satisfied their cravings and yearnings for communion with a being who, though he was partly divine, yet had much in common with themselves. Originally they looked upon Osiris as a man who lived on the earth as they lived, who ate and drank, who suffered a cruel death, who by help of certain gods triumphed over death, and attained unto everlasting life. But what Osiris did they could also do.[59]

These are the key motifs that characterize the myths of all the Mystery godmen. What Budge writes of Osiris could equally be said of Dionysus, Attis, Adonis, Mithras, and the rest. It also describes the Jewish dying and resurrecting godman Jesus Christ. Like Osiris-Dionysus, he is also God Incarnate and God of the Resurrection. He also promises his followers spiritual rebirth through sharing in his divine Passion.

CONCLUSION

The Mysteries were clearly an extremely powerful force in the ancient world. Let's review what we've discovered about them:

❖ The Pagan Mysteries inspired the greatest minds of the ancient world.
❖ They were practiced in different forms by nearly every culture in the Mediterranean.
❖ They comprised Outer Mysteries, which were open to all, and secret Inner Mysteries known only to those who had undergone a powerful process of mystical initiation.

- ❖ At the heart of the Mysteries was the myth of a dying and resurrecting godman—Osiris-Dionysus.
- ❖ The Inner Mysteries revealed the myths of Osiris-Dionysus to be spiritual allegories encoding spiritual teachings.

The question, which intrigued us, was whether the Mysteries could have somehow influenced and shaped what we have inherited as the biography of Jesus? Unlike the various Pagan Mystery godmen, Jesus is traditionally viewed as a historical rather than a mythical figure, literally a man who was an incarnation of God, who suffered, died, and resurrected to bring salvation to all humankind. But could these elements of the Jesus story actually be mythical stories inherited from the Pagan Mysteries?

We began investigating the myths of Osiris-Dionysus more closely, searching for resemblances with the Jesus story. We were not prepared for the overwhelming number of similarities that we uncovered.

3

Diabolical
Mimicry

> Having heard it proclaimed through the prophets that the Christ was to come and that the ungodly among men were to be punished by fire, the wicked spirits put forward many to be called Sons of God, under the impression that they would be able to produce in men the idea that the things that were said with regard to Christ were merely marvellous tales, like the things that were said by the poets.[1]
>
> **Justin Martyr**

Although the remarkable similarities between the myths of Osiris-Dionysus and the supposed biography of Jesus Christ are generally unknown today, in the first few centuries CE they were obvious to Pagans and Christians alike. The Pagan philosopher and satirist Celsus criticized Christians for trying to pass off the Jesus story as a new revelation when it was actually an inferior imitation of Pagan myths. He asks:

> Are these distinctive happenings unique to the Christians—and if so, how are they unique? Or are ours to be accounted myths and theirs believed? What reasons do the Christians give for the distinctiveness of their beliefs? In truth there is nothing at all unusual about what the Christians believe, except that they believe it to the exclusion of more comprehensive truths about God.[2]

The early Christians were painfully aware of such criticisms.[3] How could Pagan myths which predated Christianity by hundreds of years have so much in common with the biography of the one and only savior Jesus? Desperate to come up with an explanation, the Church fathers resorted to one of the most absurd theories ever advanced. From the time of Justin Martyr in the second century onward, they declared that the Devil had plagiarized Christianity by anticipation in order to lead people astray![4] Knowing that the true Son of God was literally to come and walk the Earth, the Devil had copied the story of his life in advance of it happening and created the myths of Osiris-Dionysus.

The Church father Tertullian writes of the Devil's diabolical mimicry in creating the Mysteries of Mithras:

> The devil, whose business is to pervert the truth, mimics the exact circumstances of the Divine Sacraments. He baptizes his believers and promises forgiveness of sins from the Sacred Fount, and thereby initiates them into the religion of Mithras. Thus he celebrates the oblation of bread, and brings in the symbol of the resurrection. Let us therefore acknowledge the craftiness of the devil, who copies certain things of those that be Divine.[5]

Studying the myths of the Mysteries it becomes obvious why these early Christians resorted to such a desperate explanation. Although no single Pagan myth completely parallels the story of Jesus, the mythic motifs that make up the story of the Jewish godman had already existed for centuries in the various stories told of Osiris-Dionysus and his greatest prophets. Let's make a journey through the biography of Jesus and explore some of these extraordinary similarities.

SON OF GOD

Despite Christianity's claim that Jesus is the "only begotten Son of God,"[6] Osiris-Dionysus, in all his many forms, is also hailed as the Son of God. Jesus is the Son of God, yet equal with the Father. Dionysus is the "Son of Zeus, in his full nature God, most terrible, although most gentle to mankind."[7] Jesus is "Very God of Very God."[8] Dionysus is "Lord God of God born!"[9]

Jesus is God in human form. St. John writes of Jesus as "the Word made flesh."[10] St. Paul explains that "God sent his own Son in the likeness of sinful flesh."[11] Dionysus was also known as Bacchus, hence the title of Euripides' play *The Bacchae*, in which Dionysus is the central character. In this play, Dionysus explains that he has veiled his "Godhead in a mortal shape" in order to make it "manifest to mortal men."[12] He tells his disciples, "That is why I have changed my immortal form and taken the likeness of man."[13]

Like Jesus, in many of his myths the Pagan godman is born of a mortal virgin mother. In Asia Minor, Attis' mother is the virgin Cybele.[14] In Syria, Adonis' virgin mother is called Myrrh. In Alexandria, Aion is born of the virgin Kore.[15] In Greece, Dionysus is born of a mortal virgin Semele, who wishes to see Zeus in all his glory and is mysteriously impregnated by one of his bolts of lightning.[16]

It was a popular tradition, recorded in the most quoted non-canonical text of early Christianity, that Jesus spent only seven months in Mary's womb.[17] The Pagan historian Diodorus relates that Dionysus' mother Semele likewise was said to have also had only a seven-month pregnancy.[18]

Justin Martyr acknowledges the similarities between Jesus' virgin birth and Pagan mythology, writing:

> In saying that the Word was born for us without sexual union as Jesus Christ our teacher, we introduce nothing beyond what is said of those called the Sons of Zeus.[19]

Nowhere was the myth of the "Son of God" more developed than in Egypt, the ancient home of the Mysteries. Even the Christian Lactantius acknowledged that the legendary Egyptian sage Hermes Trismegistus had "arrived in some way at the truth, for on God the Father he had said everything, and on the Son."[20] In Egypt, the Pharaoh had for thousands of years been regarded as an embodiment of the godman Osiris and praised in hymns as the Son of God.[21] As an eminent Egyptologist writes,

> Every Pharaoh had to be the Son of God and a human mother in order that he should be the Incarnate God, the Giver of Fertility to his country and people.[22]

In many legends the great prophets of Osiris-Dionysus are also portrayed as saviors and sons of God. Pythagoras was said to be the son of Apollo and a mortal woman called Parthenis, whose name derives from the word *parthenos*, meaning "virgin."[23] Plato was also posthumously believed to be the son of Apollo.[24] Philostratus relates in his biography of Apollonius that the great Pagan sage was regarded as the "Son of Zeus." Empedocles was thought to be a godman and savior who had come down to this world to help confused souls, becoming "like a madman, calling out to people at the top of his voice and urging them to reject this realm and what is in it and go back to their own original, sublime, and noble world."[25]

Mythic motifs from the Mysteries even became associated with Roman Emperors who, for political reasons, cultivated legends about their divine nature, which would link them to Osiris-Dionysus. Julius Caesar, who did not himself even believe in personal immortality,[26] was hailed as "God made manifest, the common savior of human life."[27] His successor, Augustus, was likewise the "savior of the universal human race"[28] and even the tyrannical Nero is addressed on an altar piece as "God the deliverer for ever."[29]

In 40 BCE, drawing on Mystery myths, the Roman poet and initiate Virgil wrote a mystical prophesy that a virgin would give birth to a divine child.[30] In the fourth century CE Literalist Christians would claim that it foretold the coming of Jesus, but at the time this myth was interpreted as referring to Augustus, said to be the "Son of Apollo," preordained to rule the Earth and bring peace and prosperity.[31] In his biography of Augustus, Suetonius offers a cluster of "signs" that indicated the Emperor's divine nature. One modern authority writes:

> They include some striking points of similarity to the gospel narratives of the birth of Christ. The senate is supposed, with ludicrous implausibility, to have decreed a ban on rearing male Roman babies in the year of Augustus' birth because of a portent indicating that a king of Rome had been born. On top of this slaughter of the innocents, we are offered an Annunciation: his mother Atia dreamed during a visit to the temple of Apollo that the god had visited his favor on her in the form of a snake; Augustus was born nine months later.[32]

An inscription written around the time that Jesus is supposed to have lived reads:

> This day has given the earth an entirely new aspect. The world would have gone to destruction had there not streamed forth from him who is now born a common blessing. Rightly does he judge who recognizes in this birthday the beginning of life; now is that time ended when men pitied themselves for being born. From no other day does

the individual or the community receive such benefit as from this natal day, full of blessing to all. The Providence which rules over all has filled this man with such gifts for the salvation of the world as designate him as savior for us and for the coming generations; of wars he will make an end, and establish all things worthily. By his appearing are the hopes of our forefathers fulfilled; not only has he surpassed the good deeds of earlier times, but it is impossible that one greater than he can ever appear. The birthday of God has brought to the world glad tidings that are bound up in him. From his birthday a new era begins.[33]

But this is not a Christian celebration of the birth of Jesus. It is not even a eulogy to the Mystery godman. It is in honor of Augustus. These mythic motifs were clearly so common by the first century BCE that they were used to fabricate legends politically helpful to a living Emperor.

Celsus catalogs numbers of figures to whom legend similarly attributes divine parentage and a miraculous birth, and accuses Christianity of clearly using Pagan myths "in fabricating the story of Jesus' virgin birth."[34] He is disparaging of Christians who interpret this myth as historical fact and regards the notion that God could literally father a child on a mortal woman as plainly absurd.[35]

THE NATIVITY

Just as Christians celebrate the nativity of Jesus, initiates of the Mysteries celebrated the birth of Osiris-Dionysus, who was "The wondrous babe of God, the Mystery"[36] and "He of the miraculous birth"[37] *(see plates 1 and 2).* The Church father Hippolytus tells about the loud voice of the Hierophant of the Eleusinian Mysteries who, "screaming," proclaims the divine birth.[38] A modern Classicist writes:

The mystic child at Eleusis was born of a maiden; these ancients made for themselves the sacred dogma "A virgin shall conceive and bear a son,"[39] by night there was declared "Unto us a Child is born, unto us a Son is given."[40]

On the birth of Osiris a voice was said to have proclaimed: "The Lord of all the Earth is born."[41] An ancient Egyptian hymn proclaims: "Thou divine man-child, King of the Earth, Prince of the Underworld."[42] Another glorious Egyptian poem, reminiscent of many Christian carols, exults:

He is born! He is born! O come and adore Him!
Life-giving mothers, the mothers who bore Him,
Stars of the heavens the daybreak adorning.
Ancestors, ye, of the Star of the Morning.
Women and Men, O come and adore Him,
Child who is born in the night.

He is born! He is born! O come and adore Him!
Dwellers in Duat,[43] be joyful before Him,
Gods of the heavens come near and behold Him,
People of Earth, O come and adore Him!
Bow down before Him, kneel down before Him,
King who is born in the night.

He is born! He is born! O come and adore Him!
Young like the Moon in its shining and changing,
Over the heavens His footsteps are ranging,
Stars never-resting and stars never-setting,
Worship the child of God's own begetting!
Heaven and Earth, O come and adore Him!
Bow down before Him, kneel down before Him!
Worship, adore Him, fall down before Him!
God who is born in the night.[44]

Jesus is born in a humble stable. In the Mysteries of Dionysus a sacred marriage, from which will issue the divine child, was performed in the *boukolion*, or "ox stall."[45] However, the word usually translated as "stable" in the gospels is *katalemna*, which literally means a temporary shelter or cave.[46] It was a widespread early Christian tradition that Jesus was born in a cave.

This is a very ancient image. The cave is the womb of Mother Earth. There were caves sacred to the Greek god Pan, another name for Dionysus, all over the ancient world. The Persian godman Mithras was said to have been born in a cave. Zeus (the mythological father of Dionysus) was born in a cave on Crete. According to Orphic myths, Dionysus was also born in a cave, where he was immediately enthroned as "King of the World."[47]

The baby Jesus is visited by the "Three Wise Men" and three shepherds. In the gospels the "Three Wise Men" are actually called the *Magi*. The Magi were followers of the Persian Mystery godman Mithras. His birthday is celebrated on December 25—exactly the same date that is celebrated as the birthday of Jesus. Mithras' birth was even said to have been witnessed by three shepherds![48]

The Magi bring Jesus gifts of gold, frankincense, and myrrh. The Pagan sage Empedocles speaks of worshiping God with "offerings of unmixed myrrh and frankincense, casting down also on the ground libations of golden honey."[49] Myrrh was used as the sacred incense during the festival of Adonis. In some myths he was said to have been born from a myrrh tree. In others his mother is named Myrrh.[50]

Jesus was said to be born in the little town of Bethlehem. The name *Bethlehem* means "The House of Bread." St. Jerome relates the intriguing fact that Bethlehem was shaded by a grove sacred to the Mystery godman Adonis, who was regarded as a god of the corn and represented by bread![51]

In the Jesus story, the Three Wise Men find Jesus in Bethlehem by following a star. The Mysteries of Adonis in ancient Antioch were celebrated by cries that the "Star of Salvation has dawned in the East."[52] This was the Morning Star, which is actually the planet Venus. Venus is one of the names for the goddess who in certain myths is the consort of Osiris-Dionysus. In Egypt she was called Isis. For millennia she was associated with the bright star Sirius at the feet of the constellation of Orion, which represented Osiris. The first appearance of Sirius was a yearly omen which announced the rising of the floodwaters of the Nile, which was associated with the world-renewing power of Osiris.[53] Thus the star foretold the coming of the Lord.

St. Epiphanius tells us that in Alexandria the birth of Osiris-Dionysus as Aion was celebrated on January 6. The previous night the temple was alive with the sound of flutes and singing, reaching its height at cockcrow. Those taking part then went by torchlight into an underground sanctuary from which they brought an image of the god carved in wood and marked with "the sign of a cross on hands, knees, and head." The highlight of this Mystery celebration was the announcement: "Today at this hour the virgin Kore has given birth to Aion."[54]

St. Epiphanius must have found this a perplexing coincidence for, along with many other early Christians, he celebrated the same date, January 6, as the birthday of Jesus—as does the Armenian Church to the present day.[55] Goodness only knows what he made of the "markings of the sign of the cross on the hands, knees, and head"!

There was quite a dispute in early Christianity about whether the birth of Christ was December 25 or January 6. Was this because no one could remember? Or could it be simply because early Christians were unsure whether to synchronize it with the birth of Mithras or with the birth of Aion, both of whom were different representations of the perennial Mystery godman?

These dates were not arbitrarily chosen. Both were once the dates of the winter solstice, the shortest day, which signals the turning point of the year and the returning of the life-giving sun. Due to the precession of the equinoxes this date changes slightly over time. So, although the solstice moved progressively from January 6 to December 25, some traditions continued to celebrate it on the familiar night.[56] Today it falls around December 22. The annual celebration of the nativity of the Mystery godman celebrated the death of the old year and its miraculous rebirth as the new year on the date of the solstice.

Osiris-Dionysus represented and was represented by the sun, as was Jesus, whom the Church father Clement of Alexander calls "The Sun of Righteousness."[57] By way of balance, Dionysus' virgin mother Semele derives her name from the virgin moon goddess Selene.[58] The angel Gabriel who comes to Mary to announce the birth of Jesus was likewise equated with the moon.

BAPTISM

Jesus' mission begins with his baptism by John the Baptist. Mythologists such as Joseph Campbell have seen ancient mythological motifs behind this story. Campbell writes:

> The rite of baptism was an ancient rite coming down from the old Sumerian temple city Eridu, of the water god Ea, "God of the House of Water." In the Hellenistic period, Ea was called Oannes, which is in Greek Ioannes, Latin Johannes, Hebrew Yohanan, English John.

Several scholars have suggested, therefore, that there was never either John or Jesus, but only a water-god and a sun-god.[59]

Examining the stories of John the Baptist and Jesus, we do seem to be clearly in mythological territory. Their two stories reflect each other perfectly. They both have miraculous births. John is born to an old woman. Jesus is born to a young woman. John's mother is infertile. Jesus' mother is unfertilized. John is born at the summer solstice when the sun begins to wane. Jesus is born six months later at the winter solstice when the sun begins to wax again—hence the Baptist's declaration about Jesus: "He must grow greater, I must become less."[60] John is born in the astrological sign of Cancer, which for the ancients represented the gate of souls into incarnation. Jesus is born in the astrological sign of Capricorn, which for the ancients represented the gate of souls out of incarnation into immortality.[61] John baptizes with water and Jesus with fire and spirit. The birthday of Jesus is celebrated on the Pagan festival of the returning sun on December 25. The birthday of John the Baptist is celebrated in June, replacing a Pagan midsummer festival of water.[62]

Baptism was a central rite in the Mysteries. As long ago as the Homeric hymns we hear that ritual purity was the condition of salvation and that people were baptized to wash away all their previous sins.[63] The Pyramid Texts show that there was a ceremonial baptism of the Egyptian Pharaoh before the ceremony of his ritual birth as the embodiment of Osiris.[64] In some Mystery rites baptism was simply symbolized by the sprinkling of holy water. In others it involved complete immersion.[65] Baptism tanks have been found at initiation halls and shrines.[66] At Eleusis initiates ritually cleansed themselves in the sea. In his initiation ceremony, after a confessional prayer, Lucius Apuleius underwent a bath of purification, and later a baptism of sprinkling.[67] In the Mysteries of Mithras, initiates underwent repeated baptisms to wash away their sins. Such initiations took place in March or April, at exactly the same time that in later centuries Christians also baptized their new converts, called *catechumens*.[68]

The similarities between Christian and Pagan rites were obvious to early Christians.[69] The Church father Tertullian tells us:

> In certain Mysteries it is by baptism that members are initiated and they imagine that the result of this baptism is regeneration and the remission of the penalties of their sins.[70]

According to St. Paul, there are three symbolic actions in a baptism of total immersion. Entering the water signifies death, immersion beneath it means burial, and emergence from it resurrection.[71] This allegorical interpretation of baptism is completely in sympathy with the Mystery rites, which also represented a mystical death and resurrection.[72] In the early Church, the newly baptized were clothed in white robes, given a new name, and offered honey to eat.[73] Likewise, in the Mysteries of Mithras, initiates who were spiritually "reborn" had honey poured on their hands and applied to their tongues, as it was customary to do with newborn children.[74]

Descriptions by Christian authors of Christian baptism are indistinguishable from Pagan descriptions of Mystery baptism. Christian initiates went to baptism naked, then after they came out of the water they put on white garments and walked in a procession to a basilica carrying a candle and wearing a crown. This is identical to the procession celebrating the Mysteries of Dionysus at Eleusis, where initiates dressed in white, wearing a crown on their heads and carrying a torch in their hands, walked to the sanctuary singing hymns.[75] Justin Martyr found the similarities between Christian and Pagan rites of baptism deeply disturbing. He resorted once again to the diabolical mimicry argument. Evil demons, he claimed, had instigated a parody of Christian baptism in Pagan rites.

In the Mysteries, however, purification through baptism was not just by water, but also by air and fire. Lucius Apuleius tells us that before he was deemed worthy to approach the divinity he had to "travel through all the elements."[76] Servius writes:

Every purification is effected either by water or by fire or by air; therefore in all Mysteries you find these three methods of cleansing. They either disinfect you with burning sulphur or wash you with water or ventilate you with wind; the latter is done in the Dionysiac Mysteries.[77]

The gospels also talk of a threefold elemental baptism. In the Gospel of Matthew, John the Baptist predicts the coming of Jesus, saying,

Now I bathe you in water to change hearts, but the one coming after me is stronger than me. I am not big enough to carry his shoes. He will bathe you in holy breath and fire. Winnowing-fan in hand, he will clean up his threshing floor, and collect the grain to be put in the silo and the husks to be burned in the unquenchable fire.[78]

In this translation the familiar term *holy spirit* is correctly translated from the original Greek as "holy breath," which clearly brings out the idea of baptism by air. John tells us that Jesus will wield a winnowing fan, used for sieving corn. In the Mysteries of Eleusis such a fan was used in baptism by air. In vase paintings and other representations, initiates are pictured veiled and seated with a winnowing fan being waved above their heads.[79] Dionysus was known as "He of the Winnowing Fan." At his birth he was said to have been cradled in a winnowing fan, just as, symbolically, the initiate was at his spiritual rebirth.[80]

In the same way that an initiate into the Pagan Mysteries was reborn through purification by air, so Jesus promises rebirth through breath. In the Gospel of John, Nicodemus asks him, "How can a person be born in old age? Can he climb into his mother's belly a second time and be born?" Jesus answers:

> Truly, truly I tell you: anyone who isn't born of water and breath can never get into the kingdom of God. What's born of the flesh is flesh, and what's born of the breath is breath. Don't be amazed because I told you you have to be born again. The wind blows where it will and you hear the sound of it, but you don't know where it comes from or where it goes; it is the same with everyone born of the breath.[81]

MIRACLES

The early Egyptian Christian Basilides believed that Jesus was baptized on January 6, a date which had been celebrated for centuries in Egypt as "the Day of Osiris."[82] Some Christians commemorated this date as the day on which Christ "sanctified the water." They offered prayers at midnight on January 5 and then all rushed with pitchers to a river to obtain water, which was believed now to be holy and possess purifying powers. For hundreds of years before Christ Egyptians had been doing exactly the same thing at exactly the same time. The night of January 5 was said to be a time when the waters of the Nile gained miracle-working powers, through the grace of Osiris. These waters were drawn in pitchers by the Egyptians and kept in their houses as a defense against every evil.[83]

The night of January 5 was also the time when Dionysus was believed to miraculously change water into wine.[84] According to Pliny, on the island of Andros a stream of wine flowed in the temple of Dionysus and continued for seven days, but if samples of it were taken out of the sanctuary they immediately turned to water. We also hear that on Naxos a spring miraculously issued forth fragrant wine.

During the Greek festival called Thyia, three empty basins were put into a room in the presence of citizens and foreigners. The room was then locked and sealed, and anyone who wanted to could bring his own seal to add to the seal on the door. On the next day the seals remained unbroken, but those entering the room found that the three basins had miraculously been filled with wine. Pausanias assures us that citizens and foreigners alike had vouched under oath for the reliability of this report.[85]

According to myth, the miracle of turning water into wine took place for the first time at the marriage of Dionysus and Ariadne.[86] The same miracle is attributed to Jesus at the wedding feast in Cana.[87] In the fourth century CE St. Epiphanius relates similar miracles still happening on January 6 and claims to have drunk of a spring that had issued forth wine. But he no longer attributes the miracles to Dionysus, but to Jesus. For Epiphanius, such miracles now occurred "at the hour when Jesus ordered the water to be taken to the master of the feast and he changed their water into wine."[88]

Other of Jesus' miracles were also attributed to the Pagan godman. Asclepius, who was followed by Hippocrates, the "father of medicine," was said to have cured the sick and raised the dead. He was known as the "lover of men." A comparison between the wonders of Asclepius and the miracles of Jesus was a standard feature of Pagan anti-Christian writings.[89] In reply, early Christians described Jesus as the physician greater than great Asclepius. The Pagan Celsus and the Christian Origen argued with equal conviction as to the relative merits of Asclepius savior or Jesus savior.[90] Many of the inscriptions to Asclepius were taken over by early Christians by simply replacing his name with that of Jesus.[91]

Many of the great prophets of Osiris-Dionysus were renowned as wandering wonder-workers who performed exactly the same supernatural feats attributed to the wandering wonder-worker Jesus. Pythagoras was particularly famous for his miracles. Like Jesus, he was said to have performed many

THE JESUS MYSTERIES

healings and as he went around from town to town the word got about that he was coming "not to teach, but to heal."[92] In his *Life of Pythagoras* Iamblichus claims that Pythagoras' innumerable miracles included "tranquillisations of the waves of rivers and seas in order that his disciples might the more easily pass over them."[93] According to the Gospel of Mark, Jesus performs the same miracle to benefit his disciples on the Sea of Galilee.[94] This miracle was clearly part of the legendary biographies of many Pagan wonder-workers, for Iamblichus adds:

> The power of effecting miracles of this kind was achieved by Empedocles of Agrigentum, Epimenides the Cretan, and Abaris the Hyperborean, and these they performed in many places.[95]

In the Gospel of John, Jesus miraculously helps his disciples land a large catch of fish.[96] This supernatural feat was also performed by Pythagoras in a legend recorded by Porphyry.[97] Pythagoras miraculously predicted the exact number of fish that would be caught, but the story does not record what this number was. In the gospel account Jesus makes no such prediction, but we are told that the catch numbers exactly 153 fish. This seems on the face of it to be an irrelevant fact that the gospel writer included just for dramatic color. But scholars have concluded that it is mentioned deliberately and is highly significant.[98]

It is likely that the number of fish that Pythagoras predicted would be caught was precisely 153. The Pythagoreans were renowned for their knowledge of mathematics and regarded 153 as a sacred number.[99] It is used in a mathematical ratio that Archimedes called "the measure of the fish" to produce the mystical symbol of the *vesica piscis* or "sign of the fish"—the intersection of two circles which yields a fish-like shape. This was an ancient Pythagorean symbol that was used by early Christians to represent their faith. The fact that this mystical fish symbol can be produced from the number of fish that were caught in the account of Jesus' miracle strongly suggests it has been adapted from the original miracle of Pythagoras and that this miracle story encoded sacred geometrical formulae.[100]

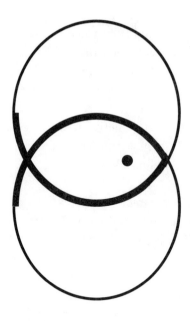

The sign of the fish is widely used today as a symbol of Christianity, but originated in Pagan sacred geometry. Two circles, symbolic of spirit and matter, are
brought together in a sacred marriage. When the circumference of one touches
the center of the other they combine to produce the fish shape known as the
vesica piscis. The ratio of height to length of this shape is 153:265, a formula
known to Archimedes in the third century BCE as the "measure of the fish." It is
a powerful mathematical tool, being the nearest whole number approximation
of the square root of three and the controlling ratio of the equilateral triangle.

Pythagoras' disciple Empedocles was another wandering wonder-worker. Like
Pythagoras and Jesus, he was a self-proclaimed godman, announcing himself to
the people of Acragas as "an immortal god, no longer a mortal." People followed him in droves, adorning him with ribbons and asking for miracles.[101]
Like Jesus, he was said to have knowledge of the future. Like Jesus, he taught
spiritual truths and cured sickness. He was known as "The Wind Stiller" and,
like Jesus, had the ability to control the wind and rain.[102] He assured his disciples that, as a result of what he would teach them, they would be able to fetch
from the Underworld the life force of a man who had died.[103] Empedocles himself was said to have raised back to life a woman who had been dead for 30 days,
just as Jesus was said to have raised Lazarus 500 years later.[104]

Apollonius of Tyana was another wandering godman who healed the sick, predicted the future, and raised the dead.[105] Although not physically present, he was said to have brought back to life the daughter of a Roman consul in exactly the same way as Jesus is said to have brought back to life the daughter of Jairus, a president of the synagogue, without even visiting her.[106] Like Jesus, Apollonius also exorcised evil spirits. He even describes witnessing a feeding miracle similar to Jesus' "feeding of the five thousand," a supernatural feat which Celsus tells us is an "illusion" performed by many holy men.[107] Yet, like Jesus, who claims that a prophet is never recognized in his own country,[108] the divine men of Pagan legends are commonly represented as rejected by their homeland. Apollonius of Tyana writes in a letter, "What wonder is it if, while other men consider me equal to God, my native place, so far, ignores me?"[109]

The gospels tell us that on one occasion Jesus exorcized a man of demons who called themselves *Legion*, because there were "about 2,000 of them." These demons are cast by Jesus into a large herd of pigs, which rush over the edge of a hillside and are drowned.[110] Exactly the same motif is found in the rites of the Mysteries at Eleusis.[111] As part of the purification ceremony before initiation, some 2,000 initiates all bathed in the sea with young pigs.[112] This bathing ritual banished all evil into the pigs, which were then sacrificed, as a symbol of the initiates' own impurities, by being chased over a chasm.[113]

Even the Pentecostal miracle of "speaking in tongues" is prefigured by Pagan myth. After Jesus' death the disciples found themselves miraculously speaking in strange tongues, which others heard as their own native language.[114] The same phenomenon was reported centuries earlier at Trophonius and Delos, where the oracular priestesses seemed to some to speak unintelligibly, while other witnesses heard them speaking in their own differing mother tongues.[115] Burkert, one of the foremost modern classical scholars, asserts that these Pagan and Christian miracles "have justly been compared."[116]

Christians asserted that Jesus' claim to being the one and only Son of God was proven by his miracles. To Celsus this was plainly ridiculous. He tells us, "Miracles and wonders have indeed occurred everywhere and in all times," and lists a number of Pagan sages and godmen renowned as wonderworkers.[117] The standard Christian response to such Pagan critics was to claim that while Jesus' miracles were a sign of his divinity, Pagan miracles were the works of the Devil. Celsus replies indignantly:

Good lord! Is it not a silly sort of argument to reckon by the same works that one man is a god while his rivals are mere "sorcerers?"[118]

THE GODMAN AND HIS DISCIPLES

Jesus surrounds himself with 12 disciples. This is usually taken to be symbolic of the 12 tribes of Israel. This notion of 12 tribes, however, is itself a symbolic reference to the 12 signs of the zodiac in Babylonian astrology, which the Jews adopted while in exile in Babylon.[119] The zodiac was an extremely important symbol in the Pagan world. Osiris-Dionysus is symbolically represented as the still spiritual center of the turning wheel of change represented by the 12 signs. As Mithras, Dionysus, Aion, and Helios, he is often depicted at the center of the circling zodiac.[120] During the initiation ceremony in the Mysteries of Mithras, 12 disciples surrounded the godman, just as the 12 disciples surrounded Jesus. The Mithraic disciples were dressed up to represent the 12 signs of the zodiac and circled the initiate, who represented Mithras himself.[121]

The circle of 12 around a central one derives from sacred geometry and for the followers of Pythagoras contained profound mystical meaning. Pythagoreans, who were renowned in the ancient world for their knowledge of mathematics, conceived of God as a perfect sphere.[122] The ancients discovered that if a sphere is surrounded by others of exactly the same dimensions, so that all the spheres are in contact with each other, the central sphere will be surrounded by exactly 12 others.[123] The image of the godman and his 12 disciples encodes such teachings from sacred geometry.

In the gospels Jesus is not at first recognized by his disciples as the Son of God, but later is transfigured before Peter, John, and James, revealing himself in all his divine glory.[124] Likewise in Euripides' *The Bacchae*, Dionysus first appears to his disciples as a wandering holy man, but later is gloriously transfigured. When they perceive his true divinity, they exclaim:

But look! Who is this, rising above the palace door?
It is he Dionysus come himself, no more disguised
As mortal, but in the glory of his divinity![125]

To his disciples, Jesus is the savior. Dionysus is likewise "He who came to bring salvation."[126] His followers call to him: "Come, thou savior."[127] In *The Bacchae* they rejoice:

> We are saved! Oh, what a joy to hear your Bacchic call ring out!
> We were all alone, deserted; you have come, and we rejoice.[128]

During his mission Jesus is attacked for his seemingly licentious behavior. In the Gospel of Luke he reproaches "the people of this generation" for first condemning John the Baptist who came "neither eating bread nor drinking wine" for being "possessed" and then also condemning the "Son of Man" who comes "eating and drinking" for being "a glutton and a drinker, a friend of tax gatherers and sinners."[129] The followers of Dionysus were likewise often accused of both possession and licentious behavior. Their "orgies" were infamous, although in fact these were no more sexual affairs than were the comparable "love feast" celebrated by early Christians. Like Jesus, Dionysus comes "eating and drinking," yet brings a profoundly spiritual message to ordinary people. He was a god of divine intoxication and a "god of the people" who was often reviled and feared by religious and secular authorities, just as Jesus was. The Mysteries also had a more ascetic side, however, comparable to the austere John the Baptist. The early Christian monastic tradition initiated by St. Anthony was modeled on ascetic Pythagorean communities found throughout the Mediterranean.[130]

RIDING ON A DONKEY

According to the gospel story, at the height of his popularity Jesus rides into Jerusalem while crowds sing his praises and lay branches in his path.[131] Traditionally the crowd is said to have waved palm leaves. The palm was symbolic in the Mysteries.[132] Plato writes of "the palm of wisdom of Dionysus."[133] The great festival of the Mystery godman Attis began with the "Entry of the Reed-Bearers," which was followed by the "Entry of the Tree," an evergreen pine upon which was tied an effigy of the godman.[134] One modern scholar remarks:

It is impossible to ignore the associations with Jesus' entry into Jerusalem surrounded by palm-bearers, and his bearing of the cross or tree which became his chief symbol.[135]

The gospels relate that Jesus goes out of his way to make sure he is mounted on a donkey. In vase representations, Dionysus is also often pictured astride a donkey, which carries him to meet his passion.[136] The playwright Aristophanes writes of "the ass who carried the Mysteries."[137] When the crowd of pilgrims at Athens walked the Sacred Way to Eleusis to celebrate the Mysteries, a donkey carried a basket containing the sacred paraphernalia, which would be used to create the idol of Dionysus, while the crowds shouted the praises of Dionysus and waved bundles of branches.[138] In this way, like Jesus entering Jerusalem, Dionysus rode in triumph to his death.

The mythical motif of "riding on a donkey" is often taken as a sign of humility. It also has a more mystical meaning, however. To the ancients the donkey typified lust, cruelty, and wickedness. It symbolically represented the lower "animal" self, which must be overcome and subdued by an initiate of the Mysteries. Lucius Apuleius wrote a story called *The Golden Ass*, which was an allegorical tale of initiation. In it Lucius is transformed into a donkey through his own foolishness and endures many adventures, which represent stages of initiation. At his final initiation he is transformed back into a human being. This story is symbolic of the initiate being overcome by his lower nature and then, through initiation into the Mysteries, rediscovering his true identity.[139]

The Egyptian goddess Isis tells Lucius that the donkey is the most hateful to her of all beasts.[140] This is because it is sacred to the god Set, who in Egyptian mythology is the murderer of Osiris.[141] Plutarch recorded an Egyptian festival in which donkeys were triumphantly pushed over cliffs in vengeance for Osiris' murder. Set is symbolic of the initiate's lower self, which slays the spiritual Higher Self (Osiris) and must be metaphorically put to death for the spiritual Self to be reborn.

The donkey was also a common symbol of the lower "animal" nature in the Greek Mysteries of Dionysus. A vase painting represents a ridiculous donkey with an erect phallus dancing among the disciples of Dionysus.[142] A design on a wine pitcher shows donkeys having sex.[143] In another design a pilgrim is shown stopping to pull the tail of a donkey.[144] A favorite representation of afterlife sufferings in the Underworld was the figure of a man condemned to forever plait a rope that his donkey continually eats away, symbolic of the lower self constantly trying to eat away the spiritual achievements of the Higher Self.[145] The figure of the godman riding in triumph on a donkey symbolized that he was master of his lower "animal" nature.

THE JUST MAN AND THE TYRANT

According to the gospels, Jesus is an innocent and just man who, at the instigation of the Jewish high priests, is hauled before the Roman governor Pilate and condemned to die on spurious charges. Exactly the same mythological motif is found five centuries earlier in Euripides' play *The Bacchae*, about Dionysus. Like Jesus in Jerusalem, Dionysus is a quiet stranger with long hair and a beard who brings a new religion. In the gospels, the Jewish high priests don't believe in Jesus and allege that "His teachings are causing disaffection amongst the people."[146] They plot to bring about his death. In *The Bacchae*, King Pentheus is a tyrannical ruler who does not believe in Dionysus. He berates him for bringing "this new disease which fouls the land" and sends out his men to capture the innocent godman, announcing:

> And once you catch him, he shall be stoned to death.
> He'll wish he'd never brought his Bacchic rites to Thebes.[147]

Like the Jewish high priests who are appalled at Jesus' blasphemous claim to be the Son of God,[148] King Pentheus rants in anger at stories of Dionysus' divine parentage:

> Whatever the man may be, is not his arrogance
> An outrage? Has he not earned a rope around his neck?[149]

Like Jesus, Dionysus passively allows himself to be caught and imprisoned. The guard who apprehends him tells King Pentheus:

> We hunted him, and here he is. But Sir, we found
> The beast was gentle; made no attempt to run away,
> Just held his hands out to be tied; didn't turn pale,
> But kept his florid colour, smiling, telling us
> To tie him up and run him in; gave us no trouble
> At all, just waited for us. Naturally I felt

A bit embarrassed. "You'll excuse me, Sir," I said,
"I don't want to arrest you; it's the king's command."[150]

The guard relates the wondrous things he had witnessed Dionysus perform and warns King Pentheus: "Master, this man has come here with a load of miracles." The king, however, proceeds to interrogate Dionysus who, like Jesus before Pilate, will not bow to his authority. When Pilate reminds Jesus that he has the power to crucify him, Jesus replies, "You would have no authority at all over me, had it not been granted you from above."[151] Likewise Dionysus answers the threats of Pentheus with: "Nothing can touch me that is not ordained."[152] Like Jesus, who said of his persecutors, "They know not what they are doing,"[153] Dionysus tells Pentheus, "You know not what you are doing, nor what you are saying, nor who you are."[154]

As Jesus is led away to crucifixion, he warns the crowd not to weep for him, but for themselves and their children, who will suffer for the crime of his execution, saying,

> For the days are surely coming when they will say, "Happy are the barren wombs that never bore a child, the breasts that never fed one." Then they will say to the mountains, "Fall on us," and to the hills, "Cover us up."[155]

As he is led away, Dionysus, likewise, threatens divine vengeance, announcing:

> But I warn you: Dionysus who you say is dead,
> Will come in swift pursuit to avenge this sacrilege.[156]

Many of the great philosophers of the Mystery tradition were also "just men" who suffered an unjust death at the hands of tyrannical authorities. One such is Socrates who, like Jesus, was accused of heresy. Under Athenian law the penalty for this "crime" was death, unless the defendant offered an alternative penalty acceptable to the judges. Like Pilate, who offers to set Jesus free because it is a custom to release one prisoner at the Passover, the Athenian authorities hoped that Socrates would escape death on a technicality by paying a fine and going quietly into exile.[157] Like Jesus, refusing to compromise with his persecutors and seeming to deliberately court his own death, Socrates offered to pay a single mina, an insultingly small sum, which forced the authorities to impose the death sentence.[158]

Some of Socrates' followers offered to pay "thirty pieces of silver" on his behalf, which was a betrayal of Socrates' own desire to remain true to his principles.[159] This motif appears in the gospel story as the 30 pieces of silver paid to Judas to betray Jesus. Socrates is executed by drinking a cup of poison. In the garden of Gethsemane, when he is contemplating his forthcoming execution, Jesus prays, "My Father, if it is possible let this cup pass me by."[160] Socrates was fearless before death for he had been told in a dream that three days after his death he would be reborn.[161] Jesus, likewise, goes to his death with confidence and foretells that after three days he will be resurrected.[162]

Jesus' behavior at his trial is exactly what would be expected of a sage of the Mysteries.[163] He is not afraid to openly condemn those in authority for hypocrisy. Likewise, Cynic and Stoic philosophers were renowned for being "hostile to authority and resistant to discipline, disdainful of kings, magistrates, or public officials."[164] There were numbers of such philosophers whose lack of respect for Roman authority earned them martyrdom which, like Jesus, they willingly accepted.[165] The Stoic sage Epictetus writes: "Take my body, or property, but do not try to rule my moral purpose."[166] He describes a philosopher facing execution announcing to an Emperor: "You will do your part and I mine, which is to go without complaint."[167] As early as the fourth century BCE, Plato had laid down the expected fate of the "just man," writing, "The just man will have to endure the lash and finally, after every extremity of suffering, he will be crucified."[168] The gospels portray the "just man" Jesus as conforming to these expectations.

The "just man unjustly accused" was so familiar a figure in the ancient world that Celsus ridicules the Christians for trying to claim that Jesus was in any way unique. With wit and biting satire, he suggests that if they wanted to create a new religion they would have been better to have based it around one of the many famous Pagan sages who also "died a hero's death," writing:

> It would have been better had you in your zest for a new teaching formed your religion around one of the men of old who died a hero's death and was honored for it—someone who at least was already subject of a myth. You could have chosen Heracles or Asclepius, or if these were too tame, there was always Orpheus, who as every one knows, was good and holy and yet died a violent death. Or had he already been taken? Well, then you had Anaxarchus, a man who looked death right in the eye when being beaten and said to his persecutors, "Beat away. Beat the pouch of Anaxarchus; for it is not him

you are beating." But I recall that some philosophers have already claimed him as their master. Well, what of Epictetus? When his leg was being twisted he smiled and said with complete composure, "You are breaking it." And when it was broken, he smiled and said, "I told you so." Your God should have uttered such a saying when he was being punished![169]

BREAD AND WINE

Before his death, Jesus celebrates a symbolic Last Supper of bread and wine. In *The Bacchae*, Euripides calls bread and wine the "two powers which are supreme in human affairs," the one substantial and preserving the body, the other liquid and intoxicating the mind.[170] The ancients credited the Mystery godman with bringing to humanity the arts of cultivating corn and the vine to produce bread and wine.

In the gospels, Jesus proclaims: "I am the bread of Life" and during the Last Supper he breaks bread and offers it to his disciples, saying, "Take this, this is my body."[171] The Mystery godman was, likewise, symbolically associated with bread and with the corn from which it comes.[172] Osiris was said to have met his death by being torn limb from limb, which is symbolic of the corn being threshed to produce flour. The bones of the dead Adonis were said to be ground on a mill then scattered to the wind.[173]

In the gospels Jesus also proclaims: "I am the true vine"[174] and during the Last Supper he offers his disciples a cup of wine, saying, "This is my blood."[175] Like Jesus, Dionysus was also associated with the vine and with wine. He was known as the "god of wine" and in some myths he dies by being dismembered, which is symbolic of the grapes being trodden to produce wine.

By partaking of the bread and wine offered by Jesus, his disciples symbolically eat his body and drink his blood, so communing with the Christ. The idea of divine communion through eating the god is a rite so ancient that it is found in the Egyptian *Book of the Dead*, in which the deceased are portrayed as eating the gods and so imbuing their powers.[176] The ritual of eating and drinking the "body" and "blood" of Jesus is celebrated by Christians as the Eucharist.[177] Such a "holy communion" was also practiced in the Mysteries, as a means of becoming one with Osiris-Dionysus.[178] The uninitiated who misunderstood these rites accused the Mysteries of practicing cannibalism—exactly the same accusation that was later leveled at early Christians who celebrated the Eucharist.[179]

Pagan practices that parallel the Christian communion appalled Justin Martyr, who complains that when Jesus told his disciples to drink of the cup, saying, "This is my blood," he gave this ritual to them alone, yet "the wicked demons in imitation, in the Mysteries of Mithras, also delivered the command to do so." He relates with horror that in these Mysteries, as in the Christian Eucharist, mystic formulas are pronounced over bread and a cup, which are then given to one about to be initiated.[180] As in Christianity, participants in the Mysteries of Mithras had to undergo a long period of preparation before being allowed to partake in the "holy communion."[181] When they did, they were offered a sacrament of water mixed with wine and bread or consecrated wafers bearing the sign of a cross![182] No wonder poor old Justin Martyr found this Pagan holy communion so disturbing.

An inscription reads:

> He who will not eat of my body and drink of my blood, so that he will be made one with me and I with him, the same shall not know salvation.[183]

This may sound like a Biblical quotation from Jesus, but it is actually the Mystery godman Mithras speaking! It is, however, uncannily similar to a passage in the Gospel of John where Jesus likewise announces:

> Unless you eat of the flesh of the Son of Man and drink his blood, you have not life in yourselves.[184] Whoever eats my flesh and drinks my blood will live in me and I in him.[185]

The holy communion in the Mysteries of Mithras was developed from older rites, which used consecrated bread and water mixed with the intoxicating juice of a psychedelic plant called Haoma.[186] The Mysteries of Mithras replaced the Haoma, a plant unknown in the Occident, with the juice of the vine. Wine probably affected the ancients far more powerfully than it does us, however, for they seldom drank it unmixed with water. Plato enthuses about its revelationary power in the Mysteries of Dionysus,[187] writing, "Rather the madness of the god than the sobriety of men."[188]

As one eminent Classicist writes, "To drink wine in the rites of Dionysus is to commune with the god and take his power and physical presence into one's body."[189] In the Christian rites of the Eucharist Jesus is said to symbolically become the wine drunk by the participant in the ritual. Likewise, Euripides tells us that Dionysus becomes the wine and is himself "poured out" as an offering.[190] In some vase representations, bread and wine are shown before the idol of Dionysus *(see plate 5)*.[191] Just as in the Eucharist a Christian is given "redemption" in the symbolic form of a wafer biscuit, in the Mysteries of Dionysus the initiate was presented with *makaria* ("blessedness") in the form of a cake.[192]

An inscription relates that in the Samothracian Mysteries the priest "shall break and offer the food and pour out the cup to the initiate."[193] Initiates of the Mysteries of Attis also had some form of communion, for they declared: "I have eaten from the tambourine, I have drunk from the cymbal." What they ate and drank from these sacred instruments is not recorded, but most likely it was also bread and wine.[194]

From the time of Justin Martyr right up to the present day, Catholic Christians have believed that the bread and wine of the Eucharist literally become "the flesh and blood of that Jesus who was made flesh."[195] Some initiates of the Mysteries seemed to have shared this rather strange literal interpretation of their "holy communion." The more enlightened initiate Cicero felt forced to explain to them that equating the god with corn and the vine was symbolic only. Impatient with such foolishness, he writes, "Is anybody so mad as to believe that the food which he eats is actually a god?"[196]

DEATH OF THE GODMAN

Jesus is generally believed to have been crucified on a cross, but the word translated by "cross" in the New Testament has a general meaning of a "stake." It was the custom of the Jews to expose on a stake the bodies of those that they had stoned to death, as a warning to others.[197] In the Acts of the Apostles, Peter does not say that Jesus was crucified, but "hung on a tree,"[198] as does St. Paul in his Letter to the Galatians.[199] The Church father Firmicus Maternus tells us that in the Mysteries of Attis a youthful image of the godman was tied to a pine tree.[200] Adonis was known as "He on the tree."[201]

In the Mysteries of Dionysus, a large bearded mask representing the god-man was hung on a wooden pole (see plates 4 and 5).[202] Like Jesus, who at his crucifixion is given a crown of thorns, Dionysus was given a crown of ivy. Just as Jesus is dressed up in purple robes when he is ridiculed by the Roman soldiers, so Dionysus was also dressed in purple robes and initiates at Eleusis wore a purple sash wrapped around their bodies.[203] Just before he dies Jesus is given wine mixed with gall to drink.[204] Wine was ritually imbibed by celebrants in the Mysteries of Dionysus, and the Hierophant, who represented Dionysus himself, was given gall to drink.[205]

Jesus meets his death alongside two thieves, one of whom ascends with him to heaven, while the other goes to hell. A comparable mythical motif is found in the Mysteries. A common icon pictures two torchbearers either side of Mithras. One of these figures has his torch pointing upward, symbolizing the ascent to heaven, and the other has his torch pointing downward, symbolizing the descent to hell.[206] In the Mysteries of Eleusis, we also find two torchbearers with their torches pointing upward and downward respectively, standing either side of Dionysus, but this time they are women.[207] The torchbearers in the Mysteries of Mithras are thought to have developed from the earlier Greek mythical brothers Castor and Pollux. On alternate days, one of the brothers would be alive and the other dead. They represented the Higher Self and lower self, which cannot both be "alive" at the same time. Castor and Pollux were known as "The Sons of Thunder"—a title which, in the Gospel of Mark, Jesus inexplicably gives to two of his disciples, the brothers James and John![208]

In some myths it is Dionysus' adversary, representing the initiate's lower self, who dies the godman's death in his stead. In *The Bacchae*, King Pentheus sets out to kill Dionysus, but is himself lifted up on a tree.[209] In a similar Sicilian myth, Dionysus' adversary King Lycurgus is crucified.[210] This suggests that while in some Mystery traditions Dionysus was hung on a tree, in others his fate was crucifixion.

Perhaps initiates of the Mysteries of Dionysus built on the image of "the just man crucified" suggested by Plato in order to bring about this development of the myth?[211] Or perhaps Plato was referring to an already existing secret myth of initiation in which the godman was crucified?[212] In a chapter of one of his books actually entitled "Plato's Doctrine of the Cross," Justin Martyr acknowledges that the Pagan philosopher had centuries earlier taught the doctrine that the "Son of God" was "placed crosswise in the universe."[213]

The cross was a sacred symbol to the ancients. Its four arms represented the four elements of the physical world—earth, water, air, and fire. The fifth element, spirit, was bound to materiality by these four elements. The figure of a man nailed to a four-armed cross would, therefore, naturally have signified the predicament of the initiate as a soul bound to a physical body. Plato refers to the desires of the body as nails that one by one fasten the soul to the body.[214] The four nails used to crucify a man through the hands and feet would have been symbolic of our sensual desires, which attach the soul to the world of the four elements.

It seems incredible that Osiris-Dionysus could have been portrayed as meeting exactly the same death as Jesus, but this is what the evidence suggests. The Church father Arnobius is scandalized that in the Mysteries of Dionysus initiates passed around a holy cross.[215] On some vase representations the idol of Dionysus is shown hanging from a cross.[216] A sarcophagus of the second or third centuries CE from Rome pictures an aged disciple bringing the divine child Dionysus a large cross.[217] One modern scholar describes this cross as "an intimation of the child's ultimately tragic fate"[218] (see plate 3).

From the same period comes the remarkable talisman which shows a crucified figure immediately recognizable as Jesus but who is actually Osiris-Dionysus (see front cover and plate 6). The inscription under this figure reads "Orpheus-Bakkikos," which means "Orpheus becomes a Bacchoi." Orpheus was a great legendary prophet of Dionysus who was so respected that he was often regarded as the godman himself. A Bacchoi was an enlightened disciple of Dionysus who had become completely identified with the god. The talisman, therefore, represents Dionysus dying by crucifixion, symbolizing the initiate's mystical death to his lower nature and rebirth as a god.

We also have a seemingly strange piece of ancient graffiti carved behind a pillar in Rome sometime between 193 and 235 CE (see plate 7). It sketches a man with a donkey's head crucified on a cross, with the caption "Alexmenos worships his god." This has been interpreted as a Pagan insult toward Christianity, but it is far more likely that it is a Dionysian representation of the crucifixion of the lower "animal" nature, which, as we have already discussed, was symbolized by a donkey.[219]

It is a remarkable fact that we have no representations of the crucified Jesus before the fifth century CE. If this piece of graffiti and the talisman of Orpheus are taken as references to Christianity, we are in the bizarre position of saying that the first portrayals of the crucifixion of Christ are a Pagan joke and a talisman in which Jesus is called Orpheus—both of which date to centuries before any genuine Christian portrayals! This does not seem very credible. The simple and obvious solution to these puzzles is that in certain myths of Osiris-Dionysus, the godman was portrayed as meeting his death by crucifixion.

THE SACRED SCAPEGOAT

Christians believe that Jesus died for the sins of the world. In ancient Greece there was a tradition of making a particular individual into a "scapegoat," who symbolically took on the sins of the people and was expelled from the city or put to death. Such an individual was called a *pharmakos*, which simply means "magic man."[220] His persecution was clearly a religious event, since before his death he was fed at public expense on especially pure foods and was clad in holy garments and wreathed with sacred plants.[221] Through his sacred sacrifice the sins of the city were banished.

Osiris-Dionysus was a sacred *pharmakos*, who, like Jesus, died to atone for the sins of the world.[222] The fate of a *pharmakos* was to be insulted, beaten, and put to death,[223] and those who walked the Sacred Way toward Eleusis to share in Dionysus' sacrificial death were likewise beaten, insulted, and terrorized by masked men.[224] In the Gospel of Mark, Jesus predicts a similar fate for the Son of Man: "They will make fun of him and spit at him and whip him and kill him."[225]

St. Paul writes: "Without the shedding of blood there is no forgiveness of sins."[226] Jesus is portrayed as the sacrificial "Lamb of God." Christians talk of being "born again" through being "washed in the blood of the lamb." Such metaphors echo the ancient Mysteries of Attis. These were bloody rites in which an animal was the sacrificial victim. In the modern world we do not see our own animals butchered for food, so this can seem a very primitive ritual. To those who regularly killed animals in order to eat, it would have seemed much less distasteful. In the rites of the Taurobolium, or bull-sacrifice, a bull was slaughtered on a perforated platform, through which the blood poured down to bathe the initiate standing in a pit beneath. Afterward the initiate was considered "born again." Poorer people made do with a Criobolium, in which a sheep was sacrificed, and were literally "washed in the blood of the lamb!"[227]

The Mysteries of Mithras, like Christianity, celebrated these sacrificial rites symbolically rather than literally. An icon of Mithras slaying a bull was used as an altar-piece, rather than enacting the actual sacrifice. This may seem a rather gruesome icon but, upon consideration, is less violent than the Christian altar-piece of a man being tortured to death on a cross.

"Thou hast saved us by shedding the eternal blood" reads an inscription—not to Jesus, but to Mithras,[228] although centuries later Christians would express gratitude to their savior godman in exactly the same language. An anonymous Egyptian poet also adores his sacrificed and resurrecting savior Osiris with words that could equally well be addressed to Jesus:

> Have they sacrificed thee? Do they say that thou hast died for them? He is not dead! He lives for ever! He is alive more than they, for he is the mystic one of sacrifice. He is their Lord, living and young for ever![229]

Like Christianity, the Mysteries had a doctrine of "original sin." Plato teaches that the soul is banished into the body as a punishment for some unnamed ancient crime.[230] According to Empedocles, we are wandering through the four elements to atone for guilt incurred in the divine world.[231] The Mysteries taught that the original sin was separation from God.[232] The sacrificial death of the godman, or the sacrificial animal he kills, represents the initiate's own symbolic death to their lower "animal" nature and rebirth into their divine nature, which unites them with God and so atones for this original crime.

EASTER

In the fourth century an anonymous author tells us that Christians and followers of the Mystery godman Attis were both struck by the remarkable coincidence between the death and resurrection of their respective deities. This gave rise to bitter controversy between the adherents of the rival religions.[233] The Pagans contended that the resurrection of Christ was a spurious imitation of the resurrection of Attis and the Christians that the resurrection of Attis was a diabolical counterfeit of the resurrection of Christ.[234]

The Megalensia was a spring festival in the Mysteries of Attis which, like Easter, lasted for three days.[235] During this time the myth of Attis was performed as a passion play, just as the story of Jesus was performed as a passion play in the Middle Ages. An effigy of the corpse of Attis was tied to a sacred pine tree and decorated with flowers sacred to both Attis and his Syrian counterpart Adonis.[236] It was then buried in a sepulchre.[237] But like Jesus, on the third day Attis rose again.[238] In the darkness of the night a light was brought to his open grave, while the presiding priest anointed the lips of the initiates with holy oil, comforting them with the words: "To you likewise there shall come salvation from your trouble."[239] The mythologist Sir James Frazer writes:

> But when night had fallen, the sorrow of the worshipers was turned to joy. For suddenly a light shone in the darkness: the tomb was opened; the god had risen from the dead; and as the priest touched the lips of the weeping mourners with balm, he softly whispered in their ears the glad tidings of salvation. The resurrection of the god was hailed by his disciples as a promise that they too would issue triumphantly from the corruption of the grave. On the morrow, the twenty-fifth day of March, which was reckoned the vernal equinox, the divine resurrection was celebrated with a wild outburst of glee. At Rome, and probably elsewhere, the celebration took the form of a carnival. It was the festival of Joy (Hilaria).[240]

According to an ancient and widespread Christian tradition Jesus died on March 25, the same day that the resurrection of Attis was officially celebrated at Rome.[241] However, another ancient Christian tradition, reported by the Church father Lactantius, places the death of Christ on March 23 and his resurrection on March 25th, which coincides exactly with the death and resurrection of Attis.[242]

The Anthesteria, the spring festival of the Mysteries of Dionysus, was another three-day festival, of which one modern authority comments, "A certain similarity with the sequence of Good Friday and Easter cannot be overlooked."[243] Easter rites observed in Greece, Sicily, and southern Italy still bear a striking resemblance to the Mystery rites of Adonis.[244] At the festival of Adonis the air was infused with the sweet aromas of incense and filled with loud lamentation at the death of the godman. The embalmed image of Adonis was then laid in a coffin and borne to his grave,[245] but the faithful afterward consoled themselves with the assurance that the godman was alive.[246] The Pagan writer Lucian records:

They make offerings to Adonis as to one dead, and the day after the morrow they tell the story that he lives.[247]

In the gospels we are told that Jesus' corpse was "wrapped in a linen sheet" and anointed with "more than half a hundred weight of a mixture of myrrh and aloes."[248] According to Plutarch, a representation of Osiris was also wrapped with linen and anointed with myrrh.[249] Likewise, in the Mysteries of Adonis an image of the corpse of the godman was washed, anointed with spices, and wrapped around with linen or wool.[250]

After his death Jesus descends to hell, then resurrects on the third day. Plutarch tells us that Osiris, likewise, is said to have descended to hell and then arisen from the dead on the third day.[251] An ancient Egyptian inscription promises an initiate that he will also be resurrected with his Lord: "As truly as Osiris lives shall he live; as truly as Osiris is not dead shall he not die."[252]

Having resurrected, Jesus ascends to heaven. The Church father Origen refers to Osiris as a young god, who was "restored to life, and went up to heaven."[253] In the Mysteries of Adonis, initiates annually mourned the death of the godman with the shrill notes of the flute, weeping and beating of breasts, but on the third day he was believed to be resurrected and to ascend up to heaven in the presence of his worshipers.[254] According to some myths acted out as part of the Mysteries of Dionysus, shortly after his death Dionysus also rose from the grave and ascended to heaven.[255]

In the Mysteries of Mithras initiates enacted a similar resurrection scene.[256] Having accomplished his mission on Earth, Mithras was said to have ascended to heaven in a sun-chariot.[257] Like Jesus, who sits at the right hand of the Father after his ascension, Mithras was believed to have been enthroned by the God of Light as ruler of the world. Also like Jesus, Mithras was said to be waiting in heaven for the End of Time, when he would return to Earth to awaken the dead and pass judgment.[258]

Echoes of these mythological motifs are, once again, found in the legends of the sages of the Mysteries. Seneca tells us that, like Jesus, the philosopher Canus foretold that he would reappear three days after his death and did indeed return from the grave to one of his friends to "discourse on the survival of the spirit."[259] Heraclides tells us that after a banquet to celebrate one of Empedocles' miracles, the great sage suddenly ascended to heaven accompanied by glorious celestial lights.[260] It was said that Pythagoras descended to Hades in search of wisdom,[261] and after his death reappeared to his disciples and ascended into heaven.[262] The ritual sequence of death, descent into the

Underworld, and regeneration is known to have been an important analogy of initiation in the Pythagorean Mysteries from the earliest times.

Given all these dying, resurrecting, and ascending Pagan godmen and sages, it is not surprising to find Celsus indignant at Christian claims that Jesus is unique. He is amazed at the Christians' literal interpretation of what to him are obviously myths, writing,

> Is your belief based on the "fact" that this Jesus told in advance that he would rise again after his death? That your story includes his predictions of triumphing over the grave? Well, let it be so. Let's assume for the present that he foretold his resurrection. Are you ignorant of the multitudes who have invented similar tales to lead simple-minded hearers astray? It is said that Zamolix, Pythagoras' servant, convinced the Scythians that he had risen from the dead, having hidden himself away in a cave for several years, and what about Pythagoras himself in Italy—or Phampsinitus in Egypt? Now then, who else: What about Orpheus among the Odrysians, Protesilaus in Thessaly, and above all Heracles and Theseus? But quite apart from all these risings from the dead, we must look carefully at the question of the resurrection of the body as a possibility given to mortals. Doubtless you will freely admit that these other stories are legends, even as they appear to me; but you will go on to say that your resurrection story, this climax to your tragedy, is believable and noble.[263]

MOTHER OF GOD

Like her divine son, Jesus' mother Mary is also said to have ascended bodily to heaven and is honored as the "Mother of God." In the same way Semele, the mortal mother of Dionysus, is later raised up to heaven and honored as an immortal alongside her illustrious son.[264]

In Christianity, Mary takes on many of the roles of the Great Mother goddess of the Pagan Mysteries. Indeed, the Christian festival of the Assumption of the Virgin in August has ousted an ancient Pagan festival of the goddess.[265] Statues of the Egyptian goddess Isis holding the divine child have been the models for many Christian representations of Mary and the baby Jesus (see plates 1 and 2). They are so like those of the Madonna and child that they have sometimes received the adoration of ignorant Christians. Statues of the black virgin, so highly venerated in certain French cathedrals during the Middles Ages, have proved upon examination to be basalt statues of Isis![266]

Talking of the influence of the cult of the Egyptian goddess Isis on Christianity, one authority writes:

> Her stately ritual, with its shaven and tonsured priests, its matins and vespers, its tinkling music, its baptism and aspersions of holy water, its solemn processions, its jeweled images of the mother god, presented many points of similarity to the pomps and ceremonies of Catholicism. And to Isis in her later character of patroness of Mariners the Virgin Mary perhaps owes her beautiful epithet of Stella Maris, "Star of the Sea," under which she is adored by tempest-tossed sailors.[267]

It was a very early tradition in Christianity that Jesus' women followers, rather than the male disciples, were the first witnesses of the empty tomb and the resurrected Christ. In the original ending of Mark's gospel it is only Mary Magdalene, Mary the mother of James, and Salome who see the risen Jesus—a tradition that the Pagan critic Celsus acknowledges.[268]

According to another early Christian tradition all three women are called Mary—Mary Magdalene, Jesus' companion; Mary his mother; and Mary her sister.[269] In the Gospel of John the same three Marys are pictured at the foot of the cross.[270] The fact that we are given three Marys is a clear indication that we are in ancient mythological territory—the triple goddess was a familiar figure in the Pagan world. At Eleusis she appears as Demeter, Persephone, and Hecate. We find her appearing as the three fates, three charities, and three graces.

Like Jesus, Dionysus is often associated with three women followers. When a new sanctuary of Dionysus was founded three priestesses called maenads would go there to establish the cult. Each one of them would assemble one of the three women choirs that helped celebrate the Mysteries.[271] The Oinotropio were three women disciples of Dionysus said to have the ability to miraculously turn water into wine at the festivals of the god-man.[272] Among the most common of ancient sacred sculptures are representations of the cave of Pan, in which three women are being led into an empty cave by Hermes the messenger of the gods, like the three Marys being led by the angel into the empty cave, which was Jesus' tomb.[273]

SPIRITUAL REBIRTH

Jesus is born to Mary in a cave and resurrects from a cave before three Marys. Such "circular" mythic motifs were important in the Mysteries. In some myths of Osiris-Dionysus, his miraculous resurrection and miraculous birth were one and the same event. Having died his sacrificial death, he would immediately be born once again as the divine child. So, the cave in which he was born and laid out is symbolic of both womb and tomb.[274] Minucius Felix, a Christian writer, tells us that in the Mysteries of Osiris priests acted out the sorrowful search of Isis for the dead Osiris, which afterward turned to celebration upon the emergence of a small boy, representing the godman reborn,[275] thus he says, "They never cease year by year to lose what they find and to find what they lose."[276]

The key to understanding the myth of the resurrection, both in the Mysteries and the story of Jesus, is that mystically death is rebirth. Plutarch tells us that sharing in the passion of Dionysus was intended to bring about a *palingenesis*, or "rebirth."[277] Initiates of the Mysteries underwent what Lucius Apuleius calls a "voluntary death" from which they emerged spiritually reborn.[278] Just as Jesus offers his followers the opportunity to be "born again," Osiris is "He who giveth birth unto men and women a second time"[279] and "He who maketh mortals to be born again."[280]

When he "dies" to his lower self, the initiate of the Mysteries is also in labor giving birth to his Higher Self. Perhaps this is why gall, which was given to women in labor, was drunk by the Hierophant in the Eleusinian Mysteries and offered to Jesus on the cross.

Jesus mystically equates death and birth in the Gospel of John when he predicts:

> A little while and you will not see me, and again a little while and you will see me. In very truth I tell you, you will weep and mourn, but the world will be glad. But though you are plunged into grief, your grief will be turned to joy. A woman in labor is in pain because her time has come; but when the child is born she forgets the anguish in her joy that a man has been born into the world.[281]

To die to the lower self is to be spiritually reborn—this is the central secret teaching encoded by the myths of Osiris-Dionysus. Could the Jesus story also be a myth, which encodes the same perennial spiritual teaching?

CONCLUSION

Either the Devil really has perfected the art of diabolical mimicry or there is a mystery to solve here. Let's review the evidence:

- ❖ Jesus is the savior of mankind, God made man, the Son of God equal with the Father; so is Osiris-Dionysus.
- ❖ Jesus is born of a mortal virgin who after her death ascends to heaven and is honored as a divine being; so is Osiris-Dionysus.
- ❖ Jesus is born in a cave on December 25 or January 6, as is Osiris-Dionysus.
- ❖ The birth of Jesus is prophesied by a star; so is the birth of Osiris-Dionysus.
- ❖ Jesus is born in Bethlehem, which was shaded by a grove sacred to Osiris-Dionysus.
- ❖ Jesus is visited by the Magi, who are followers of Osiris-Dionysus.
- ❖ The Magi bring Jesus gifts of gold, frankincense, and myrrh, which a sixth-century BCE Pagan tells us is the way to worship God.
- ❖ Jesus is baptized, a ritual practiced for centuries in the Mysteries.
- ❖ The holy man who baptizes Jesus with water has the same name as a Pagan god of water and is born on the summer solstice celebrated as a Pagan water festival.
- ❖ Jesus offers his followers elemental baptisms of water, air, and fire, as did the Pagan Mysteries.
- ❖ Jesus is portrayed as a quiet man with long hair and a beard; so is Osiris-Dionysus.
- ❖ Jesus turns water into wine at a marriage on the same day that Osiris-Dionysus was previously believed to have turned water into wine at a marriage.
- ❖ Jesus heals the sick, exorcises demons, provides miraculous meals, helps fishermen make miraculous catches of fish, and calms the water for his disciples; all of these marvels had previously been performed by Pagan sages.
- ❖ Like the sages of the Mysteries, Jesus is a wandering wonder-worker who is not honored in his home town.
- ❖ Jesus is accused of licentious behavior, as were the followers of Osiris-Dionysus.
- ❖ Jesus is not at first recognized as a divinity by his disciples, but then is transfigured before them in all his glory; the same is true of Osiris-Dionysus.
- ❖ Jesus is surrounded by 12 disciples; so is Osiris-Dionysus.

- Jesus rides triumphantly into town on a donkey while crowds wave branches, as does Osiris-Dionysus.
- Jesus is a just man unjustly accused of heresy and bringing a new religion, as is Osiris-Dionysus.
- Jesus attacks hypocrites, stands up to tyranny, and willingly goes to his death predicting he will rise again in three days, as do Pagan sages.
- Jesus is betrayed for 30 pieces of silver, a motif found in the story of Socrates.
- Jesus is equated with bread and wine, as is Osiris-Dionysus.
- Jesus' disciples symbolically eat bread and drink wine to commune with him, as do the followers of Osiris-Dionysus.
- Jesus is hung on a tree or crucified, as is Osiris-Dionysus.
- Jesus dies as a sacrifice to redeem the sins of the world; so does Osiris-Dionysus.
- Jesus' corpse is wrapped in linen and anointed with myrrh, as is the corpse of Osiris-Dionysus.
- After his death Jesus descends to hell, then on the third day resurrects before his disciples and ascends into heaven, where he is enthroned by God and waits to reappear at the end of time as a divine judge, as does Osiris-Dionysus.
- Jesus was said to have died and resurrected on exactly the same dates that the death and resurrection of Osiris-Dionysus were celebrated.
- Jesus' empty tomb is visited by three women followers; Osiris-Dionysus also has three women followers who visit an empty cave.
- Through sharing in his passion Jesus offers his disciples the chance to be born again, as does Osiris-Dionysus.

Discounting the diabolical mimicry argument, as all sane people must, how are we to explain these extraordinary similarities between Pagan myth and the story of Jesus?

The first possibility we considered was that the true biography of Jesus had been overlaid with Pagan mythology at a later date. This is a common idea often advanced to account for those aspects of the Jesus story that seem obviously mythical, such as the virgin birth. But we had found so many resemblances between the myths of Osiris-Dionysus and the supposed biography of Jesus that this theory seemed inadequate. If *all* the elements of the Jesus story that had been prefigured by Pagan myths were later accretions, what would be left of the "real" Jesus? If this theory is true then the

Jesus we know is a myth and the historical man has been completely eclipsed.

The other possibility that occurred to us was more radical and challenging. Could it be that the story of Jesus was actually yet another version of the myth of Osiris-Dionysus? If we had not been brought up in a Christian culture, would we ever have interpreted the incredible stories related by the gospels as anything other than profound myths? No one believes the myths of Osiris-Dionysus are literally true, so why should we take as historical fact the same events related in a Jewish setting?

Not knowing quite what to believe, we turned our attention to Jesus' spiritual teachings, wondering if here we might glimpse something of the man beneath the myth.

4

Perfected Platonism

Many of the ideas of the Christians have been expressed better—and earlier—by the Greeks.[1] Behind these views is an ancient doctrine that has existed from the beginning.[2]

Celsus

Just as Pagan critics of Christianity saw the story of Jesus as an adaptation of the myth of Osiris-Dionysus, so they also viewed Christian teachings as a poor copy of the ancient and perennial philosophy of the Pagan Mysteries. Celsus writes of the Christians dismissively:

> Let's speak about their systematic corruption of the truth, their misunderstanding of some fairly simple philosophical principles—which of course they completely botch.[3]

Most early Christian intellectuals had been educated in Pagan philosophy and were well aware of its profound similarities with their own doctrines. Clement of Alexandria regarded the gospels as "perfected Platonism."[4] Justin Martyr calls Heraclitus, Socrates, and other Greek philosophers Christians before Christ.[5] Yet he stops short of acknowledging a common spiritual heritage. To Justin the similarities are, once again, the results of diabolical mimicry which blinds the foolish to the essential differences between Christianity and Paganism. He writes:

For I myself, when I discovered the wicked disguises which the evil spirits had thrown around the divine doctrines of the Christians, to turn aside others from joining them, laughed both at those who framed these falsehoods, and at the disguise itself, and at popular opinion; not because the teachings of Plato are different from those of Christ, but because they are not in all respects similar, as neither are those of the Stoics, poets, and historians.[6]

The Pagans were so persistent in accusing Christianity of borrowing from Plato, however, that St. Ambrose wrote a treatise to confute them. He did not deny the resemblances, but explained them by claiming that Plato plagiarized Moses![7] Building on a fake chronology established in the fourth century by Bishop Eusebius, Augustine developed the equally ludicrous idea that Plato copied the Jewish prophet Jeremiah. He explains:

Did not the illustrious bishop show that Plato made a journey into Egypt at the time when Jeremiah the prophet was there, and show that it is much more likely that Plato was through Jeremiah's means initiated into our literature. And thus, when we reflect on the dates, it becomes much more probable that those philosophers learnt whatever they said that was good and true from our literature, than that the lord Jesus Christ learnt from the writings of Plato—a thing which it is the height of folly to believe.[8]

Justin Martyr went so far as to deny that Pagans had any right to their own prophets and claimed the wisdom of the ancient sages for Christianity! He writes: "Whatever things were rightly said among all teachers are the property of us Christians."[9] Following this tradition, St. Augustine later likewise declared:

If those who are called philosophers, and especially the Platonists, have said aught that is true and in harmony with the faith, we are not only not to shrink from it, but to claim it for our own use from those who have unlawful possession of it.[10]

Why do these Christians feel forced to adopt such convoluted arguments as the only way of resisting Pagan accusations of plagiarism? Are the teachings of Jesus and the wisdom of the Mysteries really so similar? Let's see.

MORAL PURITY

Christians were very proud of their high moral doctrines. In contrast, they often sought to portray the Mysteries as morally degenerate. But this is absolute nonsense. The initiate Diodorus of Sicily writes, "Those who have taken part in the Mysteries are said to become more pious, more upright, and in every way better than their former selves."[11] An initiate of Sabazius announces after his initiation: "I escaped evil, I found the good."[12] Sopatros tells us, "On account of initiation I shall be quite prepared for every moral demand."[13] Iamblichus, talking of the Mystery pageant, writes:

> Exhibitions of this kind in the Mysteries were designed to free us from licentious passions, by gratifying the sight, and at the same time vanquishing all evil thought, through the awful sanctity with which these rites were accompanied.[14]

Initiation into the Mysteries was seen as a source of moral purification and preparation for death. Aristophanes declares: "All those who participated in the Mysteries led an innocent, calm and holy life; they died looking for the light of the Elysian fields."[15] Porphyry adds, "At the moment of death the soul must be as it is in the Mysteries; free from any blemish, passion, envy, or anger."[16] Celsus tells us that it was announced that initiation was only open to "whoever is holy from every defilement and whose soul is conscious of no evil" and that "No one should approach unless he was conscious of his innocence."[17]

Jesus taught his followers to strive for moral purity, not only in deed, but even in thought. The Church father Clement of Alexandria writes: "He who would enter the shrine must be pure, and purity is to think holy things."[18] But Clement is merely echoing the ancient inscription over the Pagan shrine of Asclepius, which also read: "Purity is thinking only holy thoughts."[19] Likewise, in the sayings of the Pagan sage Sextus, we read: "Do not even think of that which you are unwilling God should know."[20] Celsus writes:

> What ought really to occupy our minds, day and night, is the Good: publicly and privately, in every word and deed and in the silence of reflection.[21]

The Stoic philosophers developed the idea of the conscience, which Christianity inherited.[22] *Conscience* means "with knowledge." For the Pagan sages, to listen to one's conscience was to follow the inner spiritual Knowledge, or Gnosis, possessed by the Higher Self. The followers of Pythagoras were required every night to remember all the events of the day and judge themselves morally from the standpoint of their Higher Self. The initiate Seneca describes his constant striving for moral perfection in simple homely language that could be that of a modern Christian:

> Every day I plead my case before myself. When the light is extinguished, and my wife, who knows my habit, keeps silence, I examine the past day, go over and weigh all my deeds and words. I hide nothing, I omit nothing: why should I hesitate to face my shortcomings when I can say, "Take care not to repeat them, and also I forgive you today"?[23]

The need to confess one's sins was taught by Jesus and is still an essential element of Christianity. This idea was far from new, however. Initiates into the Mysteries were required to purify themselves by making a public confession of all their failings and misdeeds. In the Mysteries of Eleusis, the priest asked the initiate to confess the worst deed that he had ever committed in his life.[24] This was not an empty formality, but a truly pious act. The despotic Roman Emperor Nero turned back from seeking initiation into the Mysteries when he realized he would have to openly admit murdering his mother. Even a tyrant accepted this loss of face, rather than lie before the most sacred institution of the ancient world.[25] A modern classical scholar writes that the Mysteries "anticipated Catholicism in the establishment of a Confessional—but less rigid—with the elements of a penitential system and absolution for uneasy devotees. The priests acted as representatives of the Mystery-god, exacting auricular confession."[26] A "Negative Confession" of the evils one had avoided committing is found in the Egyptian *Book of the Dead* as long ago as 1500 BCE.[27]

Contrary to Christian claims that the Mysteries were morally degenerate, the evidence clearly shows that initiation was designed to bring about moral regeneration.

Despite this, of course, the Pagan Mysteries were no less open to hypocrisy and abuse than any other religion. The Jewish Pythagorean Philo complains: "It often happens that good men are not initiated, but that robbers and murderers, and lewd women are, if they pay money to the initiators and hierophants."[28] But as a modern scholar remarks,

Such passages show that abuses existed, but also that it was felt to be a scandal if the initiated person failed to exhibit any moral improvement.[29]

LOVE

In contrast to the traditional Jewish God of justice, Jesus preaches a revolutionary new conception of a God of love. Jesus' first and central commandment is that his followers should love God, and to this day having a personal loving relationship with God is at the heart of Christianity. This was also at the heart of the Mysteries. A modern scholar writes:

> If one had to single out one paramount feature that distinguished all the Mystery cults from other religions of their period, it would be that they sought a personal relationship with their gods. Consequently the attitude of their devotees to the gods was one of love rather than fear or indifferent manipulation. The motive of much primitive religion seems to be to get rid of the gods, and by fair means or foul to prevent them from troubling mankind. For the Mystery religions the motive is quite the contrary: it is to get closer to them, recognizing them as man's best friends.[30]

The Christian sentiment of *brotherly love* was also a feature of the Mysteries six centuries before there were any Christians. Initiates at Eleusis were called *adelphoi*, meaning "brothers." A *philadelphian* was someone who practiced "brotherly love." The followers of Mithras were also called *brothers*. Adherents of the Mysteries of Jupiter Dolichenus were *fratres carissimi*, or "most loving brothers."[31]

However, Jesus taught his followers not only to love their fellow Christians, but also to love all their neighbors. In the Gospel of Matthew he instructs his followers: "Treat others as you wish to be treated."[32] But this teaching was nothing new either. It is a perennial and ubiquitous precept found in nearly all religious traditions.[33] Among the sayings of the Pagan philosopher Sextus, we find: "Such as you wish your neighbor to be to you, such also be to your neighbor."[34]

But Jesus goes farther than this. He teaches that we should even love our enemies. We should forgive those who wrong us and "turn the other cheek."[35] These beautiful and profound teachings are usually seen as a revolution in spirituality, replacing the old Jewish Law of "an eye for an eye." They were indeed a radical departure from such Jewish sentiments, but they were perfectly familiar to initiates of the ancient Pagan Mysteries! In *The Sayings of Sextus the Pythagorean* we find the same teachings: "Wish that you may be able to benefit your enemies."[36] Pythagoras himself had taught that even if abused, one should not defend oneself.[37]

Epictetus similarly writes:

This is the philosopher's way; to be flogged like an ass and to love those who beat him, to be father and brother of all humanity.[38]

But most famously in the ancient world, these teachings had been expressed by Socrates and recorded by his disciple Plato. Celsus writes:

You Christians have a saying that goes something like this: "Don't resist a man who insults you; even if he strikes you, offer him the other cheek as well." This is nothing new, and it's been better said by others, especially by Plato.[39]

In one of Plato's dialogues, Socrates leads Crito, step by step, to exactly the same profound understanding that 500 years later appears in the gospels. We pick up the argument as Socrates is reaching his conclusion:

Socrates:	"Then we should never do wrong?"
Crito:	"Never."
Socrates:	"And should we not even try to avenge a wrong if we are wronged ourselves, as most would do, on the premise that we should never do wrong?"
Crito:	"So it seems."
Socrates:	"So, should we do harm, Crito, or not?"
Crito:	"I should say not, Socrates."
Socrates:	"Well then, is it just or unjust to repay injury with injury?"
Crito:	"Unjust, I would think."
Socrates:	"Because doing harm to men is no different from doing wrong?"

THE JESUS MYSTERIES

Crito: "Exactly so."
Socrates: "So, we should never take revenge and never hurt anyone, even if we have been hurt."

Socrates concludes:

> It is never right to do wrong and never right to take revenge; nor is it right to give evil, or in the case of one who has suffered some injury, to attempt to get even.[40]

Celsus comments caustically:

> This was Plato's opinion, and as he says, it was not new to him but was pronounced by inspired men long before him. What I have said about it may serve, part for whole, as an example of the sort of ideas the Christians mutilate.[41]

The great sages of the Mysteries even expanded their ethic of universal love to include animals. Although some Mystery religions practiced animal sacrifice, Pythagoras was a vegetarian and Empedocles looked back to a golden age "when no altar was wet with the unholy slaughter of bulls."[42] The enlightened Pagan sages, like the enlightened masters of any religious tradition, tried constantly to lead initiates away from out-of-date practices toward understanding the spiritual meaning of their rites.[43] A modern classical scholar writes of the Mysteries of Orpheus as "imposing—perhaps for the first time in the Western world—a lofty ethic of purity and non-injury." He continues:

> The Orphics and Pythagoreans were truly the first Christians in the ethical sense, and a few Christians like St. Francis have extended their compassion in Pythagorean fashion to the animal kingdom.[44]

HUMILITY AND POVERTY

Jesus teaches his followers to emulate his own humility and poverty. He sends out his disciples, saying,

Go and announce that the kingdom of heaven is approaching. Cure the sick, raise the dead, wash lepers, throw out demons. Accept free gifts, and give for free. Don't have gold, silver, or brass in your belts. Don't take a knapsack on the road, or a second tunic or shoes, or a cane.[45]

In doing so, his followers became indistinguishable from the Pagan Cynic philosophers, who traveled from place to place giving spiritual teachings.[46] A modern scholar writes:

Among the familiar sights during the first century of the Roman Empire were the Cynics wearing rough cloaks, carrying begging bags and thorn-sticks. They used to wander from town to town preaching to the people, and hammering in their platitudes. When the apostles went preaching the gospel, they traveled about in a similarly unencumbered manner.[47]

Both Cynics and early Christians wore the same rough garments and both called their religion *The Way*.[48] Describing a Cynic, Epictetus writes in words that could equally describe Jesus and his disciples:

He is a herald from God to men, declaring to them the truth about good and evil things; that they have erred, and are seeking the reality of good and evil where it is not; and where it is they do not consider. He must then be able, if so it chance, to go up impassioned, as on the tragic stage, and speak that word of Socrates, "O men, whither are ye borne away? What do ye? Miserable as ye are! Like blind men ye wander up and down. Ye have left the true road, and are going by a false; ye are seeking peace and happiness where they are not, and if another shall show where they are, ye believe him not."[49]

Celsus sees Christian humility as an enforced copy of the voluntary humility of the Pagan sages. He rants indignantly:

Not surprisingly, they emphasize the virtue of humility, which in their case is to make a virtue of necessity! Here again prostituting the noble ideas of Plato. Not only do they misunderstand the words of the philosophers; they even stoop to assigning words of the philosophers to their Jesus. For example, we are told that Jesus judged the rich with the saying "It is easier for a camel to go through the eye of a needle than for a rich man to enter the kingdom of God." Yet we know that Plato expressed this very idea in a purer form when he said, "It is impossible for an exceptionally good man to be exceptionally rich." Is one utterance more inspired than the other?[50]

Celsus is right to be critical of Christian claims that Jesus' teachings are original and distinctive. Jesus teaches, "Lay up your treasure in heaven where no thief can get near it, no moth destroy it."[51] Sextus likewise exhorts, "Possess those things that no one can take away from you."[52]

Jesus is the king of the world because he is wise, not because he is powerful. A popular Stoic maxim was "The only true king is the wise man."[53]

Jesus teaches, "Keep awake, for you do not know when the master of the house will come. If he comes suddenly, do not let him find you asleep."[54] Epictetus writes, "Go not far from the ship at any time, lest the master should call and thou not be ready."[55]

Jesus teaches, "I assure you, anyone who doesn't receive the Kingdom of God like a little child, will never get into it."[56] Heraclitus writes, "The Kingdom belongs to the child."[57]

Jesus teaches, "Why do you call me good? No one is good, only God."[58] Four centuries previously Plato had defined God as "the Good," a quality which, by definition, only God could fully manifest. In similar fashion to Jesus, Pythagoras had refused to be called wise, explaining that no one is wise except God; Pythagoras preferred to call himself a "lover of wisdom" or *philosopher*—a term he was the first person to use.

HEAVEN AND HELL

When the Mysteries were first introduced to Greece from Egypt, the notion of an afterlife was a new and heretical doctrine to the Greeks. Likewise, the concept of heaven and hell is not found in the Old Testament, yet is a central idea in the gospels.[59] Where did these notions come from? Just as in ancient Greece, these new ideas were introduced by the Mysteries.

Christianity offers its adherents the consolation of a heavenly afterlife, while threatening the wicked and nonbelievers with the torments of hell. Sophocles writes:

> How thrice blessed are they of mortals who, having beheld these Mysteries, depart to the house of Death. For to such alone is life bestowed there: to others fall all ills.[60]

On the death of his beloved little daughter Timoxena, Plutarch wrote a beautiful letter of consolation to his wife in which he urged her to remember "the mystic symbols of the rites of Dionysus" which will prevent her from thinking that "the soul experiences nothing after death and ceases to be."[61] Plutarch is confident that through "the experience which we share together of the revelations of Dionysus," he and his wife "know that the soul is indestructible" and in the afterlife is like a bird set free from its cage.[62]

An inscription claims that initiates of the Mysteries, like the Christian faithful, are "reborn in eternity."[63] A hierophant's funeral inscription tells us that he now knows "death is not an evil but something good."[64] Glaucus writes: "Beautiful indeed is the Mystery given us by the blessed gods: death is for mortals no longer an evil but a blessing."[65] A priest of the Mysteries of Orpheus named Philip preached so enthusiastically about the bliss that awaited the initiated in heaven, that one wit asked him why he did not hurry up and die to enjoy it himself![66]

St. Augustine complains that the Mysteries "promise eternal life to anybody!"[67] Yet the Mysteries only promised eternal salvation to the initiated, just as Christianity only promises eternal life to Christians. A hymn warns:

> Blessed is he who has seen this among earthly men; but he who is uninitiated in the sacred rites and who has no portion, never has the same lot once dead down in the murky dark.[68]

The Mysteries of Orpheus were renowned in the ancient world for their vivid descriptions of the torments awaiting evildoers in the afterlife. As one modern authority tells us, "Orphics created the Christian idea of purgatory."[69] Indeed, the scholar Franz Cumont has shown that the vivid descriptions of the happiness of the blessed and sufferings of sinners found in Orphic books were taken over by the Jewish Books of Esdras, which were written in the first century CE and included among the apocryphal scriptures in some versions of the New Testament; these Pagan conceptions of the afterlife were then developed by St. Ambrose and so became the standard imagery of Catholicism.[70]

No wonder, then, that when early Christians came across passages in Plato concerning the punishment of souls in Tartarus, the Greek hell, they found it difficult to explain how Pagans could have anticipated their own doctrine of hellfire.[71] In *Phaedo*, for example, Plato describes a "huge lake blazing with much fire . . . and boiling with water and mud." In the non-canonical Christian scripture *The Apocalypse of Peter* we find the same fate awaiting sinners in the Underworld, who will be trapped in "a huge lake filled with blazing mud."[72]

Celsus is clear that Christian conceptions of heaven and hell borrow heavily from the Mysteries. He writes:

> Now the Christians pray that after their toil and strife here below they shall enter the kingdom of heaven, and they agree with the ancient systems that there are seven heavens and that the way of the soul is through the planets. That their system is based on very old teachings may be seen from similar beliefs in the old Persian Mysteries associated with the cult of Mithras.[73]

The Mysteries of Mithras did indeed, like Christianity, teach of the terrors that awaited the damned in the bowels of the Earth and of the pleasures for the blessed in a celestial paradise.[74] The belief in seven heavens has not come down to us in modern Christianity, but was prevalent among early Christians and is referred to by St. Paul, who describes himself being "caught up as far as the third heaven."[75]

Christian enthusiasm for the sufferings of the damned in hell reminds Celsus of the more superstitious initiates of the Mysteries of Bacchus:

> Christians babble about God day and night in their impious and sullied way; they arouse the awe of the illiterate with their false descriptions of the punishments awaiting those who have sinned. Thus they behave like guardians of the Bacchic Mysteries.[76]

The more enlightened sages of the Mysteries viewed such horrors as merely stories to encourage better moral behavior. Plutarch calls the terrors of the Underworld an "improving myth."[77] The Christian philosopher Origen likewise argued that the literal terrors of hell were false, but they ought to be publicized in order to scare simpler believers.[78]

Both the Pagan sages and Origen believed in reincarnation. Heaven and hell were seen as temporary states of reward and punishment followed by another human incarnation. Life and death were viewed as parts of a recurring "circular" process, not once-only events leading to eternal reward or damnation. Hell was a purgatorial experience leading to further human experience, through which every soul could make its return journey to God.

Origen, however, was posthumously condemned by the Roman Catholic Church as a heretic for his compassionate belief that all souls would eventually be redeemed.[79] The Roman Church required all Christians to believe that some souls would suffer in hell forever, while the faithful would enjoy eternal salvation. This is the one doctrine on the afterlife, which Celsus regards as distinctively Christian. He writes:

> Now it will be wondered how men so desperate in their beliefs can persuade others to join their ranks. The Christians use sundry methods of persuasion, and invent a number of terrifying incentives. Above all, they have concocted an absolutely offensive doctrine of everlasting punishment and rewards, exceeding anything the philosophers (who have never denied the punishment of the unrighteous or the reward of the blessed) could have imagined.[80]

The Roman Church also taught that at the Last Judgment there would be an apocalypse of fire at the end of time in which all non-Christians would be consumed and the faithful physically resurrected. Celsus is appalled, writing,

> It is equally silly of these Christians to suppose that when their god applies the fire (like a common cook!) all the rest of mankind will be thoroughly roasted, and that they alone will escape unscorched—not just those alive at the time, mind you, but they say those long since dead will rise up from the earth possessing the same bodies as they did before. I ask you: Is this not the hope of worms? For what sort of human soul is it that has any use for a rotted corpse of a body? The very fact that some Jews and even some Christians reject this teaching about rising corpses shows just how repulsive it is; it is nothing less than nauseating and impossible. I mean, what sort of body is it that could return to its original nature or become the same as it was

before it rotted away? And of course they have no reply for this one, and as in most cases where there is no reply they take cover by saying "Nothing is impossible with God."[81]

Yet even this rather bizarre Christian doctrine of apocalypse and physical resurrection is prefigured by the Mysteries of Mithras. This particular Mystery tradition taught that at the end of the present age God would send destruction upon the world. Then, like the "Second Coming" of Jesus, Mithras would descend to Earth again and raise the dead from their tombs. According to the Gospel of Matthew, during the last days the Son of Man will separate the good from the bad, like a shepherd separating sheep from goats, saving the one and condemning the other.[82] Likewise the followers of Mithras expected that in the last days humanity would form one grand assembly and the good be separated from the bad. Finally, acquiescing to the prayers of the "beautiful ones," they believed God would cause a devouring fire to fall from the heavens, which would annihilate all the wicked. Just as the Christian apocalypse signals the final defeat of the Devil by Christ, so in Mithraism the Spirit of Darkness and his impure demons will perish in the great conflagration and the rejuvenated universe enjoy happiness without end for all eternity.[83]

THE NEW AGE

In the Gospel of Matthew, Jesus predicts the coming apocalypse and birth of a New Age, saying,

> For nation will make war upon nation, kingdom upon kingdom; there will be famines and earthquakes in many places. With all these things the birth-pangs of the New Age begin.[84]

Based on their understanding of astronomy, Pagans also expected a New Age. The ancients believed that approximately every 2,000 years we enter a new astrological "Great Month."[85] They themselves were living in the Great Month of Aries, which began in about 2000 BCE. The Age of Aries was symbolized by the ram, hence Dionysus was often depicted with ram's horns. The New Age of Pisces began around 145 BCE and is currently changing into another New Age, the Great Month of Aquarius.

Pisces is symbolized by the fish, and Christians obviously viewed their faith as a new religion for this New Age. The most common symbol used to represent Christianity was the symbol of the fish—the Pythagorean *vesica piscis*, which we have discussed previously *(see pp. 39–40)*. The apostles were known as "fishers of men." Early Christians called themselves "little fishes." The Greek word ICTHYS, which means "fish," was used by early Christians as a code word for *Jesus*. This was regarded as an acronym for "Jesus Christ, Son of God, Savior." The great mouthpiece of Christian orthodoxy, Tertullian, writes:

> But we, the Christians, are little fishes after the type of our great Fish (ICTHYS) Jesus Christ, born in the water.[86]

However, Icthys had for centuries been the Greek name for Adonis the god-man in the Syrian Mysteries![87]

As the Age of Pisces began, its opposite sign in the zodiac, Virgo the Virgin, was on the western horizon. Pagan mythology, therefore, expected the savior of the Piscean Age to be born of a virgin. In the first century BCE the Roman poet and initiate Virgil, reputedly repeating a prophecy of a Pagan oracular priestess known as the Sibyl, predicted such a miraculous birth:

> We have reached the last era in Sibylline song. Time has conceived and the great Sequence of the Ages starts afresh. Justice, the Virgin, comes back to dwell with us. The first-born of the New Age is already on his way from high heaven down to earth. With him the iron race shall end and golden man inherit all the world. Smile on the baby's birth. This glorious Age will dawn. The ox will not be frightened of the lion. Your very cradle will adorn itself with blossoms to caress you. Enter, for the hour is close at hand. See how the whole creation rejoices in the age that is to be! Begin, then, little boy, to greet your mother with a smile.[88]

This prophecy, so reminiscent of the story of the birth of Jesus and the Christian promise that the lamb and lion will lie down together, was interpreted by Christians as anticipating the coming of Jesus. Actually, Virgil was referring to the widely held Pagan belief that the coming age of Pisces would herald a new beginning for humankind, and the divine child was Osiris-Dionysus.[89]

The ancients believed that the beginning of a New Age was marked by the destruction of the old. The Great Month of Taurus is symbolized by a bull. Scholars now understand that altar-pieces representing Mithras slaying a bull are actually star maps depicting the ending of the Age of Taurus.[90] The following Great Month of Aries is symbolized by a ram. Is it a coincidence that the end of this Great Age is similarly marked by representations of the slaying of Jesus, the "Lamb of God?"[91]

The Persian Mysteries of Mithras believed that the Great Months were each bounded by an apocalypse—at one end by a flood and at the other by fire.[92] The Greeks also held that there had been a dreadful but purifying flood, related in the myth of Deucalion. In the same way, early Christians looked back to a purging by water, the flood of Noah, and looked forward to a purging by fire, the coming apocalypse. No wonder, then, that Celsus sees in this Christian vision more plagiarism of ancient Pagan teachings:

> They postulate, for example, that their Messiah will return as a con-
> queror on the clouds, and that he will rain fire upon the earth in his
> battle with the princes of the air, and that the whole world, with the
> exception of believing Christians, will be consumed in fire. An inter-
> esting idea—and hardly an original one. The idea came from the Greeks
> and others—namely, that after cycles of years and because of the for-
> tuitous conjunctions of certain stars there are conflagrations and
> floods, and that after the last flood, in the time of Deucalion, the cycle
> demands a conflagration in accordance with the alternating succes-
> sion of the universe. This is responsible for the silly opinion of some
> Christians that God will come down and rain fire upon the earth.[93]

ONE GOD

Paganism is traditionally classified as a *polytheistic* religion, because Pagans believed in many gods. Christianity, by contrast, is classed as a *monotheistic* religion because Christians believe in only one God. In their relentless campaign to eradicate Paganism, Christians have portrayed its so-called polytheism as primitive idolatry. But this is a complete distortion of the sublime philosophical understanding of God held by the sages of the ancient Mysteries.

Five hundred years before Christ, Xenophanes had already written: "There is one God, always still and at rest, who moves all things with the thoughts of his mind."[94] The legendary Egyptian sage Hermes Trismegistus is credited with teaching: "Do you think there are many Gods? That's absurd—God is one."[95] Writing at around the time that Christians were just beginning to preach their supposedly anti-Pagan doctrine of one God, the Pagan sage Maximus of Tyre declared: "The one doctrine upon which all the world is united is that one God is king of all and father."[96]

Even Justin Martyr could not deny that Pythagoras had preached the doctrine of one God. He quotes Pythagoras' own words:

> God is one; and he himself does not, as some suppose, exist outside the world, but in it, he being wholly present in the entire circle, and beholding all generations, being the regulating ingredient of all the ages, and the administrator of his own powers and works, the first principle of all things, the light of heaven, and father of all, the intelligence and animating soul of the universe, the movement of all orbits.[97]

This idea was not even new in the time of Pythagoras, but had existed for thousands of years among the ancient Egyptians, who talked of an ineffable one God who could not be represented in stone. In the Egyptian Mysteries, Osiris represents this supreme Being and was proclaimed "Heir of the world and the One God."[98] Egyptian inscriptions reveal just how similar the Pagan and Christian conceptions of God in fact are:

> God is One alone,
> and none other existeth with Him.
> God is the One who hath made all things.
> God is from the beginning,
> and He hath been from the beginning.
> He existed when nothing else existed,
> and what existeth
> He created after He had come into being.
> He is the father of beginnings.[99]

The Egyptian god Amun was called "the One of One." The great Egyptologist Wallis Budge remarks:

It is also said that he is "without a second" and thus there is no doubt whatever that when the Egyptians declared their God to be One, and without a second, they meant precisely what the Hebrews and Arabs meant when they declared their God to be One. Such a God was an entirely different Being from the personification of the powers of nature and the existences which, for want of a better name, have been called "gods."[100]

Like every religion, Paganism had its superstitious and primitive side, and there certainly were many Pagan cults of different gods. But, as Budge explains, these so-called gods represented aspects of nature. The ancient Egyptian word, which we translate as "god" is *neter*. *Neter* refers to a spiritual essence or principle. The many *neters* of the Egyptians represented the many natures of the one all-embracing Being—the gods were different aspects or faces of the one supreme God.[101]

In the ancient world, a particular god was often chosen to represent the one ineffable God, and the epithet *pantheus*, meaning "all-god," was added to his name. Thus we find Latin inscriptions to Osiris-Dionysus, in his forms as Serapis and Liber, which address the godman as "Serapis Pantheus" and "Liber Pantheus."[102]

Pagans could all worship the same one God via any particular god or goddess that appealed to them without being in contradiction with their neighbors who chose a different divine face. Celsus writes:

> It matters not a bit what one calls the supreme God—or whether one uses Greek names or Indian names or the names used formerly by the Egyptians.[103]

By denying the validity of all other faces of the divine except Jehovah, the god of the Jews, Christians stepped outside this common understanding.

Pagans found this inexplicably small-minded. Such exclusivity was alien to the Pagan spirit of religious tolerance, beautifully captured by Maximus of Tyre:

> Let all the nations know the divine, that it is one; and if the art of Phideas arouses the Greeks to the remembrance of God, the worship of animals the Egyptians and a river others, and fire others again, I do

not find fault with their differences. Let them only know, let them only love, let them remember.[104]

This open-minded tolerance did not stop initiates of the Mysteries trying to free their fellow Pagans from pointless superstition, however.[105] When Christians criticized the Pagans for worshiping idols they were actually echoing the sages of the Mysteries, who had been gently mocking more primitive Pagan practices for centuries. Celsus complains indignantly of the Christians:

> There is nothing new or impressive about their ethical teaching; indeed when one compares it to other philosophies, their simple-mindedness becomes apparent. Take their aversion to what they term idolatry. As Herodotus shows, the Persians long before our time held the view that things that were made with human hands cannot be regarded as gods. Indeed it is preposterous that the work of a crafts-man (often the worst sort of person!) should be considered a god. The wise Heraclitus says that "those who worship images as gods are as foolish as men who talk to walls."[106]

Diagoras was renowned for mocking the gods,[107] as was Diogenes of Pontus, who, when asked why he was begging from a statue, answered sardonically, "To get practice in being refused."[108]

Xenophanes had attacked the immoral behavior of the gods as portrayed by Homer and Hesiod, commenting sarcastically,

> Human beings think of the gods as having been born, wearing clothes, speaking, and having bodies like their own. Ethiopians say the gods are black with snub noses. Thracians say they have blue eyes and red hair. If cows and horses had hands they would draw pictures of the gods looking like cows and horses.[109]

The satirist Lucian has his fictional character Momus complain to Zeus about all the bizarre representations of the gods with animal heads. In reply Zeus acknowledges, "These things are unseemly," but explains that "Most of them are a matter of symbolism and someone who is not an initiate into the Mysteries really should not laugh at them."[110] Celsus likewise explains that the Pagan representation of the gods are understood by the initiated as having symbolic meaning and should not be taken literally, since they are "symbols of invisible ideas and not objects of worship in themselves."[111]

Ironically, many Pagan philosophers thought it was the Christian conception of God that was primitive. While it was all right to personify aspects of God as the "gods," they regarded it as impossible to portray the ineffable nature of the supreme God in human terms as the Christians did. Celsus, finding such anthropomorphism ridiculous, writes:

> The Christians say that God has hands, a mouth, and a voice; they are always proclaiming that "God said this" or "God spoke." "The heavens declare the work of his hands," they say. I can only comment that such a God is no God at all, for God has neither hands, mouth nor voice, nor any characteristics of which we know. Their absurd doctrines even contain reference to God walking about in the garden he created for man; and they speak of him being angry, jealous, moved to repentance, sorry, sleepy—in short as being in every respect more a man than a God.[112] Further, for all their exclusiveness about the highest God, do not the Jews also worship angels?[113]

Not only did the Jews and Christians worship angels, which Pagans saw as directly equivalent to their many gods and goddesses, they even talked about "the gods" in exactly the same way that Pagans did! The Church father Clement of Alexandria writes of spiritual illumination "teaching us beforehand the future life that we shall lead according to God and with the gods." The illuminated, he explains, are called gods because they are "destined to sit on thrones with the other gods that have been first put in their places by the Savior."[114]

The Pagan initiate Cicero writes, "Know then, that thou art a god."[115] In the same way, in the Gospel of John we read that Jesus answers the Pharisees' accusation of blasphemy for having claimed to be the Son of God:

> Is it not written in your own law "I said: You are gods?" These are called gods to whom the word of God was delivered—and Scripture cannot be set aside. Then why do you charge me with blasphemy because I, consecrated and sent into the world by the Father, said, "I am God's Son"?[116]

The early Christian philosopher Origen used phrases such as "two Gods" in discussing the creed.[117] Justin Martyr speaks of "a second God."[118] And then, of course, there is the decidedly polytheistic Christian doctrine of the Holy Trinity.[119] The idea that God can manifest in "three persons" is identical with the Pagan concept of the many natures or faces of the one supreme ineffable God.

The notion of a divine trinity is not found in Judaism, but it is prefigured by Paganism.[120] Aristotle writes of the Pythagorean doctrine that "the whole and everything in it is comprehended by the number three, for end, middle and beginning have the number of the whole, that is the trinity."[121] Hundreds of years earlier, an ancient Egyptian text has God proclaim: "Being One I became Three."[122] Another reads:

> Three are all the gods, Amon, Ra, Ptah; there are none like them. Hidden in his name as Amon, he is Ra, his body is Ptah. He is manifested in Amon, with Ra and Ptah, the three united.[123]

On close examination the line between so-called monotheism and polytheism is not as hard and fast as some would have us believe. In fact it is so fluid as to be of no real consequence at all.

THE LOGOS

The King James translation of the Gospel of John opens with the famous and poetic passage:

> In the beginning was the Word, and the Word was with God, and the Word was God. The same was in the beginning with God. All things were made by him; and without him was not anything made that was made. In him was life and the life was the light of men.[124]

Many readers of this text find it strangely moving, but would confess to not really understanding what it means. This is not surprising, because without some knowledge of Pagan philosophy it really does make little sense.

In the original Greek, the term here translated as "Word" is *Logos*. The concept of the Logos is completely foreign to Judaism and is entirely derived from the Pagan Mysteries. As long ago as the sixth century BCE Heraclitus set out on a journey of self-discovery and discovered the "Logos shared by all."[125] He writes:

Having hearkened not unto me, but unto the Logos, it is wise to confess that all things are One.[126]

The Pagan sage Epictetus preaches: "The Logos of the philosophers doth promise us peace which God proclaimed through his Logos."[127] The Roman Vitruvius writes: "Let no one think I have erred if I believe in the Logos."[128] Clement of Alexandria acknowledges that: "It may be freely granted that the Greeks received some glimmers of the divine Logos" and quotes the legendary Pagan sage Orpheus, who proclaims: "Behold the Logos divine. Tread well the narrow path of life and gaze on Him, the world's great ruler, our immortal king."[129] But this Pagan concept is much older than the Greeks. It can be found in the ancient Egyptian Pyramid Texts of the Third Dynasty, which were written more than 2,500 years before the Christian era![130]

How should we understand this ancient concept of the Logos? In ancient Greek, Logos has many levels of meaning, which our term *Word* does not begin to capture.[131] One of these is expressed by the Church fathers Clement and Origen, who describe the Logos as "the Idea of Ideas." It is God's primal thought.[132] The legendary Pagan sage Hermes Trismegistus expresses exactly the same concept. He describes the Logos—the Idea of Ideas—emerging from the Oneness of God like a word or thought.[133] For Hermes, as for Clement and Origen, the Logos is the first thought of the great Mind of God, through which he creates the universe.

Christians personify the relationship between God and the Logos as that between a father and a son. The Logos is the "Son of God." Yet they also teach that the Father and the Son are aspects of each other. St. John expresses this paradox: "The Logos was with God, and the Logos was God."

These are actually ancient Pagan doctrines, propounded by sages such as Hermes Trismegistus, who also calls the Logos "the Son of God."[134] He explains that, like mind and thought, the Father and the Son are really One, but when separated from each other they appear as two. Likewise, in the sixth century BCE Heraclitus had written: "The Father and the Son are the same."[135] Clement acknowledges that Euripides had "divined as in a riddle that the Father and the Son are one God."[136]

How should we understand this mysterious relationship between the Logos and God, the Father and the Son?[137] Clement writes:

> The Son is the Consciousness of God. The Father only sees the world as reflected in the Son.[138]

The Logos is God conscious of Himself. It is the One Soul of the Universe, which is conscious through all beings. This is why Heraclitus sets out to find himself, but discovers a "Logos shared by all," because the Logos is our essential common identity. The Christian philosopher Origen writes:

> As our body, while consisting of many members, is yet held together by one soul, so the universe is to be thought of as an immense living being, which is held together by One Soul—the power and the Logos of God.[139]

Just as St. John tells us that Jesus is an embodiment of the Logos, so the Pagan initiate Plutarch teaches that Osiris is "the Logos in itself, transcendent and impassible."[140] By equating Jesus Christ with the Logos, St. John is making it clear that he is a personification of this One Soul of the Universe, as Osiris-Dionysus is for Pagans. Christ is in us all, because he is the essential divine nature we all share. From this perspective, the Son of God is not an historical figure who lives in time, but an eternal philosophical principle, for, as Origen writes, "The Father did not beget the Son, but ever is begetting him."[141]

So, is there any real difference between Christian and Pagan understanding of the Logos? Once again, it is only found in the Christian idea that, unlike the Pagan godman who *mythically* embodied the Logos, Jesus *literally* embodied this philosophical principle. St. Augustine writes of his studies of Pagan philosophy:

> I read there that God the Word was born not of flesh and blood, nor of the will of man, nor the will of the flesh, but of God. But that the Word was made flesh and dwelt amongst us, I read not there.[142]

The essential idea that divided the Pagans and Christians of the ancient world was the Christian belief that one man, and one man only, had literally been the Logos made flesh. To the Pagans the notion that the Logos we all share could in some way be manifest in a single human being was impossible. The extraordinary claim that a carpenter from Nazareth actually was the one and only Son of God and incarnation of the Logos was the only thing that Christians could latch onto that definitively differentiated them from their Pagan neighbors. They would, however, spend centuries arguing over what it could possibly mean.

LANGUAGE OF THE MYSTERIES

Professor Max Müller tells us emphatically that anyone who uses terms such as *logos* or "the word," *monogenes* or "the only-begotten," *protokos* or "the first-born," *hyios tou theou* or "the Son of God" has "borrowed the very germs of his religious thought from Greek philosophy."[143] The writings of early Christians, including the New Testament, are rife with such Pagan concepts, which go unnoticed because they are disguised by poor English translations of the original Greek.[144] The language used by early Christianity is in fact so similar to that of the Mysteries that we often cannot tell from burial inscriptions whether the deceased was a Christian or a Pagan![145]

St. Paul, for example, describes God speaking "divine Mysteries in the Spirit."[146] Baptism and the Eucharist are referred to as "Mysteries."[147] The bishop who leads the ceremony is called a *Mystagogue*. The mass is called a *Mystagogia*, a word which is still used by Greek Orthodox Christians to describe the passion of Jesus. As a modern authority comments, this is "the language of the Mysteries."[148]

The Christian philosopher Origen calls Christianity the *telete*, meaning "the initiation." Likewise, the Pagan critic Lucian views early Christianity as another version of the Mysteries and calls it simply a "new *telete*"—a new initiation.[149] St. Paul is usually translated as writing of "mature" or "perfected" Christians, but again the Greek would be more accurately translated as "initiated." When dealing with certain doctrines, it was common for early Christians, such as Origen, to simply announce: "The initiates know what I mean!"[150] This is exactly the same formula used by the Pagan philosophers Pausanias, Plutarch, and Apuleius when they touch upon secrets of the Pagan Mysteries.[151]

The writings of the Church father Clement of Alexandria are full of terminology taken directly from the language of the Pagan Mysteries. He writes of the Christian revelation as "the holy Mysteries," "the divine secrets," "the secret Logos," "the Mysteries of the Logos." For Clement, Jesus Christ is the "teacher of the divine Mysteries," just as Osiris-Dionysus is. "The Lord is my hierophant," Clement writes. "I am become holy while I am being initiated."[152] In language no different from that of a Pagan initiate, he enthuses:

> O truly sacred Mysteries! O pure light! In the blaze of the torches I have a vision of heaven and of God. I become holy by initiation. The Lord reveals the Mysteries. He marks the worshiper with His seal. If thou wilt, be thyself also initiated, and thou shalt dance with angels around the unbegotten and imperishable and only true God.[153]

Christianity even inherited its forms of organization from the Mysteries.[154] A modern Christian scholar acknowledges:

> The Mysteries had brought men together in those religious associations which were the harbingers of the house-churches of primitive Christianity, and had ready to hand for the new religion an organization and system of administration. The Mysteries, both Greek and Oriental, had created a favorable milieu for Christianity by making religion a matter of personal conviction; they had made familiar the consciousness of and the need of a redemption; and by their salvationist propaganda they disposed men to lend a ready ear to the Christian proclamation of Jesus as savior; they had denationalized gods and men in aiming at the brotherhood of mankind; they had stimulated cravings for immortality; they had made men zealous propagandists by laying upon them the duty of the diffusion of their faith; they had fostered monotheism by making their patron deity the representative of the Divine Unity.[155]

CONCLUSION

So was the New Testament really new? It was certainly new and heretical to traditional Jews. Through the figure of Jesus their doctrine of "an eye for an eye" was challenged by Socrates' doctrine of "Love your enemies." Their notions of the afterlife were revolutionized by Mystery teachings on the nature of heaven and hell. The New Testament was, therefore, new to the Jews—but not to Pagans. They had held such doctrines for hundreds of years. That the teachings of Jesus were anticipated by Pagan teachings would not have surprised the ancients, however. They would have expected the Truth, by its very nature, to be perennial, not original.

Let's review some of the evidence we have unearthed:

- ❖ Jesus taught his followers to be pure in thought and word and deed; so did the sages of the Mysteries.
- ❖ Christians have a personal loving relationship with God; so did the initiates of the Mysteries.
- ❖ Jesus taught his followers to love their neighbors; so did the sages of the Mysteries.
- ❖ Jesus taught his followers to love their enemies; so did the sages of the Mysteries.
- ❖ Christians love each other as "brothers"; so did initiates of the Mysteries.
- ❖ Christians embrace humility and voluntary poverty, as did Pagan sages.
- ❖ Christians have a conception of heaven and hell not found in Judaism, but taken directly from the Mysteries.
- ❖ Christians await an apocalypse of fire and the birth of a New Age; so did initiates of the Mysteries.
- ❖ Early Christian imagery of the fish is taken from Pagan astrology.
- ❖ Christians believe in one God; so did the sages of the Mysteries.
- ❖ Christians, like Pagans, talked of the "gods."
- ❖ Christians attack idolatry, as did the sages of the Mysteries.
- ❖ Christians conceive of God as a Holy Trinity, a concept that is also found in the Pagan Mysteries.
- ❖ Christians see Jesus as an embodiment of the Logos, which is a Pagan concept not found in Judaism.
- ❖ Early Christian writings, including the New Testament, are full of the language of the Mysteries.
- ❖ The organization of the early Christian Church was an adaptation of the practices of initiates of the Pagan Mysteries.

It was now obvious to us that the teachings of the Mysteries anticipated the doctrines of Christianity and that the Pagan myths of Osiris-Dionysus prefigured the story of Jesus. For 2,000 years our culture has believed that

Christianity was a unique and revolutionary revelation, but that is clearly not true!

So what is the truth? This was the question we were determined to answer. The traditional history of Christianity bequeathed to us by the Roman Church had failed to account for the historical evidence, so we decided to look elsewhere.

In the first few centuries CE the Christian community was divided into many different sects. As well as the Literalist Christians who eventually became the Roman Church there were other Christian groups collectively known as the *Gnostics*. The Gnostics had a radically different perspective on Christianity, which the Literalists regarded as dangerously misguided. When Literalist Christianity became the religion of the Roman Empire it enforced its own particular view and brutally eradicated the "heretics." So, the traditional history of Christianity is merely the perspective of the winners in the sectarian battle between Literalists and Gnostics. As this account had proved inadequate to the facts, we decided to listen to what the losers had to say. The Gnostics may have lost the battle for survival, but that does not mean we should assume that their perspective on Christianity was any less valid. What was it the Gnostics knew, we wondered, that made the Roman Church consider them so dangerous?

The Gnostics

Recent investigations have challenged the traditional outlook and the traditional conclusions and the traditional "facts." With some today, and with many tomorrow, the burning question is, or will be, not how did a particularly silly and licentious heresy rise within the church, but how did the church rise out of the great Gnostic movement, how did the dynamic ideas of the Gnosis become crystallized into dogma?[1]

Rev. Lamplugh

The Gnostics' view of Christianity was in many ways the mirror image of that of the Literalist Christians who eventually became the Roman Catholic Church. Literalists were rigidly authoritarian. Gnostics were mystic individualists. Literalists wanted to enforce a common creed on all Christians. Gnostics tolerated various different beliefs and practices. Literalists selected four gospels as holy scripture and had the rest consigned to the flames as heretical works of the Devil. Gnostics wrote hundreds of different Christian gospels. Literalists taught that the true Christian believed in Jesus as preached to them by the bishops. Gnostics taught that the true Christian experienced *Gnosis* or mystical "Knowledge" for themselves and became a Christ!

The Gnostics were so effectively suppressed that until recently almost all we knew about them came from the writings of their detractors and oppressors.[2] Literalist Christians bequeathed us the idea that Gnosticism was a perversion of Christian thought, which confused the original teachings of Jesus with alien Pagan doctrines. For 2,000 years this has been the party line of orthodox Christianity, and as it successfully eliminated the opposition and destroyed all the evidence, it has been generally accepted as the truth. In 1945, however, a library of Gnostic scriptures was discovered in a cave near Nag Hammadi in Egypt. This has revolutionized our understanding of Gnosticism and early Christianity. Now we are in a position to let the Gnostics speak for themselves.

Although remembered today as heretics, the Gnostics saw themselves as the genuine Christians. In a Gnostic gospel called *The Apocalypse of Peter*, the risen Jesus calls Literalist Christianity an "imitation church" in place of the true Christian brotherhood of the Gnostics. From the Gnostics' point of view, it was the Literalists who had distorted true Christianity. They had created a religion that required blind faith in historical events from what was originally a spiritual path through which each initiate could personally experience mystical Knowledge or Gnosis. To the Gnostics, Literalist Christianity preached only the Outer Mysteries of Christianity, which they called a "worldly Christianity" suitable for "people in a hurry."[3] Gnosticism, by contrast, was a truly "spiritual Christianity," which revealed the secret Inner Mysteries of Christianity to the chosen few.[4]

Remarkably enough, these particular quotations are not from some little known Gnostic heretic, but from the writings of two of the most eminent Christians of the early Church—Clement, the head of the first Christian philosophical school in Alexandria, and his successor, Origen.[5] These men were highly respected during their lifetimes and are still regarded as two of the greatest early Christian philosophers, yet both preached a form of Christianity more akin to Gnosticism than to modern mainstream Christianity. Clement is even honored as a saint by the Catholic Church, yet he wrote volumes on the Gnostic whom he called the true Christian.[6]

The Gnostic beliefs of such influential and respected Christian intellectuals as Clement and Origen show that the Gnostics were not strange and insignificant heretics on the fringes of Christianity, as the traditional picture would have us believe. On the contrary, Gnosticism was a broad, vibrant, and sophisticated spirituality, which was attractive to the greatest Christian intellectuals of the first few centuries CE—not only great sages such as Valentinus and Basilides, who have been all but forgotten because they were branded heretics by the Roman Church, but also men such as Clement and Origen, whose reputations have been less maligned.

PAGAN PHILOSOPHY

The central and most repeated accusation leveled at the Gnostic Christians by Literalist Christians was that they were essentially little different from Pagans. Irenaeus, the great heresy-hunter of early Literalism, condemns the Gnostics for patching together a new garment out of the useless old rags of Greek philosophy.[7] He calls the followers of the Gnostic sage Simon Magus "Mystery priests" and accuses them of worshiping "an image of Simon made in the form of Zeus."[8] Tertullian, another author of fanatically anti-Gnostic works, compares the Christian initiations offered by the Gnostics to the Pagan initiations practiced at Eleusis.[9] Hippolytus, a disciple of Irenaeus, tells us of a Gnostic group called the Sethians, of whom he asserts:

> They took the whole content of their teaching from the ancient [Pagan] theologians Musaeus, Linus, and Orpheus, who especially made known the rites and Mysteries.[10]

Irenaeus is outraged that Gnostics venerated pictures of Christ alongside "images of worldly philosophers such as Pythagoras, Plato, Aristotle, and the others."[11]

Gnostics attended Pagan festivals and welcomed Pagans to their own Christian meetings,[12] leading Tertullian to comment reproachfully:

> It has been observed that heretics have connections with very many magicians, itinerant charlatans, astrologers, and philosophers.[13]

Although such Literalist Christians grotesquely misrepresented the Gnostics, this was one thing about which they were undoubtedly right: Gnosticism did indeed resemble the Pagan Mysteries.[14] Unlike Literalists, however, Gnostics did not see Paganism as the enemy and so openly acknowledged this debt and encouraged the study of the great philosophers of antiquity.[15] Indeed, Pagan works were discovered alongside Christian texts in the Gnostic library in Nag Hammadi.[16]

Clement of Alexandria was steeped in Pagan philosophy, which he regarded as a divine gift to lead men to Christ.[17] He explains:

> Greek philosophy purges the soul, and prepares it beforehand for the reception of faith, on which the Truth builds up the edifice of Gnosis.[18]

Origen, likewise, instructed his pupils that perfect piety required a knowledge of Pagan philosophy,[19] which he calls a fine meal prepared for sophisticated palates. In comparison he claims that Christians "cook for the masses."[20] Origen had been instructed in philosophy by the Pagan sage Ammonius.[21] The Pagan philosopher Porphyry relates that he "visited for a long time" with Ammonius and Origen, both of whom he calls "Platonists" and "men who much surpassed their contemporaries in insight."[22]

As well as being the teacher of the great Christian philosopher Origen, Ammonius was also the teacher of Plotinus, one of the greatest of all Pagan philosophers. Plotinus refers to Gnostic Christians within his own philosophical school and clearly regards Gnosticism as an overly complex and inferior version of the Pagan Mysteries:

> All their terminology is piled up to conceal their debt to ancient Greek philosophy.[23] We feel a certain regard for some of our friends who happened upon this way of thinking before they became our friends, and, though I do not know how they manage it, continue in it.[24]

PAGAN MYTHOLOGY

Gnostic writings are full of figures from Greek mythology and concepts from Pagan philosophy, astrology, and magic.[25] *The Books of the Savior*, for example, states that Ieou (the Supreme God) has the assistance of five other Great Rulers—the Pagan deities Kronos, Ares, Hermes, Aphrodite, and Zeus.[26]

Gnostic texts also mix together Pagan and Jewish mythological motifs. A Gnostic text called *Baruch* presents a synthesis of Pagan astrology and the Jewish concept of angels. God the Father creates 12 angels who circle and govern the universe, just as the signs of the Pagan zodiac.[27] The text uses the Jewish name for God, *Elohim*, but equates Elohim with the Greek Zeus. It describes Elohim choosing as a prophet the Pagan hero Heracles[28] and even calls God *Priapus*, another name for Dionysus, claiming,

> The Good is Priapus who was created before there was anything; he is called Priapus because he prefabricated everything. For this reason he is erected in every temple, is honored by all creation.[29]

Hippolytus tells us of a group of Gnostic Christians called the Naassenes who claimed to teach a philosophy that underlies all mythologies—Pagan,

Jewish, and Christian.[30] The Naassenes saw Jesus as identical to the mythical figure of the young dying son of the Great Mother they called "the many shaped Attis."[31] This figure was also known in their hymns as Adonis, Osiris, Pan, Bacchus, and Shepherd of White Stars—all of which are names for Osiris-Dionysus![32] Not only did these Gnostic Christians see Jesus as identical to Osiris-Dionysus, but Hippolytus also claims they were actually initiates in the Pagan Mysteries. He writes:

> It is said, they were all initiated into the Mysteries of the Great Mother, because they found that the whole Mystery of rebirth was taught in these rites.[33]

The Great Mother goddess was a towering figure who dominated the ancient world. In Egypt she was known as Isis and in Greece as Demeter. She was the mother or sister or spouse of Osiris-Dionysus or often, in that magical way that only myth allows, all three.

When we explored the Pagan Mysteries we did not investigate the nature of the goddess very deeply, because we were looking for parallels between Paganism and Christianity, and orthodox Christianity does not have a goddess. It has only God the Father, God the Son, and a rather vague androgynous God the Holy Spirit. Gnostic mythology included a more natural and balanced Holy Trinity of God the Father, God the Son, and the Mother goddess Sophia.[34]

In Gnostic texts the goddess is called by many names, including "All-Mother," "Mother of the Living," "Shining Mother," "the Power Above," "the Holy Spirit"[35] and "She of the Left-hand," as the complement of Christ who is "Him of the Right-hand."[36]

Like the Pagan goddess, as well as being a divine heavenly being, Sophia is portrayed in Gnostic myth as a tragic figure. She searches desperately for her redeemer/brother/lover Jesus in the same way that the Egyptian goddess Isis searches the world for her redeemer/brother/lover Osiris. The Gnostics poetically imagined that "all watery substances" were tears shed by Sophia. In so doing they were echoing the Pagan sage Empedocles, who five centuries previously had described all water as the tears of the goddess Persephone.[37]

Sophia was so important to some Gnostics that they taught that it was only in the Outer Mysteries that the Eucharist celebrated the passion of Jesus. For the "spiritual" Christians initiated into the Inner Mysteries, the Eucharist recalled the passion and suffering of the goddess Sophia![38]

THE GOD OF PLATO

As we have already discussed, although the Pagan sages talked of gods and goddesses they maintained a completely mystical and transcendent understanding of the supreme God. Since the time of Plato, they had criticized viewing God as a divine "personality." The supreme God of the Pagan Mysteries was an ineffable Oneness beyond all qualities, which could not be described in words.[39] This abstract and mystical conception of God was also adopted by the Gnostics. God was not seen as some sort of big person in the sky, but was understood as the Mind of the Universe, which expresses itself through all beings.[40]

This was not the picture of God held by Literalist Christians. Their God was Jehovah, the god of the Jews, who the Old Testament reveals as a partisan, capricious, and sometimes tyrannical tribal deity.

In the same way that Plato had attacked the traditional Greek picture of God as the domineering Zeus, so the Gnostics attacked this traditional Jewish picture of God,[41] teaching that Jehovah was in reality only the image of the true God. The Gnostic sage Valentinus used Plato's term "demiurge"[42] to describe Jehovah, signifying him to be a subordinate divine being who serves as the instrument of the true God.[43] Jehovah was pictured as a presumptuous lesser deity who ignorantly believes himself to be the one true God. In the Old Testament Jehovah proclaims: "I am a jealous God, and there is no other God besides me."[44] However, the Gnostic *Secret Book of John* calls this "madness" and comments:

> By announcing this he indicated to the angels that another God does exist; for if there were no other one, of whom would he be jealous?[45]

In some Gnostic texts, when Jehovah pronounces himself the one and only God he is castigated for his arrogance, like a presumptuous child, by his mother the goddess Sophia![46]

The Gnostic Jesus was not a prophet of Jehovah, the lesser god of the Jews, but of the true ineffable God of Plato and the Pagan Mysteries. The Gnostic teacher Cerdo explains:

> The God proclaimed by the law and the prophets is not the Father of Our Lord Jesus Christ. The God of the Old Testament is known, but the Father of Jesus Christ is unknown.[47]

In complete contrast to the crass anthropomorphism of the traditional Jewish view, the Gnostic sage Basilides taught the Pagan doctrine that: "We must not even call God ineffable, since this is to make an assertion about Him; He is above every name that is named."[48]

HIEROPHANT OF THE MYSTERIES

The Literalists' Jesus is portrayed as Jehovah's promised Messiah, but the Gnostics' Jesus resembles a Hierophant of the Pagan Mysteries *(see plate 8)*. In a Gnostic gospel called *The Wisdom of Jesus Christ*, the resurrected Jesus appears to his disciples as a great angel of light and, smiling at their amazement and terror, offers to teach them "the Mysteries."[49] In a Gnostic text called *Pistis Sophia*, he teaches his followers: "Cease not seeking day and night, until ye have found the purifying Mysteries,"[50] and Mary Magdalene praises him, saying:

> Now we know, O Master, freely, surely, plainly that Thou hast brought the keys of the Mysteries of the Kingdom of Light.[51]

The Gnostic Jesus leads his disciples in Mystery initiations, including one recorded in a text called *The Acts of John*, using a "round dance." Such initiation dances were extremely common in the Pagan Mysteries. As one modern authority puts it, "Not a single ancient initiation festival can be found that is without dancing."[52] In the Mysteries at Eleusis the candidate for initiation was seated while others danced around him in a circle, mimicking the orbits of the planets and the stars.[53] In the Mysteries of Mithras, as already mentioned, the initiate representing Mithras stood in the middle of a circle of 12 dancers representing the signs of the zodiac.[54]

The Acts of John describes the disciples holding hands in a circle around Jesus in similar fashion. Jesus sings and in response the disciples intone the sacred word: *Amen*. Jesus teaches that in this "round dance" he reveals "the passion" and desires that it is "called a Mystery."[55] As one scholar notes, the round dance "is evidently some echo of the Mysteries, and the ceremony is that of a sacred dance initiation."[56] In the hymn accompanying the dance initiation three voices can clearly be distinguished: Christ, who is the initiator or hierophant, his assistants, and the candidate for initiation. In the following extract the voices have been allocated to one of these three figures to clearly demonstrate the initiatory nature of the text:[57]

Initiate	"I would be saved."
Christ	"And I would save."
Assistants	"Amen."

Initiate	"I would be freed."
Christ	"And I would free."
Assistants	"Amen."

Initiate	"I would be pierced."
Christ	"And I would pierce."
Assistants	"Amen."

Initiate	"I would be born."
Christ	"And I would bring to birth."
Assistants	"Amen."

Initiate	"I would eat."
Christ	"And I would be eaten."
Assistants	"Amen."

Initiate	"I would hear."
Christ	"And I would be heard."
Assistants	"Amen."

Christ	"I am a lamp to thee who beholdst Me."
Assistants	"Amen."

Christ	"I am a mirror to thee who perceivest Me."
Assistants	"Amen."

Christ	"I am a door to thee who knockest at Me."
Assistants	"Amen."

Christ	"I am a way to thee, a wayfarer."
Assistants	"Amen."

Christ	"Now respond thou to my dancing. See thyself in Me who speaks; and when thou hast seen what I do, keep silence on My Mysteries."[58]

SECRET MYSTERIES

The Pagan Mysteries contained both exoteric or outer Mysteries which were open to all, and esoteric or inner Mysteries, which were revealed only to the chosen few who had undergone a lengthy period of purification and spiritual preparation. Clement tells us that in early Christianity there were likewise Lesser Mysteries for beginners on the spiritual path and Greater Mysteries which were a secret higher knowledge, which led to full "initiation."[59] "The secret traditions of true Gnosis," he explains, had been transmitted "to a small number, by a succession of masters, and not in writing."[60]

Origen recognizes that in having Outer Mysteries and Inner Mysteries Christianity was following the example of Paganism. He writes:

The existence of certain doctrines which are beyond those which are openly taught and do not reach the multitude is not a peculiarity of Christianity only, but is shared by the philosophers. For they had some doctrines which were exoteric and some esoteric.[61]

Like Pagan initiates, Gnostic initiates were required to keep the Inner Mysteries a profound secret. The heresy-hunter Hippolytus tells us that the followers of the Gnostic sage Basilides "may not speak of their Mysteries aloud, but must preserve them in silence."[62] Indeed, they were required to undergo an initial five-year period of silence, just as were initiates in the Pythagorean schools of the Pagan Mysteries.[63] *The Book of the Great Logos* instructs:

These Mysteries are to be guarded with utmost secrecy, and revealed to none who are unworthy; neither to father or mother, to sister nor brother, nor to any relative; neither for meat nor drink, neither for woman nor gold nor silver nor anything in this world.[64]

Clement writes:

> It is not wished that all things should be exposed indiscriminately to all and sundry, or the benefits of wisdom communicated to those who have not even in a dream been purified in soul. Nor are the Mysteries of the Logos to be expounded to the profane.[65]

Another Gnostic sage demands:

> If you wish to know what eye has not seen or ear heard, and what has not entered the heart of man, the One who is high above all good things, swear to keep secret the Mysteries of the teaching. This is the oath: "I swear by the One above all, the Good, to keep these Mysteries and to tell them to no one and not to return from the Good to the creation."[66]

According to Clement, Mark did not preach only the familiar gospel in the New Testament, but three different gospels suitable for different levels of initiation. The New Testament Gospel of Mark contains thoughts suitable for beginners in the faith. But Mark also wrote a *Secret Gospel* to be used by those who were being *perfected* or "initiated."[67] Clement records that Mark had written both of these gospels in Alexandria, where they were still kept. The teachings of *The Secret Gospel of Mark* were regarded as so secret that Clement advises one of his students that its existence should be denied, "even under oath," for "not all true things are to be said to all men" and "the light of the truth should be hidden from those who are mentally blind." According to Clement, the *Secret Gospel* recorded "things suitable to whatever makes for progress toward Gnosis." Even in this "more spiritual gospel," however, Mark still did not "divulge the things not to be uttered, nor did he write down the esoteric teaching of the Lord, but to the stories already written he added yet others and, moreover, brought in certain sayings, the interpretation of which he knew would lead the hearers into the innermost sanctuary of that truth."[68]

Only to his closest students did Mark convey further oral teachings, which imparted Gnosis. This final gospel was so mystical that it could not be written down at all.

The fragments that remain of *The Secret Gospel of Mark* illuminate the meaning of some otherwise bizarre passages in the New Testament. They include an account of Jesus raising a young man from the dead. Scholars have speculated that this is an early version of the story of Jesus raising Lazarus from the dead in the Gospel of John.[69] In the *Secret Gospel* this story is immediately followed by the initiation of the risen young man. For the Gnostics being raised from the dead is clearly an allegory for spiritual rebirth through initiation. This suggests that the tale of Lazarus being raised from the dead in the Gospel of John was also originally an allegory for initiation.[70] This would explain the curious passage in the Gospel of John in which Thomas, rather than offering to go and help Jesus raise Lazarus from the dead as one might expect, instead suggests to the disciples, "Let us also go and die with him!"[71] If the Lazarus story were originally an initiation allegory, like the story in *The Secret Gospel of Mark*, Thomas' otherwise inexplicable words would become meaningful. Thomas is in fact exhorting the other disciples to go and be initiated—to "die and resurrect" like Lazarus.

In *The Secret Gospel of Mark*, the youth about to be initiated comes to Jesus wearing only a linen cloth over his naked body. That night, we are told, "Jesus taught him the Mystery of the Kingdom of God." This illuminates another bizarre incident in the Gospel of Mark. After the betrayal and arrest of Jesus at night in the garden of Gethsemane Mark records:

> Among those who followed Jesus was a young man with nothing on but a linen cloth. They tried to seize him, but he slipped out of the linen cloth and ran away naked.[72]

This strange character appears nowhere else in the New Testament. Many readers down the centuries must have wondered about the identity of this naked young man and what he was doing with Jesus and the disciples. The *Secret Gospel* suggests that he was a candidate for initiation.

KNOWLEDGE BEYOND BELIEF

The Greek philosopher Heraclitus writes, "Human opinions are toys for children."[73] The sages of the Pagan Mysteries were disparaging about mere beliefs or opinions; they were interested in knowledge. Plato argued that belief is concerned only with the appearances of things, while knowledge penetrates to the underlying reality.[74] The highest level of understanding, he proclaimed, is that knowledge through which the mind becomes unified with the object of knowledge.[75] The Gnostics inherited these Pagan teachings and were also disparaging of *pistis* (faith) in comparison with *Gnosis* (knowledge).

Gnosis is not an idea that is open to doubt, but a mystical experience of the Truth, which is immediate, certain, and completely non-conceptual. While Literalist Christians extolled the spiritual value of blind faith and commanded the faithful not to question what they were told by the bishops, the Gnostic masters, like the Pagan sages before them, taught that through initiation into the Inner Mysteries initiates could directly experience Gnosis and know the Truth for themselves.

For the Gnostics, faith was only a stepping-stone leading to Gnosis. The Gnostic teacher Heracleon explains that at first people believe through faith in the testimony of others, but they need to go on to experience the Truth directly.[76] Clement taught:

> Faith is the foundation; Gnosis the superstructure.[77] By Gnosis faith is perfected[78] for to know is more than to believe.[79] Gnosis is proof of what has been received through faith.[80]

Like the Pagan sages, the Gnostics taught that all doctrines were merely approaches to the Truth, which was itself beyond words and concepts, and could only be found through experiencing Gnosis for oneself.[81] *The Gospel of Philip* explains:

> Names can be very deceptive, for they divert our thoughts from what is accurate to what is inaccurate. Thus one who hears the word "God" does not perceive what is accurate, but does perceive what is inaccurate. So also with "the Father" and "the Son," and "the Holy Spirit," and "life" and "light," and "resurrection," and "the church," and all the rest—people do not perceive what is accurate, but they perceive what is inaccurate.[82]

SELF-KNOWLEDGE

The most important injunction on the spiritual path of the Pagan Mysteries was inscribed over the sanctuary of Apollo at Delphi: *Gnothi Seauton*—"Know Thy Self." The Gnosis or Knowledge which initiates of the Pagan Mysteries sought was Self-knowledge.[83]

The Gnostic *Book of Thomas the Contender* likewise teaches:

> Whoever has not known himself has known nothing, but he who has known himself has at the same time already achieved Gnosis about the depth of all things.[84]

In *The Testimony of Truth* Jesus advises a disciple to become "a disciple of his own mind," which is "the father of Truth."[85] The Gnostic sage Silvanus encourages:

> Knock on yourself as upon a door and walk upon yourself as on a straight road. For if you walk on the road, it is impossible for you to go astray. Open the door for yourself so that you may know what is.[86]

But what is the self? The Pagan sages taught that every human being has a mortal lower self called the *eidolon* and an immortal Higher Self called the *Daemon*.[87] The eidolon is the embodied self, the physical body, and personality.[88] The Daemon is the Spirit, the true Self, which is each person's spiritual connection to God. The Mysteries were designed to help initiates realize that the eidolon is a false self and that their true identity is the immortal Daemon.[89]

From the eidolon's point of view the Daemon appears to be an independent Guardian Angel.[90] Initiates who still identify with the eidolon, therefore, do not experience the Daemon as their own true Self, but as a spirit guide whose job it is to lead them to their spiritual destination. Plato teaches, "We should think of the most authoritative part of the soul as a Guardian Spirit given by God which lifts us to our heavenly home."[91]

The Gnostic sages taught exactly the same Mystery doctrine.[92] Valentinus explains that a person receives Gnosis from their Guardian Angel, but that this angelic being is actually the seeker's own Higher Self.[93] In ancient Egypt the Daemon had for millennia been pictured as a Heavenly Twin of the eidolon.[94] This image is also found in Gnosticism. The Gnostic sage Mani was said to have been conscious of having a protecting angel from the age of four and, aged 12, to have realized it was his Heavenly Twin, whom he called the "most beautiful and largest mirror image of my own person."[95]

In *The Acts of John*, John observes that Jesus sometimes held converse with a Heavenly Twin who descended to join him:

> When all of us, his disciples, were sleeping in one house at Gennesaret, I alone, having wrapped myself up, watched from under my garment what he did; and first I heard him say, "John, go thou to sleep," and thereupon I feigned to be asleep; and I saw another like unto him come down, whom I also heard saying to my Lord, "Jesus, do they whom thou hast chosen still not believe in thee?" And my Lord said, "Thou sayest well, for they are men."[96]

The *Pistis Sophia* relates a charming myth of the child Jesus meeting his own Heavenly Twin for the first time. His mother Mary recalls:

> When thou wert a child, before the Spirit had descended upon thee, when thou wert in the vineyard with Joseph, the Spirit came down from the height, and came unto me in the house, like unto thee, and I knew Him not, but thought that he was thou. And he said unto me, "Where is Jesus, my brother, that I may go to meet him?"[97]

Mary relates to Jesus that when his Twin finally found him, "He embraced thee and kissed thee, and thee also didst kiss him; ye became one and the same being."[98]

The goal of Gnostic initiation was, likewise, to bring the lower self into union with the Higher Self, for it is when they are made one that enlightenment occurs.[99] Irenaeus relates that the Gnostic "believes himself to be neither in heaven nor on earth, but to have embraced his Guardian Angel."[100] The great Gnostic master Valentinus writes:

> When the human self and the divine "I" are interconnected they can achieve perfection and eternity.[101]

THE UNIVERSAL DAEMON

The quest for Self-knowledge leads the Pagan or Gnostic initiate on a remarkable journey of discovery. At first initiates experience themselves as the eidolon, the embodied personality, and see the Daemon as a Guardian Angel or Heavenly Twin. The more mature initiate experiences the Daemon as their own Higher Self. To those blessed with the final vision of complete Self-knowledge or Gnosis, the Daemon is found to be more awesome still. It truly is the "divine 'I,'" as Valentinus puts it.

Although it appears as if each person has their own Daemon or Higher Self, the enlightened initiate discovers that actually there is one Daemon shared by all—a universal Self, which inhabits every being. Each soul is a part of the one Soul of God.[102] To know oneself therefore is to know God.

These mystical teachings are found both in the Pagan Mysteries and Gnostic Christianity.[103] The ancient Pagan teaching "I am Thou, and Thou art I" is found in the Gnostic text *Pistis Sophia* and becomes in the New Testament Gospel of John "I in Thou, and Thou in me."[104]

The Pagan sage Sextus writes: "If you would know Him by whom you were made, you would know yourself."[105] Similarly, the Christian philosopher Clement writes: "It is the greatest of all disciplines to know oneself; for when a man knows himself, he knows God."[106] Clement taught his Christian initiates to "practice being God"[107] and that the true Gnostic had "already become God."[108]

In a beautiful statement of the perennial mystical teachings inherited by Gnostic Christianity from the Pagan Mysteries, the Gnostic sage Monoimos advises:

> Seek Him from out thyself, and learn who it is that taketh possession of everything in thee, saying: "*My* God, *my* spirit, *my* understanding, *my* soul, and *my* body," and learn whence is sorrow and joy, and love and hate, and waking though one would not, and sleeping though one would not, and getting angry though one would not, and falling in love though one would not. And if thou shouldst closely investigate these things, thou wilt find Him in thyself.[109]

Gnostic means "Knower," but it is not some piece of spiritual information that a Gnostic knows. They know that by which all else is known—the knower, the experiencer, the Higher Self, the divine "I," the Daemon. The true Gnostic, like the enlightened initiate of the Pagan Mysteries, discovers that the Daemon is actually the one Soul of the Universe—the Consciousness that inhabits each one of us.[110] According to the Pagan and Gnostic sages who have traversed the path of Self-knowledge to its paradoxical conclusion, when we finally discover who we are, we discover that there is only God.

REINCARNATION

In the Pagan Mysteries it was believed that a soul progresses toward the realization of Gnosis over many lifetimes.[111] The Pagan initiate Plutarch explains that the unenlightened soul is attracted back into physical incarnation over and over again by force of habit:

> We know that the soul is indestructible and should think of its experience as like that of a bird in a cage. If it has been kept in the body for a long time and become tamed to this life as a result of all sorts of involvements and long habituation, it will alight again back to a body again birth after birth and will never stop or give up becoming entangled in the passions and chances of this world.[112]

Although it was eventually exorcised from mainstream Christianity, this Pagan idea was embraced by the early Gnostic Christians. The Gnostic sage Basilides taught that Gnosis was the consummation of many lives of effort.[113] *The Secret Book of John* teaches that a soul will continue to reincarnate until it is eventually "saved from its lack of perception, attains Gnosis, and so is perfected," after which "it no longer goes into another flesh."[114] The *Pistis Sophia* teaches that a soul cannot be brought into the Light until, through many lifetimes of experience, it has understood all of the Mysteries. Having progressed on the spiritual journey during this life, however, its next incarnation will be into a "righteous body which shall find the God of Truth and the Higher Mysteries."[115]

Plato tells us that the dead have the choice of drinking from the "Spring of Memory" and walking the right-hand path toward heaven or drinking from the "Cup of Forgetting" and walking the left-hand path toward reincarnation.[116] The Gnostic *Book of the Savior* teaches the same doctrine, explaining that a righteous man will be born into his next life without forgetting the wisdom he has learned in this life because he will not be given the "Draught of Oblivion" before his next birth. Rather he will receive "a cup full of intuition and wisdom" which will cause the soul not to fall asleep and forget, but to "seek after the Mysteries of Light, until it hath found them."[117]

Plato saw being incarnated in a human body as comparable to being incarcerated in a sort of prison.[118] The Gnostic *Secret Book of John* likewise describes incarnation as being "cast into fetters."[119] Plato explains, "The soul is suffering the punishment of sin until the penalty is paid."[120] Origen similarly teaches that incarnation is a sort of punishment for having sinned and that in proportion to the sin, souls are put into particular types of bodies. He tells us that souls are "enveloped in different bodies for punishment" many times over, until they are purified, when they will "rise again to the state in which they formerly were, completely putting away their evil and their bodies."[121] Like the Pagan sages, Origen could not believe that a just and compassionate God would condemn any soul to eternity in hell, but thought that all souls would be saved through experiencing repeated human incarnations.[122] He writes:

> Every soul has existed from the beginning; it has therefore passed through some worlds already, and will pass through others before it reaches the final consummation. It comes into this world strengthened by the victories or weakened by the defeats of its previous life.[123]

Despite his great prestige among early Christians, this brilliant Christian philosopher was posthumously condemned by the Catholic Church as a heretic for teaching this ancient doctrine.[124] This is even more ironic since such teachings are completely in keeping with the New Testament.[125] In the Gospel of John the high priests of Jerusalem ask John the Baptist if he is a reincarnation of Elijah,[126] while in the Gospel of Mark the disciples discuss the possibility of Jesus being the reincarnation of John the Baptist, the prophet Elijah, or one of the other prophets![127]

SEXUAL EQUALITY

In the Pagan Mysteries initiation was open to all, regardless of sex. Dionysus' most intimate disciples were ecstatic women followers called the maenads and in Italy the Mysteries of Dionysus were entirely run by women.[128] Under the old Greek Olympian religion women were condemned to live within four walls carrying out household chores, but with the coming of the rites of Dionysus, they ran wild in the woods![129]

There were many famous priestesses and prophetesses of the Pagan Mysteries: the great mystical poet Sappho and her sisters on Lesbos, who were priestesses in the Mysteries of Adonis; Diotima, the priestess who taught Socrates; and the Pythoness, the oracular priestess at Delphi whose advice was sought by the powerful statesmen and famous philosophers of the ancient world. The Christian Clement of Alexandria compiled a list of Pagan women whose achievements he admired.[130] As well as famous women poets and painters, he mentions philosophers such as Arignote, Themisto, and others, including two who studied with Plato and one trained by Socrates.[131]

The Pythagoreans were famous for giving freedom and respect to women.[132] Ancient Pythagorean texts often stress the equal status of women and men.[133] According to Aristoxenus, Pythagoras got most of his ethical lore from a priestess of Delphi called Themistoclea. In his letter to the women of Croton, Pythagoras says expressly that "Women as a sex are more naturally akin to piety."[134] It was to a woman, his daughter Damo, that he entrusted his writings. A woman disciple of Pythagoras called Arignote was the author of a book called *The Rites of Dionysus* and other philosophical works.[135]

Like their Pagan predecessors, the Gnostics also honored women and considered them equal to men. After all, in the gospels Jesus is portrayed as violating Jewish convention by talking openly with women, whom he included among his close companions, and it is women who first discover the risen Christ.[136] Clement teaches: "In Christ there is neither male nor female," explaining that the term *humanity* is common to both men and women.

In Gnostic gospels female figures, particularly Mary Magdalene, play central roles. In the *Dialogue of the Saviour* Mary is portrayed as "a woman who had understood completely" and with whom Jesus had a particularly close relationship.[137] A wise Mary Magdalene is often portrayed in conflict with a foolish and misogynous Peter.[138] In the *Pistis Sophia* Peter complains that

Mary is dominating the conversation with Jesus and displacing his own rightful priority and that of the other male apostles. He urges Jesus to silence her, but Jesus rebukes him. Later Mary admits to Jesus that she hardly dares speak freely because "Peter makes me hesitate; I am afraid of him, because he hates the female race." Jesus replies that whoever the Spirit inspires is divinely ordained to speak, whether man or woman.[139]

Irenaeus records with irritation that women were particularly attracted to Gnostic Christianity.[140] This is not surprising since among Gnostics women enjoyed positions of leadership and spiritual authority, unlike in the Literalist Church, where they were regarded as second-class human beings.[141] Irenaeus is appalled that the Gnostic sage Marcus encouraged women to act as priests in celebrating the Eucharist,[142] while Tertullian complains bitterly about "those women among the heretics" who hold positions of authority and is enraged that "they teach, they engage in discussion; they exorcise; they cure." He suspects that they might even baptize and act as bishops![143]

NATURAL MORALITY

In Euripides' The Bacchae, King Pentheus tries to insult Dionysus by describing him as "the god who frees his worshipers from every law," but Dionysus replies, "Your insult to Dionysus is a compliment."[144]

The Pagan Mysteries were often accused of being immoral because they taught that conventional ideas of morality were superseded by someone who had experienced Gnosis. The ultimate aim of the Mysteries was spiritual liberation, not moral servitude.

Irenaeus complains that the Gnostics likewise claimed that "Actions are not good or bad in themselves, but only in accordance with human conventions" and implies that the Gnostics' spiritual freedom was actually just an excuse for licentiousness.[145] He writes:

> They maintain that they have attained to a height beyond every power, and that therefore they are free in every respect to act as they please, having no one to fear in anything. For they claim that because of the redemption they cannot be apprehended, or even perceived, by the judge.[146]

Through mystically experiencing the true God of Jesus, the Gnostics claimed that they were "redeemed" or "released" from the power of the tyrannical Jehovah and all the rules and regulations he had imposed on the Jews. In the Gnostic initiation process the initiate ritually declared his independence from the false god.[147] According to the Gnostic sage Simon Magus, initiates who had escaped from Jehovah's power and come to know the true Father were "free to live as they please."[148]

As one modern authority puts it:

> Basilides and his successor Valentinus, the great Gnostic masters of Alexandria, favored a strict amorality: the only rule was that there are no rules. If, as many initiates preferred, one's bent was ascetic, that was fine; if one was completely promiscuous, that was also fine.[149]

Neither the sages of the Pagan Mysteries nor the Christian Gnostics were actually preaching immorality, however. They were both simply acknowledging that there was a spiritual understanding deeper than an externally imposed set of ethical rules, and that human beings who were in touch with their divine nature would act intuitively and spontaneously in harmony with the whole of life. The Gnostic sage Basilides explains that "spiritual" Christians are moral simply "by nature."[150] Obeying moral codes may be a part of the journey of purification that leads to Gnosis, but having arrived, all ethical rules can be abandoned as the initiate will naturally act well— although not necessarily conventionally![151]

Clement writes:

> Definite outward observances cease to have any value for one whose whole being is brought into an abiding harmony with that which is eternal; he has no wants, no passion; he rests in the contemplation of God, which is and will be his unfailing blessedness.[152] All the action, then, of a man possessed of Gnosis is right action; and that done by a man not possessed of Gnosis is wrong action, though he observe a plan.[153]

CONCLUSION

The Gnostics present a picture of early Christianity startlingly different from that bequeathed to us by the Roman Church. We have already seen that the story of Jesus and the teachings he gives in the New Testament are prefigured by the myths and teachings of the ancient Pagan Mysteries. In Gnosticism we find many other elements, which were central to the Mysteries but are missing in Christianity as we know it today—the quest for Gnosis, the role of the goddess, the importance of women, the Daemon/eidolon doctrine, and so on. Let's review some of these remarkable similarities between Gnostic Christianity and the Pagan Mysteries:

❖ Literalists accused the Gnostics of preaching Pagan doctrines.
❖ Gnostics taught Pagan philosophy, venerated pictures of the Pagan philosophers alongside pictures of Jesus, invited Pagans to Gnostic gatherings and were even initiated into the Pagan Mysteries.
❖ Gnostic texts contain Pagan mythical motifs, which they claimed taught a universal philosophy.
❖ Gnostics equated Jesus with "many shaped Attis" and other pseudonyms for Osiris-Dionysus.
❖ As in the Pagan Mysteries, the Gnostic Christians honored the Divine Feminine in the form of the goddess Sophia.
❖ Like the sages of the Pagan Mysteries, the Gnostics were critical of the orthodox Christians' anthropomorphic picture of God. They called the Jewish god Jehovah a false god and taught that Jesus was the Son of the true ineffable God. This indescribable ultimate Oneness was identical with the supreme God of Plato and the Pagan Mysteries.
❖ The Gnostic Jesus is like a Pagan hierophant who initiates his disciples into the Mysteries through dance and song.
❖ Gnostics taught that Christianity, like the Pagan Mysteries, had Outer Mysteries for beginners in the faith and Inner Mysteries for the initiated.
❖ Just as in the Pagan Mysteries, Christian initiates of the Inner Mysteries were sworn to secrecy.
❖ Clement tells us that Mark preached three different gospels for three different levels of initiation. His gospel in the New Testament was designed "for beginners." The *Secret Gospel* was for those being "perfected." A further oral gospel revealed Gnosis.

- ❖ As in the Pagan Mysteries, the goal of Gnosticism was the experience of Gnosis, or "Knowledge," which was contrasted with mere faith or belief.
- ❖ Like the Pagan sages, the Gnostics taught "Know Thy Self" as the means of coming to know God.
- ❖ As in the Pagan Mysteries, the Gnostics taught the doctrine of the Daemon (Heavenly Twin or Higher Self) and the eidolon (lower self).
- ❖ As in the Pagan Mysteries, the Gnostics taught that the Daemon at first appears to be a Guardian Angel, then is experienced as the initiate's own Higher Self and finally is realized to be the Mind of God in all things.
- ❖ As in the Pagan Mysteries, the Gnostics taught the doctrine of reincarnation.
- ❖ As in the Pagan Mysteries, in Gnosticism women played a prominent role.
- ❖ Both Pagan and Gnostic sages were accused of condoning immorality when actually they were both preaching the same mystical doctrine of natural morality.

Faced with this overwhelming evidence it seemed to us that the Gnostic Christians were clearly practicing an adaptation of the ancient Pagan Mysteries. Was this the clue we were looking for to solve our mystery? Could Gnosticism be the original Christianity, which developed from the Pagan Mysteries with the Jesus story as a Jewish version of the perennial myth of the dying and resurrecting Mystery godman? It seemed too incredible to be true, but we did not feel it could be ruled out. We therefore decided to take a closer look at exactly how the Gnostics saw the Jesus story. Did they base their faith on the belief in the existence of a historical man, like Literalist Christians, or was their Jesus, like Osiris-Dionysus, the central character of a mystical allegory?

6

The Jesus Code

To you it is given to know the Mysteries of the kingdom of God, but to the rest of them it is only given in allegories.[1]

Jesus in the Gospel of Luke

The Pagan sages did not regard the myths of Osiris-Dionysus as histories that must never be changed or adapted, but allegorical myths, which could be syncretized with each other and reworked. The Gnostic Christians, likewise, did not regard their gospels as historical records, but works of allegorical literature encoding eternal truths that could be creatively developed and refined. Indeed, Gnostic initiates were expected to interpret the myths and teachings they received in their own unique way to show that they had personally experienced Gnosis and were not simply repeating, parrot-fashion, what they had been told by someone else. Tertullian complains:

> Every one of them, just as it suits his own temperament, modifies the traditions he has received, just as the one who handed them down modified them, when he shaped them according to his own will.[2]

Irenaeus is likewise appalled, fuming:

> They all generate something new each day; for no one is considered initiated or mature among them unless he develops some enormous fiction![3]

The Gnostics explained that their spiritual creativity came from direct personal contact with the "Living One." They argued that it is ultimately only through one's own experience that one can judge what is true and that therefore, personal experience must take precedence over all second-hand testimony and tradition.

MYTHICAL ALLEGORIES

In the Pagan Mysteries the secret Inner Mysteries revealed the allegorical meaning of the myths of the Outer Mysteries. Likewise, the Gnostics claimed that they taught secret Inner Mysteries, which revealed Gnosis, for which the Outer Mysteries of Christianity were only a preparation.

When Literalist Christians poured scorn on the very idea that there were secret Christian teachings, Gnostics pointed to the example of Jesus, who in public spoke in parables and in private revealed the meaning of these allegories to his closest disciples.[4] In Mark, for example, we read:

> And he said to them, "Things are hidden only to be revealed, and made secret only to be brought to light. If any have ears to hear, let them hear." And he kept speaking to them in allegories, according as they could hear, and he said nothing to them without allegories, but privately to his own students he always gave the key.[5]

The idea that mystical teachings could be encoded in mythical stories was at the heart of the Pagan Mysteries. Philo, a Jewish Pythagorean, calls allegory "the method of the Greek Mysteries."[6] The Pagan philosopher Demetrius writes: "What is clear and manifest is easily despised like naked men. Therefore the Mysteries too are expressed in the form of allegory."[7] Macrobius, likewise, explains:

> Plain and naked exposition of herself is repugnant to Nature. She wishes her secrets to be treated by myth. Thus the Mysteries themselves are hidden in the tunnels of figurative expression, so that not even to initiates the nature of such realities may present herself naked, but only an élite may know about the real secret, through the

interpretation furnished by wisdom, while the rest may be content to venerate the Mystery, defended by those figurative expressions against banality.[8]

This Pagan allegorical approach toward sacred scripture was enthusiastically embraced by Gnostic Christians. The Gnostic *Gospel of Philip* teaches the same doctrine as Macrobius: "Truth did not come into the world naked, but in images. One will not receive truth in any other way."[9] Literalist Christians, on the other hand, took scripture as historical fact. The Pagan satirist Celsus is astonished at such *naïveté* and demolishes a literal interpretation of the Biblical story of creation with characteristic wit:

> God banishes man from the garden made specifically to contain him. Silly as that may be, sillier still is the way the world is supposed to have come about. They allot certain days to creation, before days existed. For when heaven had not been made, or the earth fixed or the sun set in the heavens, how could days exist? Isn't it absurd to think that the greatest God pieced out his work like a bricklayer, saying, "Today I shall do this, tomorrow that," and so on, so that he did this on the third, that on the fourth, and something else on the fifth and sixth days! We are thus not surprised to find that, like a common workman, this God wears himself down and so needs a holiday after six days. Need I comment that a God who gets tired, works with his hands, and gives orders like a foreman is not acting very much like a God?[10]

Like Celsus, Gnostic Christians viewed such literalism as superficial and simple-minded. Origen was amazed that anyone could take such stories literally, since they are clearly allegorical (he would have been shocked, no doubt, to speak to many modern fundamentalist Christians!) He writes:

> What man of sense will agree with the statement that the first, second and third days, in which the evening is named and the morning, were without Sun, Moon and Stars, and the first day without a heaven? What man is found such an idiot as to suppose that God planted trees in Paradise, in Eden, like a husbandman? I believe that every man must hold these things for images under which a hidden sense lies concealed.[11]

Origen viewed the idea that scripture was mythical allegory as a "beautiful tradition," which could reveal the hidden meaning encoded in the stories about Jesus.[12] He writes:

> I do not think anyone will doubt that these are figurative expressions which indicate certain Mysteries through a semblance of history and not through actual events.[13]

Origen explains that to those "not altogether blind the gospels are full of passages of this kind," which are "recorded as actual events, but which did not happen literally." He quotes as an example the story of Jesus being tempted by the Devil. Jesus is taken up a high mountain where he is shown all the kingdoms of the world, which the Devil offers him if he will only fall down and worship him. Origen pours scorn on the idea that anyone could actually see all the kingdoms of the world from the top of a mountain and affirms that this is meant to be understood allegorically. He tells us:

> The careful reader will detect thousands of other passages like this in the gospels.[14]

Clement also regarded the true Christian as the Gnostic who can penetrate to the allegorical meaning of scripture by understanding "the involutions of words and the solutions of enigmas."[15] He teaches that the initiate who has experienced Gnosis grasps the complete truth, piercing to the depths of scripture of which the "believer" tastes only the surface.[16]

In this spirit, Gnostics did not interpret the Jesus story literally as a historical account, but as a spiritual allegory encoding profound mystical teachings. In a text called *The Travels of Peter* Jesus himself is made to decode some of the allegorical teachings hidden in the accounts of his crucifixion. He explains:

> The Logos is symbolized by that straight stem on which I hang. The cross-piece of the cross represents that human nature which suffered the fault of change in the first man, but by the help of God-and-man, received again its real mind. Right in the center, joining twain in one, is set the nail of discipline, conversion, and repentance.[17]

SACRED MATHEMATICS

The immense challenge we face today in attempting to decode both the myths of the Pagan Mysteries and the Jesus story can only be understood when the complexity and subtlety of the code is appreciated. The Gnostics, like their predecessors the Pythagoreans, not only used symbols and images, but also numbers and mathematical formulas to encode their mystical teachings. Mathematics and geometry were regarded by the Pagan sages as sacred sciences that reveal the workings of the Mind of God. Pythagoras called numbers "immortal gods."[18] Over Plato's Academy were written the words "Let no man who knows no mathematics enter here."[19]

The Literalist Christian Hippolytus calls the Gnostics "disciples of Pythagoras and Plato" and accuses them of likewise taking "arithmetical science" as "the fundamental principle of their doctrine."[20] Clement was fascinated by Pythagorean mathematics and even applied the ratios revealed in the mathematical laws underlying harmony in music to the interpretation of scripture.[21] The Gnostic sage Monoimos instructed his students in the sacred mathematics of Plato and Pythagoras.[22] Gnostics used the image of the heavens divided into seven spheres, forming a sort of mystic ladder composed of an octave of eight gates that the initiate could ascend, which is identical to teachings found in the Pagan Mysteries.[23]

Scholars have concluded that Gnostic gospels such as the *Pistis Sophia* and the *Book of Ieou*, rather than being compendiums of mystifying nonsense, are actually based on a sophisticated form of number symbolism.[24] One central element in this symbolism is gematria—the expression of numbers and mathematical relationships through words.

In the ancient Greek alphabet, each letter also signified a number. Thus any word also had a numerical value and could be used to convey mathematical information. The Greek names of the gods were more than just words, their numerical values were also significant. For example, in its most common Greek spelling, the name of the Pagan godman Mithras expresses *360*, which in some places was regarded as the number of days in a year. Several ancient writers deliberately add an extra letter, however, to make the name's numerical value equal 365, the more accurate reckoning of the solar year.[25] Thus, as St. Jerome points out, Mithras is numerically revealed as a solar deity.

Gematria was also adopted by the Gnostic Christians. Gnostic myth even represents the youthful Jesus instructing scholars at the Jerusalem Temple in the mystical meaning of the Greek alphabet![26] Like the Pagan Mithras, the name of Abraxas, the Gnostic solar divinity, also expresses the number 365. The most striking example of Christian gematria, however, is the name *Jesus* itself.

The early Christians maintained that *Iesous*, the original Greek name we translate as "Jesus," was "a name above all names."[27] Origen boasted that it possesses more magical efficacy than the names of the Pagan divinities.[28] It is well known that according to the Revelation of John the number of the "Beast" is 666.[29] What is less well known is that according to gematria, the Greek name *Iesous* (Jesus) expresses the number 888.[30]

$$\text{I} \quad \text{E} \quad \text{S} \quad \text{O} \quad \text{U} \quad \text{S}$$

$$10 + 8 + 200 + 70 + 400 + 200 = 888$$

This number was regarded as sacred and magical by the ancients for a number of reasons, including the fact that if all the numbers associated with each of the 24 letters in the Greek alphabet are added together they come to 888. It is surely also significant that in musical harmony, which for the Pythagoreans was a sacred science, 666 is the string ratio of the perfect fifth and 888 is the string ratio of the whole tone![31]

The fact that Jesus' name equals 888 is no lucky accident. The Greek name *Iesous* is an artificial and forced transliteration of the Hebrew name *Joshua*, which has been deliberately constructed by the gospel writers to make sure that it expresses this symbolically significant number.[32]

Even Literalists are aware of the number symbolism of Jesus' name. Irenaeus states:

> Iesous is a name arithmetically symbolical, consisting of six letters, as is known by all those that belong to the called.[33]

Other names in the Jesus story also have significance when translated into numbers using gematria. Jesus gives his disciple Simon the name *Cephas*, meaning "Rock," often translated as "Peter." In the original Greek Cephas expresses 729, which was an important number to Pagans. Plutarch, a priest of Apollo at Delphi, notes that 729 is a number of the sun, being the number of days and nights in a year. Socrates remarks that it is "a number that is closely concerned with human life, if human life is concerned with days and nights and months and years."[34]

Scholars have even found that the New Testament story of Jesus helping his disciples make a miraculous catch of 153 fish is a mathematical puzzle, which reveals an "underlying and unfolding geometrical diagram."[35] As already discussed, this miracle story is based on a similar miracle performed by Pythagoras, the great Pagan guru of sacred mathematics. Both these stories encode sacred mathematical formulae understood by the initiated as revealing esoteric teachings.

The New Testament stories of the feeding of the 5,000 and the 4,000 have also been shown to yield mystical geometrical diagrams. This is clearly hinted at in Mark's gospels, where an impatient Jesus leads his disciples through what he clearly intends to be some mystical mathematical puzzle that, alas, his disciples do not understand:

> Jesus said, "Though you have eyes, you do not see, and though you have ears, you do not hear! Don't you remember, when I broke the five loaves for the five thousand, how many basketfuls of scraps you cleared away?"
>
> They said unto him, "Twelve."
>
> "And when I broke the seven loaves for the four thousand, how many basketfuls of scraps did you clear away?"
>
> And they said, "Seven."
>
> And he said to them, "And you still don't understand?!"[36]

It would seem that, like his confused disciples in the story, the Christian Church has failed to understand for 2,000 years that what it has taken as literal events are in fact carefully constructed mystical allegories. With the destruction of the Inner Mysteries of the Gnostics, the keys to decode the allegories have been lost and we can only guess at much of the profound metaphor at work in the Jesus story.

JESUS THE DAEMON

For Gnostics, the godman Jesus symbolized the Daemon, the immortal Self. Often the eidolon, the incarnate self, is represented in Gnostic myths by Jesus' "twin brother" Thomas. In *The Book of Thomas the Contender* Jesus (the Daemon) teaches his disciple and twin brother Thomas (the eidolon):

Brother Thomas, while you have time in the world, listen to me, and I will reveal to you the things you have pondered in your mind. Now since it has been said that you are my twin and true companion, examine yourself and learn who you are, in what way you exist, and how you will come to be. Since you will be called my brother, it is not fitting that you be ignorant of yourself. And I know that you have understood, because you have already understood that I am the knowledge of the truth. So while you accompany me, although you are uncomprehending, you have in fact already come to know, and you will be called "the one who knows himself."[37]

It was a widespread tradition among early Christians that Jesus had a twin brother who resembled him in every detail. This caused Literalists a great many problems, as the obvious objection to their claims that Jesus had literally resurrected from the dead was that his twin brother had been crucified in his place. This has led some scholars to conclude that this legend must be based on historical fact, for "what Christian would have been foolish enough to invent such a legend, seeing that it is most apt to undermine the very basis of the orthodox tradition concerning the resuscitation of Jesus?"[38] The answer is that the Gnostics invented the tradition of Jesus' twin brother as an allegory for the ancient Daemon/eidolon doctrine.

The authorship of *The Gospel of Thomas* is attributed to Didymos Judas Thomas. The Aramaic name Thomas and the Greek name Didymos both mean "twin." The author's name is thus "Judas the twin."[39] This suggests that in the original Jesus story, Judas the betrayer of Jesus symbolized the eidolon, which betrays the Daemon.

Another encoded reference to the Daemon/eidolon doctrine in the New Testament is during Matthew's account of Jesus' trial, when Pontius Pilate offers to spare one of two Jesuses—either Jesus Messiah or Jesus Barabbas.[40] One Jesus is an innocent man who is murdered and the other a murderer who goes free. These two Jesuses symbolize the Higher Self and lower self in each human being.

ILLUSIONISM

The Pagan Daemon/eidolon doctrine casts light on the otherwise baffling Gnostic teaching known as *Docetism* or "Illusionism."[41] The opponents of Gnosticism have portrayed this as a rather strange belief that Jesus did not actually have a flesh and blood body, but only seemed to exist physically, and that he magically made it appear as if he was dying on the cross although in reality he was not. As usual, however, by taking the Gnostics literally, the Literalists completely miss the point.

The Gnostic Illusionist view of the crucifixion was not meant to be taken as a historical account of events. It is a myth that encodes the perennial mystical teachings that a human being is made up of two parts: an earthly part which suffers and dies (the eidolon), and an eternal spiritual witness (the Daemon), which is untouched by suffering and experiences this world as a passing illusion.

A Letter of Peter to Philip explains that although from the time of his incarnation Jesus suffered, yet he suffered as one who was "a stranger to this suffering."[42] This teaches that the incarnate Higher Self (represented by Jesus) seems to suffer when the eidolon suffers, but in reality is always the untouched witness. In *The Acts of John* Jesus explains:

> You heard that I suffered, but I suffered not.
> An unsuffering one was I, yet suffered.
> One pierced was I, yet I was not abused.
> One hanged was I, and yet not hanged.
> Blood flowed from me, yet did not flow.[43]

How is it that Jesus can both suffer and not suffer? Because, as he explains, "I distinguish the man from myself."[44] He identifies with his transcendent Higher Self, the Daemon, not his suffering lower self, the eidolon.

The purpose of Gnostic initiation was to free initiates from all suffering through the realization that their true identity is not the eidolon bound to the cross of matter, but the Daemon that witnesses life as a passing illusion.[45] Thus the Gnostic Jesus teaches:

> Had you known how to suffer, you would have been able not to suffer.
> See through suffering, and you will have non-suffering.[46]

So, the eidolon of Jesus *seems* to suffer and die, but the real Jesus—the Daemon—cannot suffer or die.[47]

Five hundred years previously Euripides portrayed King Pentheus as binding Dionysus, while actually he was not. As Dionysus says:

> There I made a mockery of him. He thought he was binding me; But he neither held nor touched me, save in his deluded mind.[48]

In *The Apocalypse of Peter*, Peter sees Jesus "glad and laughing" on the cross while the nails are bring driven into his hands and feet, and Jesus explains:

> He whom you see on the tree, glad and laughing, this is the living Jesus. But this one into whose hands and feet they drive nails is his fleshy part, which is the substitute being put to shame, the one who came into being in his likeness. But look at him and me.[49]

In some Pagan myths it is not the godman who suffers and dies, but a substitute figure who represents the eidolon. In *The Bacchae*, King Pentheus, whose name means "Man of Suffering," is raised up on a tree and torn to shreds in the place of Dionysus.[50] Similarly, in certain Gnostic myths it is Simon of Cyrene who dies on the cross, while Jesus watches laughing from a distance.[51] In *The Second Treatise of the Great Seth*, Jesus explains:

> It was another, Simon, who bore the cross on his shoulder. It was another upon whom they placed the crown of thorns. But I was rejoicing in the height and laughing at their ignorance.[52]

Simon of Cyrene, like King Pentheus in the Pagan version of the myth, represents the eidolon, which suffers and dies. The laughing figure of Jesus, like the triumphant Dionysus, represents the Daemon, the witnessing Spirit. The Gnostic sage Basilides teaches that "because he was Mind, Jesus did not suffer" but Simon of Cyrene suffered in his stead, while Jesus laughed "because he could not be held and was invisible to all."[53]

The Gnostics did not believe that Jesus only seemed to exist, or that he magically avoided suffering on the cross, or, more sinisterly, that he had himself replaced by Simon of Cyrene, who was crucified instead while Jesus stood safely at a distance laughing. Such doctrines would, as the Literalists claimed, be distasteful and ridiculous. But this is a misunderstanding (or more likely a conscious distortion!) of Gnostic teachings. In fact, "Illusionism" is simply part of understanding the crucifixion story as an initiation allegory, which encodes the ancient Pagan Daemon/eidolon doctrine.

A fragment of these teachings has survived in the New Testament Gospel of Mark in which Simon of Cyrene is inexplicably dragooned into carrying Jesus' cross for him.[54] The name Simon here links this figure symbolically to the disciple called Simon "Peter" or "Rock," who also symbolizes the eidolon in many Gnostic myths.

An echo of this Gnostic doctrine also survives in the Muslim Qur'an which, when dealing with the supposed death of Jesus, declares:

> But they did not kill him, neither did they crucify him, but a similitude was made for them.[55]

THE SPIRITUAL RESURRECTION

According to the Pagan sages, we are each made up of a mortal eidolon and the immortal Daemon. If we are alive to our personal identity as the eidolon, we are dead to our eternal identity as the Daemon.[56] Initiation in the Mysteries was a way of bringing the soul back to life. By undergoing the mystical death of the eidolon the initiate could arise reborn as the Daemon.[57] The Gnostics taught the same Mystery doctrine.

The anonymous teacher of the Gnostic sage Rheginos explains that ordinary human existence is spiritual death and, therefore, we all need to be "resurrected from the dead."[58]

Just as Pagan initiates who witnessed the grand Mystery pageant at Eleusis metaphorically suffered with Dionysus and were spiritually reborn, likewise, initiates in the Gnostic Mysteries metaphorically shared in the suffering and triumph of their godman Jesus. Rheginos' teacher explains:

> We suffered with him, and we arose with him, and we went to heaven with him.[59]

Initiates who shared in Jesus' passion as an allegory for their own mystical death and resurrection could say along with Jesus in the Gospel of John:

That's why my Father loves me, because I lay down my life to get it back again.[60]

Literalist Christians rested their faith entirely on the supposed miracle that a historical Jesus had physically come back from the dead and that this was some sort of proof that those who believed that Jesus was the Son of God would also be resurrected physically at the "Day of Judgment." The Gnostics, in contrast, called taking the resurrection literally the "faith of fools!"[61] The resurrection, they insisted, was neither a historical event that happened once only to someone else, nor a promise that corpses would rise from the dead after some future apocalypse. The Gnostics understood the resurrection as a mystical experience that could happen to any one of us right here and now through the recognition of our true identity as the Daemon.[62]

For Literalists any personal experience of the resurrection was a distant hope of bodily immortality after the Second Coming. The Gnostic *Gospel of Philip*, however, ridicules such Christians, explaining, "Those who say they will die first and then rise are in error" since we should "receive the resurrection whilst alive."[63]

For the Gnostics the resurrection was simply "the revealing of what truly exists."[64] For initiates with "eyes to see," therefore, this mystical resurrection had "already taken place."[65] It could not possibly be a future event, because it was an awareness of what was real in the present moment. An initiate's true identity did not become the Daemon through the process of initiation. It had always been the Daemon. The resurrection was actually only a change in awareness. The teacher of Rheginos proclaims:

> Already you have the resurrection. Consider yourself as risen already.[66] Are you—the real you—mere corruption? Why do you not examine your own Self, and see that you have arisen?[67]

The Treatise of the Resurrection teaches:

> Everything is prone to change. The world is an illusion! The resurrection is the revelation of what is, and the transformation of things, and a transition into newness. Flee from the divisions and the fetters, and already you have the resurrection.[68]

Although the Gnostics saw the resurrection as an allegory, they did not see it as unreal. On the contrary, to the initiated the mystical experience of spiritual resurrection was more real than the so-called reality of normal consciousness. The teacher of Rheginos explains:

> Do not suppose that resurrection is an illusion. It is not an illusion; rather it is something real. Instead, one ought to maintain that the world is an illusion, rather than the resurrection.[69]

THE SACRED MARRIAGE

An important mythical motif in the Pagan Mysteries was the sacred marriage between the godman and the goddess, symbolizing the mystical union of opposites.[70] In Crete they celebrated the marriage of the goddess Demeter and the godman Iasion.[71] Upon his yearly "arrival" in Athens, Dionysus was hailed as "Bridal One"[72] and his marriage to the queen of the city, who represented the goddess, was ritually celebrated.[73]

In Mystery initiations, the initiate was often portrayed as the bride of Osiris-Dionysus. Initiations were carried out in special "bridal chambers" which have been found at Pagan sanctuaries.[74] An ancient fresco shows scenes of those preparing for initiation being dressed in the attire of brides.[75] After their initiation they were hailed as "brides."[76]

The bride represented the incarnate self or eidolon and Osiris-Dionysus represented the disincarnate Self or Daemon. The sacred marriage ritually united these two opposing parts of the initiate. Epiphanius tells us:

> Some prepare a bridal chamber and perform a mystic rite accompanied by certain words used to the initiated, and they allege that it is a spiritual marriage.[77]

The Pagan Mystery motif of the sacred marriage is missing from orthodox Christianity,[78] but was important in Gnostic Christianity, which celebrated the sacred marriage between Jesus and Sophia. In Gnostic myth, Sophia is portrayed in a "fallen" state as representing the incarnate self. She is pictured as lost in the world searching for the ineffable Source. Looking for love in all the wrong places, she becomes a prostitute. Finally she begs God the Father for help and He sends her as a bridegroom the Firstborn Son of God, her brother Jesus.[79] When the bridegroom arrives they make love passionately to become One.[80]

This is an allegory of the Daemon or Spirit coming to the rescue of the incarnate self or psyche. According to *The Gospel of Philip*, only the person who has "remarried" the psyche with the Spirit becomes capable of withstanding physical and emotional impulses that, unchecked, could drive them toward self-destruction and evil.[81]

The sacred marriage is a symbol of mystical unity, which was the goal of Gnosticism. In *The Gospel of Thomas* Jesus teaches his disciples:

> When you make the two one, and when you make the outside like the inside, and the above like the below, and when you make the male and the female one and the same, so that the male be not male nor the female female then will you enter the kingdom.[82]

Some Gnostic groups ritually celebrated the sacred marriage as part of their rites of initiation. Irenaeus tells us: "They prepare a bridal chamber and celebrate Mysteries."[83] The followers of the Gnostic sage Marcus performed an initiatory rite "with certain formulae, and they term this a spiritual marriage."[84] We are told that the followers of the Gnostic poet Valentinus practiced the rite of a spiritual marriage with angels in a nuptial chamber.[85] The Naassenes taught that the initiated "must cast off their garments and all become brides pregnant by the Virgin Spirit."[86] *The Gospel of Philip* explains that the process of initiation climaxed in the "bridal chamber" of mystical union, for "The holy of the holies is the bridal chamber. The redemption takes place in the bridal chamber."[87]

In the Jesus story, the fallen Sophia (the psyche) is represented by the figure of Mary Magdalene, whom Jesus (the Daemon) redeems from prostitution.[88] According to the Gnostic sage Heracleon, this motif of a sacred marriage also appears in the Jesus story as the marriage feast in Cana where Jesus, like Dionysus before him, changes water into intoxicating wine. This miracle, Heracleon tells us, symbolizes that "divine marriage," which transforms what is merely human into the divine.[89] The motif also occurs in a passage from the Gospel of Matthew in which Jesus explains that reaching the kingdom of Heaven will be like a maiden going to meet "the Bridegroom."[90]

In *The Gospel of Thomas* Jesus teaches that to experience this final level of initiation into mystical union, each initiate must enter the bridal chamber alone:

Many are standing at the door, but it is the solitary who will enter the bridal chamber.[91]

BECOMING CHRIST

The Pagan sages taught that in the Inner Mysteries an initiate discovered that what appeared to be their individual Daemon was actually the Universal Daemon, which they pictured as having been torn into fragments and distributed among all conscious beings. Epictetus teaches: "You are a fragment torn from God. You have a portion of him within you."[92] Osiris-Dionysus represents this Universal Daemon, the Mind of God conscious in all living things.

In many myths Osiris-Dionysus meets his death by dismemberment.[93] This is often taken to mean the threshing of the corn to produce bread and the trampling of grapes to produce wine. Initiates of the Inner Mysteries, however, understood this motif on a more mystical level, as encoding teachings about the dismemberment of the Universal Daemon by the power of evil. In the myth of Osiris, for example, the godman is murdered and dismembered by his evil brother Set, and then the goddess Isis collects together all of Osiris' limbs and reconstitutes him. This myth encodes the Mystery teaching that God needs to be "re-membered," that the spiritual path is the process of the reuniting the fragments of the Universal Daemon, of perceiving One in all.

Describing Osiris' death, Plutarch writes:

Set scatters and destroys the sacred Logos which the goddess Isis collects and puts together and delivers to those undergoing initiation.[94]

This Pagan motif of dismemberment is completely foreign to Christianity as we now know it, but was fundamental to Gnosticism. Like their Pagan predecessors, Gnostic Christians believed each individual human self to be a fragment of one single heavenly being, which had been dismembered by evil forces, robbed of all memory of its heavenly origins, and forced into individual physical bodies.[95]

Like the Pagan godman Osiris-Dionysus, the Christian godman Jesus symbolically represents the Universal Daemon or Logos, which has been dismembered. In the *Pistis Sophia*, Jesus declares: "I have torn myself asunder and come into the world."[96] In *The Acts of John*, he teaches that "the multitude that is about the cross" represents the "Limbs of Him" that have yet to be "gathered together."[97] In *The Book of the Logos* Jesus says:

> Save all my Limbs, which since the foundation of the world have been scattered abroad, and gather them all together and receive them into the Light.[98]

A Gnostic hymn to be sung on the "great day of supreme initiation," beseeches Jesus:

> Come unto us, for we are Thy fellow-members, Thy limbs. We are all one with Thee. We are one and the same, and Thou art one and the same.[99]

The Pagan sage Proclus explains that the "most secret of all initiations" reveals "the Spirit in us" as "a veritable image of Dionysus."[100] A Pagan initiate who achieved Gnosis or Self-knowledge, realized their identity as an expression of Osiris-Dionysus, the Universal Daemon. Such an initiate was known in the Mysteries as an *Osiris* or a *Dionysus*.[101]

In the same way, the Gnostic *Gospel of Philip* teaches that a true Gnostic is "no longer a Christian, but a Christ."[102] Origen also teaches that a follower of Jesus could become "a Christ."[103] In an untitled Gnostic apocalypse Jesus calls out to his "children" with whom he is working until "the Christ" is formed within them.[104] In the *Pistis Sophia* he teaches that only someone who has become a Christ will know the supreme Gnosis of the Whole.[105] In a collection of Gnostic sayings, he explains, "As ye see yourself in water or a mirror, so see ye Me in yourselves."[106] In *The Gospel of Philip* he proclaims:

> You saw the Spirit, you became Spirit. You saw Christ, you became Christ. You saw the Father, you shall become the Father.[107]

This teaching is even found in the New Testament Gospel of Luke, where Jesus promises that "the initiated student will become like his teacher."[108]

A common phrase in the Pagan Mysteries, often quoted by Plato, was *Soma sema*, "The body is a tomb."[109] Gnostic initiates also understood that those who identified with the incarnate physical self were spiritually dead and needed to be reborn into eternal Life. Initiates who experienced mystical resurrection realized their true identity as the Christ and discovered, like the women in the Jesus story, that "the tomb is empty." The body is not their identity. They are not the eidolon that lives and dies, but the eternal witness that is forever unborn and undying.

LEVELS OF INITIATION

Both Pagan and Gnostic philosophical systems described four levels of human identity: physical, psychological, spiritual, and mystical. Gnostics called these four levels of our being the body, the counterfeit-spirit, the Spirit, and the Light-power. The body and the counterfeit-spirit (our physical and psychological identities) make up the two aspects of the eidolon or lower self. The Spirit and Light-power (our spiritual and mystical identities) make up the two aspects of the immortal Daemon—the individual Higher Self and the shared Universal Self.

The Gnostics called those who identified with their body "Hylics," because they were so utterly dead to spiritual things that they were like unconscious matter, or *hyle*. Those who identified with their personality, or *psyche*, were known as "Psychics." Those who identified with their Spirit were known as "Pneumatics," which means "Spirituals."[110] Those who completely ceased to identify with any level of their separate identity and realized their true identity as the Christ or Universal Daemon experienced Gnosis.[111] This mystical enlightenment transformed the initiate into a true Gnostic or Knower.[112]

In both Paganism and Christianity these levels of awareness were symbolically linked with the four elements: earth, water, air, and fire.[113] The initiations leading from one level to the next were symbolized by elemental baptisms.[114] In *The Book of the Great Logos* Jesus offers his disciples "the Mysteries of the three baptisms" by water, air, and fire.[115] Baptism by water symbolizes the transformation of the Hylic person, who identifies solely with the body, into a Psychic initiate, who identifies with the personality or psyche. Baptism by air symbolizes the transformation of the Psychic initiate into a Pneumatic initiate, who identifies with his Higher Self. Baptism by fire represents the final initiation, which reveals to Pneumatic initiates their true identity as the Universal Daemon, the Logos, the Christ within, the "Light-power"—"the true Light which lighteth every man that cometh into the world," as John's gospel puts it.[116] Such an initiate had realized Gnosis.

These, then, are the levels of initiation in Gnostic Christianity.

Level of Initiation	Level of Identity	Gnostic Description	Element
Hylic	Physical identity	Body	Earth
Psychic	Psychological identity	Counterfeit-spirit	Water
Pneumatic	Spiritual identity	Spirit	Air
Gnostic	Mystical identity	Light-power	Fire

LITERAL, MYTHICAL, AND MYSTICAL

A Pagan initiate of the Outer Mysteries viewed the myth of Osiris-Dionysus enacted in the Mystery pageant as a marvelous and emotionally compelling spectacle. An initiate of the Inner Mysteries was instructed in the allegorical meaning encoded in the myth. A master of the Mysteries embodied these teachings in their own being. Likewise, a Gnostic initiate's relationship with the Jesus story changed as they progressed toward Gnosis. These three levels of understanding can be characterized as literal, mythical, and mystical:

❖ *Literal:* Psychic Christians had experienced the first baptism by water and been initiated into the Outer Mysteries of Christianity. They understood the story of Jesus as a historical account of a person, who literally returned from the dead.

❖ *Mythical:* Pneumatic Christians had experienced the second baptism of air (holy breath or holy spirit) and been initiated into the secret Inner Mysteries of Christianity. They understood the Jesus story as an allegorical myth encoding teachings about the spiritual path traveled by each initiate.

❖ *Mystical:* Gnostics had experienced the final baptism of fire and realized their identity as the Christ (the Logos or Universal Daemon). They transcended the need for any teachings, including the Jesus story.

As Origen writes:

> Very many mistakes have been made, because the right method of examining the holy texts has not been discovered by the greater number of readers.[117]

The right method, according to Origen, is to understand the three levels on which scripture works. The lowest level is the obvious literal interpretation. The next level, for "one who has advanced somewhat," is an allegorical level, which edifies the soul. The final level, which reveals Gnosis, is for "one who is perfected by the spiritual law." Origen taught that through following this threefold path, the Christian initiate progresses from faith to Gnosis.[118]

The pseudo-history of Jesus' life was an essential part of the Outer Mysteries of Christianity, which were designed to attract new would-be initiates, so the Gnostics did not necessarily deny the historicity of the gospels. But any literal interpretation of the Jesus story was only the first step presented to spiritual beginners. The true meaning of this myth was revealed to initiates in the secret Inner Mysteries.

Origen is dismissive of Literalist Christianity, which does not progress beyond viewing the Jesus story as historical fact, calling it a "popular, irrational faith," which leads to "somatic Christianity." As one scholar remarks:

> He makes it only too clear that by "somatic Christianity" he means that faith which is based on the gospel history. Of teachings founded upon the historical narrative, he says, "What better method could be devised to assist the masses?" The Gnostic or sage no longer needs the crucified Christ. The "eternal" or "spiritual" Gospel, which is in his possession, "shows clearly all things concerning the Son of God Himself, both the Mysteries shown by His words, and the things of which His acts were the symbols."[119]

The Naassene Gnostics taught that Literalist Christians who understood only the Outer Mysteries were "bewitched" by Jehovah the false God, whose spell has the opposite effect of the "divine enchantment" of the Logos.[120] Basilides, likewise, teaches:

> Those who confess Jesus as the crucified one are still enslaved to the God of the Jews. He who denies it has been freed and knows the plan of the unbegotten Father.[121]

As Origen puts it with startling bluntness: "Christ crucified is teaching for babes."[122]

CONCLUSION

For the Gnostics Jesus is a figure who must be understood on many levels. Since the destruction of Gnosticism we have only been taught the lowest level of understanding and have been denied access to the secret Inner Mysteries of the Gnostics, which reveal the true allegorical nature of the Jesus story. Has this led us to mistake Jesus for a historical figure? Let's examine some of the evidence again:

- ❖ As in the Pagan Mysteries, Gnostics initiated into the Inner Mysteries understood scripture as mythical allegory, which could be altered and improved upon, not literal history, which must be preserved intact.
- ❖ Like the Pagan philosophers, the Gnostics used gematria and number symbolism to encode complex sacred mathematical teachings. The name *Iesous*, which we translate as "Jesus," is an artificial transliteration of the Jewish name Joshua into Greek to make sure that it equals the mystically significant number 888. This remarkable fact was even acknowledged by Literalists.
- ❖ Like Osiris-Dionysus, Jesus symbolizes the Daemon of the initiate. As in Pagan myth, sometimes another figure representing the eidolon is symbolically portrayed as dying the godman's death as a substitute.
- ❖ In the same way that the Pagan sages understood the myths of Osiris-Dionysus as allegorical teaching stories, so the Gnostics understood the Jesus story to be a mystical initiation myth leading to spiritual resurrection.
- ❖ As in the Pagan Mysteries, the Gnostics practiced a ritual sacred marriage of the Daemon and eidolon as part of their initiations.

- Like Osiris-Dionysus, the Gnostic Jesus represents the universal Daemon, which has been dismembered and needs to be re-membered.
- Initiates in the Pagan Mysteries who realized their true nature as the Universal Daemon became an "Osiris" or a "Dionysus." Likewise, Gnostic initiates became a "Christ."
- Like the Pagan Mysteries, Gnosticism viewed a human being as having four levels of identity: physical, psychological, spiritual, and mystical. As in the Pagan Mysteries, these were linked to the four elements— earth, water, air, and fire—and initiates were led through these levels of identity by elemental baptisms.
- The Gnostics did not necessarily deny the historicity of the gospels, but viewed taking the Jesus story literally as only the first stage in their Mysteries.

Could the Jesus story have been taught as a history to beginners in the faith as part of the Outer Mysteries and then revealed in the secret Inner Mysteries to be an initiatory myth? Could this myth of Jesus have been based on the ubiquitous myths of Osiris-Dionysus? Could Gnosticism have been the original Christianity, which developed as a Jewish version of the Pagan Mysteries? Could Literalist Christianity be a later "heresy," which maintained only the Outer Mysteries of Christianity? At first such possibilities seemed outrageous, but only by rethinking the whole of the traditional history of Christianity could we begin to make sense of the evidence before us.

Seeing the Jesus story as a myth developed from Pagan mythology explained its uncanny resemblances to the myths of Osiris-Dionysus. Seeing Christianity as a Jewish version of the Pagan Mysteries explained why the teachings put into the mouth of Jesus in the gospels resemble the teachings of the Pagan sages. Seeing Gnosticism as existing before Literalism actually made more sense of the historical evidence than the traditional view that Gnosticism was a later deviation.

Even by their own evidence, the Literalists' account makes no sense. All the Literalist heresy-hunters trace the so-called heresy of Gnosticism back to a Gnostic sage called Simon Magus, whom they regard as the arch-heretic. Irenaeus tells us: "The falsely so-called Gnosis took its beginnings, as one may learn from their own assertions, from the followers of Simon."[123] Yet Simon Magus is meant to have been a contemporary of Jesus and is mentioned in the Acts of the Apostles.[124] More reliable sources suggest that Simon was a Samaritan, who received his education in Alexandria where, according to some scholars, he was directly influenced by the Jewish Pythagorean Philo.[125] Could the original teachings of a historical Jesus really have been so quickly perverted by his contemporary Simon, as the traditional picture requires? If Simon had wanted to preach an utterly different doctrine from Jesus, why would he not have simply set up his own cult, which had nothing to do with Christianity?

Moreover, the heresy-hunters tell us of a Gnostic sage called Dositheus who was the precursor of Simon and lived around 100 BCE or earlier![126] If by the evidence of the Literalists themselves, Gnosticism predates when Jesus is supposed to have lived, how can it have been a later perversion of his teachings? Not only this, but we know that even the name Jesus has been deliberately constructed to equal in gematria the mystical number 888, which strongly suggests it was invented by Gnostics. Faced with all of this evidence it seemed to us that we had no choice but to completely reverse the traditional picture and see Literalism as a degenerate form of the original "Jesus Mysteries" of the Gnostics.

A radically new picture of the origins of Christianity was emerging, which we called "The Jesus Mysteries Thesis." In essence it is this. Nearly all the peoples around the Mediterranean had at some point adopted the Pagan Mysteries and adapted them to their own national taste. At some point in the first few centuries BCE a group of Jews had done likewise and produced a Jewish version of the Mysteries. Jewish initiates adapted the myths of Osiris-Dionysus to produce the story of a Jewish dying and resurrecting godman, Jesus the Messiah. In time this myth came to be interpreted as historical fact and Literalist Christianity was the product.

These ideas seemed revolutionary, but nothing else explained the facts. But before adopting a theory as radical as the Jesus Mysteries Thesis we knew there was more important research to be done. Wasn't there incontrovertible proof that there had been a Jewish teacher called Jesus? If there was then the Jesus story obviously could not be a Jewish adaptation of the myth of Osiris-Dionysus. We therefore began looking for evidence for the existence of Jesus the man. This was someone who had supposedly thrown money-lenders out of the temple in Jerusalem, miraculously fed thousands of people, and raised the dead; at his death the whole Earth was said to have quaked and split open, the dead had risen from their graves, and a great unnatural darkness had covered the land.[127] If he really was more than mythical, surely someone somewhere would have mentioned it in the records of the times?

7

The Missing Man

There is nothing more negative than the result of the critical study of the life of Jesus. The Jesus of Nazareth who came forward publicly as the Messiah, who preached the ethic of the kingdom of God, who founded the kingdom of heaven upon earth, and died to give his work its final consecration, never had any existence. This image has not been destroyed from without, it has fallen to pieces, cleft and disintegrated by the concrete historical problems which came to the surface one after another.[1]

Albert Schweitzer

We began our quest for the historical Jesus with the Romans. Jesus is said to have been crucified by the Romans and they were renowned for keeping careful records of all their activities, especially their legal proceedings, so we felt we could be optimistic that they would mention such a celebrated case as that of Jesus. Unfortunately, however, there is no record of Jesus being tried by Pontius Pilate or executed.

This was an extremely literate period in human history. Here is a list of Pagan writers who wrote at or within a century of the time that Jesus is said to have lived:

Arrian	Pliny the Elder	Martial
Petronius	Appian	Plutarch
Seneca	Juvenal	Apollonius
Dion Pruseus	Theon of Smyrna	Pausanias

Valerius Flaccus	Damis	Ptolemy
Florus Lucius	Silius Italicus	Dio Chrysostom
Quintilian	Aulus Gellius	Hermogeones
Favorinus	Statius	Lysias
Lucanus	Columella	Valerius Maximus

The works of these writers would be enough to fill a library, but not one of them refers to Jesus. The only Roman writers to mention anything of interest are Pliny, Suetonius, and Tacitus, who were writing at the beginning of the second century.[2]

Pliny, the governor of Bithynia in Asia Minor, wrote a very short passage to the Emperor Trajan in 112 CE requesting clarification on how to deal with troublesome Christians.[3] The Roman historian Suetonius, in a list of miscellaneous notes on legislative matters (between considering the sale of food in taverns and briefly discussing the behavior of charioteers), relates that in 64 CE, "Punishment was inflicted on the Christians, a class of men given to a new and wicked superstition."[4] But all these sources really tell us is that a few Christians existed in the Roman world—which is not in doubt—and that they were not considered of any particular importance. They tell us nothing about Jesus himself.

Suetonius also relates that between 41 and 54 CE, the Emperor Claudius expelled the Jews from Rome, "since the Jews constantly made disturbances at the instigation of Crestus."[5] Although Crestus was a popular name, this is often taken as a corruption of "Christ." Even if this were true, however, Christ is simply a Greek translation of "Messiah" and there were at the time any number of would-be Messiahs rousing the Jews to rebellion, so the supposition that any reference to "Christ" necessarily refers to the Jesus Christ of the gospels is completely unfounded. Anyway, Jesus is not believed to have ever visited Rome. Again, all we are really being told is that Claudius had to deal with troublesome Jews, which was a regular occurrence in Roman history.

The Roman historian Tacitus does give us a little more. Writing about the great fire of Rome in 64 CE, he states that nothing could eliminate the rumor that Emperor Nero had himself started the blaze, so Nero blamed the Christians:

Nero fabricated as scapegoats, and punished with every refinement, the notoriously depraved Christians (as they were popularly called). Their originator, Christ, had been executed in Tiberius' reign by the procurator of Judea, Pontius Pilate. But in spite of this temporary set-back the deadly superstition had broken out afresh, not only in Judea (where the mischief started) but even in Rome. All degraded and shameful practices collect and flourish in the capital.[6]

The evidence of Tacitus is not contemporary, however, but dates from about 50 years after the event. As governor of Asia $c.112$ CE, he must have been familiar with Christian "troublemakers," as his friend Pliny obviously was. The only thing that would make Tacitus' writings an independent testimony to the existence of Jesus and not merely the repetition of Christian beliefs would be if he had gained his information about Christ being crucified under Pontius Pilate from the copious records that the Romans kept of their legal dealings. But this does not seem to be the case, for Tacitus calls Pilate the "procurator" of Judea when he was in fact a "prefect,"[7] so Tacitus is clearly not returning to the records of the time but quoting hearsay information from his own day.

Despite their obsession with records and histories, that concludes our survey of relevant Roman texts. However, it could be argued that other Roman literature, which may well have mentioned Jesus, has been lost over time. But surely any such texts would have been carefully preserved by the Roman Church once it held power in the Empire. Not only this, but it is safe to assume that well-educated early Christians, such as Justin Martyr, would have quoted these texts in support of Literalist Christianity, but they do not.

There are only two credible explanations for Jesus' conspicuous absence from Roman texts. Either there simply was no historical Jesus or Jesus seemed of so little importance to the Romans that he was deemed not worthy of mention. Let us turn, therefore, to Jewish historians. To the Jews Jesus would either have been the long-awaited Messiah or a blaspheming impostor who stirred up the masses. Either way, someone somewhere should refer to him.

JEWISH HISTORIANS

Philo was an eminent Jewish author who lived at the same time that Jesus is supposed to have lived and wrote around 50 works that still survive. They deal with history, philosophy, and religion, and tell us much about Pontius Pilate—yet make no mention at all of the coming of the Messiah Jesus.[8]

Philo's contemporary, Justus of Tiberias, was a Jew who lived near Capernaum, where Jesus was often said to have stayed. He wrote a history that began with Moses and extended to his own times, but again gave no mention of Jesus.[9]

There is still Josephus, however, a younger contemporary of the apostle Paul. He wrote two famous history books, *The Jewish Wars* and the monumental *Antiquities of the Jews*. These two works are our most important sources of information on the history of the Jewish people during the first century of the Christian era. And here at last, as one might expect, we seem to find the evidence we are looking for. Josephus writes:

> At about this time lived Jesus, a wise man, if indeed one might call him a man. For he was one who accomplished surprising feats and was a teacher of such people as are eager for novelties. He won over many of the Jews and many of the Greeks. He was the Messiah. When Pilate, upon an indictment brought by the principal men among us, condemned him to the cross, those who had loved him from the very first did not cease to be attached to him. On the third day he appeared to them restored to life, for the holy prophets had foretold this and myriads of other marvels concerning him. And the tribe of the Christians, so called after him, has to this day still not disappeared.[10]

Josephus also tells us that when the "miracle-worker" was brought before Pilate, he concluded that Jesus was "a benefactor, not a criminal, or agitator, or a would-be king." Josephus relates that as Jesus had miraculously cured Pilate's wife of a sickness, Pilate let him go. However, the Jewish priests later bribed Pilate to allow them to crucify Jesus "in defiance of all Jewish tradition."[11] As for the resurrection, he tells us that Jesus' dead body could not have been stolen by his disciples, which was a common argument advanced against Christian claims that Jesus miraculously resurrected, since "guards were posted around his tomb, 30 Romans and 1,000 Jews"![12]

For hundreds of years these passages in Josephus were seized on by Christian historians as conclusive proof that Jesus existed. That is, until scholars began to examine the text a little more critically. No serious scholar now believes that these passages were actually written by Josephus.[13] They have been clearly identified as much later additions. They are not of the same writing style as Josephus and if they are removed from the text, Josephus' original argument runs on in proper sequence. Writing at the beginning of the third century, Origen, whom modern authorities regard as one of the most conscientious scholars of the ancient Church, tells us that there is no mention of Jesus in Josephus and that Josephus did not believe that Jesus was the Christ since he did not believe in any Jewish Messiah figure.[14]

Josephus was in fact a pro-Roman Jew. He was hated by his fellow countrymen as a collaborator, which led him to flee Judea and live in Rome until his death.[15] Here he received patronage from two Emperors and a wealthy Roman aristocrat.[16]

Josephus does mention various would-be Jewish Messiah figures—about whom he is entirely uncomplimentary. At the time he was writing, the long-held belief amongst Jews that their God would send them the Messiah to free his people from oppression had become an obsession. But Josephus had his own interpretation of what he calls this "ancient oracle."[17] He did not deny that it was a divine prophecy, but believed that his fellow Jews had misunderstood it completely. According to him, the prophesied ruler of the world had come in the person of the Roman Emperor Vespasian, who had happened to be proclaimed Emperor while in Judea![18] It is absolutely inconceivable that Josephus could have, quite suddenly, broken with his style of writing, all his philosophical beliefs, and his characteristic political pragmatism to write reverentially about Jesus!

Early Christians who, like us, searched for historical evidence of Jesus' existence, would have seized on anything written by Josephus as conclusive proof. Yet early Christians do not mention Josephus. It is not until the beginning of the fourth century that Bishop Eusebius, the propagandist of the Roman Church, suddenly produced a version of Josephus which contained these passages.[19] From that point onward, Josephus became the foundation for the historicity of Jesus.

Unable to provide any historical evidence for Jesus, later Christians forged the proof that they so badly needed to shore up their Literalist interpretation of the gospels. This, as we would see repeatedly, was a common practice.

THE TALMUD

Although there is no evidence for the historical Jesus in the writings of Jewish historians, there are a handful of passages in the Jewish Talmud that are sometimes wheeled out to provide some evidence for Jesus the man. These are clearly not Christian forgeries. Here is what they say:

❖ It has been taught: On the eve of Passover they hanged Yeshu . . . because he practiced sorcery and enticed Israel astray.

❖ Our rabbis taught: Yeshu had five disciples—Mattai, Nakkia, Netzer, Buni, and Todah.

❖ It happened with Rabbi Elazar ben Damah, whom a serpent bit, that Jacob, a man of Kefar Soma, came to help him in the name of Yeshu ben Pantera.

❖ Once I was walking on the upper street of Sepphoris, and found one of the disciples of Yeshu the Nazarene.[20]

"Yeshu" is a shortened form of "Yehoshua" or "Joshua," which in Greek becomes "Jesus," so perhaps these passages are about the Jesus of the gospels?

However, dismissing the fact that we have mention of only five disciples with completely unrecognizable names, there are other reasons why these passages are not the proof we are seeking.

The fact that we have a mention of "Yeshu the Nazarene" is not extraordinary. The Nazarenes were a Jewish religious sect and the use of the word does not imply "from Nazareth." Yeshu was an extremely common name that could refer to any number of people.[21] Josephus mentions at least 10 Jesuses, although it is revealing to note that some translations of Josephus only translate the passages that they want the reader to identify with Jesus Christ using the Greek version of the name that we all recognize, while leaving the names of all the other Jesuses in the untranslated Hebrew![22]

As the scholar who unearthed these passages in the Talmud admits, even if they do refer to Jesus and not some other Yeshu, they cannot be taken as proof of Jesus' existence, because they are written so late. Although based on older writings, the Talmud was not written until 200 CE, and we do not know whether these were early passages. Anyway, the rabbis are so vague in their chronology that they differ by as much as 200 years in the dates they assign to the figure that may or may not be Jesus![23]

There does not seem to be anything substantial here. Where else can we look? Remarkably enough, that's it! We've reviewed all the potential historical evidence for the existence of Jesus. Extraordinary as it may seem, there simply is nothing else.[24] All we are left with are Christian testimonies. Can these be regarded as historical documents?

GOSPEL TRUTH?

There were actually hundreds of different Christian gospels, not just the familiar four of the New Testament. However, since no one seriously claims that the apocryphal and Gnostic gospels are other than mythological, we need only concern ourselves here with Matthew, Mark, Luke, and John. These books are traditionally said to be eyewitness accounts of the life of Jesus written by his disciples. The fact that there are four of them adds weight to the claim that they genuinely record historical events. Yet actually these gospels often do not agree at all on what happened.

The most startling contradiction is between the genealogies presented in the Gospel of Matthew and the Gospel of Luke. Both authors go to great lengths to show that Jesus is descended from the line of David, as the promised Messiah must be according to Jewish beliefs. Both authors see Jesus as fathered by Joseph. So far, so good. But is Joseph fathered by Jacob, as Matthew claims, or Heli, as Luke claims? From just one generation back the family lineages that the two gospels present are utterly different from each other. And from then on they bear no resemblance to each other at all! See for yourself:

GOSPEL OF MATTHEW[25]	GOSPEL OF LUKE[26]
Jesus	Jesus
Joseph	Joseph
Jacob	Heli
Matthan	Matthat
Eleazar	Levi
Eliud	Melchi
Achim	Jannai
Zadok	Joseph
Azor	Mattathiah

Eliakim	Amos
Abiud	Nahum
Zerubbabel	Esli
Shealtiel	Naggai
Jeconiah	Maath
Josiah	Mattathiah
Amon	Semein
Manasseh	Josech
Hezekiah	Joda
Ahaz	Johanan
Jotham	Rhesa
Azariah	Zerubbabel
Joram	Shealtiel
Jehoshaphat	Neri
Asa	Melchi
Abijah	Addi
Rehoboam	Cosam
Solomon	Elmadam
David	Er
	Joshua
	Eliezer
	Jorim
	Matthat
	Levi
	Symeon
	Judah
	Joseph
	Jonam
	Eliakim
	Melea
	Menna
	Mattatha
	Nathan
	David

Luke continues his genealogy past David all the way back through the Patri-archs to Adam and eventually to God Himself. But all of this seems a little unnecessary, since both gospel writers are also at great pains to make clear that Joseph isn't Jesus' father at all! Jesus' mother Mary is a virgin and God is the father directly, not via the line of the 77 men that Luke lists for us. Matthew tells us clearly:

> It is by the Holy Spirit that she has conceived this child. All this happened in order to fulfill what the Lord declared through the prophet "The Virgin will conceive and bear a son."[27]

Surely this is too much of a contradiction for the writers of the gospels of Matthew and Luke simply not to have noticed?

Mark, on the other hand, doesn't mention Bethlehem, the virgin birth, or Jesus' family descent from David at all. Why does he leave out these extremely pertinent facts? Something fishy is going on here!

The gospels are littered with such inconsistencies. Luke offers us what looks like a convincing piece of historical detail when he tells us that Jesus was born at the time of the census of Quirinius. This took place in 6 CE. Yet Matthew tells us that Jesus was born during the reign of King Herod, who died in 4 BCE.[28] Luke even contradicts himself, stating that John and Jesus were miraculously conceived six months apart in the reign of Herod, but still portrays Mary with child at the time of the census of 6 CE, creating one of the rarely mentioned miracles of the New Testament—a 10-year pregnancy!

John places the cleansing of the temple at the beginning of his narrative, Matthew at the end.[29] Mark has Jesus teaching only in the area of Galilee, and not in Judea, and only traveling the 70 miles to Jerusalem once, at the end of his life. Luke, however, portrays Jesus as teaching equally in Galilee and Judea. John's Jesus, on the other hand, preaches mainly in Jerusalem and makes only occasional visits to Galilee.[30]

Amazingly, since Literalist Christianity is built upon the historicity of Jesus' death and resurrection, even the events surrounding his crucifixion are not uniformly recorded by the gospels. According to Matthew and Mark, Jesus was both tried and sentenced by the Jewish priests of the Sanhedrin. Luke has it that Jesus was tried by the Sanhedrin, but not sentenced by them. Yet according to John, Jesus does not appear before the Sanhedrin at all.[31] Jesus then goes to his death by crucifixion. Or is it, as Paul says, to be "hanged on a gibbet?"[32] Or, as Peter has it in the Acts of the Apostles, that he was "hung on a tree?"[33]

The same confusion exists about the death of Jesus' betrayer, Judas Iscariot. In Matthew, Judas "went and hanged himself."[34] But the Acts of the

Apostles tells us he died from an accidental fall after betraying Jesus.[35] The gospel writers, who we are supposed to believe were Jesus' close disciples, cannot even remember their master's last words correctly! According to Matthew[36] and Mark[37] Jesus quotes Psalm 22 as his parting words, asking, "My God, my God, why have you forsaken me?" But Luke has Jesus quote Psalm 31: "Father, into your hands I commend my spirit."[38] For those who don't like either of these, there is always John's account,[39] in which Jesus says simply, "I am thirsty," and then, "It is finished."[40]

According to Mark, when Joseph of Arimathea goes to Pilate to ask if he can have Jesus' body for burial, the governor is shocked to learn that Jesus has died so quickly.[41] One wonders why he was surprised, however, since John tells us that Pilate had himself already agreed to quicken Jesus' death by breaking his legs and stabbing him with a spear.[42]

According to Matthew, Jesus had predicted that:

Just as Jonah was in the hollow of the whale for three days and three nights, so the Son of Humanity will be in the heart of the earth for three days and three nights.[43]

Alas, it seems his calculations were inaccurate, for according to the gospels, Jesus died on Friday and rose on the following Sunday, thus spending only two nights "in the heart of the earth."

The Gospel of Mark tells us that when some of Jesus' women disciples found his empty tomb they merely "saw a young man in a white robe" inside.[44] Luke, however, relates that "two men in brilliant clothes suddenly appeared by their side."[45] Matthew paints a far more dramatic picture, claiming:

All at once there was a violent earthquake, for the angel of the Lord, descending from heaven, came and rolled away the stone and sat on it. His face was like lightning, his robe white as snow.[46]

In Mark[47] and Matthew,[48] the resurrected Jesus appears to his other disciples in Galilee, where they have been specifically sent by divine decree. Yet this stupendous supernatural event does not seem to have impressed itself very clearly on the other disciples, since Luke and the author of the Acts of the Apostles have the risen Jesus appearing in and around Jerusalem.[49] Indeed, according to Acts, not only did they not receive any divine commandment to go to Galilee, but were expressly forbidden to leave Jerusalem.[50]

Even Jesus himself is not consistent. In Mark he charitably explains:

Who isn't against us is for us.[51]

But in Matthew he is more dogmatic, warning,

Whoever isn't with me is against me.[52]

Even in one and the same gospel Jesus is profoundly inconsistent. According to Matthew, Peter asks his master, "Lord, how many times shall my brother wrong me and I forgive him? Up to seven times?" Jesus replies by giving his beautiful teachings of complete forgiveness, advising him:

I'm not telling you up to seven times, I'm telling you up to seventy seven times![53]

Why Peter needed to ask is unclear, however, since merely one paragraph previously in the same gospel Jesus had already given the much less forgiving and more pragmatic advice:

If your brother wrongs you, go have it out with him, just you and him. If he listens to you, you've gained your brother back. If he doesn't listen, bring one or two along with you, so that everything said stands on the word of two or three witnesses. If he won't listen to them, speak up at a meeting. If he won't listen to the assembly, let him be the same to you as the foreigner and the tax-collector.[54]

So which did the master teach? Should we forgive 77 times or only three times?

If the gospels are a historical record of the teachings of Jesus, then we can at least conclude that he is not the Son of God. Either that or the Son of God is as fallible as any mortal. For he repeatedly predicts that the coming apocalypse will be witnessed by those still living at the time. In Luke we read:

I tell you truly, that there are some of those standing right here who will never taste death before they see the kingdom of God. And there will be signs in the sun and moon and stars, and on earth an anxious mass of people in confusion over the roar of the sea and the tides, with people dying of fear and apprehension about what's coming over the world. Yes, the powers of heaven will be shaken. And then they will see the Son of Man coming on a cloud with power and great glory. When these things start to happen, look up and raise your heads, because your redemption is approaching. When you see these things happening, you know the kingdom of God is close. I assure you that this generation will not pass away till it all happens.[55]

Likewise in Matthew, Jesus asserts:

I assure you there are some among those standing here who will never taste death before they see the Son of Man coming in his monarchy.[56] I assure you that this generation will not go by before all this happens.[57]

Yet, 2,000 years later, when all his disciples are well and truly dead and buried, none of these things have come to pass and Jesus has not returned.

The most telling moment in the gospels, however, is when Mark has Jesus quote from the Old Testament in his arguments against the Pharisees. Nothing surprising about this—except that Jesus quotes from the mistranslated Greek version of the Old Testament, which suits his purpose precisely, not from the original Hebrew, which says something quite different and unhelpful to his argument. That Jesus the Jew should quote a Greek mistranslation of Jewish Holy Scripture to impress orthodox Jewish Pharisees is simply unthinkable. It does make sense, however, if the whole incident were made up by one of the hundreds of thousands of Greek-speaking Jews who no longer spoke their native tongue and could not read their scriptures untranslated, hence attributing to Jesus their own misunderstandings.[58]

NEW TESTAMENT SCHOLARSHIP

One thing is surely indisputable from all of this: the gospels are not, as some Christians claim, the divine words of God.[59] For if they are, God is extremely confused. As, by his very nature, God is unlikely to be confused, it seems safe to conclude that we are dealing with the words of fallible men. So, can the gospels be relied on to tell us anything about a historical Jesus? What light can scholarship shed on Matthew, Mark, Luke, and John?

Well, first of all, the gospels were not originally even known by these names. They were not attributed to any particular author, each gospel being regarded as "the gospel" of a particular Christian sect. Only later did they acquire the names of their supposed authors.[60] The gospels are actually anonymous works, in which everything, without exception, is written in capital letters, with no headings, chapter or verse divisions, and practically no punctuation or spaces between words.[61] They were not even written in the Aramaic of the Jews but in Greek.[62]

The gospels have also been added to and altered over time. The Pagan critic Celsus complains that Christians "altered the original text of the gospels three or four times, or even more, with the intention of thus being able to destroy the arguments of their critics."[63] Modern scholars have found that he was right. A careful study of over 3,000 early manuscripts has shown how scribes made many changes.[64] The Christian philosopher Origen, writing in the third century, acknowledges that manuscripts have been edited and interpolated to suit the needs of the changing theological climate:

> It is an obvious fact today that there is much diversity among the manuscripts, due either to the carelessness of the scribes, or the perverse audacity of some people in correcting the text, or again to the fact that there are those who add or delete as they please, setting themselves up as correctors.[65]

To convey the enormity of the problem, one scholar describes selecting a place in the gospels completely at random (in this case he chose Mark 10–11) and checking to see how many differences were recorded between various early manuscripts for these passages. He discovered "no fewer that 48 places where the manuscripts differ, sometimes there are only two possibilities, often there are three or more, and in one case there are six!"[66]

Scholars also know that whole sections of the gospels were added later. For example, originally Mark did not contain any words beyond Chapter 16 verse 8—the fear of the women at their discovery of the empty tomb. The so-called "long ending," in which the risen Jesus appears to his disciples, is not found in any early manuscripts and yet now appears in nearly all New Testaments.[67]

Despite all of this editing and amending, the gospels remain contradictory and inconsistent, as we have seen. For centuries, the Catholic Church prevented anyone other than priests reading the New Testament for themselves, so few had the chance to discover just how confused the gospels are. That all changed with the Protestant Reformation.[68]

Eager to distance themselves from Rome, German Protestant scholars began to search the gospels for the real Jesus. Even up to the present day the majority of such scholars have themselves been Christians, since a theological career at a German university is closed to those who have not been baptized.[69] Yet despite this, rather than giving Christianity a firm historical foundation, as they hoped, Protestant scholars' three centuries of intense scholarship have undermined the literal figure of Jesus completely.[70]

From detailed research they concluded that the Gospel of John was written so late that it could not have been an eyewitness account.[71] In Matthew, Mark, and Luke, Jesus teaches in pithy parables, but John contains lengthy, apparently verbatim speeches in fluent Greek, which were clearly not the words of a Jewish carpenter's son.[72] John also describes quite different incidents from the other gospels.

The work of the Berlin philologist Karl Lachmann and other eminent scholars also revealed that, despite their differences, Matthew, Mark, and Luke shared a great deal in common. These similarities are due to the fact that Matthew and Luke are actually reworkings of Mark,[73] which is the simplest and earliest gospel. If John is written too late and Matthew and Luke are based on Mark, this leaves us only the Gospel of Mark as a possible eyewitness account of the life of Jesus.

Scholars believe that Mark was written sometime between 70 CE and the early second century.[74] If we accept the earliest possible date, it is just feasible that Mark was an eyewitness. Yet ironically, Mark does not claim to have known Jesus. Many in the early Church objected to his gospel being treated as canonical for this very reason.[75] Mark is claimed to have been at best some sort of secretary or interpreter for Peter. Even this is impossible, however, since Mark's gospel exhibits what one modern scholar calls "a lamentable ignorance of Palestinian geography":[76]

> In the seventh chapter, for instance, Jesus is reported as going through Sidon on his way from Tyre to the Sea of Galilee. Not only is Sidon in the opposite direction, but there was in fact no road from Sidon to the Sea of Galilee in the first century CE, only one from Tyre.

Similarly the fifth chapter refers to the Sea of Galilee's eastern shore as the country of the Gerasenes, yet Gerasa, today Jerash, is more than thirty miles to the southeast, too far away for a story whose setting requires a nearby city with a steep slope down to the sea. Aside from geography, Mark represented Jesus as saying, "If a woman divorces her husband and marries another she is guilty of adultery" (Mark 10 v 12), a precept which would have been meaningless in the Jewish world, where women had no rights of divorce.[77]

In the late nineteenth century, Wilhelm Wrede, Professor of New Testament Studies at Breslau University, argued that even the Gospel of Mark, the earliest and most primitive gospel, was more concerned with theological dogma than historical accuracy.[78] In 1919 another German scholar, Karl Ludwig Schmidt, published a careful study of the way in which Mark's gospel had been created. He was able to show that the author of Mark had created his gospel by linking together existing smaller stories. The Jesus story had been constructed from pre-existing fragments.[79] The way that Matthew and Luke had added to Mark the nativity story and genealogies showed how the Jesus story had evolved over time. It could no longer be assumed by scholars that these narratives were in any way factual accounts.[80] This effectively brought to an end any hope of finding a historical Jesus within the gospels.

German theologians began increasingly to date the origination of Mark, Matthew, and Luke to well into the second century CE.[81] Rudolf Bultmann (1884–1976), Professor of New Testament Studies at Marburg University, spent his life studying the gospels and was one of the greatest authorities on the New Testament. He pioneered the influential method of analyzing the gospels called "form-criticism."[82] Eventually he concluded:

I do indeed think that we can now know almost nothing concerning the life and personality of Jesus, since the early Christian sources show no interest in either and are, moreover, fragmentary and often legendary.[83]

ACTS OF THE APOSTLES?

If the gospels cannot help us in our quest to find the historical Jesus, what about the rest of the New Testament? Amazingly, the Acts of the Apostles, the letters of Paul, James, Peter, John, and Jude, and the Revelation of John do not concern themselves at all with the historical Jesus. But they do talk about the apostles. If we can substantiate their existence, perhaps we can, by implication, prove the existence of Jesus.

The gospels tell us little of most of the 12 apostles apart from their names. Yet even here, there are serious discrepancies. In the gospels of Mark, Matthew, and Luke, the disciples Peter, James, and John are Jesus' closest followers. In John's gospels, however, Peter plays only a minor role and James and John are not even mentioned.[84] John's gospel, on the other hand, presents us with the apostles Nathanael and Nicodemus, who make no appearance in the other three gospels.[85] On top of this, the list of names of the disciples is very clumsily worked into the text of Mark and Matthew, which has led scholars to conclude that the number of the disciples was what was originally important, and the names were a later consideration.[86] John's gospel doesn't even list the names. In Chapter 6 we are told that the disciples were "many," and a few verses later Jesus is suddenly and inexplicably addressing "the twelve."[87]

The traditional view of Church history is that after the resurrection the 12 apostles played a decisive role in establishing the Church. Their deeds are recorded in the Acts of the Apostles. Yet, although the author of Acts ascribes the greatest importance to the 12, he tells us nothing about nine of them apart from their names.[88] Of the 12, Acts concerns itself only with Peter. But even Peter is not mentioned after Chapter 15, and we hear only of Paul, who was not one of the 12 and was never supposed to have met Jesus.[89]

Acts does not inspire confidence as a reliable record of events. As one Christian translator of the New Testament admits, it is more like a "drugstore paperback."[90] It is full of little adventure fantasies. For example, we are told of a Christian called Anasias who had sold a property and only offered some of the proceeds to the apostles, pocketing the rest. When Peter confronts him with the truth, he simply drops down dead! Peter does not seem to be particularly upset by this and three hours later performs exactly the same trick on the poor man's wife! When he asked her, "Do you hear the feet of those who buried your husband coming to carry you out too?" she "fell down suddenly at his feet and expired." Not surprisingly, "a great fear came over all the assembly and all those who heard about these things."[91]

Peter may be able to cause dishonest property speculators to drop dead on the spot, but this is nothing. According to Acts, Philip can "teleport" himself from one place to another! He appears suddenly to baptize a eunuch in one place and then is snatched away to instantly reappear in distant Azotum.[92] Acts also wildly exaggerates. Paul is meant to have preached for two years "till all the inhabitants of Asia had heard the word, Jews and Greeks alike."[93] Surely an impossible achievement, even for a saint! And then there is the bizarre case of "Peter and the giant tablecloth":

> Peter went upon the roof to pray around the hour of noon. And he got hungry and wanted to taste some food. While they were preparing something, a rapture came over him: and he saw the sky opening and a sort of table-setting coming down, like a giant tablecloth being draped over the four corners of the earth, containing all the quadrupeds and serpents of the land and birds of the air. And a voice came to him: Get up Peter, slaughter and eat.[94]

It seems safe to assume we are not dealing with factual accounts here. Moreover, Acts is clearly not written by a single author, as is claimed. At Chapter 16 the narrative suddenly jolts from the third person into the first person, something which continues sporadically through the book.[95] So, like the gospels, Acts of the Apostles is a "cut and paste" creation.

This explains why it is not even internally consistent. For example, in Chapter 9 we are told that when Paul received his vision of light and heard a divine voice on the road to Damascus, his companions "heard the voice but could see no one."[96] Yet in Chapter 21 Paul is made to relate of the same experience: "My companions saw the light, but did not hear the voice that spoke to me."[97]

Acts also contradicts the testimony of Paul in his Letter to the Galatians. According to Acts, after his visionary experience on the road to Damascus, Paul is told to seek out a disciple called Ananias in Damascus, who will tell him what to do.[98] He then goes to Jerusalem, where Barnabas introduces him to the apostles.[99] In the Temple at Jerusalem he experiences a second vision of Jesus and receives his vocation to preach to the Gentiles.[100] Yet this is quite different from Paul's own account, in which he makes no mention of

Ananias and claims he went to Arabia and had nothing to do with Christians in Jerusalem for three years after his conversion experience.[101] He states emphatically: "What I write is plain truth; before God I am not lying." So who is lying?

Like the Gospel of Mark, the Acts of the Apostles also misquotes the Hebrew Old Testament. It portrays Peter as proving his point to the Jews of Jerusalem using a badly translated passage from the Greek version of the Old Testament, which in the original Hebrew means something else altogether. Acts also portrays James as likewise appealing to the Jews of Jerusalem by quoting a passage from the Greek Old Testament that distorts the Hebrew original.[102] The Jerusalem Jews cannot have been very impressed! From this evidence alone, scholars have concluded that Acts cannot be taken as a historical record of the Jerusalem Church.[103]

This is also borne out by the evidence of when Acts was written. It was regarded as holy scripture by Irenaeus and Tertullian, who lived at the end of the second century. But Justin Martyr, living a generation earlier, displays no knowledge of it.[104] It is not quoted before 177 CE, so it is definitely not a contemporary account, as it claims to be, and was probably written somewhere between 150 and 177 CE.[105]

There were actually many different scriptures relating the deeds of the disciples in circulation among early Christians, but no one considers the noncanonical tales of the apostles as historical documents.[106] Why should we treat the canonical Acts of the Apostles with any less skepticism, just because the Roman Church authorities decided to include it in the New Testament? The scriptures dealing with the mythical exploits of John, Peter, Paul, Andrew, and Thomas were banned and consigned to the bonfire in the fifth century by Pope Leo the Great as dangerous heretical lies.[107] The canonical Acts of the Apostles was spared such a fate simply because, unlike these other gospels, it endorsed the "party line" of the Roman Church.

THE EARLIEST EVIDENCE

So much for the Acts of the Apostles. What of the New Testament letters ascribed to the apostles Peter, James, and John? Can these help us at all? Unfortunately, modern scholars have shown that these letters are forgeries written much later to combat heretical ideas within the early Church. They are not even very good forgeries. As one translator writes of the Second Letter of Peter, "It refers to the apostles as 'our ancestors' as if they were dead and buried."[108] So it is clearly not by Peter, but uses his name so that the apostle is seen as endorsing its anti-heresy message.[109] These letters were widely seen as fakes and took a long time to become an established part of the canon of the New Testament.[110]

What about Paul's letters? Here at last we have someone who is universally agreed to have been a historical person. However, scholars believe his later letters, known as "the Pastorals," are forgeries, which contradict his earlier letters.[111] Like the letters attributed to the other disciples, they were written in the second century CE to combat internal divisions in the Church.[112] But some of the earlier letters, while suffering from editing, additions, and the usual "cut and paste" treatment, are widely believed to have been written by Paul. Paul wrote his letters before 70 CE. So, they actually predate all of the gospels. They are the earliest existing Christian documents and some of them are basically genuine. At last we have something substantial!

It is a completely remarkable fact, however, that Paul says nothing at all about the historical Jesus! He is concerned only with the crucified and resurrected Christ, whose importance is entirely mystical. Paul makes it clear that he never met a historical Jesus. He writes: "Neither did I receive the Gospel from man, nor was I taught it, but it came to me through revelation of Jesus Christ."[113] Paul doesn't mention Jerusalem or Pilate either. Indeed, as we shall explore in more detail later, he declares that Jesus was crucified at the instigation of the "Archons" or "rulers of the age"[114]—demonic powers that are talked of by the Gnostics! In fact Paul does not link Jesus with any historical time and place, including the recent past.[115] Paul's Christ, like the Pagan's Osiris-Dionysus, is a timeless mythical figure.

Paul says nothing about Nazareth and never calls Jesus a Nazarene.[116] Although he portrays Christianity as a baptist sect, he never mentions John the Baptist.[117] He tells us nothing about Jesus eating and drinking with tax collectors and sinners, his Sermon on the Mount, his parables, his arguments with Pharisees, or his clashes with the Roman authorities.[118] Paul doesn't even know the Lord's Prayer which, according to the gospels, Jesus gave to his disciples, saying, "Pray then like this," for Paul writes, "We do not even know how we ought to pray."[119]

If Paul were actually following a recently deceased Messiah, it is astonishing that he did not feel it necessary to go and see the apostles who knew Jesus personally before starting off on his own teaching mission. Yet he says he does not gain his authority from anyone. It would also seem reasonable to assume that, if Jesus were a literal figure not a mythological Christ, Paul would have quoted from his master's teachings and the example of his life on a regular basis. In fact he never mentions Jesus' life and only quotes Jesus once—and when he does, it is the universal Mystery formula of the Eucharist:

> This is my body which is broken for you: this do in remembrance of me. This cup is the new covenant in my blood: this do, as oft as ye drink it, in remembrance of me.[120]

When Paul quotes this passage, he tells us that Jesus spoke it "on the night when he was betrayed" or in some translations "on the night of his arrest." Both of these translations, however, embellish the original Greek to give the idea of historicity. The Greek actually states that Jesus spoke these words on the night he was "delivered up,"[121] a phrase reminiscent of that used to describe the fate of the Greek sacrificial *pharmakos*, who also meets his death to atone for the "sins of the world."

Paul gives his ethical teachings on his own authority, without mentioning Jesus. When he wishes to support them he draws on the Old Testament, even when quoting Jesus would have served him just as well, or even better. He teaches that Christ's death puts an end to Jewish Law, but doesn't draw on Jesus' claim that he has come to do exactly that. He doesn't back up his call for celibacy with Jesus' praise of those who renounce marriage for the sake of the kingdom of heaven.[122] When he argues that at the resurrection a person's body will be changed from flesh and blood, he doesn't quote Jesus' teachings that "when they rise from the dead, they neither marry nor are given in marriage, but are like angels in heaven."[123] If he had known the master's words, are we really to believe he would have made absolutely no reference to them?

Although Paul doesn't mention a historical Jesus, he does mention a John and a James, who are often presumed to be two of the disciples mentioned in the gospels. Paul tells us nothing about John, but he does call James "the brother of the Lord," which is sometimes seized upon to prove that Paul acknowledged a historical Christ, because he had met his brother. It was a common Christian practice, however, to call each other "brother." In both the Gospel of Matthew[124] and the Gospel of John,[125] Jesus calls his followers his "brothers" without inferring that they are his blood family, and in a Gnostic gospel called *The Apocalypse of James* we read specifically that James was "said to be the Lord's brother only in a purely spiritual sense."[126]

Mosaic from "The House of Dionysus" in Paphos Cyprus *c.* fourth century CE

1 This divine child with halo may look like the infant Jesus but is actually
  the Pagan savior Osiris-Dionysus.

Egyptian statue *c.* third century BCE

Roman painting *c.* 20 BCE

2 Christian representations of the Madonna and baby Jesus were based on ancient Pagan images of the miraculous child Osiris-Dionysus and his divine mother.

Byzantine Christian icon *c.* thirteenth century CE

Marble sarcophagus from the second or third centuries CE

3 An old man brings the holy child Dionysus a large cross as an omen of his ultimate fate. Such a cross was carried around in Athens during a three-day festival celebrating the death and resurrection of the Pagan godman.

Marble sarcophagus from the second to third centuries CE

4 A representation of Dionysus is lifted up on a tree during the Spring festival of the Mysteries. Jesus was likewise said to have been "lifted up on a tree" at Easter time. Often a cross bar was also used so that, like Jesus, the Pagan godman was raised up on a cross.

5 (Overleaf) Dionysus was represented as bearded, wearing purple robes and a crown, often made of ivy. Jesus is, likewise, portrayed as a bearded man who was dressed in purple robes and a crown of thorns before his crucifixion. On an altar before Dionysus are loaves of bread and jars of wine which will be used to celebrate the holy communion of the Mysteries, a sacred sacrament that Christians inherited and still perform today.

Greek vase *c.* fifth century BCE

Greek vase *c.* sixth century BCE

Plaster cast of a third-century CE ring-seal amulet

6 This is a plaster cast of an amulet which was housed in the Museum of Berlin until it was lost during World War II. Although it seems to portray Christ crucified, it actually depicts the passion of the Pagan godman Osiris-Dionysus.

7 (Overleaf) A Pagan initiate of the Mysteries looks on at the crucifixion of a donkey-headed man. This represents his lower "animal" nature, which he has put to death in the process of initiation so that he may be spiritually resurrected.

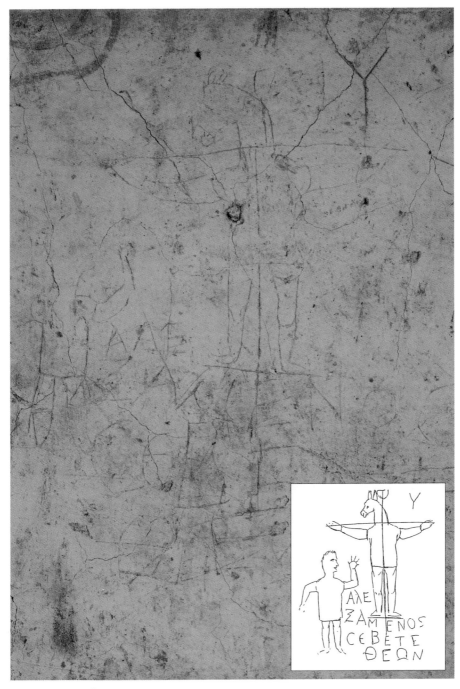

Carving on a pillar in Rome 193–235 CE

8 The "Hierophant" or High Priest of the Pagan Mysteries used a magic wand during initiation rituals. Here Hermes, patron deity of the Hierophants of the Greek Mysteries, is shown using his wand to guide souls into and out of a half-buried funerary urn. This represents the descent and ascent of souls into and out of physical incarnation. The motif of "raising from the dead" also symbolizes initiation and spiritual rebirth.

Greek vase *c.* fourth to fifth centuries BCE

Painting from the Roman catacombs *c.* fourth to fifth centuries CE

The earliest depictions of Jesus show him, like a Pagan Hierophant, using a magic wand to perform his miracles. Here he is shown raising Lazarus from the dead. The Roman Emperor Constantine referred to Jesus raising Lazarus "by using a small staff." Other paintings show Jesus using his Hierophant's wand to turn water into wine and to multiply the loaves for the feeding of the five thousand.

For picture credits see page 336.

Paul also mentions a certain "Cephas." This is traditionally taken to be the apostle Peter. Peter was originally called Simon but, in different circumstances in each gospel, was given the name "Rock" by Jesus. This is "Cephas" in Aramaic and "Peter" in Greek. Is Cephas the same person as Peter? Paul also mentions a "Peter" once in his letters, but does not equate Cephas and Peter as one and the same person. An early Christian scripture called *The Letters of the Apostles* opens with a list of 11 apostles, the third of whom is called Peter and the last of whom is called Cephas, so there certainly was a Christian tradition that Cephas and Peter were not identical. The modern tendency to assume that they are necessarily the same person is mistaken.[127]

Even if Cephas is taken to be another name for Peter, is this the Peter who supposedly knew Jesus? It is easy to assume so, because we are all so familiar with the gospel stories. However, there is nothing in Paul's letters to suggest that the Cephas he meets in Jerusalem and Antioch is the Peter of the gospels who personally knew Jesus. In fact, quite the opposite. Paul's relationship with the Cephas of his letters would certainly not suggest that Cephas was the right-hand man of a historical Messiah. Paul is extremely hostile to Cephas and opposes him with strong language:

> When Cephas came to Antioch I challenged him face to face, because he was acting inexcusably.[128]

He takes issue with Cephas for conforming to Jewish Law and refusing to eat with Gentile Christians.[129] Yet Paul does not bring up the fact that, if Cephas is the Peter of the gospels, he must have known that Jesus ate and drank with sinners and prostitutes and defended himself against criticism that he was violating Jewish Laws.[130] Paul calls Cephas a hypocrite.[131] Yet, if he is the Peter of the gospels, why doesn't Paul throw in his face the fact that he had fallen asleep in the garden of Gethsemane, and denied the Lord three times with curses,[132] and had even been compared to Satan by Jesus himself?[133]

There is only one short passage in Paul, which could justify the belief that the Cephas of his letters is the Peter of the gospels. Writing of the resurrected Jesus, Paul says,

> He appeared to Cephas and then the Twelve. Next he appeared to hundreds of the faithful at once.[134]

This is curious, because according to the gospels, Judas Iscariot was dead by this time, so Jesus could only have appeared to the 11. And none of the gospels speak of Jesus appearing to "hundreds" of people. Once again we have to acknowledge we are at a loss to know what to believe.

This passage could well be a later addition to Paul's letter. But even if it is not, all it really tells us is that a Cephas, along with hundreds of others, had the mystical experience of seeing the risen Christ, just as Paul himself had done. Is Paul describing a historical event or mystical rites? Thousands of initiates in the Pagan Mysteries of Eleusis could have made essentially the same claim of experiencing the resurrected godman without inferring that any of them had met a historical Osiris-Dionysus. This may sound like a radical interpretation, but it does make sense of a passage in Paul's Letter to the Galatians, which is otherwise incomprehensible. Paul criticizes the "Stupid Galatians," "before whose eyes Jesus Christ was openly displayed on the cross!" for looking to a "material" rather than "spiritual" understanding of salvation.[135] Are we really to believe that this Christian community in Asia Minor had witnessed the crucifixion in Jerusalem and that Paul, who never claimed to have known Jesus, felt justified in calling such witnesses "stupid?" Paul's comment would make sense, however, if the Galatian Christians had rather witnessed a dramatic representation of Christ's passion. It is this, Paul states, that will make them "perfect"—or to use the more accurate translation, "initiated!"

So what can we actually say about Paul's Cephas? Only that he is a leader of Jewish Christians in Jerusalem and a theological rival to Paul. It would seem that Paul's letters, the earliest Christian documents, cannot help us in our search for a historical Jesus. All he can tell us is that the Christian community was already internally divided by the middle of the first century between pro-Jewish Christians in Jerusalem and those, like Paul, who saw Jesus as coming to replace the old Jewish Law. It is only because of the gospels and Acts of the Apostles, both written much later, that the figures of Cephas, John, and James in Paul's letters have become associated with the gospel figures who bear their names. There is actually nothing in Paul to make us believe that the Christians he is talking about personally knew a historical Jesus. The gospels were written after Paul's letters and have been revealed as theological rather than historical documents. It is more likely, therefore, that the gospel writers picked up on the names of Cephas, James, and John mentioned earlier by Paul and developed them into the characters we find in the Jesus story.

THE HISTORY OF A DEVELOPING MYTH

The evidence suggests that the New Testament is not a history of actual events, but a history of the evolution of Christian mythology. The earliest gospel is Mark, itself created from pre-existing fragments. The authors of Matthew and Luke added to and modified this gospel to create their own versions of the life of Jesus. From this we can conclude that they did not see Mark's gospel as a valuable historical record that must be preserved intact. Neither did they see it as the inviolable "Word of God," which must never be altered. They evidently believed it to be a story that could be embellished and adjusted to their own needs—in exactly the same way that Pagan philosophers had been developing and elaborating the myths of Osiris-Dionysus for centuries.

But Mark is not our earliest evidence of the Jesus story. This is found in the letters of Paul. Despite the fact that these letters were written before any of the gospels, and by as many as 100 years before the Acts of the Apostles, they are placed in the New Testament after these books. This gives the false impression that Paul follows on from the gospels and Acts, rather than the other way around.[136] Hence, it is easy not to even notice that Paul's Christ is not a historical figure. However, if we put the elements that make up the New Testament in their correct chronological order, we see the Jesus story developing before our eyes.

The mythological dying and resurrecting Christ of Paul is developed by the primitive Jesus story of Mark. This is significantly added to by Matthew and Luke. We then have the more philosophically developed Gospel of John, with its "Logos" doctrine and long Greek speeches by Jesus. Finally we have a collection of legends about the apostles, followed by a number of forged letters, which presuppose a literal Jesus and adopt the authority of the apostles to attack heretical Christians.

Looked at in this way, the New Testament itself tells the story of how Christianity developed:

The Letters of Paul	*c.* 50	Jesus is a mystical dying and resurrecting godman.
The Gospel of Mark	70–110	The myth of Jesus is given a historical and geographical setting.

The Gospels of Matthew and Luke	90–135	Details of Jesus' birth and resurrection are added and the story embellished.
The Gospel of John	c.120	Christian theology is developed.
Acts of the Apostles	150–177	Having now created the illusion of a historical Jesus, Acts is created to account for his disciples.
Letters of the Apostles	177–220	Letters attributed to Paul and the apostles are forged by Literalists in their battles with Gnosticism, attacking "many deceivers" who "do not acknowledge Jesus Christ as coming in the flesh."[137]

The original version of the Gospel of Mark, the earliest account of the Jesus story, did not include the resurrection at all. This has been added later. Before these additions, Mark's gospel ended with the women finding the empty tomb and only the intimation that Jesus had resurrected as promised. Characteristically, the Gnostic gospels start where Mark's original gospel ends. They do not relate the events of Jesus' life, but the secret teachings of the risen Christ after the resurrection. This suggests that the original quasi-historical Jesus story related in the Gospel of Mark was, as the Gnostics claimed, the Outer Mysteries designed to appeal to spiritual beginners. These Outer Mysteries could take an initiate as far as the empty tomb and the intimation of eternal Life, but only the secret teachings of the Gnostics revealed the sayings of the risen Christ. These led initiates beyond the literal story to the true Mystery, to the mystical experience of their own death and resurrection and the realization of their deeper identity as the Christ—the ever-living Universal Daemon.

CONCLUSION

Like countless scholars who have made this quest before us, we have found that looking for a historical Jesus is futile. It is astonishing that we have no substantial evidence for the historical existence of a man who is said to have been the one and only incarnation of God throughout all of history. But the fact is we do not. So, what have we got?

- ❖ A few mentions of "Christians" and followers of someone called Crestus among all the extensive histories of the Romans
- ❖ Some fake passages in Josephus among all the substantial histories of the Jews
- ❖ A handful of passages from among the vast literature of the Talmud, which tell us that a man called Yeshu existed and had five disciples called "Mattai, Nakkia, Netzer, Buni, and Todah"
- ❖ Four anonymous gospels that do not even agree on the facts of Jesus' birth and death
- ❖ A gospel attributed to Mark written somewhere between 70 and 135 CE, which is not even meant to be an eyewitness account and certainly isn't from its ignorance of Palestinian geography and the fact that it misquotes Hebrew scripture
- ❖ Gospels attributed to Matthew and Luke, which are independently based on Mark and give us entirely contradictory genealogies
- ❖ A gospel attributed to John, which was written some time after the other three and certainly not by the disciple John
- ❖ The names of 12 disciples for whom there is no historical evidence
- ❖ The Acts of the Apostles, which reads like a fantasy novel, misquotes the Hebrew Old Testament, contradicts Paul's letters, and was not written until the second half of the second century
- ❖ A selection of forged letters attributed to Peter, James, John, and Paul
- ❖ A few genuine letters by Paul, which do not speak of a historical Jesus at all, but only of a mystical dying and resurrecting Christ
- ❖ A lot of evidence which suggests that the New Testament is not a history of actual events, but a history of the evolution of Christian mythology

Maybe (if we really want to believe it), something of this could (perhaps) be evidence of a historical Jesus. This cannot be ruled out. But the evidence that suggests that Jesus is a mythical figure is so compelling that we will need something far more substantial than any of this to undermine it.

The lack of any evidence for a historical Jesus finally made us completely abandon the idea that the true biography of Jesus had been distorted and overlaid with Pagan mythology to create the gospel stories. It also made us dismiss an extraordinary idea developed in the 1920s by a group of monks in Germany called the "Mystery Theory."[138] This explains the resemblances between the biography of Jesus and the mythology of the Mysteries by claiming that, as the climax of a divine plan, the life of Jesus finally fulfilled in history what had previously been only mythical. This is actually just the diabolical mimicry theory in a more positive disguise. There is no good reason to view the stories of Osiris-Dionysus as myths and the Jesus story as their historical fulfillment. To do so is just cultural prejudice.

It is often argued that only the existence of a historical Jesus can account for the power and appeal of Christianity. Without the inspiration of some charismatic founder how could it have originated and spread around the whole of the ancient world? The Jesus Mystery Thesis accounts for this without needing to hypothesize the existence of a man for whom we have no evidence. Christianity, as the Mysteries of Jesus, originated and spread around the ancient world in exactly the same way that the Mysteries of Dionysus had done—and the Mysteries of Mithras, and of Attis, and of Serapis, and of all the other mythical dying and resurrecting Mystery godmen.

Far from throwing the Jesus Mysteries Thesis into question, our search for a historical Jesus had endorsed it. However, our studies of the New Testament had opened up a serious area of doubt. If Paul is the earliest Christian we know of who is actually a historical figure, and the Gnostics were the original Christians, as the Jesus Mysteries Thesis claims, then surely we should expect to find that Paul was a Gnostic. But traditionally he is portrayed as vehemently anti-Gnostic. We seemed to have hit a major flaw in our thesis. Until, that is, we once again dared to challenge the received view and look more closely at the evidence for ourselves.

8

Was Paul a Gnostic?

Much of what passes for "historical" interpretation of Paul and for "objective" analysis of his letters can be traced to the second-century heresiologists. If the apostle were so unequivocally anti-Gnostic, how could the Gnostics claim him as their great Pneumatic teacher? How could they say they are following his example when they offer secret teaching of wisdom and Gnosis "to the initiates?" How could they claim his resurrection theology as the source for their own, citing his words as decisive evidence *against* the ecclesiastical doctrine of bodily resurrection?[1]

Elaine Pagels

St. Paul is the most influential Christian of all time. There are 13 letters attributed to him in the New Testament, making up a quarter of the whole of canonical Christian scripture. On top of that, most of the Acts of the Apostles is devoted to tales of Paul. But who is Paul?

Traditionally Paul is viewed as a bastion of orthodoxy and a crusader against the heretical Gnostics. Yet it is a remarkable fact that the Gnostics themselves never saw him in this light. Quite the opposite—the great Gnostic sages of the early second century CE called Paul "the Great Apostle"[2] and honored him as the primary inspiration for Gnostic Christianity. Valentinus explains that Paul initiated the chosen few into the "Deeper Mysteries" of Christianity, which revealed a secret doctrine of God. These initiates had included Valentinus' teacher Theudas, who had in turn initiated Valentinus himself.[3]

Many Gnostic groups claimed Paul as their founding father and Gnostics calling themselves "Paulicians" continued to flourish, despite persistent persecution from the Roman Church, until the end of the tenth century.[4] Paul wrote his letters to churches in seven cities, which are known to have been centers of Gnostic Christianity during the second century. These Christian communities were led by the Gnostic sage Marcion, for whom Paul was the only true apostle.[5] One thing is for sure: if Paul really were as anti-Gnostic as the Literalists claim, then it is astounding how many Gnostic texts quote him or are actually attributed to him. The followers of Marcion even had a gospel, which they claimed was written by Paul.[6] The Nag Hammadi library includes *The Prayer of the Apostle Paul* and *The Apocalypse of Paul*.[7] A scripture called *The Ascent of Paul* records the "ineffable words, which it is not permissible for a man to speak," which Paul heard during his famous ascent to the third heaven alluded to by the apostle in his Letter to the Corinthians.[8] Another text, called *The Acts of Paul*, describes Paul traveling with a companion called Thecla—a woman who conducted baptisms![9]

THE GENUINE PAUL?

Who is the genuine Paul? Could he have been a Gnostic, as the Gnostics claimed? As we have already discussed, modern scholars now regard many of the letters attributed to Paul as forgeries.[10] Of the 13 New Testament letters, only seven are now accepted as largely authentic.[11]

As already mentioned, the so-called "Pastoral" letters to Timothy and Titus are universally regarded as fakes. Computer studies have confirmed that the author of the Pastorals is definitely not the author of the letters to the Galatians, Romans, and Corinthians, which are accepted as genuinely by Paul.[12] The earliest collection of letters attributed to Paul does not contain the Pastorals.[13] In fact, we do not even hear of the Pastorals at all until Irenaeus (c. 190). They appear as a part of the Christian canon only after this time, always as a set, and are regularly dismissed by Christians of all persuasions as forgeries.[14] Even the great orthodox propagandist Eusebius does not include them in his Bible (c. 325).[15]

This is important, as it is only in the Pastorals that Paul is anti-Gnostic.[16] Unlike the genuine Pauline letters, the Pastorals present him as an organizer

of the Church, a mainstay of Church discipline, and the unswerving antago-
nist of all heretics.[17] He is made to condemn Gnostic myths as "unhallowed
old wives' tales"[18] and to recommend his followers "not to meddle with the
teachings and not to waste time on endless mythologies and genealogies,
which lead to empty speculations."[19] Obviously by the end of the second century the view of Paul as a Gnostic teacher was a sufficient threat to motivate
someone to create an indisputably Literalist Paul in response.

This Paul is made to specifically advise:

> Guard what has been handed down to you by fending off all the God-
> less prattle and contradictions of false "Gnosis," which some have
> adhered to, losing the way of the faith.[20]

He is also made to be authoritarian in enforcing the power of the Church
hierarchy, writing, "Those who do go wrong should be publicly reproved, to
give the others a scare."[21] He particularly attacks "Hymenaeus and Philetus,"
two Gnostic teachers who have "wandered afield from the truth" and are
teaching the Gnostic doctrine that "our resurrection has already occurred";[22]
although in his genuine letters Paul claims to be already "resurrected" himself! And despite the fact that there was a widespread tradition that Paul
traveled with a woman who baptized,[23] he is also made to attack the Gnostic
practice of treating women as equal to men:

> A woman should quietly receive instruction in complete obedience. I
> will not allow a woman to be a teacher nor act superior to a man.[24]

At the end of the second century, then, Paul is portrayed by Literalist Christians as anti-Gnostic and authoritarian. This has been assumed to be historically accurate, but is actually only the perspective of these Literalist
Christians.[25] Just a few decades earlier, however, their view was the complete
opposite—in the first half of the second century letters attributed to Clement,
the Bishop of Rome, vigorously attack Paul as a misguided heretic![26] These
letters describe Peter as vehemently denying Paul's status as an apostle since
only an eyewitness of the resurrection should be regarded as an apostle and
Paul did not actually see the risen Christ. Paul's vision of Jesus on the road to
Damascus is apparently not only invalid, it is a revelation from an evil
demon or lying spirit![27] Jesus is claimed to be "angry" with Paul who is his

"adversary," because what Paul preaches is "contradictory" to Jesus' teachings.[28] Peter writes of Paul as his "enemy" who has convinced some of the Gentiles to reject the Jewish Law and to embrace "foolish teachings," which are "outside the Law." Paul is accused of creating a heretical gospel and Jesus' genuine apostles have to secretly send out "a true gospel" to correct these heresies.[29] Like his contemporary the arch-heretic Simon Magus, Paul is a satanically inspired divider of the Christian community.[30] He is a dangerous man who should be expelled from the Church![31]

PAUL AND THE PAGAN MYSTERIES

If we can throw off the traditional picture of Paul and look at the evidence with an open mind this anti-Paul rhetoric is understandable, since his letters show distinct Gnostic and Pagan influences. Paul is a Jew who had embraced the ubiquitous Greek culture of the times. He writes in Greek, his first language. He quotes only from the Greek version of the Old Testament. His ministry is to Pagan cities dominated by Greek culture.[32] Of these, Antioch was a center for the Mysteries of Adonis, Ephesus was a center for the Mysteries of Attis, and Corinth was a center for the Mysteries of Dionysus.[33] Paul was a native of Tarsus in Asia Minor, which by his time had surpassed even Athens and Alexandria to become the major center of Pagan philosophy.[34] It was in Tarsus that the Mysteries of Mithras had originated, so it would have been unthinkable that Paul would have been unaware of the remarkable similarities we have already explored between Christian doctrines and the teachings of Mithraism.[35]

Paul frequently uses terms and phrases from the Pagan Mysteries, such as *pneuma* (spirit), *gnosis* (divine knowledge), *doxa* (glory), *sophia* (wisdom), *teleioi* (the initiated), and so on.[36] He advises his followers to "earnestly seek the greater charismata."[37] The word "charismata" derives from the Mystery term *makarismos*, referring to the blessed nature of one who has seen the Mysteries.[38] He even calls himself a "Steward of the Mysteries of God,"[39] which is the technical name for a priest in the Mysteries of Serapis.[40]

Paul quotes the Pagan sage Aratus, who had lived in Tarsus several centuries earlier, describing God "in whom we live, and move, and have our being."[41] He also teaches Mystery doctrines.[42] Like the Pagan sage Socrates, who was deemed wise because he knew he knew nothing,[43] Paul teaches:

If someone thinks he knows something, he still doesn't know the way he ought to know.[44]

Just as Plato had written that we now only see reality "through a glass dimly,"[45] so Paul writes, "For now we see through a glass, darkly; but then face to face."[46]

This famous passage from Paul has also been translated:

At present all we see is the baffling reflection of reality; we are like men looking at a landscape in a small mirror. The time will come when we shall see reality whole and face to face.[47]

This translation clearly brings out the Platonic nature of Paul's teachings. Plato had used the image of prisoners trapped in a cave who are only able to see the shadows of the outside world cast on the cave walls as an allegory for our present condition of mistaking for real what is in fact only a reflection of ultimate reality.[48] For Plato, as for Paul, "At present all we see is the baffling reflection of reality."

Plato teaches that philosophers are those who are released from the cave to go outside and see the reality of the dazzling light of day for themselves—"face to face." This phrase is a ritual formula of the Pagan Mysteries. In *The Bacchae* we read: "He gave these Mysteries to me *face to face*."[49] Lucius Apuleius writes of his initiation: "I penetrated into the very presence of the gods below and the gods above, where I worshiped *face to face*."[50] Justin Martyr acknowledges that: "The aim of Platonism is to see God *face to face*."[51] Plato describes how in the temple of the "true earth," which exists in the realm of ideas of which this Earth is a mere image, "Communion with the gods occurs *face to face*."[52]

THE GNOSTIC PAUL

Paul's Jesus is the mystical dying and resurrecting godman of the Gnostics, not the historical figure of the Literalists. The only place where Paul seems to treat Jesus as a historical figure is in the Letter to Timothy, where he writes of "Jesus Christ who swore out so noble a deposition before Pontius Pilate"—but this letter is a forgery.[53] The genuine Paul preaches the Gnostic doctrine of Illusionism, claiming that Jesus came not as a person but in the "likeness" of human flesh.[54]

Paul's letters are full of such distinctively Gnostic doctrines. How many modern Christians have wondered what Paul's famous claim to have ascended as far as the third heaven could possibly mean? This would not be puzzling for a Gnostic or an initiate of the Pagan Mysteries, for both would have been taught that there are seven heavens linked to the seven heavenly bodies—the five visible planets and the moon and sun.[55]

Like the Gnostics, Paul is extremely disparaging of the externals of religion—ceremonies, holy days, rules, and regulations.[56] Like the Gnostics, he claims that true Christians become like Christ: having "no veil over the face" they "reflect as in a mirror the splendor of the Lord" and are thus "transfigured into his likeness, from splendor to splendor."[57]

The Gnostics saw Paul as a teacher of secret "Pneumatic" initiations. In his Letter to the Romans Paul writes: "I long to see you, so that I may share with you a certain Pneumatic charisma,"[58] of which he says, "I would not have you remain ignorant."[59] If Paul wants to urgently share something with his correspondents, why doesn't he write it in his letter? The answer for the Gnostics is that the "Pneumatic charisma" is an initiation, which he can only transmit in person and "in secret."[60] Paul writes:

> As it is written, "Eye has not seen, nor has ear heard, nor has it entered into the heart of man, what God has prepared for those who love him."[61]

Initiated readers would undoubtedly recognize these words as a Mystery formula pronounced at the time of initiation. The vow of secrecy undertaken by the followers of the Gnostic sage Justinus incorporated these words and, among other places, they also occur in the Gnostic *Gospel of Thomas*, where Jesus offers:

> I will give you what eye has not seen, and what ear has not heard, what has not been touched, and what has not arisen in the heart of man.[62]

It is only inadequate translation that conceals the fact that Paul's letters are full of characteristically Gnostic phrases and teachings. For example, the Valentinians claim that Paul initiated Christians into the "Mystery of

Sophia," which probably included the myth of the goddess' fall and redemption, and quote as proof his First Letter to the Corinthians, in which Paul writes: "We speak of Sophia among the initiated."[63] If you are wondering why you have never come across this decidedly Gnostic line of Paul's before, it is because it is usually translated as "We speak wisdom among the perfected," which doesn't make a lot of sense but at least sounds orthodox!

The traditional translation continues:

> Howbeit we speak wisdom among the perfect: yet a wisdom not of this world, nor of the rulers of this world, which are coming to nought: but we speak God's wisdom in a mystery, even the wisdom that hath been hidden, which God foreordained before the worlds unto our glory: which none of the rulers of this world knoweth: for had they known it, they would not have crucified the Lord of glory.[64]

This translation, if intelligible at all, distorts Paul's actual meaning considerably. One modern scholar explains:

> The proper meaning of this passage is obscured at two crucial points. The Greek word translated "world" here, severally in its singular or plural forms, is *aion*, which does not mean this physical world or earth, but "time" or "age." Paul's use of *aion* here accordingly shows that he was thinking in terms of an esoteric system of "world-ages." Next, the words translated as "rulers of this world" (*archontes tou aionos toutou*) do not refer, as is popularly supposed, to the Roman and Jewish authorities who were responsible for condemning Jesus to death; they denote demonic beings, who were associated with the planets and were believed to govern the lives of men on earth.
>
> In this passage, then, Paul is found explaining that, before the beginning of a series of world-ages, God determined to send into the world, for the good of mankind, a preexistent divine being, whom the demonic rulers of the world, not perceiving his real nature, put to death and thereby in some way confounded themselves. In brief, Paul envisaged mankind as enslaved by demonic beings, connected with astral phenomena, whom he describes by a variety of terms such as *archontes tou aionos toutou* and *stoicheia tou kosmou* ("The elemental powers of the universe"). From this mortal slavery mankind had, accordingly, been rescued by the divine being, who, incarnated

in the person of Jesus, had been crucified mistakenly by these *archontes* who, presumably, by thus unwittingly exceeding their rights, forfeited their control over men.[65]

This is not Christianity as we know it today! Paul is preaching Gnosticism.

Paul writes of a *Gnosis* which can be taught only to the "fully initiated."[66] He offers a prayer "that your love may more and more be bursting with Gnosis."[67] He writes of "Christ in whom are hid all the treasures of Sophia and Gnosis" and of "the Gnosis of God's Mystery."[68] Like a Gnostic initiate Paul claims: "By revelation the Mystery was made known to me."[69] Like a Gnostic defending the secrecy of the Inner Mysteries he asserts that he has heard "ineffable words which it is not lawful for a man to utter."[70] Like a Gnostic he puts the emphasis on understanding, not on dogma, writing, "The letter kills, while the spirit gives life."[71] And like a Gnostic, he describes stories in the scriptures as "allegories"[72] and writes of "events" as "symbolic."[73]

APOSTLE OF THE RESURRECTION

Literalist Christians tried to quote Paul to endorse their bizarre belief that at the Second Coming the dead would actually rise from their graves in their physical bodies.[74] It is clear, however, that Paul had a very different perspective. In common with the Gnostics, he sees the resurrection as a spiritual event. He writes categorically: "Flesh and blood cannot inherit the kingdom of God."[75]

The Gnostic sage Theodotus calls Paul "the apostle of the resurrection."[76] Like the Gnostics, Paul does not see the resurrection as a promised future event, but as a spiritual experience that can happen right now. He writes, "This is it: the duly appointed time! This is it: the day of salvation."[77] His message is clearly mystical and allegorical—he writes of being "raised up to heaven" and "enthroned with Jesus" not as some hoped-for afterlife reward, but as something, which he and other Christian initiates have already experienced.[78]

Like the Gnostics, Paul preaches that Jesus' passion is not an event in the past, but a perennial mystical reality. Through sharing in Jesus' death and resurrection each Christian initiate can themselves die to their lower self and be resurrected as the Christ or Logos.[79] In his Letter to the Philippians

Paul writes of "participating in his suffering" and "sharing in the form of his death," and so being "resurrected from the dead."[80] In his Letter to the Galatians he writes: "I have been crucified with Christ: from now on I live no more, instead Christ lives in me."[81] In his Letter to the Romans he interprets Jesus' passion allegorically, writing:

> All of us who were initiated into Jesus Christ were initiated into his death as well. By being initiated into his death, we were buried with him, so that just as Christ was raised from the dead through the glory of his Father, so we might walk in the freshness of a new life. Because if we have grown into the likeness of his death, we shall do the same with his resurrection. This much we know: that the old was crucified with him, that sin's body was destroyed to keep us from being the slaves of sin any more.[82]

In his Letter to the Colossians Paul describes himself as having been assigned by God the task of delivering his message "in full"; of announcing "the secret hidden for long ages and through many generations," which is now being disclosed to those chosen by God. And what is this great secret? Is it, as we might expect from an orthodox apostle, the "good news" that Jesus had literally come and walked the Earth, worked miracles, died for our sins, and returned from the dead? No! It is the perennial mysticism of Gnosticism and the Pagan Mysteries—that within each one of us is the one Soul of the Universe, the Logos, the Universal Daemon, the Mind of God. Paul writes:

> The secret is this: Christ in you![83]

When Paul describes his famous vision of Jesus on the road to Damascus it is significant that he doesn't say "God revealed his Son *to* me," as we would expect from a Literalist Christian. Rather, he writes, "God revealed his Son *in* me."[84]

Paul's Jesus is not a historical figure, but a symbol of the Universal Daemon of whom we are all limbs. For Paul, "Christ is like a single body with its many limbs and organs, which, many as they are together make up one body."[85] In his Letter to the Ephesians he teaches:

> Let each of you speak the truth with your neighbor because we are parts of each other.[86]

The Gnostics claimed that Paul taught that seeing Jesus as a flesh and blood man was only a transitory stage for beginners—the Outer Mysteries for Psychic Christians. Those Pneumatic Christians initiated into the Inner Mysteries understood the Jesus story's allegorical meaning. The Gnostics claimed that this change of perspective through initiation into the Inner Mysteries is what Paul was referring to when he wrote: "Even though we have known Christ after the flesh, yet now we know Him so no more."[87] Since Paul never claimed to have known a historical Jesus "in the flesh," it is indeed difficult to see what else he could have meant!

PSYCHIC AND PNEUMATIC TEACHINGS

So how could Paul have come to be both the hero of the Gnostics and the Literalists? As we have already explored, the Gnostics taught that the Jesus story works on two levels at once: as an introductory story for Psychic Christians initiated into the Outer Mysteries and as a mystical allegory for Pneumatic Christians initiated into the Inner Mysteries. Although it was understood in two completely different ways, the story remained the same. According to the Gnostics, Paul's letters were likewise designed to work on two levels. As the Gnostic sage Theodotus puts it, Paul "taught in two ways at once."[88]

Theodotus claims that Paul recognized that "each one knows the Lord in his own way: and not all know him alike."[89] So on the one hand he preached the savior "according to the flesh" as one "who was born and suffered." This "kerygmatic gospel" of "Christ crucified" he taught to Psychic Christians "because this they were capable of knowing."[90] But to Pneumatic Christians he proclaimed Christ "pneumatically" or "according to the spirit."[91] Each level of initiate would take from these teachings whatever they were wise enough to be able to hear. Paul himself writes:

> The Psychic does not receive the things of the spirit of God; they are foolishness to him; he cannot recognize them, because they are Pneumatically discerned, but the Pneumatic discerns all things.[92]

The Gnostics claimed that like the gospel parables, Paul's letters encoded secret teachings so that uninitiated readers would hear one thing and the initiated another. Only those who had been initiated into the secret oral teachings of the Inner Mysteries were capable of understanding Paul's deeper meaning. As Elaine Pagels writes,

> The Valentinians claim that most Christians make the mistake of reading the scriptures only literally. They themselves, through their initiation into Gnosis, learned to read Paul's letters (as they read all the scriptures) on the symbolic level, as they say Paul intended. Only this pneumatic reading yields "the truth" instead of its mere outward "image."[93]

The followers of Valentinus systematically decoded the allegorical meaning of Paul's letters to show their hidden meaning. For example, in his letters to the Romans Paul uses a simple everyday situation—the relationship between Jews and Gentiles—as a parable for the relation between Psychic and Pneumatic Christians. An initiate of the Inner Mysteries would understand that where Paul writes "Jews" he means "Psychic Christians" and where he writes "Gentiles," he means "Pneumatic Christians."[94] As well as "Gentiles," the other code words used by Paul to signify "Pneumatic Christian" include "the uncircumcised," "the Greeks," "Jews inwardly," "Jews in secret," and "the true Israel."[95]

In a striking passage in his First Letter to the Corinthians Paul writes with disappointment of wanting to give his followers Pneumatic teachings, but finding them only to be on a "Sarkic" level of awareness (a term synonymous with "Hylic," meaning the lowest level of human awareness). So he is forced to teach his students only the most basic of Christian doctrines:

> And I, brothers, was not able to speak to you as to Pneumatics, but as to Sarkics, as to those uninitiated in Christ. I fed you milk, not meat, for you were not yet able to take it. Nor are you now—you are still Sarkic. For where there is strife and envy among you, are you not Sarkic?[96]

Paul is impatient that his followers are still not ready to move on from elementary teachings. In his Letter to the Hebrews he writes:

> Therefore let us leave behind the elementary doctrine of Christ and progress to another level of initiation (ten teleioteta), not laying again a foundation of repentance from dead works and of faith toward

God, with teachings of baptism, laying on of hands, the resurrection of the dead, and eternal judgment. For it is impossible for those who have been enlightened, who have tasted the heavenly gift, and have become partakers of the holy breath [holy spirit], and have tasted the goodness of God's Logos, and the powers of the age to come, to have fallen back to renew repentance again. They re-crucify for themselves the Son of God.[97]

The "elementary doctrine," which Paul wants his disciples to leave behind, as a Gnostic would expect, includes repentance, faith, baptism, the laying on of hands, the resurrection of the dead, and eternal judgment—all the rituals and dogmas so precious to the Literalist Church. To the Gnostics these were only the Psychic Outer Mysteries of Christianity. Paul wants his disciples, having tasted the holy breath of Pneumatic initiation, to progress to the Pneumatic level of understanding completely and leave behind such Psychic concerns.

PAUL AND JEHOVAH

Like the Gnostics, Paul teaches that the Mysteries of Jesus supersede the Law of the Jewish god Jehovah.[98] Jesus has given Jews a New Covenant or agreement with God and Paul does not hide his low opinion of the redundant old agreement that is traditional Judaism![99] He writes:

Calling this the "new" agreement already makes the first one the "old" one, and something so antiquated and creaky won't be around much longer.[100]

Like the Gnostics, Paul does not preach moral servitude to the Law, but spiritual freedom through Gnosis. He declares: "Where the spirit of the Lord is, there is freedom."[101] For Paul, "Nothing is unclean in itself."[102] Later Gnostics, such as Carpocrates, quote Paul to defend their own doctrines of natural morality against those who accused them of immorality. After all, it was Paul, not some "loony" Gnostic heretic, who had famously proclaimed: "All things are authorized for me!"[103]

Paul even goes so far as to declare Jehovah's traditionally sacred Law, the very basis of the Jewish religion, to be a curse, writing, "All who depend upon works of the Law are under a curse,"[104] and "Christ redeemed us from the curse of the Law."[105] For Paul, as for the Gnostics, through sharing in Christ's suffering and resurrection the Christian initiate can be redeemed from the Law and set free: "Now, having died, we are out of the purview of the Law that kept us down."[106]

Paul claims the Law is the product of the "mediator." What does he mean by calling Jehovah, supposedly the one God and creator of all, a "mediator?" A mediator between what and what? Literalists have no answer, but Gnostics immediately recognize that Paul is teaching the Gnostic doctrine that Jehovah is the "demiurge," a lesser god who mediates between the ineffable supreme God and creation. Paul certainly does not regard Jehovah as the true God, for he continues: "The mediator is not one; God is one."[107]

According to Paul, people who do not understand the gospel he is preaching have had their "unbelieving minds blinded by the god of this passing age."[108] In many translations of his letters, the editor adds a helpful little note here to explain the mysterious phrase "the god of this passing age." The general orthodox gloss on this line is that Paul is referring to the Devil, but why he should refer to a wicked angel as a "god" is left unexplained! To the Gnostics it was obvious what Paul meant. He was referring to Jehovah, the lesser god of the Jews, whose years of ruling the Jewish people were coming to an end and who was to be abandoned in favor of the true ineffable God of Jesus and Plato.

AXE-WIELDING CIRCUMCISIONARIES!

The anti-Gnostic letters of Paul have been found to be forgeries, but his authentic letters do oppose others within the early Christian Church who preach "another Jesus."[109] These are not Gnostic heretics, however, but pro-Jewish Christians who believe that the Church should maintain the old Jewish custom of circumcision and honor the Law of Jehovah.

Paul attacks them with passion. In his Letter to the Philippians he warns: "Watch out for those dogs, those evil operators, those axe-wielding circumcisionaries!"[110] In his Letter to the Galatians he proclaims: "Mark my words: I,

Paul, say to you that if you receive circumcision Christ will do you no good at all,"[111] and quips, "As for these agitators, they had better go the whole way and make eunuchs of themselves!"[112]

It is not such outer Psychic observances of religious rituals, but inner Pneumatic qualities, which mark the Mysteries Paul is preaching. He claims:

> We are the circumcised, we whose worship is Pneumatic (spiritual), whose pride is in Jesus Christ, and who put no confidence in anything external.[113]

Paul's teachings here are completely in line with those of the Gnostic Jesus. In *The Gospel of Thomas*, for example, when the disciples ask Jesus about the benefits of circumcision, he explains:

> If it were beneficial, their father would beget them already circumcised from their mother. Rather the true circumcision in spirit has become completely profitable.[114]

What characterizes Paul's rival Christians is not their Gnosticism as opposed to Paul's Literalism, or their Literalism as opposed to Paul's Gnosticism. This is not the issue at all. Their disagreement is over the relationship between Christians and old Jewish traditions, and whether Christianity should be open to non-Jews, and if so in what way. The battles in the Church of Paul's time were not between Literalists and Gnostics, but between Christians with different views on the relationship between Christianity and Judaism.

Paul's letters suggest that these more traditional Jewish-Christians live in Jerusalem. They have traditionally been taken to be Peter and others of Jesus' disciples who are mentioned in the New Testament. As we have already shown, this is actually an interpretation of the evidence based on unjustified preconceptions. There is absolutely no evidence to support the idea that there ever existed a Jerusalem Church of the apostles as envisaged by traditional Roman Christianity.[115] In fact, quite the opposite.

Indeed, when in 160 Bishop Melito of Sardis went to Judea to discover what had become of the legendary Jerusalem Church, to his dismay he found not the descendants of the apostles, but instead a small group of Gnostics![116] These Christians, who called themselves the Ebionites or "Poor Men," had their own *Gospel of the Ebionites* and also a *Gospel of the Hebrews*,[117] a

Gospel of the Twelve Apostles, and a *Gospel of the Nazarenes*.[118] All of these gospels differed significantly from the gospels of the New Testament.[119] This form of Jewish-Christian Gnosticism managed to survive for many hundreds of years.[120]

The Literalist propagandist Eusebius explains the fact that the Jerusalem Church had turned out to be made up of Gnostics by claiming that they had obviously all "apostated" from their original Literalism and become heretics—but he does not explain why or how this might have happened! Actually the evidence suggests that the Jerusalem Christians had always been Gnostics, because in the first century the Christian community was made up entirely of different types of Gnosticism!

CONCLUSION

So was Paul a Gnostic? Let's review a little of what we have discovered:

- ❖ The Gnostics claimed that their spiritual lineage stemmed from Paul and that they were privy to secret oral teachings taught by Paul to select disciples.
- ❖ Gnostics had many gospels which they attributed to Paul, their "Great Apostle."
- ❖ Many Gnostic groups claimed Paul as their founding father.
- ❖ By the middle of the second century the communities to which Paul had written his letters are known to have been centers of Marcionite Gnosticism.
- ❖ Paul's anti-Gnostic Pastoral letters are fakes, forged in the late second century. In the genuine letters Paul is not anti-Gnostic and never mentions a historical Jesus.
- ❖ Literalist Christians of the early second century attack Paul, who they claim "contradicts" the true teaching and is the "adversary" of Jesus.
- ❖ Paul was born in Tarsus, a major center for the Pagan Mysteries, and often uses terms from the Mysteries in his letters. He even calls himself a "Steward of the Mysteries of God," the term for a priest in the Pagan Mysteries of Serapis. Paul quotes Pagan sages and teaches Pagan doctrines.
- ❖ When properly translated, Paul's letters reveal a powerful Gnostic content. Paul regularly uses Gnostic terms. He is a teacher of a Pneumatic

initiation. He journeyed mystically to the third heaven. He teaches that Jesus came only in the "likeness" of flesh. He is disparaging of external religion. He describes the scriptures as "allegories" and "symbolic." He rejects the Law of Jehovah, who he calls "the mediator" and "the god of this passing age."

❖ While the Literalists saw the resurrection as the promise that they would rise from their graves and experience bodily immortality after the Second Coming, Paul teaches the Gnostic doctrine that the resurrection is a mystical experience that can be had here and now.

❖ The great secret that Paul claims to be able to reveal is not that Jesus literally walked the Earth, but the mystical revelation of "Christ in you."

❖ The Gnostics claimed that, like the gospels, Paul's letters encoded secret teachings. Paul taught in "two ways at once": the Outer Mysteries to Psychic initiates and the Inner Mysteries to Pneumatic initiates. Paul's letters can be understood in different ways because they were designed to speak on different levels simultaneously.

❖ Paul is frustrated with his disciples because they are not ready to abandon "elementary" Christianity and move on to the deeper level.

All of the evidence strongly suggests that Paul was indeed a Gnostic—just as the Gnostics themselves had claimed all along. Yet, upon reflection we felt that to call Paul a Gnostic was, in a sense, misleading. The more we looked at the evidence we had uncovered, the more it seemed that to apply the terms "Gnostic" and "Literalist" to the Christianity of the first century was actually meaningless. From Paul's letters it is clear that the Christian community of this period was deeply divided, yet this schism was not between Gnostics and Literalists, as was the case by the end of the second century. Paul is neither anti-Gnostic nor pro-Gnostic, because in his day the great schism between Gnostics and Literalists had yet to occur.

At the time of Paul, the strands of thought that would become Gnosticism and Literalism were harmoniously co-existing as the Inner and Outer teachings of the Jesus Mysteries. The theological battle that Paul is engaged in is between those initiates of the Jesus Mysteries who want to maintain a traditional and distinctively Jewish identity and those, like himself, who wish to make their new Mysteries completely "modern" and cosmopolitan.

Paul has all the characteristics we would expect to find in an initiator of the Jesus Mysteries. This was powerful confirmation of the Jesus Mysteries Thesis. When a theory is true, everything starts to fall into place. Our new vision of the origins of Christianity explained the evidence, was internally consistent, beautifully simple, and wonderfully ironic. There was still something that worried us, however.

The Jesus Mysteries Thesis proposed that the Jews had created their own version of the ancient Mysteries with Jesus as their Osiris-Dionysus. How could this have happened? The traditional history paints a picture of the Jews as an insular people, separate and distinct from the other Mediterranean cultures, staunchly nationalistic and fanatically devoted to their religion, fiercely loyal to their one god Jehovah and entirely hostile to the Paganism of their neighbors. From this perspective, the idea that the Jews could possibly have adopted the Pagan Mysteries seems unthinkable. And so it would be, if any of this were true.

The Jewish Mysteries

> That Jewish priests used to perform their chants to the flute and drums, crowned with ivy, and that a golden vine was discovered in the Temple, has led some to imagine that the god they worshiped was Dionysus.[1]
>
> **Tacitus**

The traditional picture of Jesus has him growing up among shepherds and fishermen in a rural backwater of the ancient world. Actually by the time that Jesus is supposed to have lived, Judea, like so many other countries of the time, had adopted much of Greek culture and become "Hellenized."[2] An hour's walk from Nazareth in Galilee, where Jesus is supposed to have grown up, was the Hellenized city of Sepphoris, which contained a theater with a beautiful mosaic of Dionysus.[3] Gadara, a day's walk from Nazareth, contained an important school of Pagan philosophy.[4] Scythopolis, on the southern border of Galilee, was a center for the Mysteries of Dionysus[5] and was even said to have been founded by the godman himself.[6]

Jerusalem was surrounded by thoroughly Hellenized cities, such as Larissa and Ascalon, which produced a stream of eminent Pagan philosophers whose renown spread as far as Rome.[7] A Jewish scripture called *2 Maccabees* records that the Temple of Jerusalem itself was transformed into a Greek temple to Zeus and festivals of Dionysus were celebrated.[8] The high priest Jason built a Greek-style *gymnasium*—a Pagan "university" for physical, intellectual, and spiritual education—alongside the Temple which clearly appealed to Jewish clergy more than their traditional ways. According to *2 Maccabees*:

The priests no longer showed any enthusiasm for their duties at the altar, they treated the Temple with disdain, they neglected the sacrifices, and whenever the opening gong called them they hurried to join in the sports at the wrestling school in defiance of the Law.[9]

This process of integration between Jewish and Pagan culture had been going on for centuries. The history of the ancient Jews is one of repeated conquest by other nations: in 922 BCE by the Egyptians; in 700 BCE by the Assyrians; in 586 BCE by the Babylonians; in 332 BCE by the Greeks under Alexander the Great; in 198 BCE by the Syrians; and finally in 63 BCE by the Romans, who completely destroyed the state of Judea in 112 CE.[10] These conquests inevitably led to the Jewish people coming under the cultural influence of their conquerors as well as Jews becoming dispersed throughout the Mediterranean as slaves, forming the so-called "Diaspora." Those who regained their freedom became integrated with Pagan civilization and even when they had the chance to return from exile to their homeland, the majority chose not to.[11]

Jews of the Diaspora integrated Pagan spirituality with their own religious traditions. In Babylon, for example, Jews became famous for their practice of Babylonian astrology. The great patriarch Abraham himself was a Babylonian Jew who was said to have been well-versed in astrological doctrines.[12] Indeed, eminent Jews such as the historian Josephus and the philosophers Aristobulus and Philo make the outrageous claim that Abraham invented astrology.[13]

Jews even adopted the Pagan Mysteries. In Babylon they practiced the Mysteries of Tammuz, the Babylonian Osiris-Dionysus.[14] In the Old Testament, the prophet Ezekiel describes Jewish women ritually mourning the death of Tammuz at the north gate of the Jerusalem Temple itself.[15] According to St. Jerome, there was a shaded grove sacred to Adonis, the Syrian Osiris-Dionysus, in Bethlehem.[16] In Syria striking Pagan Mystery symbols have been found painted alongside traditional Jewish motifs on the walls of the synagogue.[17] In Asia Minor Jews equated their god Jehovah with Sabazius, the Phrygian Osiris-Dionysus.[18] We are even told that Jews were expelled from Rome in 139 BCE for trying to introduce the Mysteries of Sabazius into the city![19]

The god of the Jews became known as "Iao," which is an ancient Mystery name of Dionysus.[20] A coin has been found at an archaeological site less than 40 miles from Jerusalem that depicts Jehovah as the founder of the Mysteries of Eleusis.[21] Indeed, it is a shocking fact that many ancient authors, including

Plutarch, Diodorus, Cornelius Labo, Johannes Lydus, and Tacitus, repeatedly identify the god of the Jews with Dionysus.[22] One modern scholar comments:

> Of all the ancient gods, Dionysus was most persistently associated with the Jewish god in Jerusalem.[23]

The view of Jews as united in their opposition to Paganism is an illusion fostered by Christianity to act as the foundation for its own later claims to be spiritually distinct from Paganism. The truth is that different Jews adopted different positions toward Pagan culture. Some were traditional fundamentalists. Others enthusiastically adopted Pagan ways. Many sought to synthesize their own traditions with Paganism and have the best of both worlds.

COSMOPOLITAN ALEXANDRIA

The greatest integration of Jewish and Pagan cultures occurred in Alexandria in Egypt. When Alexander the Great conquered Egypt at the end of the fourth century BCE, the Jews helped him by acting as spies and mercenaries. They were rewarded by being allowed to inhabit their own quarter of the new city of Alexandria, which Alexander founded. This initiated a mass voluntary migration of Jews into the city, where they enjoyed all the benefits of sophisticated Pagan culture.[24] It is thought that up to half of the original population of Alexandria were Jews.[25]

From the very start Alexandria was a *cosmo-polis*—a "universal city." Alexander had created a vast empire within which Greek became the common language and people from every race journeyed to Alexandria to become citizens of this new multi-racial city. Ptolemy I, the first ruler of Alexandria, decided to create a small Greece in Egypt.[26] Under his enlightened rulership a library and museum were founded, which systematically collected together the knowledge of the ancient world. At its height, the library housed hundreds of thousands of scrolls—some say perhaps more than half a million scrolls and papyri.[27] Alexandria became the greatest center of learning in the ancient world, replacing even Athens.

In Alexandria the Mysteries of Osiris-Dionysus reached new heights. The mystical pageant of Eleusis was developed into an even grander dramatic spectacle, performed in many acts on multi-level stages.[28] Unlike in Athens, the Mysteries practiced in Alexandria were not even protected by a rule of secrecy, so anyone could attend these great mystical rites.[29] Such a cosmopolitan and tolerant environment naturally encouraged the merging and combining of different spiritual traditions.[30]

The Jewish population could not help but come under the spell of the sophisticated Pagan culture they encountered in Alexandria. The religious taboos of traditional Jews prevented them attending public banquets, festivals, and the theater, because of their associations with Paganism.[31] This cut them off from the immense advantages of being a part of the great civilization that surrounded them. Not surprisingly, therefore, large numbers of Jews chose to break with their traditions and attempted to integrate themselves into Pagan society. In a remarkably short period, Jews abandoned their own tongue and adopted the universal Greek language.[32] Aramaic and Hebrew continued to be spoken, because of constant immigration of Jews from Judea into Egypt, but Greek became the dominant language, not only in dealings with other national groups in the city, but within the Jewish community itself. It was even used in the services of the synagogue and in family worship.[33]

By the second century BCE, this process of cultural assimilation had gone so far that a Jewish playwright, Ezekiel, rewrote the Jewish scripture of the Exodus as a Greek tragedy in the language and style of Euripides![34] The Jewish intelligentsia wanted to reconcile their ancestral faith with the wisdom of other peoples. They questioned the fundamentalist view of their scriptures as literal history and began to interpret them as mystical allegories.[35] Using this technique borrowed from the Pagan sages, Jewish philosophers were able to interpret their scriptures in line with Greek thought.[36] Under their influence Jewish philosophy blossomed and the Alexandrian rabbis, becoming known as the "Light of Israel," were highly esteemed by Jews everywhere.[37]

Jewish fundamentalists saw their god Jehovah as a tribal deity who had helped them throughout their history to achieve victory over their oppressors and who was in complete opposition to Paganism. The Hellenized Jews of Alexandria, however, portrayed Jehovah as a universal God, identical with Plato's vision of the supreme Oneness.[38]

To avoid accusations from fellow Jews that they were abandoning their own traditions, Hellenized Jews began to claim that Pagan philosophy was originally Jewish! Hermippus asserted that Pythagoras had received his wisdom from the Jews.[39] Aristobulus developed this ludicrous idea, announcing that Plato and Aristotle had borrowed from Moses.[40] Artapanus wrote a historical fantasy in which he equated Moses with Hermes Trismegistus, the mythical founder of the Egyptian Mysteries, and with Musaeus, the mythical founder of the Greek Mysteries.[41] Although absurd, such ideas made it easier for Jews to retain their national dignity while at the same time adopting the philosophy of their Pagan neighbors and participating in cosmopolitan society.

HELLENIZED JEWISH SCRIPTURES

In claiming a Jewish ancestry for the wisdom of the Pagan Mysteries, Hellenized Jews portrayed Paganism and Judaism as essentially parts of the same religious tradition. This justified them introducing Pagan concepts and philosophy into Judaism. In the second century, the Hebrew scriptures were translated into Greek under the influence of Platonic philosophy.[42] Hellenized Jews also wrote a number of new spiritual texts which demonstrate the interpenetration of Jewish and Pagan ideas.[43] Written between the Jewish Old Testament and the Christian New Testament, they are known as "intertestamental" works.

The Letter of Aristeas, for example, equates Jehovah and Zeus, and argues for harmony between Jews and Greeks, who are portrayed as sharing one culture and one vision of the Good Life.[44]

A modern scholar writes of another such text, called *4 Maccabees*:

This text is a wonder of contradictions, or should we say, resolution of contradictions. It is ostensibly directed against a Greek tyrant, Antiochus IV, by a devout orthodox Jew, yet it is written in exquisite Greek by a philosopher trained in Greek thought, and its methods of argument are those of Socrates.[45]

The Books of Enoch also draws on Pagan motifs. These scriptures were attributed to the ancient Jewish Patriarch Enoch, but in the hands of Hellenized Jews he becomes a grand mythological figure, equated with the legendary Egyptian sage Hermes Trismegistus.[46] One scholar notes:

In their wondrous and transcendent poetic vision, these documents contain universal stories and preoccupations which relate them to other great myths of the ancient world.[47]

This inter-testamental "Wisdom Literature" no longer divides humanity into Jews and Gentiles, but rather into the "wise and foolish." It stresses spiritual piety rather than obedience to the Laws of Moses and portrays Jehovah not as a Jewish god, but as Lord of the whole Earth.[48]

Jews even created their own version of the Pagan *Sibylline Oracles*. The original Pagan oracles were attributed to the Sibyl, a prophetess believed to be centuries old who, in a state of ecstasy, spoke the words of God. Sometime in the second century BCE, an Alexandrian Jew invented a Jewish Sibyl and composed her sayings in perfect Greek hexameters.[49]

Jewish inter-testamental literature often personifies wisdom as "Sophia," as did the ancient Pagans. As a modern scholar notes, this "is entirely Greek and has no counterpart in orthodox Jewish theology."[50] The Jewish Sophia appears from as early as the third century BCE, when she is described as Jehovah's consort in the Book of Proverbs.[51] Three centuries later, echoing Pagan Mystery doctrines, the Jewish philosopher Philo wrote of Moses as "the child of parents incorruptible and wholly free from stain, his father being God, who is likewise Father of all, and his mother Sophia, through whom the universe came into existence." For Philo, as for the Gnostics, Sophia is the "Mother of the Logos."[52] The central role given to the Divine Feminine by the Pagan philosophers, the Hellenized Jews of the inter-testamental period and later by the Gnostics, is strong evidence for a direct line of evolution linking these three traditions together.

THE MYSTERIES OF MOSES

Clearly then, Hellenized Jews wanted to integrate the wisdom of the Pagan Mysteries with their own spiritual traditions. But did they create a specifically Jewish version of the Mysteries as the Jesus Mysteries Thesis predicts?

The clues we need to answer this question are found in the works of Philo of Alexandria (20 BCE–40 CE), a well-respected Jewish leader and famous Jewish philosopher.[53] Philo was devoted to his native Judaism, but was also thoroughly Hellenized and obsessed with Pagan philosophy. He writes of philosophers as an international brotherhood of world citizens who "dwell in the cosmos as their city," looking after all alike, and eulogizes:

Such men, though comparatively few in number, keep alive the covered spark of Wisdom secretly, throughout the cities of the world, in order that Virtue may not be absolutely quenched and vanish from our human kind.[54]

Among the ancients, Philo particularly revered Pythagoras and his follower Plato, whom he called "the great" and "the most sacred."[55] The Christian philosopher Clement of Alexandria refers to Philo as "the Pythagorean."[56] Like all followers of Pythagoras, Philo was well versed in music, geometry, and astrology, as well as Greek literature from every age.[57] Also, like other Pythagoreans, he was immersed in the mysticism of the Pagan Mysteries.[58]

Philo uses what he calls "the method of the Mysteries" to reveal Jewish scriptures as allegories encoding secret spiritual teachings.[59] He interprets the "historical" story of Moses and the Exodus as a mystical metaphor for the path that leads through this world to God. The guide on this journey is the familiar Pagan figure of the "Logos." For Philo, as for the sages of the Mysteries, the Logos is "the only and beloved Son of God."[60] Like the sages of the Mysteries, he teaches that the wonders of the visible world are designed to lead humans to the experience of mystical union with God.[61]

Philo did not only adopt the philosophy of the Mysteries, but claimed to be an initiate himself[62]—but not of the Pagan Mysteries, however. He encouraged Jews not to participate in Pagan initiations, as they had their own specifically Jewish Mysteries: the Mysteries of Moses![63] According to Philo, Moses was the great initiator, "a hierophant of the ritual and teacher of divine things." Philo also calls himself a hierophant and initiator in the Jewish Mysteries.[64] He writes of "teaching initiation to those initiates worthy of the most sacred initiations."[65] As in the Pagan Mysteries, his initiates formed a secret mystical sect and were required to be morally pure. As in the Pagan Mysteries, they were sworn to never reveal the "veritably sacred Mysteries" to the uninitiated, lest the ignorant should misrepresent what they did not understand and in so doing expose the Mysteries to the ridicule of the vulgar.

For Philo, initiation was the entrance to a new world, an invisible country, the world of ideas where "the purified mind could contemplate the pure and untainted nature of those things which are invisible and only discernible by the intellect."[66] As in the Pagan Mysteries, the purpose was for the initiate to become transformed into a divine being through the experience of religious ecstasy. In the manner of the Mysteries, Philo writes of *enthousiazein* (being divinely inspired), *korubantian* (being mystically frenzied), *bakeuein* (being seized by divine madness), *katechesthai* (being possessed by the deity) and *ekstasis* (ecstasy).[67] He compares the ecstasy of the initiates of the Jewish Mysteries to both prophetic inspiration and the divine frenzy of initiates of the Mysteries of Dionysus. He writes:

> Go out from yourself filled with divine frenzy like those possessed in the mystical rites of Dionysus, and possessed by the deity after the manner of prophetic inspiration. For when the mind is no longer self-contained but rapt and frenzied with a heavenly passion this is your inheritance.[68]

THE FIRST CHRISTIANS?

Philo's works survived the mass destruction of ancient texts by the Roman Church because of a strange quirk of history. Bishop Eusebius, the fourth-century Church propagandist, could find little evidence from which to construct a history of Christianity, so he eagerly seized upon a description in one of Philo's books, of a group of Jews called the Therapeutae.[69] Philo's description of their spring festival is reminiscent of the Christian celebration of Easter[70] and Eusebius, therefore, claimed that he had discovered the earliest Christians in Alexandria.[71] He asserted that the officials of the Therapeutae were the first bishops, priests, and deacons, and that no one can fail to see in these men the first Christians.[72]

The spring, of course, was also the time when Pagans celebrated their festival of the dying and resurrecting godman, so Eusebius is unjustified in his assumption. Philo wrote about the Therapeutae in 10 CE, which would be 20 years before the supposed date of the crucifixion, so we can safely conclude that the Therapeutae are not the early Literalist Christians that Eusebius would have us believe.[73] Yet, ironically, Eusebius might well have been right in a way, which he would never have intended.[74] For the Therapeutae are a group of Jews clearly practicing a Jewish version of the Pagan Mysteries—exactly the sort of group the Jesus Mysteries Thesis proposes synthesized the Jesus story from the myths of Osiris-Dionysus.

We can tell that the Therapeutae were Jews because they celebrated the

Jewish festival of the Pentecost and kept sacred the Sabbath.[75] Yet in every other way, they resembled a Pythagorean community. As in Pythagorean communities, the Therapeutae dressed in white, shared all their goods in common[76] and admitted women as equals because they "possessed the same eager desire and had made the same deliberate choice as the men."[77] Philo tells us about the Therapeutae in a book called *On the Contemplative Life*. "The contemplative life" was a phrase used by Pythagoreans throughout the ancient world to describe the way of life in their monastic communities.[78] Indeed, Philo tells us that the Therapeutae were a "race of men found in many parts of the inhabited world, in both the Greek and non-Greek world, sharing in the perfect Good."[79]

As already discussed, Philo was himself known as "the Pythagorean" and he writes of the Therapeutae in the language of mystical mathematics characteristic of the followers of Pythagoras:

> In the first place they all come together at the end of every seventh week, for they reverence not only the simple period of seven days, but also the period of the square of seven, since they know that the seven is pure and ever-virgin.[80] Their seventh-day festival then is only a prelude to their greatest feast, which is assigned to the fiftieth, the most holy and natural of numbers, the sum of the powers of the perfect right-angled triangle, which has been appointed as the origin of the generation of the cosmic elements.[81]

Like the ancient Pagan sages, Philo contrasts the unintelligent worship of externals by the misinstructed in all religions with the worship of the true God by those, like the Therapeutae, who follow the contemplative life.[82] Like Pagan initiates, the Therapeutae saw the literal interpretation of their scriptures as only an outer covering, concealing secret mystical meaning. They believed that: "The exegesis of the sacred writings treats the inner meaning conveyed in allegory."[83] Philo writes:

> The whole interval from dawn to sunset they devote to their exercise. Taking the sacred writings they spend their time in philosophizing and interpreting their ancestral code allegorically, for they think that the words of the literal meaning are symbols of a hidden nature which is made plain only by the under-meaning.[84]

Philo even specifically compares the divine calling received by members of the Therapeutae to the mystical enthusiasm experienced by initiates of the Mysteries of Dionysus:

> They who betake themselves to the divine service do so not because of any custom or on someone's advice or appeal, but carried away with heavenly love, like those initiated into the Mysteries of Dionysus; they are afire with God until they behold the object of their love.[85]

Describing the coming together of separate groups of men and women in the rites of the Therapeutae, Philo writes:

> When each band has feasted apart by itself, drinking of God-pleasing nectar, just as in the rites of Dionysus men drink the wine unmixed, then they join together, and one chorus is formed of the two bands, in imitation of the joined chorus on the banks of the Red Sea because of the wonderful works that had been there wrought.[86]

That Philo can, in one sentence, compare the Therapeutae to both initiates of the Mysteries of Dionysus and the followers of Moses on the banks of the Red Sea shows just how integrated Pagan and Jewish traditions had become. Such passages can leave us in no doubt that certain Jews had indeed embraced Paganism and combined it with Judaism to produce a specifically Jewish version of the ancient Mysteries.

Here, then, we have found exactly the sort of community, which could have produced the Mysteries of Jesus. And they live exactly where we would expect them to—near that great melting-pot of Pagan and Jewish cultures, Alexandria.

Philo tells us:

> In Egypt there are crowds of them in every province and especially round Alexandria. For they who are in every way the most highly advanced come as colonists, as it were, to the Therapeutic fatherland, to a spot exceedingly well adapted for the purpose, perched on a fairly high terrace overlooking Lake Mareotis, immediately south of Alexandria.[87]

Lake Mareotis is a few miles from where Herodotus witnessed the celebration of the Mysteries of Osiris before tens of thousands of people 500 years previously.[88] Here, Philo tells us, the Therapeutae were also "initiated into the Mysteries of the sanctified life"[89] and, just like the sages of the Pagan Mysteries before them and the Gnostic Christians after them, sought to directly experience "that which is better than the Good and purer and more ancient than the One."[90]

CONCLUSION

Although it may at first have seemed unlikely that Jews could have adopted the Pagan Mysteries, this is clearly exactly what happened. If it were not for our Christian culture, which portrays the Jews as distinct from and in opposition to the Pagan civilizations all around them, this would not seem so extraordinary. Every other culture in the Mediterranean had embraced the Mysteries. It was inevitable that, sooner or later, Hellenized Jews would also integrate this universal mysticism with Judaism. Let's review some of the evidence:

- ❖ Pagan and Jewish cultures have met and integrated throughout history.
- ❖ By the time that Jesus is supposed to have lived, Galilee was surrounded by Hellenized cities, which were the home of eminent Pagan philosophers and centers for the Mysteries of Dionysus.
- ❖ In Babylon Jews were renowned for their knowledge of Pagan astrology and practiced the Mysteries of Tammuz. These Mysteries are recorded in the Old Testament as having been practiced by Jews in Jerusalem itself. Jews associated Jehovah with Osiris-Dionysus and were expelled from Rome for introducing the Mysteries of Sabazius.
- ❖ Jews adopted the Greek language, joined Greek *gymnasia*, rewrote the Exodus as a Greek-style play, translated Jewish scripture under the influence of Pagan philosophy, and wrote new scriptures combining Jewish and Pagan motifs.
- ❖ Jewish philosophers claimed that Greek philosophers had received their wisdom from the Old Testament prophet Moses, thus portraying Paganism and Judaism as essentially parts of the same religious tradition.

- Philo the Pythagorean claimed to be a hierophant in the Mysteries of Moses, which resemble the Pagan Mysteries.
- The Therapeutae are Jewish Pythagoreans.
- Like initiates of the Pagan Mysteries, the Therapeutae believed that their myths encoded secret mystical truths.
- Philo compares the Therapeutae to the followers of Dionysus.
- The Therapeutae lived by a lake near Alexandria where the Mysteries of Osiris had been celebrated for hundreds of years.

Were the Therapeutae of Alexandria proto-Christians? Alexandria was the center of Pagan mysticism in late antiquity, had the largest Jewish population outside Judea, and was the home of the greatest masters of the Christian Gnosis during the first few centuries CE. Clement tells us that it was here that the Gospel of Mark, the earliest New Testament gospel, was written. It is the most obvious place for the Jesus Mysteries to have been created.

Did the Therapeutae, having developed their own version of the ancient Mysteries, take the logical next step? Did they also adopt the Mystery myth of Osiris-Dionysus and rework it as the story of a Jewish dying and resurrecting godman called Jesus? The answer is we simply do not know. However, that the Mysteries were being practiced by Jews strongly supports the idea that some such group of Jewish initiates, quite possibly the Therapeutae themselves, were responsible for creating the Jesus story.

The mystical wisdom of the Mysteries was encoded in the myth of Osiris-Dionysus. Surely it would have been irresistible, having created a specifically Jewish form of the Mysteries, not to also adapt this great ancient myth? Hellenized Jews had rewritten the Exodus as a Greek play in the style of Euripides. Why not also rewrite Euripides' *The Bacchae*, in which Dionysus comes to Thebes, as a Jewish tragedy in which the godman comes to Jerusalem?

We were by now completely convinced that the Jesus Mysteries Thesis was the only credible explanation of all the evidence we had before us. But there were still a few intriguing questions that remained unanswered. We knew that the Jesus story was a myth, but how had it come to be interpreted as history? How had Paul's mythical Christ become the man from Nazareth that is portrayed in the gospels? Pagan stories of the dying and resurrecting godman did not claim to relate actual events, so why was the Jesus story presented as a literal biography?

To answer these questions we decided to deconstruct the Jesus myth itself, to discover how it had been created and how it had come to be historicized. The key to understanding its construction, we realized, is to recognize something so obvious it is staggering that it has been so easily missed. The hero of the Jewish Mystery myth is a composite character. Jesus is a synthesis of two pre-existing mythical figures: the Pagan godman and the Jewish Messiah.

10

The Jesus Myth

My favorite definition of religion is "a misinterpretation of mythology." And the misinterpretation consists precisely in attributing historical references to symbols which properly are spiritual in their reference.[1]

Joseph Campbell

When Pythagoras and his followers introduced the Egyptian Mysteries into Greece they did not simply set up a cult of Osiris. The Mysteries of Osiris contained doctrines that were deeply heretical in fifth-century BCE Athens, especially the idea that a god could die.[2] So, to avoid simply being shunned and persecuted for introducing a foreign superstition, the Pythagoreans transformed a minor Greek deity, Dionysus, into a Greek version of the mighty figure of Osiris. In this way, the Greeks were introduced to the Egyptian Mysteries in a form that seemed indigenous to themselves.[3] This approach was adopted by all other Mediterranean cultures, which embraced the Mysteries. They also transformed an indigenous deity into the dying and resurrecting godman.

A Jewish Pythagorean community such as Philo's Therapeutae wishing to introduce the ancient Mysteries to the Jews would have faced very similar problems to those encountered by the Pythagoreans five centuries previously. In order to make the Mysteries easily accessible to Jews they needed an indigenous mythological figure they could transform into a Jewish Osiris-Dionysus.

The Jews had dispensed with all gods and goddesses, and worshiped only their one God, Jehovah. But while Jehovah could be equated with Plato's supreme Oneness, he did not have a mythological biography like the Pagan gods, which could be adapted to become the Osiris-Dionysus myth. Unlike other cultures the Jews had no minor deities, so there was only one Jewish mythological figure who could possibly be transformed into Osiris-Dionysus: the Messiah.

The Hebrew word *Messiah* means "Anointed," which in Greek is "Christ." The term was originally used to designate kings and high priests, who were ritually anointed with oil. In the Old Testament it is frequently used to refer to the reigning king.[4] In later years, when the Jews were a conquered and defeated people, it came to signify a future redeemer who would come to free them from their oppressors and restore the Jewish state under a king of the line of their great King David.[5] After the Roman occupation of Judea in 63 BCE the situation for the Jews became increasingly desperate and it seemed that only a cosmic act of God could break the vast Empire, which persecuted them, so the Messiah came to be seen as a supernatural figure whose arrival would herald the end of time.[6]

The construction of the Jesus story suggests that the creators of the Jewish Mysteries took the only option available to them and synthesized the dying and resurrecting godman of the Mysteries with the Jewish Messiah. The gospels clearly state that Jesus is the Messiah. He is claimed to be born in Bethlehem from the line of David—just as the Messiah must be. He is called the Messiah by Peter.[7] He is even named Joshua (Jesus in Greek), which was the expected name of the Messiah.[8] Yet Jesus the Messiah is actually only a thin veil concealing the quite different figure of Jesus the dying and resurrecting godman.

This is particularly clear from the accounts of his birth. Both Matthew and Luke give us long and detailed genealogies to show that Joseph is of the line of David (see pp. 139–40), yet both of them also tell us that Jesus is not Joseph's son at all, but God's son. It is remarkable that so many commentators pass over the extraordinary contradiction within these two gospels without offering any convincing explanation. Did Matthew and Luke not realize the absurdity of what they were saying? Even if it is a result of later additions and bad editing, surely such a paradox could not have been unintentionally allowed to remain in the gospels!

The Jesus Mysteries Thesis, however, solves this otherwise strange enigma by suggesting that the gospel writers were well aware of the contradiction they were setting up. They knew that what they were writing was a myth encoding secret teachings. So, they each presented a genealogy to make it appear that Jesus was the Jewish Messiah, son of David, while at the same time telling those "with ears to hear" that Jesus was actually Osiris-Dionysus, the Son of God and a virgin mother.

The genealogies given by Luke and Matthew are entirely different because they are literary constructs and really have no importance. What matters is that through the vehicle of the Messiah the Jews are given access to the Mystery teachings encoded in the myth of Osiris-Dionysus. As Origen explains, "breaks in the narrative structure, irrational and impossible situations" were all placed in the scriptures deliberately to make sure that readers did not get caught in the lowest literal interpretation for too long, for "if the sequence and elegance of the narrative were obvious throughout, we would not believe that anything other than the obvious meaning could be meant in the scriptures." "Certain snares" and "obstacles and impossibilities" are interwoven into scripture to prevent the reader "sticking to the letter, and not learning its more divine meaning."[9]

In this manner, while conforming as much as possible to Jewish expectations about the Messiah, the Jesus story makes it plain that this is not his true identity.[10] For example, the Jewish Messiah was expected to be a warrior king come to liberate Judea from her enemies and re-establish the line of David. Yet at his trial Jesus clearly announces:

> My kingdom does not belong to this world. If it did, my followers would be fighting to save me from arrest by the Jews. My kingly authority comes from elsewhere.[11]

When Peter tells Jesus he believes him to be the Messiah, Jesus neither affirms nor denies it, but simply predicts that the Son of Man must die and resurrect. When Peter rebukes him because the Jewish Messiah cannot die in this way, Jesus rebukes him back, calling him Satan! Peter is condemned for being unable to make the transition from the Jewish idea of the savior as victorious Messiah to the Pagan conception of the savior as sacrificed godman.[12]

For traditional Jews it was unthinkable that the Messiah, who was expected to ride in triumph over all of Judea's enemies, could possibly die as a common criminal. Indeed, the Old Testament Book of Deuteronomy specifically says that "Anyone hanged on a tree is accursed"[13]—the very description given by Peter as the fate of Jesus.[14] In Judaism the Messiah was not thought of as someone who would save by his own sacrificial death. This is the role of Osiris-Dionysus. In his death and resurrection, therefore, Jesus is revealed not as the Jewish Messiah destined to bring military victory and national salvation, but as the godman of the Mysteries who brings spiritual victory and mystical salvation.

To help Jews over the major hurdle of Jesus' ignominious death and obvious lack of military triumph against their oppressors, Jesus is portrayed as claiming that he will return again. Having accomplished the death and resurrection of Osiris-Dionysus, he promises an imminent Second Coming when he will return in glory to smite his enemies and fulfill the expectations of the Jewish Messiah.

JEWISH MYTHICAL MOTIFS

Studying the Jesus story it is obvious that the creators of the Jesus Mysteries adapted pre-existing Jewish mythology to marry their myth of the dying and resurrecting godman with Judaism. The Jewish meal of Passover, for example, was transformed into the sacramental meal of the Mysteries simply by having Jesus offer bread and wine as symbols of his body and blood.

The Passover occurs in the Old Testament myth of the Exodus in which Moses leads his people from captivity in Egypt across the desert to the promised land. This was a favorite tale of Hellenized Jews, especially Philo, and forms the basis for a number of elements in the Jesus story. Mystical Jews understood the Exodus as an allegory of spiritual initiation. The Jewish people start off as "captives" in Egypt, are "called out of Egypt" by Moses, and are finally led as the "chosen people" to the promised land by the prophet Joshua. Here then are the three stages of initiation we have already found in both Gnosticism and the Pagan Mysteries: the initiate is first a "captive" (a Hylic), then is baptized to become one of the "called" (a Psychic) and finally is initiated to become one of the "chosen" (a Pneumatic).[15] Someone was regarded as "captive" while identified with his body and blind to his true spiritual identity. Egypt was seen as a metaphor for the body and to "come forth out of Egypt" was seen as symbolizing transcending identification with the body. The miraculous crossing of the Red Sea was understood as a metaphor for baptism by water. A baptized initiate was regarded as one of those "called" to make the spiritual journey. The afflictions experienced by the Jews during their 40 years wandering in the wilderness were seen as a metaphor for the initiate's experience of being afflicted by doubts and uncertainties. The "chosen" were those who reached the promised land, symbolizing the promise of Gnosis at the end of the spiritual journey.

The motif of being "called out of Egypt" appears in Matthew's gospel, where the pregnant Mary is portrayed as an exile in Egypt before she returns to Judea to give birth to Jesus. God then declares: "Out of Egypt I have called my Son."[16] In an age obsessed by hidden meanings, the double resonance in this motif must have delighted the creators of the Jesus myth. Here they were able to echo the initiation allegory of the Exodus story in which the Jews are called out of Egypt and at the same time tell the initiated reader the place from which the Jesus Mysteries truly originated—ancient Egypt.[17]

Moses' 40 years wandering in the wilderness, plagued by serpents and so forth, become Jesus' 40 days and 40 nights in the wilderness, in which he is plagued by doubts and temptations in the form of the Devil. Moses does not himself make it to the promised land, but appoints the prophet Joshua to lead the chosen people to their final destination in his place.[18] Hence Joshua (Greek: Jesus) was the name selected for the Jewish Osiris-Dionysus who leads his chosen people to the promised land of mystical rebirth.[19] Joshua represents the New Covenant of the Jewish Mysteries, which replaces the old laws and traditions represented by Moses. His first task is to appoint 12 followers.[20] Likewise in the Jesus myth one of Jesus' first acts is to select the 12 disciples.

Various other elements in the Jesus story were obviously suggested by Jewish mythology. Jesus' entry into Jerusalem on an ass, for example, draws on Pagan myth, but also echoes the Old Testament Book of Zechariah, which reads: "Behold the king is coming riding on an ass, rejoice daughters of Jerusalem."[21] Such passages are often referred to by the gospel writers and other early Christians as prophecies which prove the truth of Jesus' divine nature. In the light of the Jesus Mysteries Thesis, however, they can be seen as the mythological motifs from which the story was constructed.

Hellenized Jews in Alexandria had for centuries been searching the Jewish scriptures to find resemblances with Pagan philosophy and the myths of Osiris-Dionysus. Many of the Old Testament books, particularly Psalms, have their origins in Egyptian poetry and wisdom literature, so veiled references to the myths of Osiris were easy to find.[22] These could then become the basis upon which to build a Jewish myth of Osiris, which was also rooted in Judaism. This process is particularly clear in The Gospel of Peter, which didn't make it into the New Testament. Almost every sentence in the passion narrative of this gospel is based on scriptural references in the Old Testament.[23]

In the third and second centuries BCE Jewish scriptures were translated into Greek by Hellenized Jews in Alexandria. This gave them the opportunity to create similarities between Jewish mythology and Pagan mythology, which were not there beforehand. The Book of Isaiah, for example, prophesies that "a young woman will conceive and give birth to a son," but this is mistranslated in the Greek version as "a virgin will conceive and give birth to a son," bringing it into line with the Pagan idea of the virgin birth.[24] This then became a key "proof text" in Jewish scripture used by early Christians to support the claim that Jesus was the long-awaited Jewish Messiah!

In the Gospel of Mark Jesus is made to quote from Psalm 22 on the cross: "My God, why hast thou forsaken me?"[25] This psalm also contains the lines: "The assembly of the wicked have enclosed me: they pierced my hands and my feet."[26] Hence in the gospels Jesus is crucified by having his hands and feet pierced with nails. The psalm goes on: "They part my garments among them, and cast lots upon my vesture."[27] Hence in the gospels Jesus' garments are divided by lot among the Roman centurions overseeing his crucifixion.

ADAPTING THE PAST

To create the Jesus myth the initiates of the Jewish Mysteries also drew on the inter-testamental literature, which had already synthesized Pagan and Jewish mythological motifs. These inter-testamental texts not only echo the Pagan Mysteries but also prefigure Christianity, forming a bridge between the two.[28] The Jewish *Sibylline Oracles*, for example, talk of a coming apocalypse of cosmic fire on the day of judgment and peace on Earth for the faithful. They are full of missionary zeal, which is rare in Jewish literature but found both in the Mysteries and in Christianity. They also look forward to the coming of a Christ—a hope that Christianity claims to fulfill.[29]

Motifs that echo the Mysteries and prefigure Christianity are also found in the Books of Enoch.[30] Like Jesus, Enoch is said to have been physically raised up to heaven.[31] On his arrival he is greeted as "the Son of Man"[32]—a title which Jesus will inherit.

This title conveys the idea that Enoch and Jesus are both to be understood as Everyman characters who mythically represent all of mankind. The Hebrew expression *son of* means "the embodiment of."[33] The Son of Man is an embodiment of the idea of the primal Man. This is another way of conveying the same idea that St. John expresses when he says that Jesus is the Logos made flesh. Jesus and Enoch are to be understood as embodiments of the Universal Daemon, the One Consciousness that animates all beings. Just like Jesus, the embodiment of the Logos, the Son of Man in *The Books of Enoch* is a divine being who has existed with God from the beginning. Also like Jesus, the Enochian Son of Man is called "a messenger from God," "the Christ of the invisible God," and "a light to the Gentiles."[34]

The inter-testamental Wisdom Literature tells of the "righteous man" who is a divine emissary sent to bring wisdom into the world. This figure, who echoes the earlier Pagan "just man," becomes the Christian "righteous man," Jesus. Like Jesus, he is rejected by humanity,[35] makes claims that evoke hostility,[36] is maltreated, comes into conflict with the authorities, dies,[37] and is finally recognized by his enemies as the "Son of God."[38]

The Nag Hammadi library of early Gnostic gospels has given us two manuscripts which, if read together, show just how easily a pre-existing text could be Christianized.[39] A non-Christian treatise called *The Initiated Good Gnostic*[40] has been somewhat arbitrarily cut up into separate speeches, which have then been put into Jesus' mouth in answer to his disciples' questions. The result is a Christian text called *The Wisdom of Jesus Christ*.[41] The Christian and non-Christian texts are almost identical apart from the addition of Jesus and his disciples. The following are some short examples:

THE INITIATED GOOD GNOSTIC	THE WISDOM OF JESUS CHRIST
	Matthew said to him: "Lord, no one can find the truth except through you. Therefore teach us the truth." The Savior said:
"He Who Is" is ineffable. No principle knew him, no authority, no subjection, nor any creature	"'He Who Is' is ineffable. No principle knew him, no authority, no subjection, nor any creature

from the foundation of the world, except he alone . . .

from the foundation of the world, except he alone . . ."

Philip said: "Lord, how then, did he appear to the perfect ones?" The perfect Savior said to him: "Before anything is visible

Before anything is visible among those that are visible, the majesty and the authorities that are in him, he embraces the totalities of the totalities, and nothing embraces him. For he is all mind . . .

among those that are visible, the majesty and the authorities that are in him, he embraces the totalities of the totalities, and nothing embraces him. For he is all mind . . ."

Matthew said to him: "Lord, Savior, how was man revealed?" The perfect Savior said, "I want you to know that he who

The First who appeared before the universe is Self-grown, Self-constructed Father, and is full of shining, ineffable light.

appeared before the universe in infinity, Self-grown, Self-constructed Father, being full of shining light and ineffable."

MYTH BECOMES HISTORY

The Pagan Mystery godmen were clearly mythological figures whose biographies existed "out of time" in the world of dreams and images. If they were regarded as having literally lived at all, it was in ancient times indistinguishable from myth. So why does the Jesus story present the myth of the Jewish godman as if it were history?

The genuine letters of Paul, as we have seen, show no sign of the Jesus story having assumed a historical setting in the first half of the first century. Paul preaches a mystical Messiah who, through his death and resurrection, brings rebirth to his followers. Such a primitive form of the Jesus myth could well have been around for hundreds of years.[42] It would have initially been a secret myth of the Jewish Mysteries, so we would not expect any evidence of its existence to have survived. Sooner or later, however, it was inevitable that the Jesus myth would become historicized.

Jews expected the Messiah to be a historical figure who literally came to rescue his people. So, if the Jewish Osiris-Dionysus was to be convincingly portrayed as the Messiah, the myth would have to be recast as a historical drama. Yet Jesus could not be said to have existed in the distant past like the Pagan Mystery godman, because such a Messiah could not bring political salvation to his people now. He would have to be portrayed as coming in the recent past, as this alone would make him relevant. To explain why no one had heard of the coming of the Messiah, Jesus is made to deliberately keep his Messiahship a secret. Indeed, Mark portrays even Jesus' closest disciples as failing to recognize him as the Messiah until after his death.[43]

The Old Testament, although interpreted as mystical allegory by Hellenized Jews such as Philo, appears on the surface to be a historical record. Portraying the Jesus story as a record of actual events would, therefore, have fitted it into the general style of Jewish scriptures; and the time and place chosen as the setting for Jesus' life and death could be used by Jewish initiates, skilled in allegory, to encode symbolic messages.

The Jewish godman was given the name Joshua/Jesus after the prophet of Exodus Joshua ben Nun, whose name means "Jesus son of the Fish." This is perfect for a savior figure designed for the new astrological Age of Pisces, symbolized by the Fish. The time chosen for Jesus' "birth" links him to an important astrological conjunction in 7 BCE, which ushered in the New Age of Pisces.[44] This stellar conjunction also becomes the star that prefigures the birth of the godman in Pagan myth. Thus Jesus symbolically becomes the new savior for a New Age.

The time of Jesus' birth also enabled the creators of the Jesus Mysteries to symbolically convey other information. According to Matthew, Jesus is born in the reign of Herod, who tries to have him killed as a baby to prevent him becoming king of the Jews. Herod, who died in 4 BCE, was a puppet of the Romans and completely loathed by the Jews.[45] Bringing the infant Jesus into immediate conflict with the hated king already fits Jesus into the model of the "just man unjustly accused" and portrays him as the Messiah come to defend the Jews. Luke makes a similar point by having his Jesus born 10 years later at the time of the census of 6 CE. By then the Romans had finally annexed Judea and the census was to enable them to directly tax the Jews. Judea no longer even had its own puppet administration, but was now ruled by a Roman governor. This led to desperate hopes that the Messiah would arise to protect his people and by placing Jesus' birth at this time, Luke implies that this hope has been fulfilled.

The only other event that places Jesus in a historical context is his death under the Roman governor of Judea, Pontius Pilate. According to Josephus and Philo, Pilate was particularly detested by the Jews.[46] He had violated Jewish religious taboos many times, including being the first Roman to defile the Jerusalem Temple.[47] Pilate was, therefore, the perfect choice for the role of the evil tyrant who executes the godman.

It is also relevant that the Jesus story is set in Galilee. Galilee was so thoroughly Hellenized that it was known among the Jews as "the land of the Gentiles."[48] Josephus records that Galilee refused to defend Jerusalem against the Romans.[49] Galilee was not loyal to the Temple cult of Jerusalem and had close relations with Pagan cultures. So it was an ideal setting for the home of the Jewish Osiris-Dionysus.

The process through which the original timeless and locationless Jesus story became set in a particular time and place can be seen in the Gospel of Mark. Scholars have noticed that all the passages that mention Galilee are later additions.[50] For example, in the line "And passing along by the sea of Galilee he saw Simon and Andrew,"[51] the words "by the sea of Galilee" are placed quite ungrammatically in the Greek syntax.[52] This has led most New Testament scholars to believe that they were added to give a geographical location to a story that previously lacked it.[53]

AN ALTERNATIVE MESSIAH

In 66 CE Jews in Judea revolted against their Roman oppressors, leading to horrendous reprisals. Josephus claims that out of a population of 3,000,000 Jews 1,000,000 died and a further 100,000 were sold into slavery.[54] When Jerusalem finally fell it was left nothing more than smoldering ruins. Josephus writes:

> All the rest of the fortifications encircling the city were so completely leveled with the ground that no one visiting the spot would believe it had once been inhabited. This then was the end to which the mad folly of revolutionaries brought Jerusalem, a magnificent city renowned to the ends of the earth.[55]

Traditional Judaism had been in its death throes since 63 BCE when the corrupt Temple priests had themselves invited in the Romans to settle their internal disputes and in so doing put their country on the road to Roman domination. By 70 CE, when the Romans destroyed Jerusalem, many Jews felt completely betrayed by their god Jehovah, who had clearly failed to protect them from their enemies. Such sentiments were expressed in the Jewish literature of the time. In *The Apocalypse of Baruch*, for example, the prophet Baruch insistently interrogates Jehovah as if he were a defendant on trial: why has God allowed Jerusalem to be captured, its Temple destroyed, its people dispersed? Baruch tells the Jewish priests to "take the keys of the sanctuary and hurl them at the heavens," commanding Jehovah to guard his own house![56] The only hope that is offered in this bleak work is that the Messiah will finally come.

It was at some point after these disastrous events that the Jesus myth was first put into a historical context by the Gospel of Mark. This suggests that it was this crisis that forced the creators of the Jesus Mysteries to transform their myth of the dying and resurrecting godman into pseudo-history. In the face of complete national catastrophe Jews needed more than Paul's mystical Christ. They needed a Messiah who had actually come to save them as promised.

The crisis in Judaism did throw up many would-be Messiahs, all of whom failed. These men, known derogatorily as *zealots* or *bandits*, combined the role of political revolutionary and religious fanatic in a way comparable to modern Muslim fundamentalists. The pro-Roman Josephus writes:

> These cheats and deceivers who claimed to be inspired schemed to bring about revolutionary changes by inducing the mob to act as if possessed, and by leading them out into the wild country on the pretense that there God would show them signs of approaching freedom.[57]

Many of these would-be Messiahs took the name of Joshua/Jesus. Josephus describes Judea as being full of such "brigands," "impostors," and "miracle-workers" who "deceive the people" and "promise deliverance." Some tried to repeat the miracle of the Exodus by leading their followers out into the desert where Jehovah would deliver them. One assembled a great company on the Mount of Olives, promising, like a second Joshua, that the city's walls would fall at his command and that he would lead his followers to slaughter the Roman garrison.[58]

In contrast, the Jesus myth presents a quite different Messiah. Jesus is not a political revolutionary. When questioned about taxes, he tells his followers to give to Caesar what is Caesar's.[59] His message is of mystical salvation, not national liberation. It is interesting to note that his betrayer, Judas, is given the same name as Judas of Galilee, the most infamous of all the zealot leaders, casting the fundamentalist zealots in a negative light.[60]

The Jesus story would seem to be consciously created to give disillusioned Jews an alternative to the disastrous revolutionary Messiahs who were merely making matters worse. Hellenized Jews, while loyal to their national traditions and having nationalistic aspirations, regarded the zealots with the same horror that modern Westernized Muslims regard fanatical Muslim fundamentalists. They realized that the zealots were in the process of bringing disaster upon their country and the events of 70 CE confirmed all their worst fears. Hellenized Jews living in Alexandria looked for some way of helping their compatriots streaming out of Judea as refugees.

The desperation of the times cannot be exaggerated.[61] In the face of the failure of the nationalist Messiah to arrive in their hour of need, the Jesus Mysteries presented to Jews a mystical alternative, a way of restoring meaning to their shattered lives, rekindling some pride in their national identity, and integrating themselves into wider Pagan society. New initiates were attracted to the Jesus Mysteries by being told the quasi-historical story of Jesus, but later, when their understanding had increased, they were initiated into the Inner Mysteries, which revealed the Jesus story as a mystical analogy. Thus, dispossessed and disaffected Jewish refugees were offered hope. The expected political savior who would set the Jewish people free was transformed into a spiritual savior who could set each individual free through mystical Gnosis.

Ironically, however, the Jesus Mysteries did not really take off within the Jewish community. The fate of this new faith was to be far stranger than anyone could possibly have imagined at the time. Within 100 years the Pagan godman disguised as the Jewish Messiah, who was designed to introduce the Pagan Mysteries to the Jews, was actually bringing Jewish traditions to Pagans!

A UNIVERSAL SAVIOR

Jesus was destined not to remain a Jewish Messiah but to become a universal savior. This process of internationalization had already begun by the time of Paul's heated debates with the Ebionite Christians. Paul was fighting to free the Jesus Mysteries from unnecessary ties to Judaism and to make them attractive to more Hellenized Jews like himself. For him, the traditional Jewish Law was only relevant, if at all, to Psychic Christians. The new (essentially Pagan) teachings of the Jesus Mysteries had rendered the old Jewish ways redundant. The "circumcisionaries" against whom Paul argued, by contrast, wished to keep the Jesus Mysteries distinctively Jewish. These more traditional Jewish-Christians were found in Jerusalem, the heart of Judaism, whereas Paul was a highly Hellenized Jew traveling from one Pagan city to another.

For all his zeal, Paul failed in his mission of winning Jewish converts to the Jesus Mysteries. At Ephesus he is said to have preached for three months in the synagogue without any results. At Antioch the Jews even attacked him. Disguising Osiris-Dionysus as the Jewish Messiah in order to smuggle the Pagan godman into Judaism was a cunning idea, but most Jews saw through this ploy very easily. A Messiah who was crucified as a criminal was not the savior they were waiting for. Christianity appeared to them as a confusing and heretical doctrine of a failed Messiah.

But when Paul turned to the Greeks he at once achieved extraordinary successes.[62] As one modern scholar remarks:

> We are compelled to admit there was something which on the one hand offended Jewish ideas, and on the other, conformed to Greek ideas. I hope I shall not be misunderstood if I say that Christ must have appeared to the Greeks as a hero. Christianity is, from a merely historical viewpoint, an enormous Greek hero cult devoted to a Jewish Messiah.[63]

To Pagans this was a new exotic Mystery cult that incorporated elements of the intriguing Jewish tradition with the perennial wisdom of the Pagan Mysteries. As the unattractive baggage of the old Jewish Laws had been dumped by Paul, there was nothing to stop Gentiles from embracing the Jesus Mysteries. Moreover, once the myth had become historicized, the new cult of

Christianity had the added appeal that it made a genuinely revolutionary claim—that the godman had actually walked the Earth in the recent past.

By the middle of the second century the Jesus Mysteries had been largely rejected by the Jewish community but embraced by Gentiles. Jesus was no longer portrayed as coming to save the Jews, but as coming to save the whole of humanity. Gentile Christians rejected the old Jewish traditions, as Paul had desired, so this was no longer an issue. But by this time, however, the Christian community had begun to split again into two distinct and antagonistic factions—Literalism and Gnosticism.

THE BIRTH OF LITERALISM

After 70 CE when the Romans laid waste to Jerusalem, Jews were spread throughout the Roman Empire as slaves and refugees. Jews who had been initiated in only the Outer Mysteries, with limited half-baked ideas of what Christianity was all about, would have been flung far and wide around the ancient world, taking what they believed to be the "biography" of Jesus the Messiah with them. Those in the western areas of the Empire became cut off from the established centers of the Jesus Mysteries in Alexandria and the eastern areas of the Empire, and so were prevented from completing the process of initiation.

With no masters of the Gnosis within hundreds of miles, it is easy to imagine how a confused form of the Jesus Mysteries would quickly develop. Within a few decades these western Christians had created a religion in which the belief that Jesus was literally the dying and resurrecting Son of God was the central doctrine. Their Literalist Christianity had no place for any Inner Mysteries. It did not view the gospels as allegories, but as historical records of actual events.

During the second century, the leaders of local groups of Christians became known as *overseers* or bishops. Without any Inner Mysteries to impart, these bishops taught that eternal salvation was guaranteed to anyone who simply believed the story of Jesus to be literally true. It is this limited form of Christianity, based only on the Outer Mysteries, which would eventually become the Roman Catholic Church.

The original Jesus Mysteries, which we now call Gnosticism, continued to flourish where they had originated, in Alexandria. This city produced the great second- and third-century Gnostic masters Carpocrates, Basilides, Valentinus, Clement, and Origen. Literalism, on the other hand, gathered strength in those areas of the Empire that were cut off from the masters of the Gnosis in the East, eventually becoming centered on Rome itself, where it took on a narrow autocratic Roman character.

Early initiates of the Jesus Mysteries formed many separate groups in different places, often centered around a particular master of the Gnosis and working with their own gospels. The Gnostics maintained this tradition of mysticism, variety, and tolerance. The Literalists, by contrast, began to build a centralized authoritarian religion.

It is easy to imagine how those initiated in the Inner Mysteries would have looked on aghast at the growth of Literalism, now completely out of their control and beginning to spring up across the ancient world as a new religious cult. Many masters of the Inner Mysteries visited Rome in order to initiate Christians into the Gnosis, but they were not welcomed. Literalist bishops were not at all pleased to have some foreign mystic proclaim them to be mere "Psychic Christians" in need of a further Pneumatic initiation. They were resentful of Gnostic sages "stealing their flock" by belittling Literalist teachings and offering initiation into the secret Inner Mysteries.

The Gnostics, who had created the Jesus story in the first place, were now accused of perverting the sacred teachings of the savior. Irenaeus, the mouthpiece of Literalism, protested that Gnostics "overthrow the faith of many, by drawing them away under the pretense of superior Knowledge."[64] Conflict was inevitable and a bitter battle for the soul of Christianity ensued.

CONCLUSION

At last we felt we had found the real Jesus. He is the Mystery godman incognito! He is the mythical "Son of God" camouflaged as the historical "Son of David."

It was now clear to us why, unlike all the other myths of Osiris-Dionysus, the Jesus story had been given a historical setting and how, once this had happened, the growth of Literalism was unavoidable.

Let us review some of what we have discovered about the Jesus myth and its development:

- Jesus is Osiris-Dionysus thinly disguised as the Jewish Messiah in order to make the Pagan Mysteries accessible to Jews. His composite nature is particularly clear from the contradictory accounts of his birth, which portray him both as the Messiah in the line of David and Osiris-Dionysus the Son of God.
- In the gospels Jesus makes it clear that he is really the dying and resurrecting Son of God, not the expected Jewish Messiah.
- Although he conforms to Jewish expectations about the Messiah as much as possible, by his death and resurrection Jesus is shown to actually be Osiris-Dionysus.
- As well as Pagan mythological motifs, the Jesus story draws on Jewish mythological motifs, especially from the story of the Exodus.
- The Jesus story draws on concepts and images developed in Jewish intertestamental literature that synthesize Jewish and Pagan ideas.
- In some texts the name Jesus has simply been added to turn pre-Christian treatises into Christian documents.
- The Jewish Messiah was expected to be a historical figure, which meant that the Jesus story would have to be cast in a historical setting.
- The creators of the Jesus Mysteries used the time and place chosen as the setting for Jesus' life to encode symbolic messages. The time of Jesus' birth links him to the birth of the New Age of Pisces and brings him into conflict immediately with the hated King Herod and the Romans. The time of his death brings him into conflict with the particularly loathed Roman official Pontius Pilate.
- In 70 CE the Romans laid waste to Jerusalem, fueling the Jews' desperate desire for a savior. This crisis put external pressure on the historicization process of the Jesus story and produced the Gospel of Mark from the mystical timeless Christ preached by Paul.
- The Jesus Mysteries presented to Jews a mystical Messiah as an alternative to all the fundamentalist zealot Messiahs causing havoc in Judea at the time.
- Although transforming the Jewish Messiah into Osiris-Dionysus in order to introduce the Pagan godman to the Jews was a clever idea, it didn't work. The Jesus Mysteries were rejected by Jews but embraced by Pagans as a new Mystery cult.
- After 70 CE Jews with knowledge only of the Outer Mysteries of Christianity were spread around the Roman Empire as slaves and refugees. Those in the West, cut off from the masters of the Gnosis in the East,

developed a new religion, based only on the Outer Mysteries, which preached a historical Jesus.

❖ The original Jesus Mysteries, now called Gnosticism, continued to flourish in the East.

❖ By the middle of the second century the Gnostics, who had created the Jesus story in the first place, were being attacked by Literalist Christians as heretics who had perverted genuine Christianity.

In synthesizing the perennial myth of the dying and resurrecting godman with Jewish expectations of a historical Messiah the creators of the Jewish Mysteries took an unprecedented step, the outcome of which they could never have guessed. And yet, upon analysis, the end was already there in the beginning. The Messiah was expected to be a historical, not a mythical, savior. It was inevitable, therefore, that the Jesus story would have to develop a quasi-historical setting. And so it did. What had started as a timeless myth encoding perennial teachings now appeared to be a historical account of a once-only event in time. From this point it was unavoidable that sooner or later it would be interpreted as historical fact. Once it was, a whole new type of religion came into being—a religion based on history not myth, on blind faith in supposed events rather than on a mystical understanding of mythical allegories, a religion of the Outer Mysteries without the Inner Mysteries, of form without content, of belief without Knowledge.

One final part of the puzzle was left for us to put into place. How did Christianity develop from a minor Mystery cult into the most influential religion of all time? And why was it that the Christianity that eventually came to dominate the world was not the grand and ancient mysticism of the Gnostics, but the narrow authoritarianism of the Literalists?

11

An Imitation Church

And there shall be others who are outside our number who name themselves bishop and also deacons, as if they have received their authority from God. These people are dry canals. They do business in my word. They praise the men who propagate falsehood. They cleave to the name of a dead man, thinking that they will become pure.[1]

Jesus in *The Apocalypse of Peter*

From the beginning of its history up to the present day, Christianity has been a religion of schism and conflict. There is not a single document in the New Testament that does not warn of false teachers or attack other Christians! At the end of the second century the Pagan satirist Celsus writes:

> Christians, it is needless to say, utterly detest each other. They slander each other constantly with the vilest forms of abuse, and cannot come to any sort of agreement in their teaching.[2]

He explains:

> At the start of their movement, they were very few in number, and unified in purpose. Since that time, they have spread all around and now number in the thousands. It is not surprising, therefore, that there are divisions among them—factions of all sorts, each wanting to have its own territory. Nor is it surprising that as these divisions have become so numerous, the various parties have taken to

condemning each other, so that today they have only one thing, if that, in common—the name "Christian." But despite them clinging proudly to their name, in most other respects they are at odds.[3]

In the first century, the battles in the Christian community were over the relationship of the Jesus Mysteries to traditional Judaism. By the middle of the second century they were between Gnostics and Literalists. The central idea of Literalist Christianity is that the Jesus story, bizarre and mythical as it may appear to be, is in fact a true history of miraculous events. In the face of Gnostic insistence that the Jesus story was actually a mystical allegory, Literalists began categorically asserting that Jesus Christ suffered and was crucified under Pontius Pilate—a statement that was repeated with such fanatical insistence that it reveals just how weak the Literalists felt at this time.[4]

The forged Second Letter of Peter, for example, defensively asserts that Literalist Christians are not following "some well-composed fiction!"[5] The author of letters attributed to Ignatius urges the faithful "not to yield to the bait of false doctrine, but to believe most steadfastly in the birth, the passion, and the resurrection, which took place during the governorship of Pontius Pilate."[6] He insists:

> Jesus Christ, David's offspring and Mary's, was really born of a virgin and baptized by John, really persecuted by Pilate and nailed to the cross in the flesh.[7]

At the end of the second century various letters attributed to the apostles Peter, John, and James were forged to advance the Literalism campaign and to portray the Gnostics as heretics from the true teachings of those who had actually known Jesus. The First Letter of John teaches that the way to discriminate between true teachers and false teachers is that the former acknowledge that Jesus Christ came "in the flesh."[8] In the Second Letter of John (a one-page diatribe against Gnostics!) the author warns:

> The world has been invaded by a host of wrong-headed people who won't accept that Jesus has come as the Messiah in the flesh. If you even say hello to them you're a partner in their evil deeds.[9]

To bolster Literalism, the Jesus story was adapted. The Gospel of John affirms "the Word became flesh," changing Paul's formula "in the likeness of flesh."[10] As well as such adaptations, scholars have isolated numerous additions to the gospels designed to emphasize that Jesus literally resurrected from the grave as a physical human being. In their original form the gospels portrayed the resurrected Jesus as a ghostly spiritual figure. Luke and Mark both relate that Jesus appeared "in another form" to two disciples on the road to Emmaus. According to Luke it was only after the disciples had talked with the stranger for some length of time and invited him to break bread at dinner that they suddenly recognized him as Jesus. At that moment "he vanished out of their sight." However, later verses have been added to portray the resurrected Jesus parading his "flesh and bones" and eating fish to prove his physical existence.[11]

John has the mourning Mary Magdalene see a man she takes to be the gardener at Jesus' grave. When he speaks her name, however, she suddenly recognizes him as Jesus, but he orders her not to touch him.[12] Just after this account, however, the story of "doubting Thomas" has been added, in which Thomas declares that he will not believe that Jesus had actually risen from the grave unless he can personally see and touch him. When Jesus appears, he tells Thomas:

> Put your finger here, and see my hands; and put out your hand, and place it in my side; do not be faithless, but believing.[13]

TAKING THINGS LITERALLY

Literalists took literally what for Gnostics were mystic metaphors. Because they believed that Jesus had literally resurrected from the dead in his physical body, they taught that after death all Christians would likewise literally be resurrected from the grave in their physical bodies. Tertullian declares that anyone who denies the resurrection of the flesh is a heretic, not a true Christian. The Literalists even claimed that the Eucharist bread and wine literally became the flesh and blood of Jesus during the mass—an extraordinary assertion that is still made by the Catholic Church to this day![14]

Taking the Jesus myth as history led Literalists to abandon the Gnostic doctrine of reincarnation. Because Literalists believed that the godman had died and resurrected once only in time, they also conceived of a human life as a once-only event. Afterlife reward or punishment was, therefore, for all time, not a temporary precursor to another human life. This left them with what the Pagan Celsus calls the "offensive doctrine" that a good God could countenance abandoning those who didn't make the grade to an eternity of suffering.[15]

Literalists also interpreted literally the idea of the apocalyptic Second Coming. In the gospels Jesus is made to promise that he will return in glory within the lifetime of some of his audience. The Gnostics, of course, saw this as a mystical metaphor about the resurrection of the initiate as the Christ or Universal Daemon. The Literalists took this "prophecy" at face value and so were left with the difficult task of explaining Jesus' failure to appear as promised.

The forged Second Letter of Peter conveys the obvious unease and confusion in the Literalist Christian community over this issue, and offers its own desperate solution, proclaiming:

> In the final days schemers will come along with their schemes following the lead of their greedy desires and saying "Where is the Second Coming that he promised us? In the meantime our fathers and mothers have died, and the whole world is still just the same as it has been since the beginning of creation." Let this one thing not escape you, dear friends; that a single day for the Lord is like a thousand years, and a thousand years is like a single day. The Lord isn't late in fulfilling His promise; what some call His lateness really is His patience with you. He doesn't want to lose anybody, he wants repentance to include everybody.[16]

Justin Martyr likewise explained that God was delaying the End because he wished to see Christianity spread throughout the world first.[17] Other Literalists came up with the ludicrous idea that St. John had turned into a sort of immortal and was living in Patmos or Ephesus and so Jesus had not got his prophecy wrong after all.[18]

Basing his bizarre and convoluted reasoning on the fact that the Ark of the Covenant was said to have been five-and-a-half cubits long, Hippolytus somehow fixed the End for 202. When this date passed uneventfully it was deferred to 500.[19] By the middle of the third century, for most Christians "the End" was no longer an imminent concern. In the early fifth century, translators of second-century Christian texts omitted all mentions of the imminent

THE JESUS MYSTERIES

apocalypse as they were now just an embarrassment.[20] Despite all of this, of course, many Literalist Christians continued to warn "The End is nigh," as they still do today.

A CHURCH OF BISHOPS

Gnostics offered initiates Gnosis, a here-and-now spiritual experience of a truth beyond the illusion that is the world. Literalists offered the hope of a heavenly afterlife through believing in the historicity of the gospel stories. By doing this, however, they created a difficult dilemma for themselves: why should anyone believe such a supernatural tale as the Jesus story to be literal history? Writing at the end of the second century, Tertullian admits that anyone who judges in terms of ordinary historical experience would find the claim that a man physically returned from the grave to be too incredible to be believed.[21] In the face of this rational doubt, the best he can manage is to argue: "It is true because it is absurd, I believe it because it is impossible."[22] And this from a man routinely claimed in history books to be a great Christian theologian!

In order to present a convincing justification for interpreting the Jesus story as historical fact, the Literalists invented a spiritual lineage, which they claimed connected them directly to the apostles, who had lived some 150 years previously. This meant they could argue that the historicity of the Jesus story was guaranteed by the personal testimonies of those living at the time, testimonies that had been faithfully passed down to them through successive bishops.

Literalists used this fabricated lineage as a powerful weapon in their battles with the Gnostics. Gnostics claimed to teach secret Inner Mysteries of which the Literalists were ignorant. Literalists counter-claimed that they alone were the representatives of a line of apostolic succession stretching back to the 12 disciples.[23] Literalists argued that this invested their bishops with the authority of the original apostles. Even today the Pope traces his primacy to Peter on the basis that, in some accounts, he was meant to be the first eyewitness of the resurrection.[24]

The claim to be heirs to the original disciples was used by Literalist bishops to legitimize their demand for blind obedience from the Christian faithful.[25] Anyone, such as the Gnostics, who opposed their authority was therefore in revolt against Christ. The forged letters attributed to Clement of Rome complain of "rash and self-willed people" who have undertaken a "rebellion."[26] They proclaim that God had delegated his authority to the bishops and so whoever refused to "bow the neck" was guilty of insubordination against Christ.[27] They even go as far as to demand that whoever disobeys the divinely ordained authorities "receive the death penalty!"[28]

Letters attributed to Ignatius likewise warn that the bishop presides "in the place of God." Indeed, the faithful should "revere, honor, and obey the bishop as if he were God!"[29] Without the bishops, priests, and deacons, "there is nothing that can be called a church."[30] The author writes:

> Let no one do anything pertaining to the church without the bishop. Let that be considered a valid eucharist which is celebrated by the bishop, or by the person whom he appoints. It is not legitimate either to baptize or to hold an agape (cult meal) without the bishop. To join with the bishop is to join the church; to separate oneself from the bishop is to separate oneself not only from the church, but from God himself.[31]

These letters argue that as there is only one God in heaven there should be only one head bishop in the Church to whom all are obedient. "One God, one bishop" became the slogan of Literalist Christianity.[32]

The Gnostics, by contrast, organized themselves without hierarchies of bishops and priests. They used the method of drawing lots to decide who should take the role of bishop, priest, reader of the scripture, prophet, and so on. Each time they met they would draw lots once more, so that the roles were constantly circulated. In this way they believed the hand of God would choose the right person for the right job at the right time.[33] The Literalist Tertullian tells us disapprovingly:

> And so it happens that today one man is their bishop, tomorrow another; today someone is a deacon, and tomorrow a reader; today someone is a presbyter who tomorrow is a layman. For even on laymen too, they impose the functions of priesthood.[34]

While the orthodox were constructing a permanent hierarchy of power, Gnostics were demonstrating that they could function as spiritual equals.[35] Tertullian is appalled, writing:

THE JESUS MYSTERIES

I must not omit an account of the conduct of the heretics, how frivolous it is, how merely human, without seriousness, without authority, without discipline, as suits their creed. To begin with, it is doubtful, who is a catechumen and who a believer; they all have access alike, they hear alike, they pray alike—even with Pagans, if any such happen to come among them. As for peace, they observe it with everyone, observing no distinctions. Nor is there any distinction between them, although they hold different doctrines, since they have sworn to join together in fighting against the one truth. All are puffed up, all offer you Gnosis.[36]

Originally men and women sat together in all forms of Christian worship. While the Gnostics continued to respect women as spiritual equals, around the middle of the second century Literalists began to segregate the sexes. By the end of the century women were being prohibited from participating in worship at all and Christian groups in which women held positions of leadership were branded as heretical![37] Tertullian decrees:

It is not permitted for a woman to speak in the church, nor is it permitted for her to teach, nor to baptize, nor to offer the eucharist, nor to claim for herself a share in any masculine function—not to mention any priestly office.[38]

It is extraordinary that at the same time that Gnostics were honoring the goddess and encouraging women priests, the vehemently misogynous Tertullian was berating women on behalf of Literalist Christianity with:

You are the Devil's gateway. You are she who persuaded him whom the Devil did not dare attack. Do you not know that every one of you is an Eve? The sentence of God on your sex lives on in this age; the guilt, of necessity, lives on too.[39]

By the end of the second century, the Literalists had begun to establish rules for who was and who was not a Christian. According to them, a Christian must confess the Literalist creed, be baptized, and above all obey the bishops.[40] For the Gnostics, however, the true Church was "invisible" and only its members could perceive who belonged to it and who did not.[41] Gnostics insisted that it took more than baptism to become a Christian. *The Gospel of Philip* explains that many people "go down to the water and come up without having received anything" and yet claim to be Christians. Nor did profession of a creed or even martyrdom make someone a Christian, since "anyone can do these things." The Gnostics quoted Jesus' saying "By their fruits you shall know them" and demanded evidence of spiritual maturity to demonstrate that a person belonged to the true Church.[42]

Not surprisingly, Literalist bishops saw such Gnostic individualism as a dangerous threat to their authority. Their attacks on Gnosticism became ever more fanatical and extreme. Irenaeus urges that Gnostics should "be recognized as agents of Satan" and warns that: "God has prepared eternal fire for every kind of heresy."[43] "Better a Pagan than a heretic" becomes a constant Literalist refrain.[44] With characteristic lunacy Justin Martyr even insinuates that Gnostics indulge in "cannibalism!"[45]

The author of the New Testament Letter of Jude, a short and rather paranoid polemic written for no other reason than to attack Gnostics, writes:

Dear friends, having every intention of writing to you about our shared salvation, I found myself obliged instead to write you a letter of warning to keep up the fight for the faith as transmitted to the holy ones, once and for all. It seems that certain persons whose damnation is already on the books, with no respect for religion, have insinuated themselves in amongst you, twisting God's good will toward us into a license for debaucheries and defying our one and only overlord and master, Jesus Christ. They pollute the body, disregard authority, and even blaspheme the powers of the universe.[46]

The Gnostics are not merely followers of an alternative form of the Christian faith, but are portrayed as the enemy within—a surreptitious cancer. They "calmly sit beside you, being a blotch upon our love-feasts." They are "stars gone off course whose eternal destiny is the darkness of the pit." The Letter of Jude recommends "avoiding with revulsion so much as a piece of clothing polluted by contact with their bodies."[47] The forger of the letters of Paul to Timothy describes Gnostic teachings as an "infestation" which spreads like "gangrene."[48]

In response, the Gnostics called the Literalist Church authorities "vulgar" and "ecclesiastical."[49] The Gnostic sage Heracleon describes the dogmas of the Literalist Church as "unnourishing, stagnant water" in contrast to the "living water" Christ offers to the elect through Gnosis.[50] *The Testimony of Truth* attacks Literalists who claimed to be Christians, but who "do not know who Christ is."[51] *The Second Treatise of the Great Seth* laments that Gnostics are "hated and persecuted, not only by those who are ignorant, but also by those that think they are advancing the name of Christ," who are "unknowingly empty, not knowing who they are, like dumb animals."[52] In this Gnostic text the savior explains that an "imitation church" has been created which "proclaims a doctrine of a dead man and lies, so as to resemble the freedom and purity of the perfect church."[53]

The Tripartite Tractate contrasts Gnostics who are children of the true Father God with the Literalists who are offspring of the Jewish false-god Jehovah. The Father's children come together in love as equals and spontaneously help one another. Literalist Christians, on the other hand, "want to command one another, outrivaling one another in their empty ambitions." They are inflated with "lust for power, each one imagining that he is superior to the others."[54]

Origen, likewise, complains:

> In many so-called churches, especially those in large cities, one can see rulers of the people of God who do not allow anyone, sometimes not even the noblest of Jesus' disciples, to speak with them on equal terms.[55]

THE VALENTINIANS

Although Literalist Christians had clearly decided that Gnostics were heretics, some Gnostics tried valiantly to maintain the original vision of the Jesus Mysteries by attempting to hold together the ever-widening gulf between the Outer and Inner Mysteries. Following in the original Christian tradition of Paul, sages such as Valentinus viewed the Church as necessarily comprised of both Psychic and Pneumatic Christians. Paul had constantly advised his disciples on how to keep these two levels of the Church living together harmoniously. Valentinus and his followers saw it as their duty, therefore, to try and reconcile Psychic (Literalist) and Pneumatic (Gnostic) Christians.

Paul discriminated between his *logos* (his Pneumatic teachings) and his *kerygma* (his Psychic teachings),[56] yet he also insisted that all Christians "confess the same thing" to avoid destructive schisms within the community.[57] Paul advised Pneumatics[58] to keep their understanding a secret "between yourselves and God,"[59] so as to not offend the Psychics and so that "together you may glorify God."[60] The Valentinians, likewise, did not disguise the fact that they taught Inner Mysteries, but also participated in the outward ceremonies of the Church alongside Literalist Christians.[61]

Irenaeus found it frustrating trying to argue theology with the Valentinians, for they simply agreed with everything he said![62] He complains:

> They keep asking us how it is that when they confess the same things and hold the same doctrine, we call them heretics![63]

But the old heresy-hunter is quick to uncover what he takes to be a devious Gnostic conspiracy. "They do indeed confess with the mouth one Jesus Christ," he agrees, but they are only "saying one thing and thinking another." "From what they say in public" the Valentinians appear to be Literalist Christians "in outward appearance," but "in private they describe the ineffable Mysteries."[64] Irenaeus complains that they even "assemble in unauthorized meetings," that is, in meetings not authorized by the bishop—who was of course Irenaeus himself![65]

By the beginning of the third century Valentinian Christians were also split between those in the East who had given up on the Literalists as a lost cause, regarding them as being outside the "Body of Christ," and the western Valentinians, such as Ptolemy and Heracleon, who still fought to unite Christianity.[66] Quoting Jesus (who is in turn quoting Plato![67]) they argued that "many are called, but few are chosen," and explained that the majority who did not have Gnosis were the "called," while the Gnostics were the chosen elect who must teach the many and bring them to Gnosis.[68] Ptolemy taught that Christ combined within the Church both "spiritual" and "unspiritual" Christians so that eventually all may become spiritual. Elaine Pagels explains:

> Meanwhile, both belonged to one church; both were baptized; both shared in the celebration of the mass; both made the same confession. What differentiated them was the level of their understanding. Uninitiated Christians mistakenly worshiped the creator, as if he were God; they believed in Christ as the one who would save them from sin, and who they believed had risen bodily from the dead; they

accepted him by faith but without understanding the mystery of his nature—or their own. But those who had gone on to receive Gnosis had come to recognize Christ as the one sent from the Father of truth, whose coming revealed to them that their own nature was identical with his—and with God's.[69]

The Valentinians even conceded that the Literalist bishops, like Jehovah the demiurge, could legitimately wield authority over Psychic Christians. But the bishops' demands, warnings, and threats, like those of Jehovah himself, were irrelevant to Christians initiated into the Inner Mysteries who had been redeemed and set free through the mystical experience of Gnosis.[70]

NO ORTHODOXY

The carefully fostered traditional picture of the Gnostics is of a small group of lunatic extremists on the fringes of orthodox Literalist Christianity to which the vast majority of Christians subscribed. But this is simply anti-Gnostic propaganda.[71] Actually, as Gibbon writes in *The Decline and Fall of the Roman Empire*, the Gnostics "covered Asia and Egypt, established themselves in Rome, and sometimes penetrated into the provinces of the West."[72] In the first few centuries CE there really was no such thing as "the Church," only competing factions, of which the Literalists were one.

Justin Martyr, a Literalist; Marcion, an uncompromising Gnostic; and Valentinus, who tried to heal the Gnostic/Literalist division, were all important Christian teachers in Rome at exactly the same time.[73] This is how diverse the Christian community was in the middle of the second century. Although Justin Martyr would come to be remembered as a great Christian hero and the other two would be dismissed as minor heretics, in their own lifetimes Valentinus and Marcion were far more influential than Justin. They both inspired Christian movements bearing their names, which flourished for centuries.

The truth is that the Gnostics were the great intellectuals of early Christianity who commanded the respect of large numbers of Christians until Gnosticism was violently suppressed in the fourth and fifth centuries. Valentinus, for example, was a highly educated Alexandrian philosopher and poet who was elected Bishop of Egypt. He was a major force in early Christianity, and Irenaeus deplores the fact that many bishops, deacons, widows, and martyrs from the Literalist community had sought initiation into Valentinian Christianity.[74] Even the bigoted Tertullian admitted that Valentinus was "a capable man, both in intelligence and eloquence."[75] Likewise, the Literalist St. Jerome admits that Marcion was a "veritable sage."[76] The hero of Literalism Justin Martyr, on the other hand, desperately wanted to be regarded as a great philosopher, but had been refused entry into Pythagorean and Platonic schools of philosophy for his lack of knowledge of mathematics.[77] It was only after these rebuffs that he became a Christian.

The Gnostic sages authored a huge number of gospels and spiritual treatises, including of course the original version of the Jesus story that became the New Testament Gospel of Mark. As well as this they also wrote the first commentaries on the gospels. Basilides was reputed to have written 24 books of commentaries, though without specific reference to the gospels, which later became canonical. He was also said to have written a gospel himself and a book on Hindu teachings![78] Ptolemy and Heracleon (c.170) are both credited with writing a commentary of the Gospel of John—so the first commentary on any book in the New Testament was also written by a Gnostic.[79]

Literalists, by comparison, produced little of real substance, concentrating on polemics against heretics. These anti-Gnostic works only began to be written around the middle of the second century, when Literalism started to emerge as a force in its own right. According to the fourth-century Church propagandist Eusebius, the first anti-heresy writer was a certain Agrippa Castor (c.135).[80] Justin Martyr (c.150) is also known to have composed a work against heresies. Neither of these works survive, however. Some scholars have conjectured that this is because they were themselves far too "unorthodox" for later orthodox Christians.[81] No refutations of heretics survive until the work of Irenaeus at the end of the second century. All subsequent refutations were based more or less on Irenaeus and frequently just copy his comments and prejudices.

But these documents attacking heretics are not the definitive statements of orthodox Christianity. In the first few centuries CE we simply do not find any orthodoxy as we understand it today. Literalism can only be regarded as orthodox in retrospect, because Literalists eventually came to control the Church in later centuries. In the first few centuries, different factions wielded more or less power at different times and even the most fanatically orthodox of Christians could find themselves ending up as heretics.

In the first quarter of the third century the Literalist Hippolytus objected to policies being proposed in Rome by a Gnostic teacher and former slave

Callistus. Callistus wanted Christians to recognize marriages between believers and their own slaves and extend forgiveness of sins to cover sexual transgressions.[82] Hippolytus slandered Callistus as a common criminal, but the majority of Christians in Rome respected him as a teacher who had been imprisoned and tortured, and elected him bishop. The arch–heresy-hunter Hippolytus now found himself a heretic from the Church of Rome whose authority he had worked so hard to endorse.[83]

Some of the greatest mouthpieces of Literalism actually defected to Gnosticism at the end of their lives, including Tatian, Justin Martyr's protégé,[84] and even the fanatical heresy-hunter Tertullian! Tertullian joined a group of Gnostics inspired by Montanus, who had previously been a priest in the Mysteries of the Pagan godman Attis![85] Using the same venom with which he had previously attacked heretics, Tertullian now condemned the "orthodox" Church for being a Church of mere Psychics, an organization of "a number of bishops" rather than "a spiritual church for spiritual people."[86] It is particularly ironic, considering Tertullian's previous misogyny, that the Montanists were famous for their ecstatic women priests! One modern authority writes:

> If Montanus had triumphed, Christian doctrine would have been developed under the superintendence of wild and excitable women.[87]

Eventually Tertullian left the Montanists and set up a Christian sect of his own—the Tertullianists.[88]

Unsurprisingly, traditional Christian history glosses over Tertullian's conversion to Gnosticism. His writings against the Gnostics, however, were endlessly copied, becoming standard texts in the Literalist Church's battle to eradicate all alternative forms of Christianity.

The idea of orthodoxy suggests there was always one perspective held in common by the majority of Christians, but there is no evidence to suggest that this is actually true. There only becomes such a thing as orthodoxy when Literalist Christianity was adopted as the state religion of the Roman Empire. Only at this time did the Literalist faction acquire the power to enforce its particular perspective. Even then, Gnosticism continued to flourish for centuries. What was considered orthodox never reflected the majority views of practicing Christians. It always reflected the views of the powerful bishops.

CHRISTIANITY AND JUDAISM

As we have seen, the Christian community was divided right from the start on the vexed issue of its relationship with traditional Judaism. By the middle of the second century most Christians were Gentiles, not Jews, and had rejected circumcision and all the other prescriptions and proscriptions laid down by Moses. But controversy still raged.

Most Gnostics wanted to completely reject the Jewish god Jehovah in favor of a more mystical conception of God as the supreme Oneness, identical to the God of Plato and the Pagan Mysteries. The influential Gnostic teacher Marcion argued for the complete separation of Christianity from Judaism. He produced a text called *The Antitheses*, which juxtaposed quotes from the Old and New Testaments to demonstrate how they contradict each other.[89] For Marcion, Jehovah was a "committed barbarian"[90] and the Old Testament merely a catalog of his crimes against humanity.[91] Christianity was a new revelation of the Good God, a universal doctrine, which had nothing to do with the imperfect creed of one small nation.[92]

Most Literalists also rejected the traditions of Judaism. Indeed, Justin Martyr relates with approval the fact that many Literalists would not even talk to their fellow Christians who followed the Law of Moses, believing that such Christians would not enjoy eternal salvation.[93] However, Literalists did want to keep the Old Testament. It was regarded as relating a divine "history," which endorsed their claim that the New Testament was also factual, not mythical. It could also be used, often in the most ridiculous of ways, as a source of "prophecies" about the coming of Jesus, which were felt to prove the truth of their Literalist perspective. Having an ancient heritage was regarded as prestigious, so keeping the Old Testament also meant they could claim, as Tertullian does, that Christianity "rests on the very ancient books of the Jews" and that these are far older than any book, city, cult, or race of the Pagan world.[94]

Literalist Christians wanted Jewish scriptures, but not Judaism. They therefore proclaimed that since the Jews had rejected the savior whom God had sent them, they had forfeited the right to their own spiritual heritage, which now legitimately belonged only to Christians. These Jewish texts became known for the first time as the *Old* Testament, which foretold the *New* Testament of Christianity. The scriptures of the Old Testament were even suitably rearranged so that they ended with a prophesy, which appeared to lead seamlessly into its apparent fulfillment in the gospels.[95]

As Literalist Christianity became more and more Romanized, so the blame for the death of Jesus was shifted from the Roman governor Pilate to the Jewish nation as a whole.[96] In the Gospel of Matthew the Jewish crowd who demand that Jesus be put to death are made to chant: "His blood be on us and on our children."[97] As a modern authority writes:

> The legacy of these words has been terrible. They have been cited to justify centuries of Christian persecution of the Jews. It is significant that only at the recent Vatican council has a formal declaration been made exonerating subsequent generations of Jews from responsibility for the murder of Christ.[98]

From the second century onward Literalist Christians wrote numbers of long and abusive tracts against the Jews.[99] Bishop Melito of Sardis (c.170) denounced them as "God-killers"[100]—criminals who had invented an "entirely new sort of crime."[101] The devastation the Jewish nation had suffered at the hands of the Roman Empire was deemed to be God's just revenge. The Jews had brought their sufferings upon themselves.[102]

Circumcision, which the opponents of Paul had regarded as a prerequisite for being a true Christian, became a sign of sharing in the blood-guilt of murdering the Lord. In his devastatingly hostile attack on the Jews, Justin Martyr writes:

> For the circumcision according to the flesh was given to you from Abraham as a sign so that you might be distinguished from other nations and from us, and so that you alone might suffer what you now rightly suffer; so that your land might become desolate, and your cities burned, and strangers eat the fruits of your land before you, and not one of you set foot in Jerusalem. Therefore these things have rightly and justly come upon you, for you put the just one to death, and before him his prophets and now you deal treacherously with those who hope in him, and with him who sent him, Almighty God, the Creator of all things.[103]

While the Jews were increasingly vilified, traditions were fabricated which portrayed Pontius Pilate as a just and holy man—even a Christian! By the fourth century both Pilate and his wife were honored as saints! This is how ludicrous and contradictory the history of early Christianity actually is.

THE CREATION OF THE NEW TESTAMENT

To wrest Christianity away from the Gnostics and build a centralized religion based on common dogmas the Literalist bishops needed to counteract the influence of the large number of Gnostic gospels circulating at the time. They therefore set out to create a limited canon of acceptable scriptures as a definitive statement of Christianity and dismiss all other texts as spurious and heretical. The foundation for this was the Old Testament appropriated from the Jews. However, the selection of other texts to include was a problem. Different Christian communities had by this time adopted different texts as sacred and all argued that their preferred collection of gospels, letters, and legends should comprise the canon. The argument raged from the end of the second century until the fourth century and beyond.[104] It is a remarkable fact that although nearly all modern forms of Christianity do not question the texts included in the New Testament, in the first four centuries every single document was at some time or other branded as either heretical or forged![105]

The first attempt at constructing a Christian canon was supposedly made by Papias of Hierapolis c.110. He is a vague figure of whom little can really be said, although, interestingly, he refers to the Gospel of Matthew as a collection of "oracles," which suggests the text that he had before him was significantly different from the text that has come down to us.[106] There is clearly no New Testament in Justin Martyr's time (c.150). The "memoirs of the Apostles," to which he refers, are far from the same as the four canonical gospels.[107] In all his works he never mentions Matthew, Mark, Luke, or John. Tatian (c.170) attempted to synthesize one gospel out of the others, and so cover up the contradictions between them, but this failed to achieve general acceptance in the Christian community.[108] At the end of the second century Irenaeus tried canonizing the four gospels we have today using as a criterion of authenticity the claim that each of them derived from one of Jesus' disciples—which is ironic, because Mark and Luke do not even pretend to be eyewitnesses of the events they describe![109]

The New Testament excluded some of the earliest and most quoted Christian texts, such as *The Gospel of Thomas*, *The Shepherd of Hermas*, and *The Gospel of the Hebrews*, because none of them contain any reference to the quasi-historical story of Jesus. *The Gospel of Thomas* claims to be a collection of "secret sayings" of Jesus, as recorded by Thomas his "twin." *The Shepherd of Hermas*, which was extremely popular among early Christians, is a thinly veiled reworking of an originally Pagan text in which Hermas meets a Pagan oracular priestess disguised as an embodiment of "the church."[110] As one modern authority remarks, although ignored today, the author of this work is actually "the early Christian whom we know best after St Paul."[111] *The Gospel of the Hebrews* is the gospel most frequently mentioned by name in the early Church.[112] However, it is easy to see why, despite its early popularity, it did not make it into the New Testament either. Among other heresies it relates that Jesus was in his mother's womb for only seven months—a strange claim that, as we have seen, was also made of the Pagan godman Dionysus![113]

Many Gnostic works, such as *The Acts of Thomas*, were too popular to simply dismiss, so they were purged of their heretical content and adapted to suit a Literalist agenda. As one scholar writes:

> Catholic bishops and teachers knew not how better to stem this flood of Gnostic writings and their influence among the faithful, than by bodily adopting the most popular narrations from the heretical books, and after carefully eliminating the poison of false doctrine, replacing them in this purified form in the hands of the people.[114]

The Acts of the Apostles may well have been such an adaptation of originally Gnostic texts. At the end of the second century Irenaeus and Tertullian regard it as a holy scripture, yet just a generation earlier Justin Martyr has not even heard of it.[115] Acts was fabricated in the form we now have it just in time to be a powerful tool against Gnosticism, confirming the historicity of the disciples and legitimatizing the bishops who claimed to maintain their lineage. It also portrayed Paul as an apostle of Literalism, and has him clearly acknowledge the primacy of Peter and the other apostles.[116] Acts was, of course, rejected by the Gnostics, who pointed out that the Paul of the letters was obviously incompatible with the Paul of Acts.[117]

GLORIOUS GORE

The conflict between Literalists and Gnostics came to a head under the pressure of the Roman persecution of Christianity, to which Gnostics and Literalists reacted in very different ways.

For the Literalists Jesus had been a martyr, therefore to meet one's death was a sign of following gloriously in his footsteps. Cyprian (died 258 CE) vividly describes the delight of the Lord with the "sublime, the great, the acceptable spectacle" of "flowing blood which quenches the flames and the fires of hell by its glorious gore."[118] Literalist martyrs were idealized as spiritual athletes and holy warriors in much the same way that Muslim extremists are today.[119] To be martyred was to be guaranteed a place in heaven. With such a prize on offer, many Literalist Christians actively sought their death. They believed that "through suffering for one hour, they purchase for themselves eternal life."[120] Tertullian declares that he desires to suffer "that he may obtain from God complete forgiveness," by giving in exchange his blood.[121]

In many ways these fanatics, gathered together in small groups on the fringes of society, resemble those modern religious cults, which also offer their adherents heavenly rewards for willingly seeking out death through mass suicide—although it is notable that somehow Tertullian and Irenaeus, two of the most vocal enthusiasts for glorious martyrdom, themselves manage to avoid this apparently desirable fate![122]

The Gnostics, by contrast, viewed the idea that martyrdom ensures salvation as a complete misunderstanding of Christianity. They believed that one should accept one's God-given fate, including meeting a martyr's death,[123] but they regarded it as ridiculous and deluded to actively seek out martyrdom as a quick way into heaven. Spiritual enlightenment was to be found through the mystical realization of Gnosis, not grand gestures.

A Gnostic text called *The Testimony of Truth* declares that those who are enthusiastic to be martyrs are the "foolish" who simply say the words "We are Christians" yet who do not know "who Christ is." They are "empty martyrs, since they bear witness only to themselves." Theirs will be only a "human death" and will not lead to the salvation, which they expect, for 'these matters are not settled in this way" and "they do not have the Word which gives life." Those who teach that God desires "human sacrifice" are making God into a cannibal.[124] These Literalist Christians are "the ones who oppress their brothers," by encouraging naïve fellow believers "to the executioner" under the illusion that if they "hold fast to the name of a dead man they will become pure."[125] The author of *The Apocalypse of Peter* is particularly horrified at Literalist exclamations of joy over acts of violence done to the "little ones."[126]

Clement of Alexandria writes of those who court martyrdom more sympathetically as children who have "not yet become men in love with God, as the Gnostic is." He explains:

No one, then, who is irrationally brave is a Gnostic; since one might call children brave who through ignorance of what is to be dreaded, undergo things that are frightful. So they touch fire even. And the wild beasts that rush close on the points of spears, having a brute courage, might be called valiant. And such people might perhaps call jugglers valiant, who tumble on swords with a certain dexterity, practicing a mischievous art for sorry gain. But he who is truly brave, with the peril arising from the bad feeling of the multitudes before his eyes, courageously awaits whatever comes. In this way he is distinguished from others that are called martyrs, inasmuch as some furnish occasions for themselves, and rush into the heart of dangers. For some suffer from love of glory, and others from fear of some other sharper punishment, and others for the sake of pleasures and delights after death, being children in faith, blessed indeed, but not yet become men in love with God, as the Gnostic is. For there are, as in the gymnastic contests, so also in church, crowns for men and for children.[127]

The Gnostics did not believe that Jesus literally died as a martyr, but that his death symbolically represented a profound mystical truth. To imitate Jesus was not to court martyrdom, but to die to one's own lower self and resurrect as the Christ within.

To the Literalists such Gnostic attitudes made the sufferings of the martyrs appear to be futile. The author of a letter attributed to Ignatius writes indignantly:

But if, as some say, Jesus' suffering was only in appearance, then why am I a prisoner, and why do I long to fight with the wild beasts? In that case, I am dying in vain.[128]

Literalists saw Gnostics as traitors who were undermining their attempts to unite the Church in the face of oppression by offering a theological justification for cowardice.[129] Gnostics, on the other hand, saw Literalists as fanatical extremists leading the gullible to pointless suffering with false promises.[130]

THE ROMANS AND THE PERSECUTIONS

The traditional history of the persecution of Christianity paints the Roman Empire as having a particular hatred of this new religion, but this was not so. Rome was constantly purging itself of mystics, philosophers, and religious cults, which it saw as a threat to its stability.[131] The Romans had a love/hate relationship with the Mysteries, of which the Christian cult was just another example. They were attracted to the exotic spirituality and profound philosophy of these foreign cults, yet also terrified by the radical challenge they presented to Roman political authority. The followers of the Mysteries of Dionysus, for example, like the later followers of the Mysteries of Jesus, were accused of a conspiracy to overthrow the state. From as early as 186 BCE the Mysteries of Dionysus had been prohibited in Rome and the shrines destroyed throughout Italy.[132] Huge numbers of initiates were executed, sometimes many thousands at a time.[133]

At various times during the first few centuries it was, in effect, a crime to philosophize in Rome.[134] Even the great Stoic philosopher Epictetus was exiled, along with countless others. Like Christian martyrs after them, many philosophers were sent to their death for refusing to compromise with the tyrannical Roman authorities. A text called *The Acts of the Pagan Martyrs* glorifies the courage and integrity of those persecuted initiates.[135] Philosophers are recorded as having gone to the stake "laughing at the sudden collapse of human destinies" and dying "unmoving in the flames."[136]

According to the traditional history of Christianity, from the earliest of times large numbers of Christians were horribly persecuted by the Romans. In fact, until the middle of the third century there was no legalized persecution of Christians. Previous persecutions had been against individuals only or limited to a particular city. Christians were not seen as a particular threat and therefore were not particularly oppressed. In the second century, the Emperor Trajan wrote to one of his governors that Christians must be given a proper trial and that judges must not give weight to anonymous attacks. Christians were "not to be hunted out" and accusers had to pay the costs of any prosecution.[137]

In 250 CE, however, plague swept the ancient world, decimating whole populations. The Empire was on the verge of collapse, and the Christian cult found itself being scapegoated for Roman misfortunes. The Emperor Decius ordered Christians to offer animal sacrifices to the gods for the health and well-being of the Empire and instigated the first general persecution against those who refused. It lasted only a year, but was repeated under Valerian in 257–9 and again under Diocletian in 303–5. In the whole of its history, therefore, Christianity was officially persecuted for a total of five years.[138]

The scale of these persecutions, even the so-called "Great Persecution" under Diocletian, is now known to have been wildly exaggerated by Christian propagandists.[139] Writing in the middle of the third century, Origen tells us that the "few" Christians who had died for their faith were "easily numbered."[140] Under the persecutions of Decius, in the huge city of Alexandria, only 10 men and seven women suffered for being Christians![141]

Roman governors actually often showed no desire to deliberately harm the Christians. Christians who refused to participate in the compulsory rituals of the Empire were offered a compromise. If they refused to eat sacrificial meat, might they not offer incense? One governor pleads with a would-be martyr:

> Do you want to wait a few days to think it over? Don't you see the beauty of this pleasant weather? No pleasure will come your way if you kill yourself.[142]

Ironically, it was the Christians themselves who often courted martyrdom. One group of Christians approached the governor of Asia and begged him to put them to death, but he refused, telling them that they were free to use cliffs and ropes if they wanted to die so much![143]

Like the Gnostics, the Emperor and Stoic philosopher Marcus Aurelius saw such volunteering for martyrdom as empty posturing rather than an example of enlightened acceptance of fate. He writes:

> Readiness to die must come from a man's own judgment, not from mere obstinacy as with the Christians: it must come considerately and in such a way as to persuade others that death is not horrible, not with tragic displays.[144]

Some Roman Emperors were actually sympathetic toward Christianity, regarding it as another interesting and exotic Mystery religion. Alexander Severus (c. 230) was even said to have had a statue of Christ in his private chapel alongside those of other godmen of the Pagan Mysteries.[145] His mother was a patron of the Christian philosopher Origen, as well as famous Pagan philosophers.[146]

THE GROWTH OF CHRISTIANITY

Despite the traditional claims, there is no evidence that the Roman persecutions led to a significant increase in the number of Christians. Christianity did not really take off until Emperor Constantine adopted the religion, at which point martyrdom was no longer an option as Christians were a favored and protected group.[147]

Christianity is usually pictured as spreading rapidly, especially among the poor and dispossessed, until it was the dominant force in the ancient world, waiting to take its destined place as the religion of the Roman Empire. But this is complete fantasy, first cultivated by Tertullian (c. 200), who makes the outrageous claim that: "Nearly all the citizens in nearly all the cities are Christians."[148] Scholars now recognize that this is a ridiculous exaggeration.[149] The more trustworthy Origen (c. 240) admits that Christians were actually only a tiny fraction of the ancient world's inhabitants.[150]

The question of how many Christians there were in the first few centuries is very difficult to answer. Inscriptions and Pagan texts make next to no references to Christians before 250. They are not mentioned either in the two most substantial histories written in the early third century.[151] We have only one actual statistic, and that from the fourth-century Christian "historian" Eusebius, who is an extremely unreliable source. He tells us that in 251 "more than fifteen hundred widows and poor people" were supported by Rome's Christians, who included 154 ministers of varying rank (52 of whom were exorcists)![152] Scholars estimate that by 250 about 2 percent of the Empire's population was Christian.[153] After this time, it may have risen to around 4–5 percent of the population.[154] Even in the fourth century, however, Eusebius still knows of only three little townships which are Christian in the entire Holy Land.[155]

The growth in the popularity of Christianity in the first three centuries CE was not unique, but part of a general upsurge in the popularity of the Mysteries throughout the ancient world. As it entered the new millennium, religious skepticism was rife within the Roman Empire. As Gibbon remarks, "All gods were seen by philosophers as equally true, by the politicians as equally false, and by the magistrates as equally useful."[156] But Plutarch tells us that the oracles that had been in decline during his youth were flourishing again at the beginning of the second century. During this century in Athens the ceremonies of Dionysus, which had lapsed completely, were reinstated and the number of people seeking initiation at Eleusis grew considerably. The Mysteries of Mithras also became hugely popular across the whole of the Empire.[157]

PAGAN REACTIONS TO CHRISTIANITY

Christianity was another Mystery cult gaining ground alongside many other such cults. However, it was attracting the attention of Pagan intellectuals. Their reactions to this new religion were similar to those of mainstream society to the many fringe religious cults of today. When Christianity became too popular to be simply ignored, its claims to originality were (justifiably) derided and its leaders accused of manipulating the gullible to line their own pockets and bolster their own egos.

Tacitus and Pliny (c.112), the first Pagan writers to take any notice of Christianity, saw the Christians as just superstitious fanatics given to over-emotional enthusiasm.[158] Celsus (c.170) described them as "a people who have cut themselves off from the rest of civilization" by claiming their faith to be unique and in opposition to ancient Paganism.[159] In his view, Christians are irrational, for they "do not want to give or receive a reason for what they believe" but rather win converts by telling them "not to ask questions but to have faith."[160] Celsus writes:

> Taking its root in the lower classes, the religion continues to spread among the vulgar: nay one can even say it spreads because of its vulgarity, and the illiteracy of its adherents. And while there are a few moderate, reasonable, and intelligent people who are inclined to interpret its beliefs allegorically, yet it thrives in its purer form among the ignorant.[161]

His friend, the satirist Lucian, lampooned Christianity as just a confidence scam aimed at making money from the gullible:

> If a professional sharper who knows how to capitalize on a situation gets among them, he makes himself a millionaire overnight, laughing up his sleeve at the simpletons.[162]

The Christian philosopher Origen, writing in the middle of the third century, is equally uncomplimentary toward the Christian community, describing it as made up of men concerned about how to make money and women gossiping so loudly nothing could be heard![163] Origen sadly acknowledges that as Christianity became an established religion, so it became corrupt:

> I admit that at the present time perhaps, when on account of the multitude of people coming to the faith even rich men and persons in positions of honor, and ladies of refinement, and high birth, favorably regard adherents of the faith, one might venture to say that some become leaders of the Christian teaching for the sake of a little prestige.[164]

In the middle of the third century a wealthy woman called Lucilla actually paid to have her servant Majorinus made Bishop of Carthage![165] Paul of Samosata, Bishop of Antioch in 260, is reported to have found the service of the Church a very lucrative profession. He extorted frequent contributions from the rich among his flock, a large part of which he pocketed for himself to pay for his luxurious lifestyle.[166]

In 270 the Pagan philosopher Porphyry wrote the most devastating critique of Christianity in 15 volumes. He demonstrated that the Christian gospels were full of inconsistencies, exaggerations, impossibilities, and falsehoods, and could not be inspired by the true God. He derided the belief in the physical resurrection as materialistic and absurd. He regarded it as ignorant and vulgar for anyone to assert that the great and beautiful cosmos would perish in an apocalypse while his own insignificant physical body would be preserved by God for eternity. For Porphyry, promising any criminal that he would be absolved and enter paradise as long as he was baptized before he died undermined the very foundations of an organized society of decent human beings.[167] He objected to Christian claims to have discovered the one and only way to God, and presented in contrast the "universal way" of Pagan philosophy. He included in his books an oracle of Apollo, which praised Christ but asserted that the Christian cult was absurd because God Incarnate was a myth.[168] Not surprisingly, when the Roman Empire became Christian, Porphyry's works were promptly banned and consigned to the flames.[169]

THE ROMAN CATHOLIC CHURCH

It is one of the great ironies of history that the mighty Roman Empire eventually came to embrace Christianity—not only as another Mystery cult, but as the one and only true religion. It seems incredible that having completely laid waste the state of Israel, Rome should end up adopting a religion with Jewish history as its sacred texts, based around a Jewish prophet said to have been executed by a Roman governor. How could this possibly have happened? The traditional history, of course, suggests that it could only have been the hand of God guiding humanity away from the darkness of Paganism. Leaving aside the possibility that Christianity is God's religion of preference, however, there are other reasons for its success.

Christianity was not the only foreign Mystery cult adopted by the Roman Empire. In 304, just 17 years before Christianity became the state religion, another godman who was miraculously born on December 25 and whose devotees also celebrated a symbolic meal of bread and wine was declared the "Protector of the Empire"—the Persian savior Mithras. The Persians were the main rivals and ancient enemies of the Romans, so the Romans' adoption of Mithras is actually even more shocking than their adoption of the Jewish savior Jesus.

The Mysteries of Mithras spread extremely rapidly throughout the Roman Empire in the first century CE.[170] At the height of its popularity in the third century Mithraism was practiced from one end of the Empire to the other; as one modern authority puts it, "from the banks of the Black Sea to the mountains of Scotland and to the borders of the great Sahara Desert."[171] Mithraic monuments often tell us that slaves as well as freemen were initiates of the Mysteries and that often it was the former who achieved the highest ranks; in Mithraism the last indeed became the first.[172] At the end of the second century Emperor Commodus himself was initiated into the Mysteries of Mithras, which created an immense stir in the Roman world and led to a great swell in the cult's popularity.[173] A number of Emperors after Commodus attempted to make Mithraism the religion of the Empire.

Other Roman leaders had flirted to different degrees with different Mystery religions. Marc Antony had styled himself on Dionysus. Claudius had looked to Attis. Vespasian had worshiped Serapis. Domitian honored Osiris. Elgabalus tried to enforce the monotheistic cult of Helios.[174] To endorse their claim of "one Empire, one Emperor" in the face of increasing fragmentation, the Roman Emperors needed "one faith"—a universal or "catholic" religion. All these cults were proposed at different times, but without success.

In the first half of the fourth century Emperor Constantine tried Christianity. It was an ideal candidate for the role. The Romans needed a Mystery religion because they were always popular with the people. But Mystery religions were led by mystics and philosophers, who had the audacity to question and undermine the authority of the state. Literalist Christianity, however, was a Mystery religion that had purged itself of all its troublesome intellectuals. It was already an authoritarian religion, which encouraged the faithful to have blind faith in those holding positions of power. It was exactly what the Roman authorities wanted—a religion without mystics, the Outer Mysteries without the Inner Mysteries, form without content.

In 321 Constantine became the first Christian Emperor. Although his motivation was clearly political, not spiritual, many years after the event he claimed that his conversion had come about through a holy vision.[175] On the eve of battle, he and "all the troops" had seen a "sign of the cross" in the noonday sky, inscribed with the words "By this conquer." This was not the familiar Christian cross, however, but the Pagan *chi-rho* symbol.[176] Having gone to bed wondering what the sign in the sky had meant, Constantine had been visited in his dreams by Christ, who was bearing the same symbol, and who commanded him to "use its likeness in his engagements with the enemy."[177] Constantine emblazoned the emblem on his troops' shields, won the battle as promised, and became a Christian. If he is to be believed, it would seem that Jesus the "Prince of Peace" won over the most terrible Empire of the ancient world by offering its Emperor a magical military talisman!

The chi-rho monogram originated in Pagan papyri where scholars used it as a sign to mark prophetic passages with chi-rho, standing for the Greek *chreston*, meaning "auspicious." With Constantine's conversion to Christianity the chi-rho became interpreted as an abbreviation for Christ. This symbol therefore had a double meaning, one for Pagans and one for Christians, which suited Constantine's purposes perfectly.

Constantine was above all a pragmatist. His Christianity was only prominent when it was politically expedient. When the victory he had been promised in his vision was honored with a monument, the inscription made no reference to Christianity and depicted Roman soldiers receiving divine assistance from the usual Pagan heavenly helpers.[178] Despite his miraculous conversion to Christianity, Constantine had his own head put on the massive statue of the sun god Helios in the forum in Rome and had coins minted that depicted him alongside Helios.[179] And he still accepted the title of Pontifex Maximus, the high priest of the Pagan world—as did all Christian Emperors up until 382![180]

Like most Roman Emperors, Constantine was a vicious and ruthless man. During his wars in Gaul (306–12) it is recorded that:

Even heathen feeling was shocked when he gave barbarian kings to the beasts, along with their followers by thousands at a time.[181]

Constantine clearly did not become more compassionate after his conversion to Christianity. Almost immediately after presiding over the Christian Council of Nicaea in 325 he had both his son Crispus and his stepmother Fausta murdered.[182] Indeed, he deliberately postponed being baptized until his deathbed so that he could continue sinning and yet be assured of a heavenly afterlife.[183] Constantine's reputation was such that not even the Roman Church could face making him a saint.[184]

The inspiration for Constantine's Christianity was his mother Helena, who had become a Christian sometime before. Forced into exile after being implicated in the murder of Constantine's stepmother, she went on a tour of the Holy Land. Here she miraculously found the tomb and birth cave of Christ, along with the remains of the three crosses used to crucify Jesus and the two thieves at Golgotha. This truly was an extraordinary miracle, since thousands of other Jews had been executed in the 300 years that had elapsed since Jesus supposedly met his death![185] Constantine erected churches on these fortuitously discovered sacred sites, which are still honored as holy to this day. Bits of the holy cross were sent all around the Empire and Helena became honored by the Catholic Church as "St. Helena, Discoverer of the True Cross!"[186] Constantine also erected a giant basilica on the site of the shrine, supposedly marking Peter's grave in Rome, which would become the Vatican—the powerhouse of Roman Catholicism.[187]

Constantine found the Christian community deeply divided, as always—not just between Literalists and Gnostics, but also within the Literalist community itself. At the Council of Nicaea, Christians are said to have begun by piling the Emperor's lap with petitions against fellow Christians![188] Constantine himself had no grasp on theology. Indeed, he gave speeches that were embarrassingly close to heresy.[189] However, he knew he needed unity. He therefore enforced it.

A creed was established at Nicaea that is still repeated in churches throughout the world today. Those bishops who refused to agree with the creed were exiled from the Empire as criminals by decree of the Emperor himself.[190] Those who signed up were invited to stay on at Nicaea as Constantine's guests for his twentieth anniversary celebrations.[191] Many bishops signed up and later regretted doing so. One subsequently wrote to Constantine, lamenting, "We committed an impious act, O Prince, by subscribing to a blasphemy from fear of you."[192]

After Constantine, the Roman Empire became increasingly Christianized under successive, ever more intolerant, Christian Emperors—that is, apart from a brief spell under Julian (360–3), who tried to reinstate Paganism.[193] He was himself a Platonic philosopher noted for his humility who wrote a beautiful hymn to the One God and was an initiate of the Mysteries of Mithras and Dionysus. He proclaimed toleration for all religions[194] and even attempted to rebuild the Jewish temple in Jerusalem but, much to the delight of the anti-Semitic Christian Church, he never succeeded.[195] Julian's Pagan renaissance was short-lived and after it Christianity was reinstated and enforced with even greater vehemence.

Despite the creed of Nicaea, the Christian Church remained forever divided against itself, engaging in constant political in-fighting thinly disguised as theological debate. In the authoritarian atmosphere of the times, the losers were excommunicated and their views made anathema. Yet no one was secure. An "orthodox" point of view today could be "heretical" tomorrow. Toward the end of the fourth century Hilary, Bishop of Poitiers, wrote despondently:

> Every year, nay, every moon we make new creeds to describe invisible mysteries. We repent of what we have done, we defend those who repent, we anathematize those whom we defended. We condemn either the doctrine of others in ourselves, or our own in that of others; and reciprocally tearing one another to pieces, we have been the cause of each other's ruin.[196]

By now even Literalist Christians had begun to see the Roman Church no longer as the fulfillment of Christ's plan but as the work of "the antichrist!"[197]

THE FALSIFICATION OF HISTORY

The Roman Church required a suitable history of its faith that vilified its enemies and celebrated its triumph as a sign of its God-given destiny. The truth of Christianity's origins was, therefore, rigorously suppressed and a more acceptable history was concocted—a fabrication, which is still taken to be accurate by the vast majority of people to this day.

The Gnostics regularly and unashamedly created fantasy gospels. But they acknowledged that they were mythologizing. Their works, of which the Jesus story itself is an example, were never meant to be taken as anything other than allegorical ficton. When the Literalists created their fantasies, however, they attempted to pass them off as historical records. These works, which form the basis of the traditional history of Christianity, are blatant forgeries.[198]

At the end of the second century Paul's original letters were interpolated and new ones forged to bring him into line with Literalist Christianity and distance him from Gnosticism. As part of the general Romanization of Christianity, a tradition was even fabricated that Paul had been in close communication with the eminent Roman statesman Seneca. Three hundred manuscripts still survive containing eight letters from Paul and 11 letters of Seneca in reply—all complete fakes, of course, but believed genuine until the last century! In them, Seneca is made to embrace Christianity and Paul to nominate him as official preacher of the gospel at the imperial court![199] In the fourth century, on the basis of these fabrications, Jerome included Seneca among his catalog of Christian saints.[200]

Letters were also forged in the names of various apostles. These are now included in the New Testament and regarded as holy scripture, but at the time were viewed with suspicion. Even Eusebius, the mouthpiece of Catholic propaganda, regarded the authenticity of the letters of James, Jude, Peter, and John as dubious and the Revelation as entirely spurious.[201] Letters attributed to early Christians such as Justin Martyr, Ignatius of Antioch, and Clement of Rome continued to be forged, adulterated, and added to well into the fifth century.[202]

Translating works into Latin afforded opportunities for distortion. In this way teachings such as those of the Christian philosopher Origen were made to appear in sympathy with what was regarded as orthodox at the time.[203]

Fictitious biographies were routinely constructed for Christian saints, often directly based on the lives and legends of dead Pagan holy men.[204] Stories were invented of Peter coming to Rome and being crucified upside down to give credence to the Church of Rome being the center of Christian power. But these tales were invented so late that no one even considered including them in the New Testament.

Popular Gnostic works were edited to remove their Gnostic teachings and replace them with doctrinally correct material.[205] Christians even adapted Pagan works to endorse their own dogma. Oracles by the Pagan Sibyl, which prophesied the coming of Jesus, were forged early in the fourth century and quoted by Constantine himself at the Council of Nicaea as proof of Jesus' divinity.[206] They even forged a *Testament of Orpheus* in which the ancient prophet of the Mysteries was made to deny his former Pagan teachings.[207]

Clumsy Christian additions were made to the works of the Jewish Pythagorean Philo,[208] and ridiculous legends invented that he had held discussions on the Law with the disciple John and met Peter in Rome![209] The Jewish historian Josephus was likewise transformed into a Christian and was even equated with the New Testament figure of Joseph of Arimathea![210] As previously discussed, additions were made to his works that reverentially testify to the historical existence of Jesus.[211]

A further document attributed to Josephus called *On the Essence of God* was also forged to reinforce the previous forgery by putting Christian doctrines into Josephus' mouth. Through careful linguistic studies, scholars now know "beyond any doubt" that the forger of this text was none other than Hippolytus (c. 222), the arch–heresy-hunter and protégé of Irenaeus![212] Scholars have also shown similarities in language and style between this forgery and Paul's Second Letter to the Thessalonians, which was written to call into question the authenticity of the first (genuine) letter.[213] So, Hippolytus may well have also been the forger of this letter of Paul.[214]

ST. PONTIUS PILATE!

The ludicrous nature of what passed for history in the early years of Christianity is graphically illustrated by the whitewashing of Pontius Pilate. This brutal Roman governor was so hated by the Jews that he had been made responsible for the savior's death by those who had originally put the Jesus myth into a historical context. But by the second century Tertullian relates the ludicrous tale that Pilate had washed his hands of Jesus' death because "in his secret heart" he was actually a Christian![215] According to Tertullian the earliest news of Christianity to reach Rome was a report from Pilate indicating that Christ (whom he supposedly had just executed) was indeed divine.[216] Emperor Tiberius (who was well known for despising all religion) immediately wanted to place Christ among the pantheon of Roman gods, but had his plans rejected by the Senate. For some reason this powerful Emperor did not question his normally servile senators, but instead contented himself with shielding Christians from the severity of repressive laws. This in itself is something of a miracle, as Tiberius was living many years before such laws were enacted![217]

Subsequently a document called *The Acts of Pilate* was forged based on Tertullian's fantasy. Then a later text called *The Gospel of Nicodemus* was based on this text to create what one modern scholar calls "a fiction three levels deep."[218] In *The Gospel of Nicodemus* we are told that when Pilate's report of Jesus' execution reached Rome, the Emperor ordered Pilate to be brought before him in chains. In front of the whole Senate, the gods and the army, the Emperor then declared:

> How could you dare to do such a thing, you most impious one, when you had seen such great signs concerning that man? By your wicked daring you have destroyed the whole world. As soon as they handed him over to you, you should have kept him secure and sent him to me, and not have followed them and crucified such a man who was righteous and did such wonderful signs as you mentioned in your report. For it is clear from these signs that Jesus was the Christ, the king of the Jews.[219]

Once the Emperor had spoken Christ's name all the statues of the gods fell down and became as dust. Pilate excused himself by claiming that the "insubordination of the lawless and godless Jews" had made him do it. So the Emperor issued a decree against the Jews, demanding:

> Obey and advance against them, and dispersing them amongst all the nations enslave them, and expel them from Judea, making the nation so insignificant that it is no longer to be seen anywhere, since they are men full of evil.

Pilate was then led to his execution uttering a prayer to the Lord. As he finished the voice of Jesus announced from heaven:

> All generations and families of the Gentiles shall call you blessed, because in your governorship all was fulfilled which the prophets foretold about me, and you shall appear as my witness at the Second Coming.

We are then told that Pilate's head was cut off and he was received by an angel of the Lord, at which point his wife Procla was so overcome with joy (sic!) that she immediately gave up the ghost and was buried with her husband.[220] Pilate ended up being revered as a saint in the Coptic Church and has his own feast day on June 25![221] His wife Procla was also revered as a saint in the Eastern Church.

Although this may have been believed as history at the time, to modern ears it sounds like obvious nonsense. Yet the more acceptable traditional history that has been taken as "gospel truth" for 1,500 years was created by the same people who gave us this baloney. It is just as fanciful and inaccurate, and if it were not for its familiarity it would be just as easy to dismiss.

EUSEBIUS, THE CHURCH PROPAGANDIST

The whole fictitious history of Christianity was finally organized and definitively collated in the fourth century by Bishop Eusebius, who is known as the "father of Church history." He was one of the bishops who completely changed their theological position at the Council of Nicaea to court the favor of Emperor Constantine.[222] He subsequently became Constantine's personal biographer, glossing over his murders with obsequious flattery.[223] Eusebius explained to the faithful that just as the Word of God guides and governs the heavens, so the Roman Emperor expresses the will of God in the government of the civilized world.[224] The Emperor was the voice of Christ on Earth!

Eusebius' job was to provide Roman Christianity with a suitable history, a task he performed with little regard for truth.[225] With beautiful understatement, one modern authority describes reading Eusebius as entering a "tantalizing, literary world where not everything said is to be taken entirely at face value."[226] Another modern scholar more bluntly calls him "the first thoroughly dishonest and unfair historian of ancient times."[227] Another describes Eusebius' "dishonesty" in his "deliberate falsification of dates."[228] Another describes Eusebius' history as "superficial" and "intentionally falsified" and created in "a very unscrupulous and arbitrary spirit."[229] As another historian rightly observes, "What can be gleaned of Eusebius does not endear him much to modern scholars."[230]

Eusebius himself indirectly confesses that he has included in his account of Christian history only that which "might redound to the glory" of the Church, while suppressing whatever could disgrace it.[231] A modern scholar concludes:

We are bound therefore to regard his labors with the greatest mistrust, and to pronounce it a most uncritical course to quote him as a competent authority; as is the custom of so many in spite of this delinquency, whenever it suits their purpose.[232]

Eusebius is quoted as an authority on Christian history simply because his is the only surviving "history" of the Church during the first three centuries.[233] His account has, therefore, been adopted by all Church historians after him, thereby perpetuating the lies, which have become the traditional history of Christianity.

In his "history" Eusebius repeats all of the standard accusations against the Gnostics. To justify the claims of the Literalist bishops to represent the original Christian tradition, he presents apostolic lines of succession that link them back to Jesus' disciples. These supposed lineages were forged earlier, probably by Irenaeus, but Eusebius makes his own additions.[234] Often he gives no more than a list of names that he has worked into a history by guesswork and invention, often creating inconsistencies and obvious errors in the process.[235] He has bishops leading the Church in Rome from early in the first century, although of course there is absolutely no evidence that a single leader of the Christian community in Rome emerged until much, much later.[236]

Eusebius also wildly exaggerates the numbers of Christians who suffered in the persecutions and creates biographies for Christian martyrs, which are actually derived from the legends of Pagan martyrs.[237] Although he is keen to catalog the works of earlier Christian writers, he wisely avoids telling us any of the ideas they expressed and thus does not lay them or himself open to accusations of heresy. Even in his account of Origen, who had been the great inspiration of his youth, Eusebius tells us nothing of Origen's ideas, which were beginning to become highly suspect in the orthodox community.[238]

As for the Jews, Eusebius delights in their tragic fate at the hands of the Romans, believing it is no more than they deserved for murdering the savior. Having written pages relating every gruesome detail of their suffering with obvious relish, he concludes, "Such was the reward of the Jews' iniquitous and wicked treatment of God's Christ."[239]

Eusebius constructs the absurd story that God told the original Christians of the Jerusalem Church to flee to safety in neighboring Pella before, in his wrath, he destroyed Jerusalem in 70 CE (with a little help from the Romans!).[240] Yet he also relates that when later Christians went in search of the Jerusalem Church they found only a group of Ebionite Gnostics. Why God should have wanted to save these "original" Christians only to have them turn into heretics Eusebius doesn't explain! But then he never seems to notice just how crazy and contradictory his fantasies are.

Without even the slightest trace of conscience, Eusebius even miraculously produces from "the archive" a letter written by Jesus himself to the Prince of Edessa, congratulating the Prince for believing in the savior without ever having seen him![241]

This then was the man who gave us what has passed for the history of Christianity, an obsequious employee of a tyrannical Roman Emperor who based his work on a 200-year tradition of deceit and forgery.[242]

THE DESTRUCTION OF PAGANISM

In the second century Tertullian, who claimed to have been converted to Christianity by witnessing Christians going to their death as martyrs, admitted he too had once enjoyed watching "the ludicrous cruelties" of Roman public persecutions.[243] This love of gore and suffering does not seem to have deserted him after he became a Christian. With obvious relish he paints a grim and violent picture of the fate awaiting Pagans at the "Final Judgment":

> You are fond of spectacles, expect the greatest of all spectacles, the last and eternal judgment of the universe. How shall I admire, how laugh, how rejoice, how exult, when I behold so many proud monarchs, and fancied gods, groaning in the lowest abyss of darkness; so many magistrates who persecuted the name of the Lord, liquefying in fiercer fires than they ever kindled against the Christians; so many sage philosophers blushing in red hot flames with their deluded scholars; so many celebrated poets trembling before the tribunal, not of Minos, but of Christ; so many tragedians, more tuneful in the expression of their own sufferings; so many dancers . . .[244]

And on he goes, delighting in the gruesome terrors his opponents will endure for all eternity. Little did he know that within a few generations such terrors would indeed afflict many Pagans, not at the Final Judgment, but in the fourth century at the hands of the Roman Catholic Church.

Having been adopted as the religion of the Roman Empire, the Literalist Church terrorized Pagans with relentless brutality. Pagan prophets were seized and tortured until they acknowledged that their gods were frauds.[245] Priests were chained to their shrines and left to starve to death.[246] Without any evidence to endorse the accusations, Pagans were condemned for sacrificing children, sprinkling their blood on altars to the gods, and making guitar strings from their guts—fantasy crimes to which they duly confessed after suffering agonizing tortures. Many were then burnt alive.[247]

Some ancient shrines were desecrated and razed to the ground while others were commandeered and forcibly transformed into Christian churches.[248] The great works of Pagan spirituality were thrown onto enormous bonfires and lost for all time. One witness records:

> Innumerable books were piled together, many heaps of volumes drawn from various houses, to be burnt under the eyes of the judges as prohibited. Owners burnt their entire libraries. So great was the terror that seized everyone.[249]

Paganism was not attacked for mistakenly worshiping non-existent gods. Nor was it ever disputed that the gods could indeed perform miracles such as healing the sick and predicting the future. Rather, Pagan gods were deemed to be devils who worked their magic to deceive and mislead the gullible.[250] Pagan "Daemons" became evil "demons" whose worship must be stamped out.[251] In the middle of the fourth century a bishop demanded of the Christian Emperor Constantius Constans:

> It is enjoined on you by the law of the supreme God, that you severely prosecute in every way the crime of idolatry. Hear and entrust to your holy consciousness what God commands concerning this crime. God orders that neither son nor brother be spared, and directs the sword as an avenger through the beloved limbs of a wife. A friend he also persecutes with lofty severity, and all the people are roused to arms to rend the bodies of sacrilegious people. Destruction is determined even for whole cities, if they are apprehended in this crime.[252]

In 383 Symmachus, a distraught Pagan Roman senator, appealed to the Christian Emperor Valentinian II for religious tolerance. In vain he wrote:

THE JESUS MYSTERIES

It is reasonable that all worship be considered one. We look at the same stars, the sky belongs to all, the same universe surrounds us. What does it matter by what method each seeks the truth. One cannot arrive at so great a secret by only one road.[253]

By 386 bands of mad monks, frenzied with fundamentalist religion, were running amok throughout the Empire, completely beyond the control of the law. The Pagan Libanius appealed to the Emperor to intervene:

You have not ordered either that the temples be closed or that no one should enter them. You have not driven out from the temples and altars fire or incense or the offerings of other perfumes. But this black-garbed mob, who eat more than elephants and drain huge amounts from the cup—these people, O King, although the law remains in force, run against the temples carrying cudgels and stones and bars of iron, while some, without these, use hands and feet. Then there is complete destruction as roofs are pulled down, walls demolished, statues are dragged down, altars pulled up, and the priests must either be silent or die. When the first is destroyed, there is a rush to a second and a third, and, contrary to law, trophy is heaped on trophy. Most take place in the countryside, but some even in the cities. The attacking forces in each case are numerous, but after countless abuses these separate groups come together and demand an account from each other of what they have done, and it is shameful not to have done the greatest damage.[254]

An anonymous Pagan (c. 390) sadly predicts:

When I die there will be no shrines, and the great holy temples of Serapis will depart into formless gloom, and a fabulous and insubstantial darkness will hold sway over the fairest things of earth.[255]

Finally, on June 16, 391 Emperor Theodosius issued an edict that closed down all Pagan temples.[256] A Christian mob immediately took the opportunity to destroy the wondrous temple of Serapis in Alexandria, leaving only its foundations.[257] An imperial decree demanded: "Burn all books hostile to Christianity lest they cause God anger and scandalize the pious,"[258] and in response illiterate monks destroyed thousands of years of accumulated wisdom and scientific knowledge as so much Pagan superstition.

The Pagan writer Eunapius, who describes "monks who resemble men but live like pigs," writes despairingly that "Anyone who had a black robe had despotic power."[259] In 415 Archbishop Cyril of Alexandria had his monks incite a Christian mob to murder the last Pagan scientist of the Alexandrian Library, a remarkable woman called Hypatia.[260] She was torn limb from limb, and Cyril was made a saint.[261]

In the reign of Constantine Christianity had been accorded equal status with the Pagan religions of the Empire. Half a century later, in the reign of Theodosius, it was declared to be the only religion that a person was permitted to practice.[262] Theodosius died in 395. Exactly 15 years later the Visigoths ravaged Rome.

This proud city, the center of the greatest empire of the ancient world, had flourished for a millennium under its own gods. Within a few decades of turning to Christianity, it had destroyed all the wonders and achievements of antiquity and then perished itself.[263] Christianity did not succeed as the one religion of the Roman Empire where Mithraism and the other Pagan cults had failed. In fact, Christianity was the religion that accompanied its downfall.

THE DESTRUCTION OF GNOSTICISM

Even after Literalist Christianity had become the state religion of the Roman Empire, Gnosticism remained a powerful force. In the fourth century heretical Christians were still so common that Cyril of Jerusalem had to warn the faithful to be careful not to step into a Gnostic church by mistake.[264] In the reign of Theodosius there were so many heretics among the clergy and monks in Egypt that the Patriarch Timothy made eating meat compulsory on Sundays, to flush out the vegetarian Gnostics![265]

Despite his obvious Gnosticism, the philosopher Synesius was even elected Bishop of Cyrene.[266] He had studied Platonic philosophy with Hypatia the Pagan scientist of Alexandria and considered the resurrection to be an allegorical representation of an ineffable Mystery. He taught that the only true religion is philosophy and that the stories and practices of religion are, at best, no more than helpful popular expressions of philosophic truth for non-philosophers.[267] In the contemporary climate of orthodoxy, however, he was forced to promise that as bishop he would toe the line in public but "philosophize in private."[268] Yet he still transformed his Easter Eve ceremony for the newly baptized into an initiation that had more in common with the Pagan Mysteries than orthodox Christianity.[269]

In response to the continuing popularity of Gnosticism the Roman Church set out to unify Christianity by force—an intention it carried out with ruthless efficiency. Theodosius passed over 100 laws against Gnostics, declaring illegal their beliefs, meetings, proselytizing, ownership of property, and eventually their very existence![270] One decree reads:

> Understand now by this present statute; Novatians, Valentinians, Marcionites, Paulicians, with what a tissue of lies and vanities, with what destructive and venomous errors, your doctrines are inextricably woven! We give you warning: Let none of you presume, from this time forward to meet in congregations. To prevent this we command you be deprived of all the houses in which you have been accustomed to meet and that these should be handed over immediately to the Catholic Church.[271]

In 381 Theodosius finally made heresy a crime against the state. Gnostic writings were condemned as a "hotbed of manifold perversity" which "should not only be forbidden, but entirely destroyed and burned with fire."[272] All philosophical debate was entirely suppressed. A proclamation declares:

> There shall be no opportunity for any man to go out to the public and to argue about religion or to discuss it or give any counsel.[273]

Early in the fifth century an abbot, working as a "heavy" for Cyril, the powerful Archbishop of Alexandria, led attacks on heretical Christian communities, threatening,

> I shall make you acknowledge the Archbishop Cyril, or else the sword will wipe out most of you, and moreover those of you who are spared will go into exile.[274]

Augustine, the great spokesman for Catholic Christianity, expressed the mood of the times perfectly when he explained that coercion was necessary since many people respond only to fear.[275] Military force was "indispensable" to suppress heretics—for their own good, of course. Augustine proclaims: "Filled with fear myself, I fill you with fear."[276] St. Paul's spirituality of love and Gnosis had become the Roman Church's religion of obedience and terror.[277]

INHERENT INTOLERANCE

Although modern Christianity is made up of countless diverse sects with opposing approaches, nearly all of them—Catholics, Orthodox, Protestants, Non-Conformists, and others—are fundamentally shaped by the triumph of Literalism in the fourth century. Most Christians today base their faith on the historical existence of Jesus. They assent to the apostolic creed formulated under the direction of the tyrannical Constantine. They read only those few texts that happened to have been selected for inclusion in the New Testament through a process of constant doctrinal conflict, flagrant forgery, and corrupt power politics in the early Church. We have been left with the mistaken idea that Literalism *is* Christianity, not merely one current of thought within it.

Why did Literalism triumph over Gnosticism? By its very nature, Gnosticism attracted people of a mystical nature. Literalism, on the other hand, attracted those interested in establishing a religion. Gnostics were concerned with personal enlightenment, not creating a Church. They could never have triumphed over the Literalists, because they could never have had the desire to do so.

Literalism was originally the Outer Mysteries of Christianity, designed to attract initiates to the spiritual path. With their fascinating tales of magic and miracles, and promise of immortality through the simple acts of baptism and belief, the Outer Mysteries were meant to be more popular and widely appealing than the Inner Mysteries. As Jesus says, "Many are called but few are chosen."[278] If the original integrity of the Jesus Mysteries had survived, the popularity of the Outer Mysteries would have naturally led more and more initiates into the Inner Mysteries of Gnosis. Once Gnosticism and Literalism were two distinct traditions in conflict with each other, it was inevitable that Literalism would prove the more popular. The eventual triumph of Literalism over Gnosticism was a foregone conclusion. What is surprising is that it took so long.

Above all, however, Literalist Christianity's success was due to one great quality it had from the beginning and continues to foster—intolerance. This is not a quirk of history, it is a logical by-product of taking the Jesus story as historical fact.

Paganism and Gnosticism were inherently tolerant because they were based on myths.[279] Different cults believed in different myths, but this didn't mean that they were in opposition to each other. Plurality was acceptable because what mattered was the inner meaning, not the particular expression. But intolerance is inherent in Literalism. If Jesus is the one and only Son of God who requires the faithful to acknowledge this as historical fact, then Christianity must be in opposition to all other religions who do not teach this. Moreover, if all unbelievers are to be damned for eternity it becomes the moral duty of Literalist Christians to spread their beliefs, by force if necessary, to save as many souls as possible, even if it means destroying their bodies to do so. The Roman Church's attacks upon Paganism and Gnosticism were a religious crusade, a God-given duty. Self-righteous intolerance had become holy.

CONCLUSION

As we reviewed the evidence, it seemed to us that the traditional "history" of Christianity was nothing less than the greatest cover-up of all time. Christianity's original Gnostic doctrines and its true origins in the Pagan Mysteries had been ruthlessly suppressed by the mass destruction of the evidence and the creation of a false history to suit the political purposes of the Roman Church. All those who questioned the official history were simply persecuted out of existence until there was no one left to dispute it.

Parallels with more recent history helped us to understand what had happened. At the beginning of the twentieth century a small handful of Communists took power in Russia. Yet within a few years huge numbers of people, including many of the civil servants who had administered the previous regime, had joined the Communist Party. Why? Because if you wanted to get on, you now had to be a Party member, and if you associated yourself in any way with the past regime, you were branded an enemy of the people. Similarly, once Christianity became the religion of the Roman Empire, its numbers began to swell enormously. Why? Because Christians were given preferential treatment. The clergy were not even required to pay tax![280] If you wanted a peaceful and successful life, you became a Christian. If you did not, you risked becoming branded as a Pagan "dissident"—an enemy of God. Just as Stalin's propaganda machine unscrupulously falsified a history for itself, which disguised its tyranny and proved its dogmas to be true and good, so the Christian propaganda machine likewise fed its lies to the faithful.

Like Communism, Christianity began with a message of freedom and equality but ended up creating an authoritarian and despotic regime. In recent years dogmatic intolerance has led fanatical young Communists in China and Cambodia to launch disastrous cultural revolutions that have destroyed the ancient riches of their civilizations and exterminated large numbers of the intelligentsia, leaving their societies in deep crisis. Likewise, 15 centuries previously, fanatical Christian monks launched a cultural revolution that laid waste the ancient wonders and achievements of Paganism, setting Western civilization back 1,000 years.

The wanton destruction of our Pagan heritage is the greatest tragedy in the history of the Western world. The scale of what was lost is hard to comprehend. Pagan mysticism and scientific inquiry were replaced by dogmatic authoritarianism. The Roman Church imposed its creed with threats and violence, denying generations of human beings the right to think their own thoughts and find their personal route to spiritual salvation. While the great literature of antiquity was being consigned to the flames, St. Augustine announced the triumph of Literalist fundamentalism, writing:

> Nothing is to be accepted except on the authority of scripture, since greater is that authority than all powers of the human mind.[281]

The ancients had built the pyramids and the Parthenon, but within a few hundred years of Christianity people in many areas of Europe had forgotten how to make brick houses. In the first century BCE Posidonius had created a beautiful revolving model of the solar system that faithfully represented the orbits of the planets.[282] By the end of the fourth century CE it was sacrilegious not to believe that God placed the stars in the heavens each night.[283] In the third century BCE, the Alexandrian scholar Eratosthenes had correctly calcu-

THE JESUS MYSTERIES

lated the circumference of the Earth to within a few percent, but now it had become a heresy not to believe that the Earth was flat.[284]

We found ourselves asking, if Paganism was so primitive and Literalist Christianity is the one true religion, why was Pagan civilization replaced by the 1,000 years we appropriately call the Dark Ages?

12

The Greatest Story
Ever Told

There is one river of Truth which receives tributaries from every side.[1]

Clement of Alexandria

The ancients would no doubt regard it as fitting that we should re-evaluate Christianity at this moment in time. According to Pagan astrology, Christianity was created at the beginning of the Great Month of Pisces. This Age is presently coming to an end and the New Age of Aquarius is dawning. From the ancient perspective, therefore, we stand at a similar turning point in the flow of history as the early Christians. The times we are living in are in many respects reminiscent of the last change of Ages. Apocalyptic fears abound. Strange new eclectic cults are springing up everywhere. Established religion is discredited and in decline. What form will spirituality take in the coming Age of Aquarius?

To move confidently forward into the future it is necessary to come to terms with the past, so it is appropriate to critically examine the Literalist Christianity that has dominated the last 2,000 years of our culture.

Spiritually this truly has been a "Dark Age" characterized by authoritarian religion, religious bigotry, and religious wars. By assuming the role of the only true faith Literalist Christianity has created an unbridgeable gulf between itself and all other spiritual traditions. Its self-proclaimed superiority has been used to justify the violent destruction of other societies around the world. It has even horribly persecuted its own mystics and free-thinkers. By adopting the Jewish father god Jehovah as the only acceptable face of God, it has subjugated the Divine Feminine, a theological perspective it has used to legitimize the subordination of women. Its insistence on blind faith in dogma and opposition to intellectual inquiry has led many to reject all forms of spirituality as mere superstition. For more and more people today religion is at best a joke and at worst a source of prejudice, intolerance, and conflict.

Whereas other cultures honor their ancestors as the source of their wisdom and civilization, we have vilified ours as Devil worshipers. What has this done to the Western psyche? We have been a culture cut off from its roots. Only after the rediscovery of Pagan philosophy in the fifteenth century, during the appropriately named Renaissance, or "rebirth," was Western civilization able to climb out of the morass of superstition and strife into which it had descended, a process which in recent years has yielded the fruit of modern science. Yet, unlike the ancients, we have not viewed science and spirituality as two aspects of the same Mystery, but as implacably hostile to each other.

Although it set out to unify the world under the banner of one religion, Literalist Christianity has actually been the cause of deep divisions: Christians against heathens, men against women, science against religion, faith against reason. The Jesus Mysteries Thesis is not just a new history of Christianity, it is an opportunity to heal the wounds left in the Western soul by these dreadful schisms.

If Christianity were to acknowledge its debt to the ancient Mysteries it could connect again to the universal current of human spiritual evolution and become a partner, not an adversary, of all the other religious traditions it has branded as the work of the Devil. If it were to cast off the deadweight of the Old Testament and its jealous tribal deity, it could rediscover the wisdom of the Divine Feminine. If it were to relinquish its dogmatism, it could reawaken the ancient sense of wonder that united science and mysticism in one human adventure of discovery. If it could finally concede that the New Testament is the work of men and women, not the word of God recording actual events, there would be nothing to stop it recovering its own mystical Inner Mysteries. Is this too much to hope for?

Only a century ago most thinking people believed that the story of Adam and Eve was literally true. Darwin's idea of natural evolution was regarded as ridiculous and heretical. Today Darwin's "unthinkable thought" has been overwhelmingly accepted. *The Jesus Mysteries* proposes a comparable shift in our understanding of Christianity. Today it may seem outrageous to claim that Christianity evolved from Paganism and that the Jesus story, like Genesis, is an allegorical myth. But tomorrow this will be obvious and uncontentious.

Christianity did not arrive as a unique divine intervention. It evolved from the past, like everything else. There are no sudden breaks in history, only a continuum of change. The ancient Pagan Mysteries did not die. They transformed into something new—into Christianity. The spirituality of the West has been shaped by these two great traditions. The time has come to rediscover their common ground and claim all of our rich heritage.

Of course this will never be accepted by fundamentalists, but if Christianity bows to reactionary pressure to return to its authoritarian past it will be consigning itself to the dustbin of history. The modern world is simply too sophisticated to fall for the "it must be true because it says so in the Bible" routine. Already Christianity is no longer the dominant force it once was. With its demise our culture has been left desperately searching for a new spiritual direction. Only by returning to its mystical roots will Christianity play a role in the creation of a new spirituality for the New Age of Aquarius. Literalist Christianity is built on the unsteady foundations of historical lies. Sooner or later it must topple over. But mystical Christianity rests securely on the bedrock of timeless mythical truth and is as relevant today as it always has been.

ONE TRUTH

Mystics of all spiritual traditions have taught that there is only one Truth, ever present and never changing. It was not suddenly revealed for the first time 2,000 years ago. Christianity is only a chapter in the perennial human quest for meaning, a current in the sea of evolving human consciousness, another attempt at articulating the timeless Gnosis toward which mystics have reached from the most ancient of days. God did not come to Earth on a once-only excursion. Nor do we have to wait for his promised apocalyptic return. The truth is, God never left.

Although there is now no tradition that can initiate modern Christians into the secret Inner Mysteries encoded in the Jesus story, these profound mystical teachings are still there for those with "eyes to see" and have been continually discovered by the greatest Christian mystics throughout the centuries. Thoroughly exploring what these teachings are is too large a task for this present book and must await a later work. All we hope to have established is that there is essentially one perennial philosophy at the heart of both the Pagan Mysteries and Christianity, and that these two traditional enemies are in fact close relatives.

Our desire is not to attack Christianity, but to point to the possibility of it regaining something it has lost—the Inner Mysteries, which reveal the secrets of Gnosis. We do not feel that the Jesus Mysteries Thesis undermines Christianity, but rather that it reveals the ancient grandeur of the Jesus story. It truly is the "greatest story ever told"—a story that has been thousands of years in the making.

In his *Study of History*, Arnold Toynbee wrote:

> Behind the figure of the dying demigod there looms the greater figure of a very God that dies for different worlds under diverse names—for a Minoan world as Dionysus, for a Sumeric world as Tammuz, for a Hittite world as Attis, for a Syriac world as Adonis, for a Christian world as Christ. Who is this God of many epiphanies but only one passion?[2]

The answer is each one of us. The ancient Mysteries taught that we are all sons and daughters of God and by understanding the myth of the sacrificed godman we also can be resurrected into our true immortal, divine identity. The Pagan philosopher Sallustius wrote of the myth of the Mystery godman Attis:

> The story of Attis represents an eternal cosmic process, not an isolated event in the past. As the story is intimately related to the ordered universe, we reproduce it ritually to gain order in ourselves. We, like Attis, have fallen from heaven; we die mystically with him and are reborn as infants.[3]

The same is true of the myth of Jesus. It is not "an isolated event in the past," but points toward the perpetual possibility of spiritual rebirth, here and now. It can still reveal the Mystery that Paul proclaimed, "Christ in you." As the Gnostic Jesus promises in *The Gospel of Thomas*,

> He who will drink from my mouth will become like me. I myself shall become he, and the things that are hidden will be revealed to him.[4]

Notes

CHAPTER 1: THE UNTHINKABLE THOUGHT

[1] *The Gospel of Thomas*, 62
[2] Mithraic inscription quoted in Godwin, J. (1981), 28
[3] Taylor, L. R. (1931), 27. Within a generation of the death of Alexander, Hecateus of Abdera, in *Aegyptiaca*, and Leon of Pella were using the composite name Osiris-Dionysus.
[4] Please note that in line with the modern convention all dates are given as BCE or CE—"Before the Common Era" or "Common Era." These religiously neutral terms replace the more usual BC and AD.
[5] Conventionally these two camps are known respectively as *orthodox* or *catholic* Christians and Gnostics. In order to prevent confusion with the institutions that use these names today, we have chosen to use the term *Literalist* instead of *catholic* or *orthodox*.
[6] Robinson, J. M. (1978), 362, quoting *The Second Treatise of the Great Seth*, 60, 20
[7] Pagels, E. (1979), 147

CHAPTER 2: THE PAGAN MYSTERIES

[1] Euripides, *The Bacchae*, 194, lines 74–83
[2] Kirk and Raven, (1957), 393, Anaxagoras fr. 532; *see* 141, Anaximander fr. 140
[3] The earliest mention of a spherical Earth in the West is in Plato, *Phaedo*, 110b, although Diogenes Laertius tells us that it was Pythagoras who first called the Earth round, *see* Guthrie, K. S. (1987), 154. The Alexandrian scholar Eratosthenes (275–194 BCE) asserted that if one sailed westward from Spain one would eventually reach India, *see* Marlowe, J. (1971), 72.
[4] Kirk and Raven, op. cit., 257, fr. 329: "Most people say that the earth lies at the center of the universe but the Italian philosophers known as Pythagoreans take the contrary view. At the center they say, is fire, and the earth is one of the planets creating night and day by its circular motion about the center." The Pythagorean theory was later adopted by the astronomers of the Alexandrian library: "Aristarchus of Samos hypothesises . . . that the earth is borne around the sun on the circumference of a circle." *See* Walbank, F. W. (1981), 185. Aristarchus was Eratosthenes' successor as Chief Librarian; *see* Marlowe, op. cit., 74.
[5] Marlowe, J. op. cit., 71. Eratosthenes' calculation was correct with an error of less than 1 percent.
[6] Lane-Fox, R. (1986), 47. Augustus ruled over an empire of over 100 million people. In Egypt, for example, the population did not approach eight million again until the mid-nineteenth century.
[7] Quoted in Kerenyi, C. (1967), 11. Zosimos is commenting on the laws passed in the fourth century CE by the Christian Emperor Valentinian to prohibit the celebration of the Greek Mysteries of Eleusis. They were regarded by local authorities as unworkable because the Mysteries were still held in such high esteem.
[8] Campbell, J. (1964), 268, quoting Cicero, *On the Laws*, 2.36

9 Burkert, W. (1985), 291: "Dionysus is the god of the exceptional. As the individual gains in independence, the Dionysus cult becomes a vehicle for the separation of private groups from the polis. Alongside public Dionysiac festivals there emerge Dionysus mysteries." Guthrie, W. K. C. (1952), 50: "It is this emergence of mystery religions into the stream of history that is meant by those who refer to the great religious revival of the sixth century. Henceforth . . . the choice of belief being a matter of individual temperament." *See* Wallis, R. T. (1992), 28, which records Jaeger's view that "From the fourth century BC on, the form of Greek religion that appealed to most people of higher education was not the religion of the Olympic gods but that of the mysteries, which gave the individual a more personal relationship with the godhead." The Mystery religions were ideally suited to the conditions following Alexander's conquest, when previously discrete cultures were thrown together. The science of comparative religion was born and old national and racial deities reinvented. The new Mediterranean *koine* presented to the individual new challenges and new opportunities. The individualistic salvation cults of the Mysteries flourished in this environment.

10 Burkert, op. cit., 289. The mystical understanding that the end and the beginning are One is a sentiment expressed by many initiates. In Greek initiation is *telete*, meaning "to finish," but when Cicero translated the concept into Latin he used *initiatio*, meaning "to begin." That both terms can be true is a reflection of this paradox. To the initiate the moments of birth, death, and initiation are the same.

11 Lucius Apuleius, *The Golden Ass*, 187, Chapter 18: "This was the happiest day of my initiation, and I celebrate it as my birthday . . . I remained for days longer in the temple, enjoying the ineffable pleasure of contemplating the Goddess's statue, because I was bound to her by a debt of gratitude that I could never hope to repay."

12 Plato, *Phaedrus*, 250b–c

13 Kingsley, P. (1995), Chapter 24. Kingsley states that the current state of research on the Presocratic philosophers has reached crisis point. Post-enlightenment classical scholars were as embarrassed by the mysticism and "miracle-mongering" of men like Pythagoras and Empedocles as they were by the supernaturalism of the New Testament. Consequently Plato's indebtedness to the Mysteries and to Orphic/Pythagorean doctrines was ignored or misunderstood. Only now are historians beginning to acknowledge that "rational" philosophy emerged from a wave of Oriental mysticism that swept Greece in the sixth and fifth centuries BCE. *See* Boardman, Griffin, and Murray (1986), 115: "The development of science and philosophy was concurrent with, and to some extent implicated in, the spread of untraditional doctrines derived not from pure reason but from oriental myth."

14 Plato, *Symposium*, 220c–d

15 Kirk and Raven, (1957), 183. Orphaned children in Ephesus were looked after in the Temple of Artemis, the "Great Mother" of Asia Minor. It was to this temple that Heraclitus donated his famous book. The bear was Artemis' totem animal, probably on account of its fiercely protective mother instinct. The children of the temple were known as "cubs."

16 Plutarch, *Life of Pericles*, 16

17 Diogenes and Antisthenes were the disciples of Plato and the originators of Cynic philosophy.

18 Euripides was the last of the Classical Greek tragedians; *The Bacchae* was his last work. The cave in which it is thought Euripides worked and meditated has recently been discovered near Salamis.

19 Kingsley, op. cit., 112, making clear his belief that large parts of Plato's philosophy derive from the teachings of the Mysteries. The Mysteries were shaped by the religious movement of Orphism and Pythagoreanism that swept Greece in the sixth and fifth centuries BCE. Pausanias, referring to a secret Pythagorean doctrine, says, "Whoever has seen the Mysteries or read the books of Orpheus will know what I mean," implying that the sayings of Orpheus formed a liturgical accompaniment to the performance of the sacred rites. A recently discovered fragment by Plato's nephew Speusippus, who took over the Academy after Plato, leaves us no doubt that he saw Plato as the successor of Pythagoras, *see* Burkert, W. (1972), 62. Aristotle also points out the dependence of Plato on Pythagoras, *see* Kingsley, op. cit., 111. Photius said that Plato was entirely dependent on the Italian Pythagoreans, and Numenius of Apamea claimed that Plato derived all his doctrines from Pythagoras, *see* Boardman, Griffin, and Murray, op. cit., 700. Proclus tells us that "Plato received all his knowledge of divine matters from Pythagorean and Orphic writings" and Moderatus of Gades severely criticized Plato, accusing him of using the ideas of Pythagoras without giving him credit where it was due, *see* Guthrie, K. S. (1987), 41. The Mysteries, Orphism, Pythagoreanism, and the philosophy of Plato can only be understood as a unified whole.

Unfortunately the key to this mystery was the secret imparted during initiation, a secret that initiates invariably took with them to the grave.

20 Kahn, C. H. (1979), 95, quoting an epigram attributed to Cleanthes
21 Angus, S. (1925), 70, quoting from *Concerning the Gods and the Universe*, 4
22 Quoted in Gregory, J. (1987), 188; slightly adapted
23 Burkert, W. (1992), 90, quoting Sopatros, *The Rhetorician*, 8.114
24 Angus, op. cit., vii. Eleusis was destroyed by Alaric the Goth aided by Christian monks.
25 Burkert, W. (1985), 286, and *see* Willoughby, H. R. (1929), 38, which also presents evidence that women and slaves were admitted to the rites. Numerous Roman nobles and Emperors were initiated at Eleusis, including Sulla, Mark Antony, Cicero, Augustus, Claudius, Domitian, Hadrian, and Marcus Aurelius, *see* Magnien, V. (1938), 25ff.
26 Kerenyi, C. (1967), 100ff. The Brahmin priest Zarmaros went as an ambassador to Emperor Augustus from King Poros of India. Augustus, initiated himself in 31 BCE, decreed that the Eleusinian Mysteries should be celebrated out of season to initiate his guest. At the climax of the Mysteries, when the sanctuary opened and the great fire blazed forth, Zarmaros astonished onlookers by walking directly into the flames.
27 Herodotus, *The Histories*, 544, Book 8, 63–8. Thirty thousand, the number of Dionysus revelers seen in the miraculous vision of 479 BCE, is the figure that Herodotus elsewhere gives for the entire population of Athens.
28 Burkert, op. cit., 287
29 The oath of secrecy taken by initiates was extracted from them before their admittance into the Telesterion, which seated 3,000 at a time. The Mysteries were performed at Eleusis for over 1,100 years during which time hundreds of thousands of people must have been initiated. Despite this, not one direct account of what took place inside survives to gratify the historian. What has been assembled so far is the indirect evidence from pottery, sculpture, poetry, plays, philosophers, and other literary sources.
30 Kerenyi, op. cit., 55: "The Hierophant at Eleusis appears as a second Dionysus." The Hierophant's costume was taken over from the actor in the tragedies of Aeschylus, a testimony to the close link between the origins of the Mysteries and the birth of theater.
31 Angus, S. (1925), 61
32 The development of theater from the cult of Dionysus is a well known fact, but how this happened is little understood and insecurely researched. Gasset writes: "Tragedy was a religious ceremony . . . Greek scholars are baffled by the faith of the Athenians, they are unable to reconstruct it. Until they have done so, Greek tragedy will be a page written in a language to which we possess no dictionary." *See* Kerenyi, C. (1976), 315. We do know that the circular orchestra of the theater was taken over from the circular threshing places used at harvest-time and that theater arose from widespread popular rituals performed in honor of Dionysus. Guthrie, W. K. C. (1952), 32, presents evidence that the first tragedy performed in the service of Dionysus was a mimetic performance—a passion play accompanied by song. The first tragedy was therefore probably concerned with the death and dismemberment of the god. Guthrie also notes that in Greek theater, "The number of plays which dealt with the tearing in pieces of heroes, some of them closely akin to Dionysus, is surprising." Understanding that the Mysteries and theater arose in the same culture, at the same period, under the aegis of the same patron deity, offers a valuable insight into what might have taken place in the dramatic spectacle enacted at Eleusis.
33 Otto, W. F. (1965), 49. *See also* Macchioro, V. D. (1930), 75, where the two traditions as to who introduced the death of Dionysus into the Mysteries are noted. One says Orpheus himself, another that the Orphic poet Onomacritus made the innovation in the sixth century BCE. Clement of Alexandria confirms that the symbols revealed in the Mysteries refer to the death of Dionysus.
34 A term meaning purification. Aristotle, in *Poetics*, states that tragedy should result in a purging (catharsis) of the emotions by pity and terror. The Mysteries too were meant to be a catharsis. Empedocles' poem *Catharmoi*, of which a few intriguing fragments remain, is believed to have been a liturgy of initiation.
35 Angus, op. cit., 93, quoting Synesius on Aristotle. Aristotle writes that initiates of the Mysteries were not expected to learn something (*mathein*), but to suffer something (*pathein*).
36 Quoted in Burkert, W. (1992), 11
37 Fidler, D. (1993), 6: "The teachings of the mystery religions were characteristically embodied in allegory, myth, and symbolic imagery, both as "teaching stories" and as basic paradigms of human experience. Certain philosophical schools, especially the Stoics and Platonists, drew upon traditional myths to illustrate insights, which transcend merely logical description.

Moreover, they held that the interpretation of the traditional myths, like the pursuit of philosophy itself, constituted, at its core, a process of initiation."

38 Plato, *Phaedo*, 69c

39 Ibid., 69d: "As those who understand the mysteries say, 'There are many who bear the wand, but few who become Bacchoi.'" Becoming one with the godman was the goal of the Mysteries.

40 Quoted in Fidler, op. cit., 23. Sallustius also writes: "The universe itself can be called a myth, since bodies and material objects are apparent in it, while souls and intellects are concealed," *see* Ehrenberg, V. (1968), 5.

41 Heliodorus, *An Ethiopian Story*, 9.9, quoted in Fidler, op. cit., 322, note 46

42 Kingsley, P. (1995), 367. A beginner was called a *mystae*, which means "eyes closed" and is the root of our words "mystery" and "mysticism." The *mystae* were those who had not yet understood the secret Inner Mysteries. The higher level of initiates were called *epoptae*, meaning "to have seen." The *epoptae* were those who had understood the Inner Mysteries.

43 Kerenyi, C. (1976), Preface, xxiv. Despite this abundance of physical evidence for the popularity of the Dionysus cult, Kerenyi reiterates Nietzsche's lament that "Even today virtually everything in the field of the Dionysian still remains to be discovered." *The Jesus Mysteries* is a part of this ongoing discovery.

44 Harrison, J. (1922), 413. Dionysus is often simply referred to as Dionysus Polynomous, "Many-named Dionysus."

45 Herodotus, *The Histories*, 197, Book 2, 172: "It is on this lake that the Egyptians act by night in what they call their Mysteries, the Passion of that being whose name I will not speak." Like all initiates of the Greek Mystery religion Herodotus had taken a solemn vow to keep its secrets, but here in Egypt he found the same rites being performed openly. Often, therefore, he is deliberately cryptic or maintains an eloquent silence, which would only be understood by other initiates. Herodotus must have been astonished to see a public enactment of the same drama that in Eleusis was performed for the chosen few in strictest secrecy. He writes cryptically, "All the details of these performances are known to me, but I will say no more."

46 Murray, M. A. (1949), 39: "The Sacred Drama of the dedication and sacrifice of the Incarnate God can be followed in the Pyramid Texts." These date to 2700 BCE.

47 Psammetichus I allowed the Ionian Greeks to establish a trading post in the delta in 670 BCE.

48 Aelian tells us of Pythagoras' gold crown, white clothing, and trousers. This has been interpreted as the traditional clothing of an Ionian poet by some scholars, but Burkert, W. (1972), 165, notes that "in exactly the same attire, the highest God, lord of death and rebirth appears in the 'Mithras liturgy.'" It is likely therefore that the account of Pythagoras' costume is meant to portray him as an initiate. D'Alviella, G. (1981), 114, notes that this was the traditional dress of initiates into the Mysteries and was later worn by Christian catechumens undergoing baptism.

49 Guthrie, K. S. (1987), 60

50 Harrison, op. cit., 365: "In Homer, Dionysus is not yet an Olympian. On the Parthenon frieze he takes his place among the seated gods." Harrison's work does much to explain the revolution that took place in Athens in the sixth and fifth centuries BCE. During this time Greece was swept by the cult of Dionysus in what amounted to a religious revival. In the Homeric Olympian religion there was a strict boundary between the gods who were immortal and men who were doomed to die. Dionysus broke through this religious taboo— a god who became a man, he died and crossed the Olympian boundary to become a god. Unlike the archaic gods of Olympus, Dionysus is always portrayed surrounded by a band of human followers and his triumph at Athens accompanied the creation of the first democracy. Harrison calls Dionysus "the people's god."

51 *See* Iamblichus, "The Pythagoric Life" and Porphyry, "The Life of Pythagoras" in *The History of Philosophy*. The followers of Pythagoras established religious communities dedicated to the "Orphic Life" in southern Italy in the sixth century BCE. Men and women were admitted as equals, all possessions were shared in common, and neophytes took a five-year vow of silence. The Pythagoreans rose at dawn to worship the rising sun, spent the day in philosophical study and religious observances, and at a communal evening meal there were readings from sacred scriptures. They were strict vegetarians, wore white, and practiced celibacy. These practices are distinctly reminiscent of the practices of the medieval monasteries, but this similarity is not accidental. St. Anthony, the founder of the first Christian monastery, was himself a Pythagorean and modeled his monastic community on the Pythagorean communities of Croton in southern Italy. *See* Lietzmann, H. (1961), Book 4, 136ff.

52 Osiris-Dionysus is the most useful title for understanding the nature of the Mystery godman. Herodotus states that the rites of Dionysus derive from those of Osiris and that "Osiris is Dionysus." In the first century BCE Diodorus confirms this, saying, "The rite of Osiris is the same as that of Dionysus and that of Isis very similar to that of Demeter; the names alone having been interchanged, and the punishments in Hades of the unrighteous, the Fields of the Righteous and the fantastic conceptions, current among the many—all these were introduced by Orpheus in imitation of the Egyptian funeral customs." Plutarch, in the second century CE, also states unequivocally that "Osiris is the same as Dionysus," see Plutarch, De Iside et Osiride, 35. Walter Burkert, a leading authority on Greek religion, wrote in 1977: "To what extent the myth, and indeed the very cult of chthonic Dionysus and the beliefs in blessedness and punishments in the nether world are dependent on the Egyptian Osiris cult from the start remains a question that must be seriously asked." See Burkert, W. (1985), 298.

53 Burkert, W. (1992), 37. Timotheus, an Eleusinian priest, came to Alexandria in 300 BCE to found the Mysteries there.

54 Turcan, R. (1992), 201

55 Angus, S. (1925), 202

56 Ibid., 283. In Cicero, On the Good Life, 109, Cicero relates that "When Socrates was asked which country he belonged to, he replied, 'The World.'" Diogenes, the follower of Socrates' disciple Antisthenes, likewise called himself a cosmopolitan. A fragment of Democritus records: "To a wise man the whole earth is open; for the native land of a good soul is the whole earth," see Lindsay, J. (1970), 93.

57 Angus, op. cit., 195, slightly adapted

58 Wallis Budge, E. A., Egyptian Religion (1899)

59 Ibid., 59

CHAPTER 3: DIABOLICAL MIMICRY

1 Justin Martyr, First Apology, 54, quoted in Hoffmann, R. J. (1987), 24

2 Quoted in Hoffmann, 120

3 D'Alviella, G. (1981), 119, surveys the extensive similarities between Christianity and the Mysteries and notes that "All these points of contact with pagan institutions could not fail to amaze and annoy the Christians who had to wage war against the last defenders of paganism."

4 King, C. W. (1887), 122–3. Justin Martyr claimed that the story of Dionysus was "invented by demons" to correspond with a certain prophesy in Genesis and bring the true Christ into doubt, see Guthrie, W. K. C. (1952), 266. Two centuries later the Christian father Firmicus Maternus was still explaining the story of the resurrection of Dionysus as an attempt to ridicule the true faith. He states indignantly, "The devil too has his Christians," D'Alviella, G. (1981), 119, quoting The Error of Profane Religion, 23.

5 Quoted in Kingsland, W. (1937), 99. In First Apology, Chapter 62, Justin also accuses the Mithraists of telling "their worshipers to 'put off their shoes'" in imitation of the command given to Moses," see Apology, 1.62.

6 "We believe . . . in one Lord Jesus Christ his son, the only-begotten God." The "Dedication Creed" of 341 CE, see Doran, R. (1995), 102.

7 Euripides, The Bacchae, 222, line 836

8 The King James version of Holy Communion, based on the "Dedication Creed."

9 Harrison, J. (1922), 444, quoting The Bacchae, line 723

10 John 1 v 14

11 Romans 8 v 3

12 Euripides, op. cit., 191, line 5

13 Ibid., 192, line 22

14 Lane, E. N. (1996), 40. Cybele the virgin goddess was known as Mater Deum, the Mother of God. In the fourth century Mary took over this title.

15 See The Hermetica (Stobaeus fr. 23), where Isis is hailed as Kore Kosmu, the Virgin of the World.

16 Campbell, J. (1964), 26. The mythologist Joseph Campbell writes of similarities between the birth of Jesus and the Orphic myth of the miraculous birth of Dionysus, "While the maiden goddess sat there, peacefully weaving a mantle on which there was to be a representation of the universe, her mother contrived that Zeus should learn of her presence; he approached in the form of an immense snake. And the virgin conceived the ever-dying, ever-living god of bread and wine, Dionysus, who was born and nurtured in that cave, torn to death as a babe

and resurrected... In Christian legend, derived from the same archaic background, God the Holy Ghost in the form of a dove approached the Virgin Mary and she—through the ear—conceived God the Son, who was born in a cave, died and resurrected, and is present hypostatically in the bread and wine of the Mass."

17 One of the few remaining fragments of *The Gospel of the Hebrews* says of Mary that "Christ was in her womb for seven months," *see* Barnstone, W. (1984), 335, and Metzger, B. M. (1987), 170. *The Gospel of the Hebrews* is believed to have been written in Egypt, *see* Stanton, G. (1995), 101. According to Clement it also quoted from Plato's *Timaeus, see* Barnstone, W. (1984), 335.

18 Kerenyi, C. (1976), 106. Semele's seven-month pregnancy is recorded by Diodorus of Sicily and Lucian.

19 Justin Martyr, *Apology*, 3

20 Lactantius, *Divine Institutions*, 4.27,20, quoted in Turcan, R. (1992), 279. The Church father makes clear that this doctrine of the identity of Father and Son was "implicit in the divine mysteries."

21 Murray, M. A. (1949), 45. The kings and queens of the Ptolemaic period had a birth chamber built in every temple. Here the divine birth of the King, the Son of God, was celebrated annually.

22 Ibid., 39

23 Guthrie, K. S. (1987), 58, quoting Iamblichus, *Life of Pythagoras*

24 Grüber and Kersten (1985), 223

25 Kingsley, P. (1995), 380, charts the transmission of the hidden Orphic/Pythagorean tradition from Empedocles through to the Sufi mystics of Islam. Jewish and Christian Gnostics and the Hermeticists and alchemists of Alexandria are all stops along this path; all derive from one esoteric classical tradition.

26 *See* Sallust, *Cataline*, 51.20

27 Angus, S. (1925), 227

28 Dittenberger, *Sylloge*, 2nd ed., 1.347, 3rd ed., 760, quoted ibid., 109

29 Ibid., 227

30 Virgil, *The Pastoral Poems*, 53. Virgil's fourth *Eclogue*, the so-called Messianic poem, was written in 40 BCE. The poets of the Augustan age were deeply immersed in Greek philosophy and mysticism, and through them the doctrines of Orpheus and Pythagoras and astrological teachings on the New Age were pressed into the service of imperial propaganda. Although Augustus' birthday was September 23, he portrayed himself as a Capricorn, like Mithras and Jesus. On coins he is depicted with the sign of Capricorn. That this was the "Gate of the Gods" in the zodiac—the rebirth of the sun at the winter solstice—was a commonplace of Graeco-Roman thought.

31 Mayor, Fowler, and Conway, (1907), 22. The earliest recorded attempt to interpret the poem in this sense was that of Emperor Constantine the Great. He declared that the poet knew that he was writing of Christ, but "wrapped the prophecy in an allegory in order to escape persecution." This belief was accepted for centuries but *see* p.12, where a modern scholar writes about "the ridiculous, and if it were not sincere, I might have said blasphemous, notion that the *Eclogue* contains an inspired Messianic prophecy."

32 Wallace-Hadrill, A. (1993), 86. Similar tales were told of the birth of Alexander the Great.

33 Dittenberger, *Orientis Graeci Inscriptiones Selectae*, 458. The Augustan scholar Andrew Wallace-Hadrill writes of the recently discovered inscription set up in 9 BCE in Asia Minor, "If we had more of this sort of thing, links with the thought and language of Paul might seem less strange." *See* Wallace-Hadrill, A. (1993), 93.

34 Quoted in Hoffmann, R. J. (1987), 57

35 For Pagans, the myth of the divine birth was a metaphorical teaching story. To the initiates of the Mysteries, a human being consisted of a material body and a spiritual soul. Our divine "father" is God, who gives us our immortal soul, our material "mother" is the Earth (matter), who gives us a mortal body. Matter cannot give birth alone, but is mysteriously impregnated by invisible Spirit to produce Life, and so is portrayed as a perpetual virgin. To the Pagan philosophers, we are all sons and daughters of God. The miraculous birth of Osiris-Dionysus is an allegory, which to the initiated expressed this spiritual truth.

36 Euripides, *The Bacchae*, line 519, quoted in Harrison, J. (1922), 436

37 Ibid. Dionysus was conceived mystically.

38 Kerenyi, C. (1967), 202, an event, which he acknowledges as "symbolic"

39 Harrison, J. (1922), 552

40 Ibid., 548. "The marriage of this mother, and the birth of this Son" was the climax of the Mysteries.

41 Wallis Budge, E. A., *Egyptian Religion* (1899), 43
42 Ibid., 37, *Hymn to Ra* from 1100 BCE
43 Duat is a name for the Underworld inhabited by the dead.
44 Murray, M. A. (1949), 68
45 Harrison, J. (1922), 548ff, *see also* Burkert, W. (1985), 239. Of this ancient ritual and the three-day festival at which it was celebrated Burkert says, "A certain similarity with the sequence of Good Friday and Easter cannot be overlooked."
46 Wilson, I. (1984), 52
47 Burkert, W. (1985), 297, quoting the *Orphic Rhapsodies*: "To the child Dionysus he hands over the rule of the world and places him on a throne." This took place in the birth cave.
48 Cumont, F. (1903), 131
49 Guthrie, W. K. C. (1952), 197. The Pythagoreans rejected animal sacrifice and this was Empedocles' alternative.
50 Frazer, J. (1922), 337
51 Ibid., 346
52 Ibid., 347
53 Campbell, J. (1964), 339. The heliacal rising of Sirius (the brightest star in the northern hemisphere), which heralded the rising of the Nile, was for millennia associated by Egyptians with the resurrection of Osiris.
54 Ibid.
55 Lietzmann, H. (1961), Book 3, 314: "Epiphanius followed the same custom [celebrating the birth of Jesus on January 6] in Cyprus in AD 380. The Syrian church did likewise in the fourth century; and when preaching on Whit-Sunday in AD 386 in Antioch, John Chrysostom mentions only three Christian festivals; Epiphany, Easter, and Whitsuntide, and he expressly describes Epiphany as the festival of the appearance of God on earth i.e., the festival of Christ's birth."
56 Kerenyi, C. (1976), 299: "In Egypt January 5th had since 1996 BCE been a festive date marking the birth of light."
57 According to inscriptions Dionysus is the "Light of Zeus," *see* Kerenyi, C. (1976), 279. The Church father Firmicus Maternus relates that Dionysus was welcomed with "Hail, New Light," *see* Angus, S. (1925), 115. Attis likewise was hailed as "New Light," *see* ibid., 136. Clement of Alexandria repeats the Mystery formula "Hail, O Light," but this time to greet Jesus as the sun, *see* Stevenson, J. (1957), 181–2.
58 Graves (1955), 58
59 Campbell, J. (1964), 349
60 John 3 v 30
61 Porphyry (1991), 44: "Cancer is the gate through which souls descend but Capricorn that through which they ascend." Porphyry attributes this doctrine to Plato. In astrology Cancer is ruled by the Moon, the mistress of life, Capricorn by Saturn, the god of death.
62 Frazer, J. (1922), 360
63 Inge, W. R. (1899), 353, quoting the *Homeric Hymn to Demeter*
64 Murray, M. A. (1949), 39
65 Cumont, F. (1903), 157
66 Angus, S. (1925), 82: "In the Hall of Initiation of the temple of Men at Antioch there was found an oblong depression, of which the most obvious explanation is that it is for baptisms. In the underground pagan shrine, discovered a few months ago on the Via Salaria, the most striking feature is a tank sunk deep in the floor which may well have served as a baptistery."
67 Ibid., 81
68 Cumont, op. cit., 167
69 Angus, op. cit., 81. Clement of Alexandria says, "In the Mysteries current among the Greeks lustrations hold the premier place."
70 Quoted ibid.
71 Romans 6 v 1–8; *see also The Shepherd of Hermas*, in which "the seal of the Son of God" is water "into which they descend dead and come up alive."
72 Wells, G. A. (1975), 184
73 Ibid.
74 Cumont, op. cit., 157
75 D'Alviella, G. (1981), 114, notes that Christianity took over the Pagan ritual almost in its entirety. The Christian baptism ceremonies recorded by John Chrysostom, Cyril, and Dionysius can be set alongside those of Pagan initiation written by Claudius, Themistius, and Plutarch.
76 Lucius Apuleius, *The Golden Ass*, 286

77 Quoted in Eisler, R. (1920), 208
78 Matthew 3 v 11–12; *see also* Harrison, J. (1963), 34, which notes that baptism by fire was symbolized in the early Church by immersing a blazing torch into the font, and D'Alviella, G. (1981), 113, which records that in the early Roman Church the Pope leads the "Chosen Ones" to the baptistery where he consecrates the water in the baptismal font by blowing over the surface of the water. The deacons then dip their candles in the water. In the *Missale Romanum*, which is still in force today, the priest dips an Easter candle in the baptismal font, praying "that it may fully impregnate this water with its power." Among the Greeks pieces of firewood or torches lit from the altar flame were added to the lustral water and purification by air was also used. As D'Alviella notes, "The baptismal font of Christianity therefore contains the three principal elements through which the candidates for the Mysteries formerly had to pass."
79 Harrison, J. (1922), 547
80 Frazer, J. (1922), 388
81 John 3 v 3–12
82 Lietzmann, H. (1961), Book 3, 320. *See also* p. 314, where Clement of Alexandria tells us that the Gnostic followers of Basilides celebrated the baptism of Jesus on the night of January 5. One hundred and fifty years after the Basilideans, the Literalists adopted this date as the epiphany and baptism of Jesus.
83 Ibid. The birthday of Osiris celebrated the rising of the Nile and was taken over by the Christians as the day on which Christ sanctified the water.
84 Ibid. Lietzmann, an orthodox Church historian, relates the numerous connections between the wine miracles of Jesus and Dionysus and then declares: "No explanation is needed to show how this very day came to be adopted for commemorating the marriage at Cana when Jesus performed the miracle which used to be performed by Dionysus." On this matter we disagree—an explanation *is* needed.
85 Otto, W. F. (1965), 98
86 Ibid., *see also* Lietzmann, op. cit., 314
87 John 2 v 1–11
88 Lietzmann, op. cit., 321
89 Hoffmann, R. J. (1987), 133, note 59
90 Angus, S. (1925), 307, offers a detailed description of the Asclepius/Jesus confrontation
91 Ibid., 309. Statues of Asclepius became models for the fourth- and fifth-century depictions of Jesus.
92 Kingsley, P. (1995), 342
93 Quoted in Guthrie, K. S. (1987), 91. The same miracle is recorded by Porphyry.
94 Mark 4 v 35–41
95 Guthrie, op. cit.: "Many admirable and divine particulars are unanimously and uniformly related of Pythagoras, such as infallible predictions of earthquakes, rapid expulsions of pestilences, and hurricanes, instantaneous cessations of hail, and tranquillizations of the waves of rivers and seas, in order that his disciples might the more easily pass over them. The power of effecting miracles of this kind was achieved by Empedocles of Agrigentum, Epimenides the Cretan, and Abaris the Hyperborean, and these they performed in many places." Pythagoras even had the ability to appear in two places at once. Porphyry relates, "Almost unanimous is the report that on one and the same day he was present at Metapontum in Italy, and at Tauromenium in Sicily, in each place conversing with his friends, though the places are separated by many miles, both at sea and land, demanding a journey of many days," Guthrie, 128.
96 John 21 v 11
97 Guthrie, op. cit., 128. Porphyry writes: "Meeting with some fishermen who were drawing in their nets heavily laden with fishes from the deep, he predicted the exact number of fish they had caught. The fishermen said that if his estimate was accurate they would do whatever he recommended. They counted them accurately, and found the number correct, he then bade them to return the fish alive into the sea; and, what is more wonderful, not one of them died, although they had been out of the water a considerable time."
98 In *Orpheus the Fisher* Dr. Eisler explores the connection between the gospel story and Pythagoras.
99 It is the square root of 3, the controlling ratio of the equilateral triangle, is found in the ratio of the *vesica piscis* (the length divided by the height) and is an indispensable mathematical formula, *see* Fidler, D. (1993), 305.
100 Fidler, D. (1993), 108: "Anyone who knew a bit about mathematics would have immediately recognized the tale of the 153 fish in the net for what it is: a geometrical problem, though

one, in this case, with a cosmological dimension." Fidler has clearly demonstrated that the miraculous feeding of the 5,000 and the story of the fish in the net belong together. Every number in the feeding story, from the people sitting down in units of 50 and 100 to the five loaves and two fishes, is part of a formula that eventually yields a beautiful 12-rayed star with the measurement 888.

[101] Kirk and Raven, (1957), 354–5, quoting fr. 354

[102] According to Iamlichus' *Life of Pythagoras*, 28

[103] Kingsley, P. (1995), 40

[104] *See* Ava Chitwood, "The Death of Empedocles" *AJP*, 1986, p.180; *also* John 11 v 43

[105] Apollonius of Tyana was a sage of the first century CE. His biography was written up at the beginning of the third century CE, by which time it had acquired numerous legendary accretions. Many scholars have noted the similarities with the Jesus story, a fact which led early Christians to suggest that it was written to discredit their own miracle-man. Both stories in fact draw on a standard biography, which is attributed to numerous wonder-workers in the ancient world.

[106] Anderson, G. (1994), 32

[107] Mark 5 v 22 and *see* Anderson, op. cit., 96

[108] Luke 4 v 24

[109] Quoted in Eisler, R. (1931), 149

[110] Mark 5 v 10–14 and Luke 8 v 32–3

[111] Burkert, W. (1985), 286; *see also* Harrison, J. (1922), 153. When Eleusis was permitted to issue her own autonomous coinage it was the pig that she chose as the sign and symbol of her Mysteries, an animal that since Neolithic times has been associated with the Underworld. In some myths Adonis is killed by a wild boar.

[112] Harrison, op. cit., 152. The initiates bathed in the sea under the full moon, each with his sacrificial piglet.

[113] Burkert, op. cit., 242

[114] Acts 2 v 5–13

[115] Herodotus, *The Histories*, Book 8, 135; *see also* Athanaissakis, A. P. (1976), 20, *Homeric Hymn to Apollo*, 158–64. This report probably has a connection to the Pythagoreans. The altar at Delos offered only bloodless sacrifices, and the island is often mentioned in connection with the vegetarian Pythagoras.

[116] Burkert, op. cit., 110: "This has justly been compared to the Pentecostal miracle and the speaking in tongues in the New Testament."

[117] Hoffmann, R. J. (1987), 69

[118] Quoted ibid., 66

[119] The Jewish Menorah was taken over from Babylonian depictions of the "seven lights"— the sun, moon, and five visible planets. Babylonian astrology swept Greece and Italy in the four centuries BCE, to the benefit of the Jews. By the Roman period they were well known as peddlers of talismans and horoscopes and were often indistinguishable from Chaldaeans. In 139 BCE we hear of Chaldaeans and Jews alike being driven out of Rome. Intriguingly, these Jews are recorded as worshipers of Sabazius, another name for Dionysus. In *Mystery Religions in the Ancient World*, Godwin presents several Jewish depictions of the zodiac from the Roman period.

[120] Kerenyi, C. (1976), figure 146. The fourth-century BCE Brindisi Disc is the earliest known depiction of the zodiac in Europe. In the center Dionysus and Ariadne ascend to heaven in the chariot of the sun. In the sixth century BCE the Orphic poet Onomacritus rewrote the story of Dionysus and introduced the motif of the divine child killed and eaten by the 12 Titans. In so doing he brought the myth into conformity with the astrological motif of the one soul of the world manifesting in 12 archetypes. At the same time the numerous trials of Heracles were reworked into the familiar 12 for the same reason. Heracles is shown as an archetypal initiate on numerous vases, the earliest dating to 530 BCE. With the admission of Demeter and Dionysus into Olympus, the 10 gods recognized by Homer were made up into the 12 that became canonical from this period on. Various attempts were then made in the Hellenistic period to equate the Olympians each with a particular sign.

[121] *See* Godwin, J. (1981). Godwin has collected numerous depictions of mystery gods encircled by the zodiac.

[122] Kirk and Raven (1957), 326. Empedocles, the disciple of Pythagoras, called God "a rounded sphere rejoicing in his solitude . . . a sphere equal to himself from every side."

[123] This archetype thus plays a vital role in the organization of everything from atoms to cells. If equal pressure is brought to bear on these spheres so that the central thirteenth becomes flattened, it takes on the shape of a dodecahedron—a solid shape with 12 pentagonal sides.

The dodecahedron was a cult object of the Pythagoreans and was equated with "the All" and the "cosmic sphere" of the heavens. It is one of the five sacred solids described by Plato in *Timaeus*, four of which were equated with the elements earth, water, air, and fire. The fifth, the dodecahedron, was regarded as the most sacred and was associated with the fifth element, ether or spirit. In *Timaeus*, 22, Plato equates the dodecahedron with the zodiac. As a sign of completeness it appears in the 12 trials of Hercules, the 12 months of the year, the disciples of Christ, the followers of Mohammed, the gods of Olympus, the members of a jury, etc.

[124] Luke 9 v 28–36

[125] Euripides, *The Bacchae*, 241, lines 22–5. This play is mostly intact apart from losses to the scene of Dionysus' divine epiphany.

[126] Harrison, J. (1922), 541, quoting a ritual hymn of Delphi about Dionysus' epiphany at Eleusis

[127] Angus, S. (1925), 310

[128] Euripides, op. cit., 211

[129] Luke 7 v 31–5. *The Epistle of Barnabas* demonstrates that this was a widespread ancient tradition about Jesus and his followers: "In his choice of the Apostles he truly showed himself the Son of God, for those men were ruffians of the deepest dye," *see* Louth, A. (1968), 164.

[130] Lietzmann, H. (1961), Book 4, 136ff. Antony's biographer Athanasius does not disguise the fact that Antony's life followed the example of Pythagoras. Like Pythagoras, Antony is described as coming onto the public scene "as a consecrated mystic filled with God" and "as one initiated into sacred Mysteries, with knowledge of the unseen world and power over it." He then began to organize his theocracy of monks along the same lines that Pythagoras had organized a philosophical polis in southern Italy for his disciples. *See* Burkert, W. (1985), 303, where Burkert records some of the similarities between Christian monasticism and the Pythagorean communities of the sixth and fifth centuries BCE.

[131] Mark 11 v 2 and Matthew 21 v 2

[132] Lucius Apuleius, *The Golden Ass*, 170. To walk on palms was the sign of triumph, as in Apuleius' description of Isis: "On her divine feet were slippers of palm leaves, the emblem of victory."

[133] Plato, *Symposium*, 175e

[134] Frazer, J. (1922), 349; *see also* Lane, E. N. (1996), 39. The Church fathers Firmicus Maternus and Arnobius were both aware of the parallel between the pine tree and the cross.

[135] Godwin, J. (1981), 12

[136] Harrison, J. (1922), 617

[137] Ibid. Harrison connects the "ass who carried the Mysteries" with the Golden Ass of Apuleius.

[138] Burkert, W. (1985), 287

[139] Lucius Apuleius, *The Golden Ass*, 13. At one point in the story a young woman escapes from a bandit's cave and rides to safety on the back of a donkey. Apuleius remarks that it is an extraordinary sight to see a virgin riding in triumph on an ass—meaning that she had dominated the lusts of the flesh.

[140] Ibid. Graves (1955) discusses the symbolism of the donkey.

[141] The Greeks knew this figure as Typhon.

[142] Kerenyi, C. (1976), plate 54b

[143] Ibid., plate 55

[144] Ibid.

[145] Burkert, W. (1992), 11, i.e., the uninitiated never reach consummation.

[146] Luke 23 v 2

[147] Euripides, *The Bacchae*, 203, line 384

[148] Mark 14 v 63

[149] Euripides, op. cit., 199, line 246

[150] Ibid., 205, lines 435–44

[151] John 19 v 10–11

[152] Euripides, op. cit., 208, line 547

[153] Luke 23 v 34

[154] Euripides, op. cit., 208, line 484

[155] Luke 23 v 28–30

[156] Euripides, op. cit., 209, lines 548–50

[157] The authorities even contrive a one-month delay in Socrates' execution and ensure that security at his prison is lax so that he can escape. Socrates also declines this opportunity to let his prosecutors off the hook and declares that they are more afraid of imposing the sentence than he is of suffering it.

158 Plato, *Defense of Socrates*, 37b
159 Ibid., b–c
160 Matthew 26 v 39
161 Plato, *Crito*, 44b. Socrates quotes from *The Iliad*, 9.363, to imply that three days after his death he will return to his true home.
162 Walker, D. P. (1972), 45. The account of Socrates' death is found in the books of Plato, all of which were banned from the Christian Empire. When they turned up in Florence in the fifteenth century they caused a great stir. They were translated by the Renaissance scholar and Catholic priest Marsilio Ficino, who was struck by the comparisons between Socrates and Jesus. Both were examples of humility, total lack of ambition for worldly honor, and the willing acceptance of an unjust death. Ficino also wondered about the 30 pieces of silver, the crowing of the cock at dawn, and the cup of poison. The parallels between Socrates and Jesus are now well known. A modern classical scholar writes of Socrates' death: "It has often been compared with the story of the gospels," *see* Ehrenberg, V. (1968), 377.
163 Guthrie, K. S. (1987), 267, Saying number 12. In the short ethical sayings of Sextus the Pythagorean, which were found among the Gnostic gospels, we read: "The sage whose estimation with men is but small while he was living will be renowned when he is dead." Jesus also fits this expectation completely.
164 Seneca, *Letters from a Stoic*, 236: "A number of Stoics whose lack of respect for emperors earned them martyrdom."
165 Ibid. Seneca himself was implicated in a conspiracy against Nero and "suicided."
166 MacMullen, R. (1966), 64
167 Ibid., 55. MacMullen traces the depth and extent of philosophical resistance to the tyranny of the Empire. The stories of the philosophers' heroic outspokenness were eventually formed into a book called *The Acts of the Pagan Martyrs*.
168 Plato, *The Republic*, Book 2, 361e; *see also* Plato, *Apology*, 41a. Socrates wonders whether he too will join the ranks of the unjustly accused and compare notes with them in the afterlife.
169 Hoffmann, R. J. (1987), 112–13
170 Euripides, *The Bacchae*, 200, line 242. Euripides equates Demeter with bread and Dionysus with wine.
171 Mark 14 v 22
172 Frazer, J. (1922), 376. Such motifs led Frazer to see the godman of the Mysteries as "a personification of the corn," whose death and resurrection represented the harvesting and regrowth of the crops. The Egyptians beat their breasts and sang a lament as they cut the first corn and trampled it on the threshing floor, because Osiris was "dying" so that they could have bread to live from. Likewise, the Greeks wore Dionysus masks and sang sacred songs to the god while they trod the grapes, because Dionysus was "dying" to provide them with intoxicating wine. During their great festival of sowing, Egyptian priests used to bury effigies of Osiris made of earth and corn which, when exhumed later, were found to have sprouted. Frazer explained, "This sprouting of the grain would be hailed as an omen, or rather as the cause, of the growth of the crops. The corn-god produced the corn from himself; he gave his body to feed the people, he died that they might live." As we have observed, however, Osiris-Dionysus was much more than just a god of corn or wine. Egyptian hieroglyphs call Osiris the "Life-Force." He represents the mysterious process of death and resurrection that is Life itself. Pagan commentators, such as Plutarch, acknowledged the more superficial agricultural allegories in the myths of Osiris-Dionysus, but pointed to the deeper mystical meaning. To them, the harvesting and regrowth of the crops was itself an allegory for human death and rebirth. Just as corn grows from seeds planted in the ground, so human beings could be spiritually reborn after they were dead and buried. The Mysteries may have perhaps begun as magical rites to ensure the continued fertility of the land, as Frazer suggests, but in their developed form they came to embody the promise of immortality to human beings.
173 Ibid., 338
174 Mark 14 v 24
175 John 15 v 1–6
176 Wallis Budge, E. A., *Egyptian Religion*, (1899), 172: "The ancient Egyptians believed that the deceased must eat the gods and so be imbued with their powers."
177 Inge, W. R. (1899), 355. As well as the Eucharist, early Christians also regularly celebrated an "agape" or "love feast." In nearly all the Pagan Mysteries an agape, or sacramental meal, preceded initiation. Plutarch explains: "It is not the wine or the cookery that delights us at these feasts, but good hope, and the belief that God is present with us, and that He accepts our sacrifice graciously."

[178] Guthrie, W. K. C. (1952), 114. Before the Mysteries came to Greece from Egypt the old Olympian rites made sacrifice to the gods on the principle of reciprocity—that having sacrificed to the gods, the gods would then give something back to the people. The uneaten sacrificial offerings of the Olympian religion were replaced by the Mystery rites in which initiates mystically communed with the divinity by symbolically eating the body of the god. The Christian priest Dean Inge writes: "There have always been two ideas of sacrifice, alike in savage and civilized cults . . . the mystical, in which it is a communion, the victim who is slain and eaten being himself the god, or a symbol of the god; and the commercial, in which something valuable is offered to the god in the hope of receiving some benefit in exchange. The Mysteries certainly encouraged the idea of communion, and made it easier for the Christian rite to gather up into itself all the religious elements which can be contained in a sacrament of this kind." See Inge, W. R. (1899), 355.

[179] Burkert, W. (1992), 111

[180] Justin, First Apology, 66, quoted in Stevenson, J. (1957), 64

[181] Cumont, F. (1903), 158

[182] Grüber and Kersten (1985), 230. The Mithras cult had six other sacraments that correspond exactly with those of the Catholic Church.

[183] Godwin, J. (1981), 28

[184] John 6 v 53

[185] John 6 v 56

[186] Haoma is the Persian equivalent of the Soma of the Hindus, repeatedly praised in the Rig Veda scriptures. Mithras is the Persian equivalent of the god Mittra, who also figures in these sacred texts. The etymology of these names points to the ancient identity of the two races, derived from an original stock known to historians as "Indo-European." Lindsay, J. (1970), 89, explores the Iranian-Indian mythology as it was developed in Greco-Roman times. The Persians identified the Haoma plant with the primordial man Gayomart, who was murdered by his enemies. The plant was identified with the Son of God who was bruised and mangled in the mortar so that the life-giving fluid from his body might give new strength to his worshipers.

[187] Plato, The Laws, 775b

[188] Plato, Phaedrus, 244d

[189] Campbell, J. (1964), 112. Another scholar comments: "The eating of the god is the origin of Greek tragedy," see Carpenter and Faraone (1993), 28.

[190] Euripides, The Bacchae, 200, line 284; see also Carpenter and Faraone, op. cit., 65

[191] Carpenter and Faraone, op. cit., 52, figure 6

[192] Burkert, W. (1992), 111

[193] Angus, S. (1925), 129

[194] Godwin, J. (1981), 28

[195] Justin Martyr, Apology, 66, quoted in Stevenson, J. (1957), 64

[196] Cicero, The Nature of the Gods, Book 3, 201, line 41

[197] Mead, G. R. S. (1906), 342

[198] Acts 5 v 30

[199] Galatians 3 v 13

[200] Dunlap, S. F. (1866), 115

[201] Harrison, J. (1922), 429

[202] Otto, W. F. (1965), 217. See Chapter 6, note 2, for details of August Frickenhaus' collection of many such depictions.

[203] Mark 15 v 17 describes the dressing of Jesus in the purple robe and crown of thorns in a way that is indistinguishable from the setting up of the Dionysus idol depicted on numerous Greek vases dating from the sixth century BCE. Initiates at Eleusis wound a purple sash around their bodies as a symbol of Dionysus, who wore the purple robe of Persephone during his stay in the Underworld, see Burkert, W. (1985), 283. Initiates into the Mysteries in nearby Andania wore purple headbands during the ceremony, see Meyer, M. W. (1987), 59.

[204] Metzger, B. M. (1987), 57. The Epistle of Barnabas refers to gall. All four gospels mention that vinegar was offered to Jesus, but only Matthew 27 v 34 refers to wine mixed with gall.

[205] Harrison, J. (1922), 569, quoting Psellus, On the Mysteries: "There is the draught of gall and the throes of pain."

[206] Campbell, J. (1964), 260. Campbell remarks, "They have been compared to the two thieves crucified with Christ, one of whom was to ascend to heaven and the other descend to hell."

[207] Kerenyi, C. (1976), figure 85. The torches were symbolic in the Mysteries of the anodos and cathodos, the way up and the way down of the soul, into and out of incarnation.

[208] Mark 3 v 17

[209] Burkert, W. (1985), 165, notes that Pentheus is dressed like Dionysus before his death, which is then carried out in exact imitation of the fate usually inflicted on the god himself.

[210] Diodorus of Sicily, 3.65. In Book 1.20, Diodorus tells us it was Osiris who slew Lycurgus "who opposed his undertakings" (i.e., the worldwide dissemination of his teachings). This only confirms that by the first century BCE it was widely known that the two figures were synonymous.

[211] Plato, *The Republic*, Book 2, 361e

[212] Guthrie, W. K. C. (1952), 266, records Dr. Eisler's evidence that there was an ancient tradition of a crucified Orpheus.

[213] Justin Martyr, *First Apology*, Chapter 60

[214] Plato, *Phaedo*, 83d: "Each pleasure and pain is a sort of nail which nails the soul to the body."

[215] Arnobius, *Against the Gentiles*, 2.344, quoted in Dunlap, S. F. (1866), 106. Arnobius was steeped in Neoplatonism and Hermeticism before he converted to Christianity. *See* Turcan, R. (1992), 333. He was very familiar with the Mysteries and their rituals.

[216] Burkert, W. (1985), 240, describes the setting up of the Dionysus idol as it is depicted in the Lenaia vases: "A cloth is wound about the column to indicate the body, and is occasionally held by a cross-bar." This is done at the same festival that the scholar elsewhere likens to Easter.

[217] Kerenyi, C. (1976), figure 137

[218] Ibid., 378: "He is bringing the child the mysterious cruciform structure that was carried about in Athens at the feast of the Anthesteria, an intimation of Dionysus' impending stay in the underworld."

[219] King, C. W. (1887), 279; *see also* Wilson, I. (1984), flyleaf. It is only Christian prejudice that prevents us from seeing this graffito for what it is—a pious depiction by a devotee of the Osiris cult who believed that he had overcome Set, the enemy of his god. The imagery is entirely in keeping with Apuleius' romance of initiation *The Golden Ass*. In addition the graffito depicts another well known Pythagorean symbol, the letter "Y." Cumont records numerous grave inscriptions with this symbol (*see* Cumont [1922], 26–7, 76, 148, 150). To the Pythagoreans it was a symbol of the two paths open to man in life and in death. In life the left-hand path leads to dissolution and the right to virtue, likewise after death the left-hand path led to Tartarus, the Greek purgatory, followed by subsequent reincarnation, while the right-hand path led to the Elysian Fields.

[220] Harrison, J. (1922), 220. The word *pharmacy* derives from this source. A *pharmakos* is a formula or magical spell of banishment. In an early Christian writing Ignatius of Antioch describes the Eucharist as the *pharmakon tes Zoes*, "the medicine of immortal life," *see* Hoffmann, R. J. (1987), 16.

[221] Otto, W. F. (1965), 38–9: "The *pharmakos* was led throughout the city to absorb every miasma."

[222] We are familiar with the scapegoat ritual from the Old Testament. Leviticus 16 v 21: "Aaron shall lay both his hands upon the head of the live goat and confess over him all the iniquities of the children of Israel. The goat shall bear upon him all their iniquities into a land not inhabited." The myth of the scapegoat was a Mediterranean-wide motif, however. Greek tragedy developed from the Dionysus rituals carried out in archaic times, the *tragodoi* being the singers who led the goat to sacrifice, *see* Burkert, W. (1985), 102. An intriguing development of this motif took place in the Hellenistic period when Socrates' birthday was claimed as the day "when the Athenians purify the city," *see* Harrison, J. (1922), 97. Lysias also tells us that the Thirty Tyrants designated their political murders of Socrates and others as a purification—a purge in both the medicinal and the ominous political sense of the word, *see* Burkert, W. (1985), 83. These fragments suggest that in the centuries after his death, Socrates' disciples were attempting to link his fate with that of the *pharmakos*, a scapegoat who willingly took on his sacrificial role in order to purge the sins of the city. The very same motifs appear in the life of Jesus.

[223] Harrison, J. (1922), 99

[224] Burkert, W. (1985), 105

[225] Mark 15 v 17–20

[226] Hebrews 9 v 22

[227] Godwin, J. (1981), 111

[228] Turcan, R. (1992), 226

[229] Murray, M. A. (1949), 74

[230] Plato, *Cratylus*, 400c: "For some say that the body is the grave of the soul which may be thought to be buried in our present life. The Orphic poets . . . were under the impression that the soul is suffering the punishment of sin until the penalty is paid."

[231] Kirk and Raven, (1957), 352. According to Empedocles, the fallen soul is banished "from the blessed, being born throughout that time in the forms of all manner of mortal things and changing one baleful life for another."

[232] Guthrie, W. K. C. (1952), 72–3. After collecting together a mass of newly discovered Orphic material, the classical scholar Guthrie writes, "Looking back like this, we are struck not only by contrasts with the prevailing religious types of fifth-century Greece, but no less by resemblances with Christianity. Features it has in common with Orphism include the idea of conversion, religion as a way of life, original sin, communion and parts of its eschatology," (1952) 207.

[233] Frazer, J. (1922), 360

[234] Ibid. Once again the Christians fell back on the "subtlety of Satan" argument. *See* Lane, E. N. (1996), 37, which records St. Augustine's defensiveness about the many similarities between Attis and Jesus.

[235] The primal model for all the myths of all the Mystery gods is Osiris in Egypt. The Egyptian harvest does not fall in the autumn, but in the months of March, April, and May—Eastertime. This may be the reason why the death of the godman is celebrated not in the autumn, as one might expect, but in the spring.

[236] Kerenyi, C. (1967), 349

[237] Angus, S. (1925), 60: "The tree, prepared like a corpse, was carried into the sanctuary. The next night the resurrection of Attis was celebrated by the opening of the grave."

[238] Lane, E. N. (1996), 39: "The youthful Attis was miraculously brought back to life after three days." This cult was a favorite target for the invective of Christian writers because of this and many other parallels. Both St. Augustine and Firmicus Maternus dwell on the nearness of the rituals to those of Christianity. Augustine records in disgust the statement of a priest of Attis—that Attis himself was a Christian!

[239] Angus, S. (1925), 60

[240] Frazer, J. (1922), 350

[241] Ibid., 360

[242] Ibid. *See also* Campbell, J. (1955), 368, where Rahner notes that priests of the Attis cult complained that the Christians were imitating their vernal celebration, and Lane, E. N. (1996), 39, where a classical scholar remarks, "When I go to the Good Friday service it is difficult for me to decide whether the god being buried is Attis or Christ."

[243] Burkert, W. (1985), 241. The archaic festival of the Anthesteria was the model on which the Mysteries at Eleusis were based. In the Classical period the Anthesteria continued to be celebrated as the "Lesser Dionysia," while the Eleusinian Mysteries became the "City Dionysia." Regarding the myth enacted at this earlier festival, Burkert writes: "Dionysus, the god of wine, was himself killed and dismembered to serve as wine for sacramental drinking. Late Hellenistic allegorists are the first to say this openly. For the early period under the sway of Homer a god is by definition immortal and cannot be killed. In the secret myths of the mysteries the stories told were doubtless different; the myth of the dismemberment of Dionysus may perhaps be as old as the Anthesteria festival itself."

[244] Frazer, op. cit., 359

[245] Cicero, *On the Good Life*, 104

[246] Dunlap, S. F. (1866), 23

[247] Lucian, *The Syrian Great Mother*, 4.262

[248] Matthew 27 v 59 and John 19 v 39–40

[249] Plutarch, *Isis and Osiris*, 16

[250] Dunlap, S. F. (1866), 104

[251] Plutarch, op. cit., 39 and 42. A Greek magical papyri of the same period records: "At the port of Bousiris I'll cry the name of him who remained three days and three nights in the river, Osiris the drowned one," *see* Lindsay, J. (1970), 172.

[252] The Pyramid Texts, quoted in Angus, S. (1925), 46

[253] Fidler, D. (1993), 173, quoting Origen, *Against Celsus*, 5.17: "He was put together again and was, as it were, restored to life and went up to heaven."

[254] Frazer, J. (1922), 335

[255] Ibid., 389. *See also* D'Alviella, G. (1981), 118, which observes that the gods of the Pagan Mysteries, by their suffering and resurrection, "filled no less the role of savior which we find in the concept of the Christian Messiah."

[256] Fidler, op. cit., 144, quoting Tertullian, *Prescription against the Heretics*, 40

257 Cumont, F. (1903), 138

258 Ibid., 146. Cumont collates a mass of Mithraic eschatological doctrines identical to Christianity.

259 MacMullen, R. (1966), 96. MacMullen attributes this to the "penetration of obvious Pythagoreanism into the higher social classes with which Seneca and his like were acquainted."

260 Kingsley, P. (1995), 234; *see also* 297, note 27. Heraclides was a disciple of Plato. On the parallels between the story of Empedocles' death in *Heraclides of Pontus* and the story of Jesus' death in the Gospel of Mark, *see* Ava Chitwood, "The Death of Empedocles," *AJP*, 1986.

261 In *The Histories*, Book 4, 94–8, Herodotus cryptically retells the myth of Pythagoras' descent into the Underworld, which he undertook in order to prove his doctrine of the immortality of the soul. The mythical motif of a descent into hell is also found in the legends of Odysseus, Hercules, Orpheus, Pythagoras, Empedocles, Aeneas, and many others.

262 MacMullen, R. (1966), 317, note 6. In 1927 Levy wrote a book entitled *La Légende de Pythagore de Grèce en Palestine*. It records Pythagoras' double nature of man and god (8–15), his being raised to the heavens corporeally (67), and the stories of his reappearance to his disciples (78).

263 Hoffmann, R. J. (1987), 67. Macchioro, V. D. (1930), 13, records the numerous Pagans who allegedly died and came back to life. Beginning with Er, whose story is told in the last book of Plato's *Republic*, similar stories were told of Thespesius, Cleonimus, Rufus, Hieronymus, Machates, Cleodemus, and Empedotimus.

264 Guthrie, W. K. C. (1952), 61

265 Frazer, J. (1922), 360. The Assumption of the Virgin in August ousted the Pagan festival of the virgin Diana.

266 King, C. W. (1887), 173. King also records the inscription "Immaculate is our Lady Isis."

267 Frazer, op. cit., 383

268 Stanton, G. (1995), 43. The original version of Mark did not contain any words beyond 16 v 8. *See* Hoffmann, R. J. (1987), 132, where Celsus confirms that this is the story that he is familiar with.

269 Robinson, J. M. (1978), 139

270 John 19 v 25

271 Otto, W. F. (1965), 67. *See* Guthrie, W. K. C. (1952), 136, where three maenads are imported from Thebes to Magnesia to found a new cult of Dionysus. The three priestesses perhaps played the role of the three fates said to be present at the birth of every soul. In Plato's vision of the afterlife souls are led to the three fates before they are then led "to their birth like shooting stars," *see The Republic*, Book 10, 620e.

272 Kerenyi, C. (1967), 135

273 Harrison, J. (1922), 290–1

274 Lietzmann, H. (1961), Book 3, 147. In the fourth century a church was ordered to be built over the cave in Jerusalem in which Jesus was supposedly buried. First, however, a shrine of Aphrodite above it had to be demolished. This would suggest that the cave in fact originally belonged to her lover Adonis.

275 Frazer, J. (1922), 374

276 Angus, S. (1925), 125

277 Macchioro, V. D. (1930), 77

278 Lucius Apuleius, *The Golden Ass*, 284: "The rites of initiation approximate to a voluntary death for which there is only a precarious hope of resurrection. So she usually chooses old men who feel that their end is fast approaching yet are not too senile to be capable of keeping a secret: by her grace they are, in a sense, born again and restored to a new and healthy life."

279 Wallis Budge, E. A., *Egyptian Religion* (1899), 71

280 Ibid., 72

281 John 16 v 19–22

CHAPTER 4: PERFECTED PLATONISM

1 Quoted in Hoffmann, R. J. (1987), 91

2 Ibid., 55

3 Ibid., 91

4 Inge, W. R. (1899), 78

5 Kingsland, W. (1937), 139. *See also* Justin Martyr, *First Apology*, Chapter 46.

[6]   Justin Martyr, *Second Apology*, 13, quoted in Stevenson, J. (1957), 61

[7]   Inge, W. R. (1899), 77–8. Inge calls this "a curious notion."

[8]   St. Augustine, *Confessions, City of God, Christian Doctrine*, Chapter 28.43

[9]   Justin Martyr, op. cit., quoted Stevenson, op. cit., 62

[10]   St. Augustine, op. cit., Chapter 40, entitled: "Whatever has been rightly said by the heathen, we must appropriate to our uses."

[11]   Quoted in Inge, W. R. (1899), 351

[12]   Quoted in Angus, S. (1925), 239

[13]   Ibid.

[14]   Iamblichus, *On the Mysteries*, 1.11.12

[15]   Aristophanes the Alexandrian scholar, not the Athenian playwright, although he too wrote, in *The Frogs*, that the Elysian Fields, the Greek heaven, were only open to those who had "been initiated and lived piously," *see* Angus, op. cit., 239.

[16]   Porphyry, *On the Special Laws*, quoted in Blavatsky, H. P., *The Esoteric Writings*, Theosophical Publishing House, 1907, 214

[17]   Angus, op. cit., 79, quotes three ethical injunctions of the Mysteries from Celsus. *See also* Burkert, W. (1985), 283.

[18]   Quoted in Inge, op. cit., 86

[19]   From an inscription in the museum at Epidaurus, the foremost sanctuary of Asclepius in the ancient world.

[20]   Guthrie, K. S. (1987), 268, Saying number 22

[21]   Quoted in Hoffmann, R. J. (1987), 123

[22]   The Stoic doctrine of the conscience derives from the Daemon of Socrates, the inner voice, which guided the philosopher's conduct. In Plato, *Phaedo*, 107d, the Daemon is called the "Guardian Spirit" which guides the soul in life and also after death. It is difficult not to conclude that the Catholic teaching of the Guardian Angel derives from the Platonic doctrine of the Guardian Spirit.

[23]   Quoted in Angus, S. (1925), 208

[24]   Faulkner, R. O. (1972), 29, Spell 125, known as the "Negative Confession" or "The Declaration of Innocence." *See also* Angus, op. cit., 78ff. Angus has collected numerous examples of confession before initiation.

[25]   Suetonius, *Life of Nero* 34: "He came to Athens where the Eleusinian Mysteries were being held, but dared not participate when a herald ordered all impious and criminal persons present to withdraw before the ceremonies began."

[26]   Angus, S. (1925), 80.

[27]   Campbell, J. (1955), 45. Confession was also extracted from initiates into the Samothracian Mysteries. The following anecdote conveys what was probably a typical Hellenic attitude to this innovation. When asked to confess his most terrible crime, a Spartan initiate replied, "Who desires to know this, you or the gods?" To which the priest replied, "The gods." Unconvinced, the Spartan replied laconically, "Then begone, for if they wish to know, I will tell them."

[28]   Quoted in Inge, W. R. (1899), 354

[29]   Ibid.

[30]   Godwin, J. (1981), 27

[31]   Angus, S. (1925), 204

[32]   Matthew 7 v 12

[33]   Freke, T. (1997), 80–1

[34]   Guthrie, K. S. (1987), 268, Saying number 20

[35]   Matthew 5 v 39

[36]   Guthrie, op. cit., Saying number 55

[37]   De Vogel, C. J. (1966), 109, 125. Pythagoras taught the people of southern Italy that "they must not start to insult others, and if others abused them they must not defend themselves against the offenders."

[38]   Epictetus, *The Teachings of Epictetus*, 31, Chapter 8 v 12

[39]   Quoted in Hoffmann, R. J. (1987), 113

[40]   Plato, *Crito*, 49b–e

[41]   Quoted in Hoffmann, op. cit., 114

[42]   Quoted in Guthrie, W. K. C. (1952), 197. The Orphic life preached strict vegetarianism.

[43]   *See* Plato, *The Republic*, Book 2, 364b–e. Plato was often critical of the wandering Orphic initiators who carried out the rites but could give no explanation of what they were doing.

[44]   Godwin, J. (1981), 146

[45]   Matthew 10 v 9–10

46 It is commonly thought that the Cynic philosophy originated with Diogenes and Antisthenes, the disciples of the barefoot Socrates. Burkert traces it instead to the Pythagoreans:
"The cynicism of Diogenes is in a way a continuation of Pythagoreanism . . . there are
unmistakable coincidences." *See* Burkert, W. (1972), 203. Prior to Diogenes and contemporary with Antisthenes was Diodorus of Aspendus. Satirized by Stratonicus as wearing a
"crazy garment of skin," he "gathered followers and wore long hair, long beard, folded
tribon, wallet, and staff." As Burkert notes, threads lead from here to the Stoa as well; both
Zeno and Chrisyppus were interested in aspects of Pythagoreanism. Stratonicus' description
of Diodorus is uncannily like that of John the Baptist several centuries later.

47 Lietzmann, H. (1961), Book 4, 126–7. Later Christian fathers castigated the monks for being
indistinguishable from Cynics, with bare feet, cloak, staff, and beard. As MacMullen notes,
"Certain stereotypes of superhuman virtue were too deeply fixed in the ancient mind to be
eradicated." *See* MacMullen, R. (1966), 93.

48 Epictetus, *The Teachings of Epictetus*, 196. A coarse cloak called the tribon was worn
by both Cynics and early Christian ascetics. *See also* 209, where Epictetus uses the term
odos, "way." It also turns up in Acts 22 v 4 and 19 v 9 and 23. By the time of Jesus, Cynic
philosophers were everywhere. "They were to the ancient world what palmers and friars
were to the medieval, a familiar sight everywhere, both suspect and sacred," MacMullen,
R. (1966), 60. Epictetus, the crippled Phrygian slave, was the most famous of these; his life is
contemporaneous with that of Jesus. In Epictetus, 193, a classical scholar writes: "The
parallelisms in thought and expression between Epictetus and the New Testament have
often been noticed, and the reader will discover many others, to which I have not thought
it necessary to draw attention."

49 Epictetus, *The Teachings of Epictetus*, 26, Book 8 v 5–6. *See also* MacMullen, R. (1966), 57,
where Epictetus describes the danger in attempting to make converts in the streets of Rome,
declaring, "Nowadays this activity is not a very safe one." In 71 CE Vespasian banished all
philosophers from Rome, as did Domitian in 90, a purge which included Epictetus.

50 Quoted in Hoffmann, R. J. (1987), 94

51 Luke 12 v 33

52 Guthrie, K. S. (1987), 268, Saying number 28

53 Mack, B. L. (1993), 126

54 Mark 13 v 35

55 Epictetus, *The Teachings of Epictetus*, 81, Chapter 12

56 Mark 10 v 14–16

57 Heraclitus, fr. 94, quoted in Kahn, C. H. (1979), 71. Macchioro, V. D. (1930), Chapter 8,
positively identifies the child with Dionysus who "received the kingdom from Zeus after his
resurrection." It is significant that in Heraclitus's work we find the first references in Greek
literature to the "Mystae and the Bacchoi." The only gods he mentions, apart from Zeus and
Apollo, are Hades and Dionysus. The last two he tells us are the same.

58 Mark 10 v 18

59 *Abingdon Bible Commentary*, New York, 1929. Heaven and hell are "religious develop-
ments of the inter testamental period," according to *The Unvarnished New Testament*, 499.
Job, for example, 21 v 23–6, resents the lack of distinction in death between the wicked and
the just: "They lie down alike in the dust." *See also* Bernstein, A. E. (1993), 158, which notes
that the Deuteronomic system measures justice according to standards of prosperity and
adversity in life—all its rewards and punishments are confined to this world. Although he
explores several other possible options in the Bible, Bernstein admits these are preserved as
"minority opinions." In *The Jewish War*, 2.14.163–5, and *Antiquities*, 18.14, Josephus
records that the Sadducees, the traditionalists among Jewish sects denied both the
immortality of the soul and postmortem sanctions. In his opinion the Pharisees gained the
support of the majority of the people because they taught that the soul survives death and
receives either the reward of a new life in another body or eternal punishment in the
Underworld. The Pharisees were considered modernizers and Hellenizers.

60 Sophocles, fr. 719, quoted in Angus, S. (1925), 238–9. In *The Republic*, Book 2, 364e, Plato
refers to priests who "make not only ordinary men but states believe that there really are
remissions of sins and purifications for deeds of injustice ... and that there are also special
rites that deliver us from evils in that other world, while terrible things await those who
have neglected to sacrifice."

61 Plutarch, *The Moral Essays*, 176, "A Letter of Consolation."

62 Ibid., 184. Plutarch continues, "At first there are wanderings and toilsome running about in
circles, and journeys through the dark over uncertain roads and dead ends; then just before
the end, there are all kinds of terrors, with shivering, trembling, sweating, and utter

amazement. After this, a strange and wonderful light meets the wanderer; he is admitted into pure and verdant pastures, where he discerns gentle voices, solemn dances, and the majesty of blessed spirits and sacred visions. Here he is free, being now fully initiated, and walks at liberty like a crowned and sacrificial victim, joining in the revelry."

63 Quoted in Angus, S. (1925), 95
64 Quoted in Burkert, W. (1985), 289
65 Quoted in Godwin, J. (1981), 36. The rites of the Mysteries not only prepared the initiate for death, but were also seen as representing the process of death. Plutarch writes: "Death and initiation closely correspond," fr. 178, Loeb edition. In a delightfully paradoxical passage, he explains, "The highest of our initiations in this world is only a dream of the true vision and initiation of death. The Mysteries have been carefully conceived to awaken memories of sublime things to come."
66 Dunlap, S. F. (1866), 32, quoting Plutarch
67 St. Augustine, *City of God*, 7.24
68 Quoted in Burkert, op. cit., 289. Pindar writes: "Blessed is he who has seen this and thus goes beneath the earth; he knows the end of life, he knows the beginning given by Zeus."
69 Guthrie, W. K. C. (1952), 269, traces most Christian doctrines on the afterlife to the Orphics with one exception: the Orphics would have found the doctrine of the resurrection of the body "repulsive."
70 Cumont, F. (1922), 198, documents the route of transmission of Orphic doctrines from the Greeks to the Jews and finally to the Christians.
71 Kingsley, P. (1995), 203–4
72 Ibid., 119, note 26
73 Quoted in Hoffmann, R. J. (1987), 95
74 Cumont, F. (1903), 191, records this and other parallels between Christian and Mithraic doctrines.
75 2 Corinthians 12 v 2
76 Quoted in Hoffmann, op. cit., 76–7
77 Plato was the first to record these views in *The Republic*, Book 10. At the end of the second century BCE Polybius wrote that: "The ancients were by no means acting foolishly or haphazardly when they introduced to the people various notions concerning the gods and belief in the punishment of Hades." But like most sophisticated Greeks and Romans, he regarded such myths as merely a necessary superstition for restraining "lawless desires, unreasoning anger, and violent passions." See Polybius, *The Rise of the Roman Empire*, 349. Timaeus of Locri likewise regarded such tales as "salutary fictions," Cumont, F. (1922), 78. Other philosophers, however, violently attacked these myths, which they regarded as "life-poisoning beliefs" and a perversion of the true doctrine. See Cumont, 176. In *The Nature of the Universe*, 126, Lucretius, the Epicurean philosopher of the first century BCE, writes, "As for all those torments that are said to take place in the depths of Hell, they are actually present here and now, in our own lives." In the view of these philosophers, "The only penalty which can overtake the sinning soul is metempsychosis, which forces it to reincarnate itself in a fleshly prison," Cumont, 78. In *Meno*, 76e, Plato relates that evildoers suffer in a new incarnation exactly the violence they have inflicted in this one; in *The Laws*, 870d–e, he states that this was taught by the priests of the Mysteries.
78 Lane-Fox, R. (1986), 327
79 Cumont, F. (1922), 188. Cumont says that although we know this doctrine through Origen, "He merely reproduced a theory to which the evolution of pagan ideas had led."
80 Quoted in Hoffmann, R. J. (1987), 70. And, as Celsus notes, these were often extreme. Plato, in *The Republic*, Book 10, 615–16, relates how wicked souls were seized and flayed of their skin while their tormentors explained to purer souls passing by why their victims were being punished.
81 Quoted in Hoffmann, op. cit., 86. In contrast Celsus approvingly quotes the Pagan sage Heraclitus, who says, "Corpses should be disposed of like dung, for dung they are." Diogenes requested that his body be thrown in a ditch and covered with a little earth. For the Orphics the body was the tomb of the soul.
82 Matthew 25 v 31–3. The judgment of the dead in an afterlife court goes back to ancient Egypt, but their division into those on the right and the left can be seen evolving as these beliefs steadily penetrated the West. In *The Republic*, Book 10, 614b–d, Plato discourses on the Orphic teachings of the fate of the soul after death. About the afterlife judgment he writes, "After every judgment they bade the righteous journey to the right and upward through the heaven with tokens attached to them of the judgment passed upon them, and the unjust to take the road to the left and downward, they too wearing behind signs of all

that had befallen them..." In the Sethian Gnostic scheme, *see* Perkins, P. (1993), 57 and 209, souls on the right ascend to the light of the divine world, souls on the left return to Earth/Hades. Exactly the same doctrines, specifically in the context of Pythagorean and Orphic teaching, can be found in Virgil's *Aeneid*, Book 6. Finally, in Matthew 25 v 31–3, Jesus becomes the judge who places "the sheep at his right hand, but the goats at the left."

83 Cumont, F. (1903), 146

84 Matthew 24 v 7–8

85 The precession of the equinoxes was discovered by Hipparchus in 170 BCE. His theory explained why the constellation lying behind the sun at the spring equinox changes over time and the sun appears to move slowly backward through the signs of the zodiac over a period of 25,000 years. Hipparchus' calculation of this "Great Year" was accurate to within six seconds of a degree per year, an incredible achievement. *See* Walbank, F. W. (1981), 187. The sun spends roughly 2,000 years in each sign and the ancients called this a "Great Month." During the lifetime of Hipparchus the month changed from Aries to Pisces; in c. 2040 CE it will change into Aquarius. By the first century CE speculation on the New Age was rife, as was the practice of astrology with which it was intimately associated.

86 Quoted in Eisler, R. (1920), 71. Dr. Eisler has collated a vast amount of evidence for the closest contacts between Orphism and Christianity in the first few centuries, showing how Orpheus the Fisher slowly became Jesus the Fisher of Men.

87 Ibid., 22. The Syrians worshiped a fish god variously called Nun, Dagon, or Adonis, whom the Greeks called Icthys.

88 Virgil, *The Pastoral Poems*, 53, Eclogue 4

89 The poets of the Augustan period made frequent use of New Age imagery; their work also contains many veiled references to Orphic and Pythagorean mystical doctrines.

90 Ulansey, D. (1989), Chapter 5

91 According to Pagan doctrines Jesus represents the last sacrificial ram and the first sacrificial fish.

92 Cumont, F. (1903), 191, and Ulansey, D. (1989), 73. In the Roman period these doctrines were commonplace.

93 Quoted in Hoffmann, R. J. (1987), 77

94 Kirk and Raven, (1957), 169. It is axiomatic among Presocratic philosophers that God is One. Zeno, Mellissus, Heraclitus, Empedocles, and Pythagoras are all in agreement with Xenophanes.

95 Quoted in Freke and Gandy (1997), 47

96 Quoted in Fidler, D. (1993), 22

97 Justin Martyr, *Exhortatory Address to the Greeks*, 19.1, quoted in Guthrie, K. S. (1987), 298. Justin continues: "When Pythagoras says that Unity is the first principle of all things and that it is the cause of all good, he teaches by an allegory that God is one and alone." Justin also quotes Sophocles, Orpheus, and Plato as evidence that the wisest of the Greeks had believed in the One God, although in Justin's opinion all of these had learned from Moses while traveling in Egypt.

98 Wallis Budge, E. A., *Egyptian Religion* (1899), 83

99 Quoted ibid., 19–20

100 Ibid., 107

101 Ellis, N. (1988), 21

102 Angus, S. (1925), 190

103 Quoted in Hoffmann, R. J. (1987), 56

104 Quoted in Anderson, G. (1994), 84

105 Socrates, Anaxagoras, and Diagoras were accused of not believing in the gods. Protagoras' book *On the Gods*, which called into question the nature of the gods, was publicly burned in Athens and the author put on trial for heresy. The heresy trials that occurred in Athens at the end of the fifth century are unique in Greek history, Socrates was their most famous victim, but Plutarch tells us that another 1,500 citizens were executed.

106 Quoted in Hoffmann, op. cit., 53

107 Freke and Gandy (1998), 26. Diagoras was admiring with a friend the many expensive votive monuments to the gods surrounding a temple in Samothrace. His friend explained to him that these had been erected in gratitude by those who, while in peril on the sea, had promised to honor the gods if divine intervention rescued them from a watery grave. The monuments were therefore proof of the efficacy of prayer and the power of the gods. Diagoras replied sardonically, "Just think how many more there would have been if all those who had drowned had also been able to set one up."

108 Reported by Diogenes Laertius in *Lives of the Famous Philosophers*, quoted in Mack, B. L. (1993), 116
109 Quoted in Freke and Gandy (1998), 27
110 Lucian, *The Parliament of the Gods*, 9–11, quoted in Godwin, J. (1981), 6
111 Quoted in Hoffmann, op. cit., 71
112 Ibid., 103
113 Ibid., 56
114 Clement of Alexandria, *Stromata*, 31
115 Cicero, *The Republic*, 6.17, quoted in Angus, S. (1925), 108
116 John 10 v 31–6
117 Doran, R. (1995), 78
118 Quoted ibid., 75. *See Dialogue with Trypho*, 58–61
119 Islam regards Christianity as a polytheistic religion, which worships three gods. *See* the Qur'an, Sura 4 v 171, which advises: "Believe in God … but do not call him 'trinity.'" Unlike the Christian view of Jesus, the Muslims are careful to make clear that Muhammad is not divine, stating, "There is no God but God, and Muhammad is his prophet."
120 Lane-Fox, R. (1986), 191. A Christian sermon that has survived from the mid-fifth century called "On the Trinity" quotes in profusion the words of the Pagan gods. The doctrine of the trinity probably derives from sacred geometry: the "transcendental number" pi is hidden within the circle, a symbol of the All and so of God.
121 Quoted in Burkert, W. (1972), 265
122 Quoted in Wallis Budge, E. A., *Egyptian Religion* (1899), 24
123 Quoted in Murray, M. A. (1949), 46
124 John 1 v 1–5
125 Kahn, C. H. (1979), 250. From Kahn's commentary: "Wisdom begins with self-knowledge, Heraclitus went in search of himself but what he found within his psyche was a logos deep enough to be co-extensive with the universe."
126 Heraclitus, fr. 36, quoted ibid., 45
127 Epictetus, *The Teachings of Epictetus*, 134, Chapter 9.2
128 Vitruvius, *De Architectura*, from the Introduction to the Loeb edition
129 Clement of Alexandria, *Clement of Alexandria*, 167. Clement calls Orpheus an "interpreter of the Mysteries."
130 Murray, M. A. (1949), 46. In the Pyramid Texts of Saqqara creation takes place by and through words. By the Eighteenth Dynasty (c.1550 BCE) the theory of the Word of God as the creative power was well developed, as was the concept of the Pharaoh as the Word of God incarnate.
131 Fidler, D. (1993), 38
132 Mead, G. R. S. (1906), 388. According to Hessychius the Logos is "the cause of action." It is what instigates creation. Logos could also be rendered "Reason." This can be justifiably interpreted in many ways: as the "reason for things" and as "the ordering principle" and also as "the faculty by which the mind understands." St. John's gospel could be translated: "In the beginning was the Reason." St. John writes that the Logos "was life and the life was the light of men," Sextus the Pythagorean likewise states, "The reason that is in you is the light of your life," *see* Guthrie, K. S. (1987), 268, Saying number 31.
133 *The Hermetica*, Book 1.5. *See* Freke and Gandy (1997), 38: "My calming Word is the Son of God."
134 Copenhaver, B. P. (1992), 1, Book 1.6: "The light giving word who comes from Mind is the Son of God."
135 Quoted in Guthrie, W. K. C. (1952), 227. Hippolytus says, "Everyone knows he said that the Father and the Son are the same."
136 Quoted in Harrison, J. (1922), 480
137 Logos also means "Ratio" or "Relationship." St. John's gospel could also be rendered as beginning: "In the beginning was the Relationship." What is this relationship? It is the primal relationship between Father and Son, mind and thought, consciousness and what it is conscious of, the Creator and the creation, the Oneness and the manyness of things. This relationship is one of connectivity, because the two are One. It is, therefore, as Jesus teaches, essentially a relationship of love. This doctrine can be traced back to the Greek tradition. Eros was a favorite deity of Socrates, Plato, the Pythagoreans, and the Orphics. According to the Orphic creation myth, Night laid a silver egg in the darkness from which hatched the "First-Born" god Eros, *see* Graves, R. (1955), 30. The myth relates that the original Oneness split into two halves, which became the pattern of all dualities, heaven and Earth, spirit and matter, male and female. The immediate impulse to arise from this was the desire to reunite what had

been divided and in consequence love was born. Eros is sometimes called Phanes, or Light, but as the Orphic myth developed he came to be personified by the philosophers as the Logos.

138 Quoted in Inge, W. R. (1899), 87. A Christian Gnostic gospel likewise explains: "When first the Father, the not even the One, beyond all possibility of thought and being, who is neither male or female, willed that His ineffability should come into being, and His invisibility take form, He opened His mouth and uttered a Word, like unto Himself; who appearing before Him, became the means of His seeing what He himself was—namely Himself appearing in the form of His own invisibility," Mead, G. R. S. (1906), 363. In a Gnostic Christian tract, Jesus likewise explains, "I am the Son of the Father who is beyond all existence ... while I, His Son, am in existence," Mead, 381.

139 Quoted in Fidler, D. (1993), 48. The Logos is what connects all things together, what makes them one Whole. It is the image of an otherwise transcendent God, the mediating principle through which a mystic can experience the transcendental Oneness. This is why Clement teaches: "The man with whom the Logos dwells is made like God and is beautiful. That man becomes God." For Clement, one may have many teachers in life, but the ultimate spiritual teacher is the Logos itself, "the Teacher from whom all instruction comes."

140 Plutarch, *Isis and Osiris*, 372e–3b, quoted in De Vogel, C. J. (1966), 211. As early Church fathers admitted, Hermes was actually called "the Logos" by the Greeks. A text of the Gnostic Christians even echoes the words of St. John about Christ: "Hermes is the Word who has expressed and fashioned the things that have been, that are and that will be." *See* Fidler, D. (1993), 46, quoting the Naassene Gnostics attacked by Hippolytus.

141 Origen, *The Eternal Generation of the Son*, quoted in Stevenson, J. (1957), 204

142 St. Augustine, *Confessions*, Book 7 v 14

143 Quoted in Kingsland, W. (1937), 135

144 Inge, W. R. (1899), 349, notes that in the original Greek many Christian terms reveal their debt to Pagan Mystery terminology. Baptism with water: *mystikon loutron*; baptism generally: *myesis*, which in the Mysteries also meant "initiation"; a baptized person: *memyemenos*, *mystes* or *summystes*; an unbaptized person: *amyetos*; unction: *crisma mystikon*; a celebrant of the mass: *mystrios lanthanontos mystagogos*; the sacraments: *mysteria* and also *telete*, *tele*, *teleiosis*, *teleionsthai*, or *teleiopoios*, all of which could equally be translated as referring to initiation.

145 Angus, S. (1925); Barnstone, W. (1984): "The language could equally point to a member of a church or a mystery cult."

146 1 Corinthians 14 v 2

147 Burkert, W. (1992), 3

148 D'Alviella, G. (1981), 108

149 Quoted in Burkert, op. cit., 134, note 11

150 Quoted in Campbell, J. (1955), 367. Early Christianity presented itself as an arcane mystery, "Mysteries that make men freeze with awe." "This is known to the initiates" is a phrase running through all the Greek sermons. St. Dionysius the Areopagite writes: "Take care that you do not reveal the holy of holies, preserve the mysteries of the hidden God so that the profane may not partake of them and in your sacred illuminations speak of the sacred only to the saints."

151 D'Alviella, G. (1981), 111. Sozomenus refrains from mentioning the symbol of Nicaea in his Church history "because the book may fall into the hands of the uninitiated." In the churches of the East a deacon drove the uninitiated from the church at the moment of the Mass with almost the same formula, which opened the Mysteries.

152 Clement of Alexandria, *Clement of Alexandria*, 257

153 Ibid., 256

154 Eisler, R. (1920), 69. *Ekklesia*, Greek for "assembly," was used in the Hellenistic period for the complex hierarchies of Mystery societies. The Church later borrowed both structure and name from these societies.

155 Angus, S. (1925), 276

CHAPTER 5: THE GNOSTICS

1 From the Introduction to *The Gnosis of the Light* (the Bruce codex discovered in 1769), first translation by Rev. Lamplugh, cited in Kingsland, W. (1937), 100

2 The Bruce codex was discovered in 1769, the Askew codex, containing the *Pistis Sophia*, was brought to London in 1785. Neither of these was published in English until the nineteenth century. The Akhmim codex was not discovered until 1896. In 1851 two lost books of

Hippolytus were found on Mt. Athos in Greece containing valuable information on the Gnostics, including direct quotations from Gnostic texts. It seems that later heresiologists, who based themselves mainly on Hippolytus' work, had excised these books at an early date and they were prudently not passed on by his successors, see Cross, F. L. (1958), 641. In 1945 the study of Gnosticism was revolutionized when 52 Gnostic texts were discovered at Nag Hammadi in Upper Egypt. For the first time in 1,600 years scholars could control the hostile polemics of the Patristic sources point by point.

3   Inge, W. R. (1899), 86: "Faith is a summary knowledge of urgent truths, suitable for people who are in a hurry, but gnosis is scientific faith."

4   Freke and Gandy (1997), 101

5   It is important to note that the Catechetical school existed before it became Christian under Clement's authority. Runia, D. T. (1993), 133, questions Eusebius' account of the history of the school: "Eusebius' words definitely imply that the school existed before Pantaenus took charge. Why then does he only mention it here for the first time? Is it because he lacks information, or is he—from his own apologetic viewpoint on behalf of orthodox tradition—engaged in a cover-up?" Runia proposes that: "Pantaenus took over the school from earlier members who had a more Gnostic orientation. Eusebius would then have a reason for denying real continuity." Marlowe, J. (1971), 251, records that Pantaenus' teacher was a Pythagorean. Putting all this information together would yield the following scenario. Arising from Jewish/Pythagorean groups like the Therapeutae and basing themselves on the work of Philo, a school of Jewish Gnosticism develops in Alexandria. During the first century its teaching spreads widely in Egypt, Palestine, and Syria. Roberts (1979) considers it likely that: "If Valentinus and Basilides taught in Alexandria, the obvious place for their teaching would have been this school." See also Runia, 133, note 4. Following the destruction of the Alexandrian Jewish community in the first quarter of the second century there is a period of chaos. Out of this emerges the school run by Pantaenus and finally the Christian Gnostic school of Clement.

6   Clement, Stromata, 7.1: "The Gnostic alone is truly pious ... the true Christian is the Gnostic." See Stevenson, J. (1957), 184ff.

7   Irenaeus, Against Heresies, 2.14.1–6, quoted in Perkins, P. (1993), 179–81

8   Ibid., 1.23.2–4, quoted in Barnstone, W. (1984), 607

9   Pagels, E. (1975), 158. See also D'Alviella, G. (1981), 105.

10 Quoted in Barnstone, W. (1984), 656

11 Irenaeus, Against Heresies, 1.24.6–7, quoted ibid., 649

12 Pagels, E. (1979), 67

13 Quoted in MacMullen, R. (1966), 208

14 The first conference bringing together "specialists in Platonism on the one hand, and specialists in the 'wild underworld' of the Gnostics on the other" was held in 1992 in New York. In his contribution to the debate, John Kenney described one of the Nag Hammadi texts as reading like "a riot in Plato's cave," see Wallis, R. T. (1992), 204. A. D. Nock describes Gnosticism as "Platonism run wild," see Wallis, R. T. (1992), 187. See also D'Alviella, G. (1981), 103, where D'Alviella calls the Gnostics "half Pagan," and 122, where Wobbermin refers to Gnosticism as "Christian Orphism."

15 Lane-Fox, R. (1986), 308. In 180 CE we hear of Christians from Asia Minor living in Rome. They studied Euclid, Aristotle, and "almost worshiped Galen." Ironically, Galen mocked the Christians' reliance on blind faith, but these Christians seem to have been a living reply to his criticisms. In due course they were excommunicated by the Bishop of Rome. See Eusebius (1965), 177, where Eusebius expresses the orthodox view of these heretics who "with godless rascality corrupt the simple Faith of Holy Writ."

16 Robinson, J. M. (1978), 18. The Nag Hammadi codex has an ankh, the Egyptian hieroglyph meaning life, tooled on the cover. Found among the Gnostic texts were the Pagan works of Sextus the Pythagorean, parts of Plato's Republic dealing with the fate of the "Just Man," and extracts from The Hermetica.

17 Lane-Fox, R. (1986), 307. Clement mentions over 300 Pagan authors, of whom we now know nothing. See Clement of Alexandria, Clement of Alexandria, xiii. The Loeb editor considers Clement to be so well acquainted with the Mysteries that he was probably an initiate. See Gregory, J. (1987), 25–6.

18 Clement of Alexandria, Stromata 6.26. See also 7.55 and 6.109.

19 Lane-Fox, R. (1986), 520–1. One of Origen's pupils recalls how, using the "protreptic" style of speaking of the Pagan masters, Origen tutored him in a godlike mastery of soul over the body with the age-old Pagan objective of "Self-knowledge."

20 Quoted in Pagels, E. (1988), 85
21 Origen and Plotinus were both taught by Ammonius.
22 Porphyry, *Life of Plotinus*, 20. *See* Doran, R. (1995), 32-3.
23 Quoted in Wallis, R. T. (1992), 112
24 Quoted in Robinson, J. M. (1978), 9. *See also* Wallis, op. cit., which notes that Plotinus does not mention his opponents by name, or refer to them as Gnostics, but their identity as "Christians and other sectaries" is confirmed by Porphyry. Plotinus charges his opponents with "abandoning the ancient philosophy" in favor of revelations by Zostrianos, Allogenes, and others. (Works attributed to these authors have now been found at Nag Hammadi.) He regards them as friends who had been so badly contaminated by the new teachings that they could not get over it, even after they had been taught the true doctrine by him. Plotinus wrote against them in order to enlighten his fellow pupils that a) whatever is worthy in the apostates' teaching had been taken from Plato, and b) what had been added to it is far from being true. His work was taken up by his follower Porphyry and enlarged into 15 volumes, *Against the Christians*. A few fragments survive but the rest was consigned to the flames in the fourth century.
25 Robinson, J. M. (1978), 171. *On the Origin of the World* is a good example of Gnostic syncretism between Greek myths and philosophy and Christian ideas. A Gnostic text called *The Book of the Great Logos* has Jesus commanding his disciples to go to Galilee and find a man or woman in whom the greater part of evil is dead, and take two jars of wine from them to the place where he is, and also two vine branches. When they have done so, Jesus creates a place of offering, placing one wine jar on the right and one on the left, and strews certain berries and spices around the vessels. He then makes the disciples clothe themselves in white linen robes. This image is almost identical to representations of the Greek Mysteries of Dionysus found on ancient vases *(see plate 5)*.
26 Mead, G. R. S. (1906), 510-11
27 Barnstone, W. (1984), 639
28 Ibid., 640. As in Pagan myth the 12 trials of Heracles are equated with the signs of the zodiac. In this Gnostic text Heracles is set his trials by Elohim, thereby equating Zeus with the Jewish God.
29 Ibid., 640-1
30 Mead, op. cit., 199-200. Hippolytus' polemic against the Naassene Gnostics is invaluable for pointing out that the teachings of Gnostic Christianity and the doctrines of the Mysteries are identical. *See* Barnstone, W. (1984), 635, for the Naassene Psalm, one of the most beautiful of all Gnostic texts.
31 Hippolytus, *Elenchos*, 5. 9.5, quoted in Segal, R. A. (1992), 70
32 Jung, C. (1959), 199. In *Elenchos* Hippolytus quotes a Naassene hymn giving many of the godman's titles: Adonis, Osiris, Adam, Korybas, Pan, and Bacchus. Osiris is the shepherd who guides souls (each soul is a star in Egyptian mythology) back to the Fields of the Righteous (the star-fields of the night sky, or heaven) after death.
33 Mead, op. cit., 203
34 Robinson, J. M. (1978), 455. Mother, Father, and Son are praised as the primal triad in Sethian Gnosticism. The Egyptian trinity of Osiris, Isis, and Horus is probably the ultimate origin of both Gnostic and Christian conceptions of the divine trinity. The Gnostic myth dramatizes the fall of Sophia from heaven and her lost wanderings in the world, where she is ignored or abused by men, *see* Mead, G. R. S. (1906), 333. This is the same doctrine that is found in Paganism. Only the attainment of Wisdom could lead the fallen soul back to its heavenly origin. Pythagoras, for example, was the first man to call himself a philosopher—literally a "lover of Sophia."
35 Robinson, J. M. (1978), 143. *The Gospel of Philip*, 25, wryly observes, "Some said 'Mary conceived by the holy spirit.' They are in error. They do not know what they are saying. When did a woman ever conceive by a woman?"
36 Mead, op. cit., 334. Many of these names betray their derivation from the Isis cult.
37 Kingsley, P. (1995), 355, notes the "extensive resemblances" between the doctrines of Empedocles and the Gnostics.
38 Pagels, E. (1975), 23
39 Plato, *Timaeus*, 3.28: "To discover the maker and father of this universe is indeed a hard task, and having found him it would be impossible to tell everyone about him."
40 Anaxagoras likened God to a Universal Mind: "All things contain a portion of everything, but Mind is infinite and self-ruled, it is mixed with nothing but is all alone by itself. And all the things that were to be, all things that were but are not now, all things that are now or

that shall be, Mind arranged them all, including this rotation in which are now rotating the stars, the sun and moon, the air and the ether." Kirk and Raven, (1957), 372. This was echoed by Empedocles: "He is a holy, unspeakable mind, darting with swift thoughts over the whole world," quoted ibid, 350, and Xenophanes, "One God, greatest among gods and men, in no way similar to mortals either in body or in thought. Always he remains in the same place, moving not at all. Without toil he shakes all things by the thought of his mind," ibid., 169.

[41] Fidler, D. (1993), 18

[42] Plato, *Timaeus*, 41. The demiurge (craftsman) is a lesser god who serves the higher powers.

[43] Pagels, E. (1979), 62

[44] Exodus 20 v 5

[45] *The Secret Book of John*, quoted in Pagels, op. cit., 56

[46] McEvedy, C. (1967), 162. In *Hypostasis of the Archons*, Sophia rebukes the false creator, calling him Samael, the god of the blind. Irenaeus refers to a Gnostic system in which when Jehovah claimed, "I am Father and God, and above me there is no one," his mother the goddess Sophia "cried out against him, 'Do not lie for above thee is the Father of All, the First Man, and Man the Son of Man.'" Quoted in Mead, G. R. S. (1906), 189.

[47] Irenaeus, *Against Heresies*, 1.27.1, quoted in Barnstone, W. (1984), 644

[48] Quoted in Inge, W. R. (1899), 110. St. Augustine repeats this verbatim, not as Platonism but as orthodox Christian doctrine.

[49] Pagels, E. (1979), 46

[50] Quoted in Mead, G. R. S. (1906), 489

[51] Ibid., 506

[52] Burkert, W. (1985), 102

[53] Harrison, J. (1922), 514. The Christian Dion Chrysostom tells us that in the Mysteries the initiate is seated as if enthroned while his instructors dance around him. Aristophanes parodies the same ritual in *The Clouds* and Plato refers to it in *Euthydemus*, 277d. Kerenyi, C. (1967), 9, discusses the lamps discovered at Eleusis. These were worn by the dancers led by Dionysus and mimicked the dance of the "starry ether." The Mysteries dramatized the descent and reascent of the soul during incarnation, the lights symbolizing the planets and stars, which were imagined as a celestial ladder connecting Earth and heaven. Dio of Prusa gives us the clearest exposition of this ritual and its significance: "If one would bring a man, Greek or barbarian, for initiation into a mystic recess, overwhelming by its beauty and size, so that he would behold many mystic views and hear many sounds of the kind, with darkness and light appearing in sudden changes and other innumerable things happening, and even, as they do in the so-called enthronement ceremony—they have the initiands sit down, and they dance around them—if all this were happening, would it be possible that such a man should experience just nothing in his soul, that he should not come to surmise that there is some wiser insight and plan in all that is going on, even if he came from the utmost barbarity?" Kerenyi comments: "The intended reference is to the cosmos, the dance of stars and sun around the earth, and other marvels of nature that surpass the artful contrivances of mystery ceremonies; the comparison of the cosmos with a huge mystery hall goes back to the Stoic philosopher Cleanthes, who lived in Athens and in all probability was thinking of Eleusis." See Burkert, W. (1992), 90.

[54] Cumont, F. (1903), 153. The sacred animal masks worn by initiates of Mithras symbolized the signs of the zodiac and the simulated murder of the initiate symbolized the death of the soul and its descent into the prison of the body.

[55] *The Acts of John*, 97–102. The Gnostic *Book of Jehu* also contains an allusion to the round dance, *see* Campbell, J. (1955), 171.

[56] Mead, G. R. S. (1906), 431. *See also* Campbell, J. (1955), 173, which notes that in the fourth century the fact that *The Acts of John* was a ritual of initiation was widely known. Christ is a *mystagogue*, his disciples are *mystae* who are to become the *symmystae* of Christ. This accounts for the violent denunciation of it at the Second Council of Nicaea.

[57] The voices are not allocated in the original. This has been done by Mead.

[58] Mead, G. R. S. (1906), 431ff

[59] Quoted in Inge, W. R. (1899), 88

[60] Clement, *Stromata*, 1.12 and 7.61

[61] Origen, *Against Celsus*, 1.7, quoted in Fidler, D. (1993), 33. *See also* Wallis, R. T. (1992), 14.

[62] Quoted in Barnstone, W. (1984), 628

[63] Mead, G. R. S. (1906), 278. The Pythagoreans imposed a five-year silence on novices, which Eusebius tells us was also practiced by the followers of Basilides.

64 Quoted in Mead, op. cit., 521
65 Clement, *Stromata*, 5.9. *See* Inge, W. R. (1899), 88, where Dean Inge asserts that here Clement has borrowed "verbatim from a NeoPythagorean document."
66 Quoted in Barnstone, W. (1984), 638
67 In 1973 Morton Smith published a previously unknown letter of Clement referring to *The Secret Gospel of Mark*. Controversy surrounds the document, with some dismissing it as a forgery and others accepting it as genuine. Stanton, G. (1995), 93, gives the current state of the debate. The document itself can be found in Barnstone, W., op. cit., 339.
68 Barnstone, op. cit., 341
69 Stanton, G. (1995), 95
70 Barnstone, op. cit., 340
71 John 11:16
72 Mark 14 v 51
73 Quoted in Kahn, C. H. (1979), 55. *See also* 109, where Kahn notes Heraclitus' favored use of *ginoskein* for the knowledge, which goes beyond opinion.
74 Plato, *Phaedrus and Letters vii and viii*, 53. The editor of this version of *Phaedrus* notes that Plato repeatedly contrasts *episteme*, "knowledge," with *doxa*, "opinions." True knowledge can only be obtained by the pursuit of pure philosophy. The sensible world can only ever be the source of *doxa*.
75 Fidler, D. (1993), 9
76 Pagels, E. (1979), 48
77 Clement, *Stromata*, 6.26
78 Ibid., 7.55
79 Ibid., 6.109
80 Ibid., 7.57
81 Pagels, op. cit., 125
82 Quoted in Robinson, J. M. (1978), 142; *see also* Pagels, op. cit., 59
83 It was this command which set Socrates on his quest for true knowledge. *See* Plato, *Apology*, 22e–3c.
84 Quoted in Pagels, op. cit., 141
85 Quoted in Robinson, J. M. (1978), 448
86 Quoted in Pagels, op. cit., 136, 141
87 Socrates is the most famous exponent of the doctrine of the Daemon. *See Apology*, 31d, *Phaedrus* 242, and *The Republic* 496c. He describes his Daemon as an inner voice, which has come to him with advice throughout his life. *See* Plato, *Phaedrus and Letters vii and viii*, 43, note 3. That the doctrine predates Socrates is evidenced by Empedocles, fr. 132. Empedocles believed in a divine self alien to the body—which he calls not psyche but Daemon, an exile from the gods to whom it longs to return. *See* Guthrie, W. K. C. (1962), 318.
88 The relationship between Daemon and eidolon—between the Higher and lower self—was sometimes conceived as like that between the body and its shadow. This doctrine underlies the myth of Plato's cave, in which chained men watch their flickering shadows cast on the wall and mistake them for real life.
89 Burkert, W. (1985), 202, notes that in Greek myth the god often has a mortal double. The twins Castor and Pollux became part of Mithraic iconography for this reason: on alternate days one is alive and the other dead, a symbol of the relationship between the Daemon and eidolon. The Gnostic *Gospel of Thomas* records Jesus' cryptic saying: "Two will rest on a bed, the one will die and the other will live."
90 *See* Epictetus, *The Teachings of Epictetus*, 145, and *On Providence*, 4. Epictetus explains: "God has placed at every man's side a guardian, the Daemon of each man, who is charged to watch over him; a Daemon that cannot sleep, nor be deceived. To what greater and more watchful guardian could he have committed us? So, when you have shut the doors, and made darkness in the house, remember, never to say that you are alone; for you are not alone, but God is there, and your Daemon is there."
91 Quoted in Freke and Gandy (1998), 40
92 Mead, G. R. S. (1906), 599. An anonymous Gnostic recounts his vision of the Daemon and eidolon, which appeared to him as a giant and a dwarf: "I stood on a lofty mountain, and saw a gigantic man and another, a dwarf; and I heard as it were a voice of thunder and drew nigh for to hear; and he spake unto me and said, I am thou and thou art I, and wheresoever thou mayest be I am there. In all am I scattered, and whencesoever thou willest, thou gatherest me; and gathering me thou gatherest thyself."
93 Valentinus, in Segal, R. A. (1992), 237, describes how the Guardian Angel, which is the Self, gives the person Gnosis. Only when the eidolon and Daemon become One can the individual

achieve perfection and eternity. Segal writes: "It is becoming ever clearer that this is the characteristic and basic assumption of Gnosis."

94   Pyramid Text Utterance 215 assures the deceased: "You shall not perish and your double shall not perish. For you are your double."

95   Quoted in Lane-Fox, R. (1986), 565. Mani began preaching his universal Gnostic religion in 242 CE in Babylon. It spread rapidly throughout the Roman Empire. St. Augustine was a Manichaean "hearer" for eight years. In 304 Manichaeanism was made a capital offense in the West, for its Persian background made it highly suspect. In the more tolerant East it eventually spread as far as China. It reappeared in the West in the Middle Ages and was vigorously persecuted.

96   Quoted in Hollroyd, S. (1994), 69

97   Quoted in Mead, G. R. S. (1906), 475ff

98   Ibid.

99   See Segal, R. A. (1992), 51. Quispel refers to the *mysterium conjunctionis* between angel and man. Carl Jung used this as the title of one of his many works that were inspired by Gnosticism.

100   Quoted in Inge, W. R. (1899), 82

101   Quoted in Segal, R. A. (1992), 237

102   Marcus Aurelius, in *Meditations*, 139, writes that the Daemon "which God has given to every man for his guardian and guide" is in fact "a portion" of God himself.

103   Pagels, E. (1979), 141. The Gnostic sage Simon Magus proclaims: "Each human being is the dwelling place of an infinite power—the root of the universe."

104   Inge, op. cit., 353, notes that the Gnostics "had much in common with the Orphic Mystae" who coined this saying. See also Angus, S. (1925), 112, which records several Hermetic prayers on this theme including the following, "For thou art I, and I am thou; thy name is mine, for I am thy eidolon."

105   Guthrie, K. S. (1987), 270, Saying 92

106   Clement of Alexandria, *Paedagogus*, 3.1

107   Quoted in Angus, S. (1925), 111

108   Ibid., 106

109   Quoted in Mead, G. R. S. (1906), 223

110   This is identical to the Hindu doctrine that Atman is Brahman—the Self is God. The Katha Upanishad states: "Dwelling within all beings is the Atman, the Self, a little flame in the heart. Anyone who knows his Atman, his Higher Self, reaches Brahman the Supreme Spirit." The Mandukya Upanishad states unequivocally: "Brahman is all and Atman is Brahman."

111   Herodotus, in *The Histories*, Book 2, 122, tells us that the doctrine of reincarnation originated with the Egyptians but had been "adopted by certain Greek writers." Although he "refrains from mentioning them," there is no doubt that he is referring to the Orphics and Pythagoreans. Kingsley, P. (1995), 368, states that this was well known even in Classical times: "The Pythagoreans maintained a secrecy which was quite exceptional, but that the teachings of theirs which were 'best known by everybody' were the immortality of the soul and reincarnation." According to Diogenes Laertius, Pythagoras taught that: "The soul, revolving around the circle of necessity, is transformed and confined at different times in different bodies," quoted in Guthrie, K. S. (1987), 145. In *The Laws*, 870e, Plato attributes this doctrine to the priests of the Mysteries, by whom it was taught with the associated doctrine of *karma*: "They will also state a truth firmly believed by many who have learned it from the lips of those who occupy themselves with these matters at the Mysteries, that vengeance is taken on such crimes beyond the grave, and when the sinner has returned to our own world once more, he must infallibly pay nature's penalty—must be done by as he did." In *Meno*, 81b–c, Socrates tells us: "The soul, having been born again many times, and having seen all things that exist, has knowledge of them all."

112   Plutarch, *The Moral Essays*, 184, "A Letter of Consolation," 10

113   Mead, G. R. S. (1906), 282

114   Quoted in Barnstone, W. (1984), 60

115   Quoted in Mead, op. cit., 485

116   Plato, *The Republic*, Book 10, 614ff

117   Quoted in Mead, op. cit., 516

118   Plato, *Cratylus*, 400c: "The body is an enclosure or prison in which the soul is incarcerated." The Gnostic Carpocrates taught the same doctrine and also called the body a prison. He claimed that souls are reincarnated until they have completed all sins and that this was the true meaning behind Jesus' teaching in Luke 12 v 58: "You will not be let out till you have paid the last penny." See Barnstone, W. (1984), 649.

119 Quoted in Barnstone, op. cit., 61

120 Plato, *Cratylus*, 400c: "For some say that the body is the grave of the soul which may be thought to be buried in our present life. The Orphic poets ... were under the impression that the soul is suffering the punishment of sin until the penalty is paid."

121 Origen, *De Pricipiis*, 2.8.3, quoted in Stevenson, J. (1957), 203

122 Bernstein, A. E. (1993), 307. Origen's view was that of the Pagans—all would eventually be restored to God in a total *apokatastasis* or restoration. He used the axiom of Neoplatonic philosophy that the end must be as the beginning. All who are punished will be cured and on this basis he denied eternal punishment.

123 Origen, *De Pricipiis*, 3.1.20–1. *See also* Kingsland, W. (1937), 138. Origen asks how could someone be born blind unless they are being punished for a previous sin. Reincarnation he says, allows souls sufficient time to purge their sins and complete their cycle of lives, *see* Bernstein, op. cit., 311.

124 Bernstein, op. cit., 307. Jerome, at the end of the fourth century, was the first to condemn Origen. (Jerome denied the pre-existence of souls but taught that God was "daily creating new ones." This doctrine of *creationism* is still accepted today, *see* Brandon, S. G. F. [1969], 84. That a good God could continue to daily make millions of souls, many of whom he knows will ultimately be condemned to eternal torture, is just one of the many cruelties and absurdities of this theology.) Under Justinian in 543 CE the Greek text of Origen was burned as heretical. As Stevenson, J. (1957), 203, notes, no other opinion of Origen's was more vehemently opposed than his doctrine of "Ultimate salvation for all."

125 *See* Josephus, *The Jewish War*, 2.14.165. In Josephus' opinion the Pharisees gained the support of the majority of the people because they taught that the soul survives death and receives either the reward of a new life in another body or eternal punishment in the Underworld. The Pharisees, of whom Paul was one, were modernizers and Hellenizers who were violently opposed by the traditionalist Sadducees. Mark 12 v 18 states that: "The Sadducees teach that there is no resurrection," but unlike Josephus, who was writing at the same time, it does not go on to state that the Pharisees were teaching the Orphic doctrine of reincarnation.

126 John 1 v 19

127 Mark 8 v 27. How Jesus could be a reincarnation of his contemporary John the Baptist is not explained.

128 The paintings of the Villa of the Mysteries in Pompeii show only women priestesses of Bacchus officiating at the initiations. Livy's story of the Bacchanalia of 186 BCE, and the *Senatus Consultum*, which authorized the ruthless purge of the cult, both confirm the central role played by women.

129 Turcan, R. (1992), 292. The Bacchic cult notably liberated women, who are associated with it from its earliest appearance in Greece.

130 Pagels, E. (1979), 87

131 Ibid.

132 Harrison, J. (1922), 645–7, gives details of several Pythagorean women.

133 Kingsley, P. (1995), 162, notes that: "One of the—by classical standards—most extraordinary features of ancient Pythagoreanism was the equal status of women side by side with men."

134 Quoted in Harrison, op. cit. Iamblichus says that Pythagoras praised women for their justice, as they were willing to share what was their own with others—a quality that was rarely found in men, *see* De Vogel, C. J. (1966), 134.

135 Harrison, op. cit., 646–7. In addition, after his death the house of Pythagoras was dedicated as a sanctuary to the goddess Demeter and the street it was in was named after the Muses.

136 Pagels, op. cit., 81

137 Robinson, J. M. (1978), 245. The *Pistis Sophia* also portrays Mary as the most spiritual of all the disciples, *see* Mead, G. R. S. (1906), 467.

138 Robinson, op. cit., 524. The confrontation between Mary and Peter is a mythic scenario also found in *The Gospel of Mary*, *The Gospel of Thomas*, the *Pistis Sophia*, and *The Gospel of the Egyptians*. Mary Magdalene represents Sophia, the "Wisdom" of the Inner Mysteries of Christianity, while Peter represents the Outer Mysteries practiced by those Christians who have not yet received these secret teachings. Peter, whose name, given to him by Jesus, means "Rock," represents the teaching that the Outer Mysteries should create a solid rock within the initiate on which to build the temple of Gnosis. But the danger is that the beginner becomes arrogant and believes he understands the Mysteries when in fact he has only taken the first step. To represent this, Peter is often portrayed as foolish and fickle, both in the Gnostic gospels and in the New Testament. It is Peter who denies Jesus three times and at whom Jesus yells, "Get thee behind me, Satan," *see* Mead, G. R. S. (1906), 580. The

ignorant misogyny mythically represented by the figure of Peter has of course come to dominate orthodox Christianity and the results have been disastrous. The Divine Feminine that played a vital part in Pagan and Gnostic teachings has all but disappeared from Literalist Christianity.

139 Pagels, op. cit., 85

140 Ibid., 80

141 Among the Valentinians women were considered equal to men. They acted as prophets, teachers, evangelists, healers, and priests.

142 Quoted in Pagels (1979), 80

143 Ibid., 66

144 Euripides, *The Bacchae*, 657–9

145 Quoted in Pagels, op. cit., 62

146 Quoted in Pagels, E., (1975), 45

147 Pagels, E. (1979), 61, *see also* Pagels, E. (1975), 45. Five centuries earlier Heraclitus had declared: "For God all things are fair and good and just, but men have taken some things as unjust, others as just." *See* Kahn, C. H. (1979), 61, Heraclitus' Saying 68.

148 Quoted in Pagels, E. (1979), 63

149 Godwin, J. (1981), 86

150 Quoted in Pagels, E. (1975), 19. Basilides quotes Paul's Letter to the Romans 2 v 12–16 in his support.

151 Stevenson, J. (1957), 163ff. The Gnostic does not need to follow ethical codes to be loving because, as Clement explains, "He who is free through Gnosis is really a slave because of love for those who have not yet been able to attain to the freedom of Gnosis." The Gnostic, then, is not a depraved hedonist, as the Literalists would have us believe, but someone who chooses to naturally express love for its own sake, rather than following an imposed moral code from fear of evil or hope of reward. Clement explains further: "The man of understanding and perspicacity is the Gnostic. And his business is not abstinence from what is evil (for this is a step to the highest perfection), or the doing of good out of fear. Nor any more is he to do so for hope of promised recompense. But only the doing of good out of love, and for the sake of its own excellence, is to be the Gnostic's choice."

152 Quoted in Kingsland, W. (1937), 203

153 Clement, *Stromata*, 7.33

CHAPTER 6: THE JESUS CODE

1 Luke 8 v 1. In Matthew 13 v 11 Jesus tells the disciples: "To you it has been given to know the *mysteria* of the kingdom of heaven, but to them it has not been given."

2 Quoted in Pagels, E. (1979), 51

3 Irenaeus, *Against Heresies*, 1.18, quoted ibid., 48. The Gnostics' creativity is a sign of the vitality of this new movement. As Burkert notes in another context, "Only dead dogma is preserved without change, doctrine taken seriously is always being revised in the continuous process of reinterpretation." Burkert, W. (1972), 135.

4 Pagels, op. cit., 44

5 Mark 4 v 11–12. In the Gospel of John 16 v 12 and 25, Jesus promises his disciples more explicit teachings when they are ready to receive them: "I have yet many things to say unto you, but you cannot bear them now. These things I have spoken to you in parables: the hour is coming when I shall no more speak in parables, but shall tell you plainly of the Father." Kingsland, W. (1937), 25–6, notes that none of these "Mysteries" are in fact explained by Jesus in the canonical gospels. Instead we must turn to apocryphal and Gnostic texts to find them.

6 Quoted in Inge, W. R. (1899), 355

7 Demetrius, *On Style*, quoted in Burkert, W. (1992), 79. Strabo, following Posidonius, refers to "concealment in Mysteries," which "imitates Nature that shuns direct perception."

8 Quoted ibid. Heraclitus put it most simply when he said, "Nature loves to hide."

9 Quoted in Robinson, J. M. (1978), 150. Inge finds evidence for the Gnostics' allegorical approach to the gospels in the Gospel of John. He writes: "The fourth Gospel is steeped in symbolism of this kind. The eight miracles which St. John selects are obviously chosen for their symbolic value; indeed, he seems to regard them mainly as acted parables. His favorite word for miracles is signs or symbols." Inge, W. R. (1899), 58.

10 Quoted in Hoffmann, R. J. (1987), 102–3

11 Quoted in Stevenson, J. (1957), 206

[12] Lane-Fox, R. (1986), 524. A Jewish mystic had taught Origen that scripture was like a house full of locked rooms, that God had confused the keys and it was up to his heirs to fit the right key to each lock.

[13] Quoted in Stevenson, op. cit.

[14] Ibid. *See also* Marlowe, J. (1971), 255, where Marlowe notes that although Origen writes of the literal story as a necessary starting-point in the pursuit of Divine Knowledge, "One senses in his writing a belief that the incarnation was an unnecessary and even regrettable concession to human ignorance, which the true Christian philosopher might well have done without."

[15] Clement, *Stromata*, 6.10, quoted in Fidler, D. (1993), 31. Clement advises, "Knowing that the savior teaches nothing in a purely human way, but teaches all things with divine and mystic wisdom, we must not listen to His utterances carnally; but with due investigation and intelligence must search out and learn the meaning hidden in them."

[16] Kingsland, W. (1937), 203

[17] Quoted in Mead, G. R. S. (1906), 449

[18] Guthrie, K. S. (1987), 19ff. To the Pythagoreans numbers were "the principle, the source, the root of all things."

[19] Quoted in Lemprière, J. (1949), 3

[20] Quoted in Mead, op. cit., 335. *See also* Fidler, D. (1993), 23. Gnostic masters who employed numerical symbolism in their teachings include Basilides, Valentinus, Marcus, Colarbasus, and Monoimos.

[21] Guthrie, op. cit., 297

[22] Mead, op. cit., 222. Monoimos believed, along with the Pythagoreans, that the universe was constructed from the five elements, which were represented by the five Platonic solids.

[23] *See* D'Alviella, G. (1981), 106, which considers that Gnosticism not only borrowed from the Mysteries of Eleusis but that its doctrine of the fate of the soul "resembles too closely the Mithras Mysteries" for there not to have been some influence. Origen reveals the Mithraic doctrine about the planets and the stars "and the soul's passage through these. The symbol is this. There is a ladder with seven gates and at its top an eighth gate." Celsus suggests, however, that this is not new to Mithraism. He calls it an "ancient system that there are seven heavens and that the way of the soul is through the planets." Celsus also clearly states that the Christians that he knew in the second century were teaching exactly the same doctrines as Mithraism. *See* Hoffmann, R. J. (1987), 95.

[24] Fidler, D. (1993), 35

[25] Ibid., 73

[26] Ibid., 321

[27] Ibid., 32. The Gnostic Marcus speaks of the spoken name of the Savior Iesous as consisting of six letters, while his ineffable name consists of 24—8 + 8 + 8—the number of letters in the Greek alphabet, *see* Mead, G. R. S. (1906), 375. A Christian Sibylline Oracle also refers to the mystic number of Jesus: "Four vowels he has, twofold the consonants in him. And now will I declare to thee also the whole number. Eight monads, and to these as many decads, and eight hundreds also his name will show." Above the seven planets in the Gnostic system is the sphere of the fixed stars, where Sophia and Jesus dwell in the region of the "ogdoad." Hence, the mystic name of Jesus equates to "the fullness of the eights": 888. Rahner notes that although absent from modern Christianity, the ogdoad was at an early stage a part of orthodox Christianity. Theodotus, in a work edited by Clement, writes: "He whom the Mother generates is led into death and into the world, but he whom Christ regenerates is transferred to life into the Ogdoad," quoted in Campbell, J. (1955), 392. Cyril of Alexandria in the fourth century calls the consecration the "*mysterion Christi*, which is symbolized by the Ogdoad," Campbell, 390.

[28] Fidler, op. cit., 264

[29] Revelation 13 v 18: "Here is wisdom. He who has understanding, let him count the number of the beast: for it is the number of a man and its number is 666."

[30] Fidler, op. cit., 29

[31] Ibid., 84

[32] Ibid., 264. *See also* Dr. Eisler's study of the gematria of the Jesus story; Eisler, R. (1920), 115.

[33] Irenaeus, *Against Heresies*, 1.14.4, quoted in Fidler, D. (1993), 30

[34] Quoted ibid., 278. It was an important number to Plato, who states that the tyrant is "729 worse than the good man."

[35] Ibid., 108

[36] Mark 8 v 19

[37] Quoted in Robinson, J. M. (1978), 201

38 Eisler, R. (1931), 450
39 Robinson, op. cit., 124. Pagels is right to suggest that the opening lines of both *The Gospel of Thomas* and *Thomas the Contender* can be read as if "you, the reader, are Jesus' twin brother." This is an axiom of Gnostic teaching. *See* Pagels, E. (1979), 47.
40 Matthew 27 v 17
41 Mead, G. R. S. (1906), 217
42 Quoted Robinson, op. cit., 436
43 *The Acts of John*, 97–102
44 Ibid. The text ends with a clear exposition of Docetism: "The Lord carried out everything symbolically for the conversion of men."
45 Hence Jesus' advice in *The Gospel of Thomas*: "Become passers-by."
46 Campbell, J. (1964), 372ff, quoting *The Acts of John* and commenting on Docetism.
47 The followers of the heretical Christian Mani conveyed these teachings by differentiating between Jesus the son of Mary and Jesus the Son of God. It was the son of Mary (the eidolon) who suffered death on the cross, not the Son of God (the Daemon).
48 Euripides, *The Bacchae*, 622–5
49 *The Apocalypse of Peter*, quoted in Robinson, J. M. (1978), 377
50 Euripides, op. cit., 1044–121
51 Robinson, op. cit., 377, *The Apocalypse of Peter*
52 Quoted ibid., 365; *see also* 341, *The Paraphrase of Shem*. After his baptism the Savior foretells that in its anger Nature will try to seize him, but will only manage to crucify Soldas, another name for the earthly Jesus.
53 Barnstone, W. (1984), 628, quoting Hippolytus on Basilides
54 Mark 15 v 21
55 The Qur'an, Sura 4 v 156–7
56 Heraclitus writes: "Mortals are immortal and immortals are mortal; while one is alive the other is dead, and when one is dead the other is alive," *see* Kahn, C. H. (1979), 71. Pindar also stated that: "While the body is subject to death, the soul remains alive, for it alone comes from the god. But it sleeps while the limbs are active," *see* Cranston, S. (1977), 208.
57 Angus, S. (1925), 96. Initiation was considered as a death from which believers arose through rebirth. In Greek the words for death and initiation are very similar and were a familiar pun. "To die is to be initiated," says Plato. The resurrection promised by the early Christians is the same as that offered by Osiris-Dionysus and other mythical godmen of the Mysteries. In John 3 v 1–21 Jesus' disciple Nicodemus is confused because he takes Jesus' teaching of rebirth literally. He asks, "How can a man be born when he is old? Can he enter a second time into his mother's womb and be born?" The Egyptian sage Hermes Trismegistus likewise preached spiritual rebirth and, like Nicodemus, his student Tat interprets this literally and confesses to his master, "I know not, Trismegistus, from what womb a man can be born again, nor from what seed," *see The Hermetica*, Book 13. Jesus and Hermes both explain that this rebirth is not to be understood literally, but mystically.
58 Quoted in Robinson, op. cit., 52ff. The *Treatise on the Resurrection* explains that ordinary human existence is spiritual death but the resurrection is spiritual enlightenment, *see* Pagels, E. (1979), 42. Again this teaching is derived from Paganism. Socrates, in *Gorgias*, 493a, says, "I should not be surprised, you know, if Euripides was right when he said, 'Who knows, if life be death, and death be life?' [quoting Polyidus fr. 7] And perhaps we are actually dead, for I once heard one of our wise men say that we are now dead, and that our body is a tomb." Heraclitus a century earlier had stated that: "When we live our souls are dead, but when we die our souls revive and live." The purpose of initiation was to awaken the soul from this death-like state. This is the true doctrine, which lies behind Empedocles' claim to be able to resurrect a man from the dead. With the triumph of Literalist Christianity this doctrine became completely misunderstood as the bringing back to life of people who had actually died.
59 Quoted in Robinson, op. cit., 55
60 John 10 v 17
61 Pagels, E. (1979), 41; notes 36 and 37 give Pagels' sources
62 Ibid., 43. Pagels writes: "What interested the Gnostics far more than past events attributed to the 'historical' Jesus, was the possibility of encountering the risen Christ in the present."
63 *The Gospel of Philip*, 73.5
64 Robinson, op. cit., 56
65 In 2 Timothy 16–18 two Gnostics are accused of teaching "that our resurrection has already taken place" and of "upsetting people's faith."

66 The idea that the resurrection has already taken place occurs in several texts in the Nag Hammadi library, *see The Treatise on the Resurrection, The Exegesis of the Soul,* and *The Gospel of Philip.*

67 Quoted in Robinson, op. cit., 56

68 Ibid., adapted to form one quote

69 Ibid.

70 That the sacred marriage was at the heart of the Mysteries of Eleusis is clear from the ritual that was carried out at its culmination. Two jars were poured out, one to the East and one to the West, while the *mystae* cried out to heaven, "Rain!" and to the Earth, "Conceive!"

71 Harrison, J. (1922), 564. Demeter had a sacred marriage with the mortal Iasion which Theocritus tells us was a mystic rite giving joy "that the uninitiated will never learn."

72 Angus, S. (1925), 114. Angus devotes several pages to the theme of the sacred marriage in Paganism.

73 Kerenyi, C. (1976), 308. The wife of the Archon Basileus celebrated "the ineffable sacred ceremony" which Aretaios calls a *mysterion.* This took place in the *boukolion,* or cattle shed, near the temple of Dionysus. Burkert writes of this ritual: "Nowhere else does Greek literature speak so clearly of a sacred marriage ritual." *See* Burkert, W. (1985), 239.

74 Harrison, op. cit., 643-4. At Phlya in the southwestern part of the Peloponnesus the Mysteries of Andana were celebrated, *see* Meyer, M. W. (1987), 49ff. In age and venerability they were second only to those of Eleusis. At Phlya there was a Telesterion, a bridal chamber and a cult of Eros. It was also a haunt of many famous Pythagoreans, among them Hippasus (*see* Burkert, W. [1972], 206), Philolaus (*see* Burkert, 237), Aristoxenus, (*see* Guthrie, K. S. [1987], 243) and Echecrates (*see* Guthrie, W. K. C. [1962], 310). Diogenes Laertius mentions four Pythagoreans from Phlius, *see* De Vogel, C. J. [1966], 28.

75 Angus, op. cit., 114; *see* Macchioro, *Zagreus,* 69, for illustration.

76 Harrison, op. cit., 538. Firmicus Maternus tells us that: "The *mystae* hail those just initiated by the name of brides."

77 Ibid. Harrison notes that although the Christian Fathers "grossly libeled" the Pagan Mysteries, "when they seek an illustration for their own mysteries, they confess that the sacred marriage was believed by the celebrants to be spiritual."

78 It is not completely absent, however. Tertullian reminds his flock, "You married Christ," while Cyprian taught that to lapse was to commit "adultery to Christ," *see* Lane-Fox, R. (1986), 370.

79 Barnstone, W. (1984), 288. There are several versions of this Gnostic myth of the fall and redemption of Sophia: the *Pistis Sophia* (*see* Mead, G. R. S. [1906], 459), *The Exegesis of the Soul* (*see* Robinson, J. M. [1978], 190) and *The Gospel of Truth* (*see* Barnstone, W. [1984], 290). *See also* Mead (1906), 385ff. In the Valentinian system the marriage of Jesus and Sophia occurs after she is redeemed from her fallen state.

80 Robinson, J. M. (1978), 190

81 Pagels, E. (1988), 68-9

82 Quoted in Robinson, op. cit., 129

83 Irenaeus, *Against Heresies,* 1.21.3

84 Harrison, J. (1922), 539, quoting Epiphanius

85 Angus, S. (1925), 116

86 Ibid., quoting Hippolytus, *Philosophoumena,* 5.8

87 Quoted in Robinson, op. cit., 151

88 In the Gnostic myth *Exegesis of the Soul,* Sophia (the soul) becomes lost looking for reflected light in the world created by the demiurge (the eidolon or lower self). In the world she looks for satisfaction in all the wrong places, polluting herself with many lovers who treat her like a whore. Ashamed of herself, the soul remains in slavery, living in a brothel. The only gift she receives from her lovers is their polluted seed, but her children (her thoughts) are dumb, blind, sick, and feeble-minded. The soul remains in this sexual and psychic captivity until the day she perceives her situation and repents. She asks help from the Father who sends as a bridegroom her brother (the Daemon or Higher Self). The fruit of their union are good and beautiful children (good and virtuous ideas). *See* Robinson, op. cit., 190.

89 Pagels, E. (1975), 68

90 Matthew 25 v 1-13

91 Quoted in Robinson, J. M. (1978), 134, Saying 75. The solitary (*monarchos*) is a term used to designate the Gnostic and is frequently used in *The Gospel of Thomas,* see Pagels, E. (1979), 130. From it derive the terms *monastic* and *monk.*

92 Quoted in Freke and Gandy (1998), 40

93 Segal decodes the Orphic myth: "The young god Dionysus was set upon a throne as soon as he had been born in a cave on the isle of Crete. But the Titans gave him a mirror to distract his attention, and while the child gazed in the mirror and was fascinated by his own image, the Titans tore the child into pieces and devoured him. Only the heart of the god was saved. This means that Dionysus, when he saw his eidolon, his reflection in the mirror, in a sense was duplicated and vanished into the mirror and so was dispersed in the universe. According to the Orphic sages, this means the world soul is divided and dispersed through matter. But the world spirit remains undivided and pure from every contact with matter." *See* Segal, R. A. (1992), 254. When Zeus discovered the crime he blasted the 12 Titans and from their ashes created mankind. This Orphic myth explains how the divine spark manifests first in 12 archetypal men, the signs of the zodiac, and later in the multitude of humanity who are born under the influence of one or other of these signs. At the Last Supper Jesus' body is symbolically consumed by 12 followers as a type of this sacrifice.

94 Plutarch, *Isis and Osiris*, 2

95 Wells, G. A. (1975), 191

96 Quoted in Mead, G. R. S. (1906), 505

97 Ibid., 426

98 Ibid., 539

99 Ibid., 462; *see also* Pagels, E. (1975), 28, where the Gnostic Theodotus explains Paul's meaning in Romans 4 v 15-21. Jesus is the "one" who willingly allowed himself to be "divided" in order to restore "the many" into unity.

100 Angus, S. (1925), 97

101 The Egyptian *Book of the Dead* guaranteed immortality for the deceased by assimilation with Osiris. The dead person became Osiris and received the new name Osiris, *see* Angus, op. cit., 138. Likewise in Greece the initiate became assimilated with Bacchus and became a Bacchoi. The Orphic gold plates that have been found buried with initiates in southern Italy contain teachings on the afterworld derived from the Egyptian *Book of the Dead*. So important was this assimilation in guaranteeing afterlife bliss that initiates preserved their ritual purity even in death. An inscription from a cemetery in Cumae insists that "No one may be buried here who has not been made Bacchus," *see* Guthrie, W. K. C. (1952), 202.

102 *The Gospel of Philip*, 67.26.7, quoted in Robinson, J. M. (1978), 150

103 Origen, *Contra Celsum*, 6.79, quoted in Fidler, D. (1993), 50

104 Quoted in Mead, G. R. S. (1906), 558

105 Ibid., 484

106 Ibid., 596, *see* 270. According to the Gnostic sage Basilides, the Savior is the perfected man within the animal man.

107 *The Gospel of Philip*, 61.30, quoted in Robinson, J. M. (1978), 147

108 Luke 6 v 40

109 Plato, *Cratylus* 400c, *Gorgias* 493a, and *Phaedo* 70c. Wili argues that the myth of the Titanic/Dionysian nature of man was the origin of the doctrine that the body was the tomb of the soul, *see* Campbell, J. (1955), 75. He notes that beginning with Philolaus and Plato all ancient thinkers regarded the *soma/sema* doctrine as Orphic. Clement, Claudianus Mamertus (fifth century CE), and Macrobius all quote Philolaus in support of the Orphic-Pythagorean origin of the *soma/sema* doctrine, *see* Guthrie, W. K. C. (1962), 311.

110 The Gnostic text *The Tripartite Tractate* explains that "Humankind came to be in three essential types," which it calls the spiritual, the psychic, and the material, *see* Robinson, J. M. (1978), 94. The Naassene Gnostics called these three classes the captive, the called, and the chosen, *see* Mead, G. R. S. (1906), 199, 496. Clement repeats in a slightly altered fashion this same system. He regards those Christians who have yet to reach Gnosis as being of three different types, defined by their relationship to God as the slave, the faithful slave, and the friend, *see* Clement of Alexandria, *Stromata*, 3. The Naassene Gnostics regard "the captives" as caught up in the illusion of the world. Clement calls Hylics God's "slaves" because they unwillingly obey the will of God. Such people are the "hard of heart" whom the Teacher trains through "corrective discipline." The Gnostics regarded "the called" as those who were called to follow the path and had begun to spiritually awaken. Clement calls Psychics the "faithful slaves" of God, because they willingly follow his will. Such Christians are "believers" in need of signs and miracles to strengthen their faith, whom the Teacher trains through "good hope." The Gnostics regarded "the chosen" as those on the higher mystical path that leads beyond belief to Gnosis. Clement calls them "the friends" because they are intimate with God. Such Christians are aspirant Gnostics whom the teacher trains through "Mysteries." Origen develops Clement's work and relates these three psychological

types to their ability to penetrate through to the correct interpretation of the gospels, *see* Fidler, D. (1993), 120, quoting Origen, *Philocalia* 1.8.

111 A Hylic person is unconscious of the Daemon. The Psychic initiate is aware of the Daemon as a Guardian Angel. The Pneumatic initiate is aware of the Daemon as his/her own Higher Self. The initiate who has achieved Gnosis is aware of himself/herself as an expression of the Universal Daemon.

112 Like Gnostic, Buddha also means "Knower," from the Sanskrit *budh*, "to know."

113 *The Gospel of Philip* gives an exegesis of the teachings alluded to by St. Paul in 1 Corinthians 13 v 13 on the spiritual qualities that can be developed in these four states of being symbolized by the four elements. "The husbandry of God is ... through four: faith, hope, love, and gnosis. Our earth is faith, in which we take root. The water is hope, through which we are nourished. The wind is love, through which we grow. But the light is Gnosis, through which we ripen to maturity." *See* Pagels, E. (1975), 80.

114 In the Pagan system the initiate was led through these states of awareness by three initiations. In the Pagan Mysteries they were called *catharmos*, "purification"; *paradosis*, the transmission of the esoteric doctrine; and *epopteia*, seeing through to the Truth. Kingsley, P. (1995), 367, calls this "the basic physiognomy of the mysteries and stages of initiation in the ancient Greek world." Servius confirms that in the initiations, "Every purification is effected either by water or by fire or by air," *see* Eisler, R. (1920), 208. The Gnostic system also taught that for the highest Mysteries a threefold baptism was required, of water, fire, and spirit, *see* Angus, S. (1925), 83. This doctrine is also found in the New Testament. Matthew 3 v 11–12 tells us that John the Baptist brought baptism with water, while Jesus brought the higher initiations of baptism by breath (air) and fire.

115 Mead, G. R. S. (1906), 522

116 John 1 v 8

117 Origen, *Philocalia*, 1.8, quoted in Fidler, D. (1993), 120

118 Doran, R. (1995), 76

119 Inge, W. R. (1899), 89

120 Pagels, E. (1975), 106

121 Quoted in Barnstone, W. (1984), 626ff

122 Quoted in Inge, W. R. (1899), 56. Dionysius the Areopagite likewise taught that the scriptures contain truths that can only be understood by those who have freed themselves from the stories in which they are embedded. In comparison with the encoded mystical truths, Dionysius (who is honored as a saint by the Roman Church) calls the stories "puerile myths!" He explains that the lower self perceives the Divine by means of symbols through which the initiate may "mount to the One undivided Truth by analogy." From this exalted level of awareness the Higher Self can perceive the Divine directly. *See* Inge, op. cit., 109.

123 Irenaeus, *Against Heresies*, 1.23.2–4

124 Acts 8 v 9–24. According to the apocryphal *Acts of Peter* there was a statue erected to Simon by the time that Peter came to Rome. Here the fearless apostle engaged in a battle of magical powers with the great heretic, including a flying competition over the forum! Simon loses, of course, and crashes to the ground, *see* Barnstone, W. (1984), 426ff.

125 Eisler, R. (1931), 576

126 Mead, G. R. S. (1906), 162ff. The Pseudo-Clementine literature suggests this.

127 Matthew 27 v 51–4. Gibbon notes that these events are said to have occurred during the lifetime of Seneca and the elder Pliny, men "who recorded all the phenomena of Nature, earthquakes, meteors, comets, and eclipses." And yet, Gibbon observes, "This miraculous event, which ought to have excited the wonder, the curiosity, and the devotion of mankind, passed without notice in an age of science and history." *See* Gibbon, E. (1796), 512.

CHAPTER 7: THE MISSING MAN

1 Quoted in Wilson, I. (1984), 37. Schweizer's words, written at the beginning of this century, might stand as an epitaph to the centuries of work done by the German theological colleges.

2 The Roman historian Dio Cassius, writing in 229 CE, is silent on Jesus and never mentions Christians.

3 Quoted in Pagels, E. (1979), 94: "I have never participated in investigations of Christians: hence I do not know what is the crime usually punished or investigated, or what allowances are made."

4 Suetonius, *Life of Nero*, xvi. 2. At the same time we hear that Nero "likewise expelled from the city all pantomime actors and their hangers-on."

5   Suetonius, *Life of Claudius*, xxv
6   Tacitus, *The Annals of Imperial Rome*, 365. It is regrettable that the years 29–32 CE are missing from Tacitus' *Annals*, but if these years had contained a reference to Jesus it is inconceivable that they would not have been preserved by an early Roman Christian such as Justin Martyr.
7   Wells, G. A. (1975), 14. An inscription found in 1961 reads "Tiberieum Pontius Pilatus Praefectus Iudaeae." *See* Scullard, H. H. (1959), 476.
8   Kingsland, W. (1937), 105
9   Grüber and Kersten (1985), 6
10 *Antiquities of the Jews*, 18.63–4. This passage, recorded only in the *Antiquities*, is known as the *Testimonium Flavianum*. Scholars are agreed that it has suffered at the hands of later Christian interpreters and that the original wording is now lost. *See* Wilson, I. (1984), 60.
11 Josephus, *The Jewish War*, 406. The spurious passages are confined to an appendix known as the "Slavonic additions."
12 Ibid., 407
13 Anyone still doubting this should read *The Messiah Jesus and John the Baptist* by Dr. Eisler: "As a matter of fact, not a single Greek, Latin, Slavonic or other Josephus text has come down to us which has not passed through the hands of Christian scribes and Christian owners," Eisler, R. (1931), 38. Regarding the interpolations, Eisler says: "The critics of the passage are philologists, its defenders theologians," ibid., 41.
14 Grüber and Kersten (1985), 6, and *see* Wells, G. A. (1975), 11. Josephus was full of contempt for the numerous "Messiahs" who were active in his time. *See* Josephus, *The Jewish War*, 135. He lumped "religious frauds and bandits" together and regarded them as the cause of Jerusalem's annihilation.
15 Josephus, *The Life and Contra Apion*, ix
16 Ibid., xi. Josephus' work was seen in Rome as a "manifesto, inspired by his imperial patrons, and intended as a warning to the East of the futility of further opposition." Josephus was patronized by Vespasian and Titus and then Epaphroditus, to whom the scholar dedicated all his later works. The editor of his *Life* notes that Josephus even managed to survive under the tyrant Domitian when writers like Tacitus, Pliny, and Juvenal all preferred to keep silent.
17 The prophecy was that a king would arise in the East and bring Rome to her knees. Similar oracles circulated that Cleopatra would preside over a reborn Eastern empire that would conquer Rome.
18 Brandon, S. G. F. (1969), 307. Dio Cassius states that Vespasian was proclaimed Emperor in Alexandria, but Eusebius repeats Josephus' claim that this happened in Judea.
19 Gibbon, E. (1796), 529, footnote 36. Gibbon regarded the "vulgar forgery" to have taken place "between the time of Origen and that of Eusebius."
20 Quoted in Wilson, I. (1984), 62
21 Ibid., 66: "In the first century AD it would have been an extremely common name." Of the Jesuses mentioned by Josephus, some are revolutionaries, like Jesus son of Saphias, who with 600 followers massacred all the Greek residents in Tiberias, *see* Josephus, *The Life and Contra Apion*, 29. The most colorful of them is surely the lunatic Jesus, son of Ananias. For seven years prior to the destruction of the Temple he wandered the streets crying, "Woe to Jerusalem!" until one day his cry changed to "Woe to me!" when suddenly a stone from the siege engines struck him dead, *see* Josephus, *The Jewish War*, 328.
22 *See* Josephus, *The Jewish War*, 403, where this particularly disingenuous trick is most apparent. The lunatic Jesus of Chapter 21 is inexplicably translated as Jeshua, while in the spurious Slavonic additions the editor uses the name Jesus. In defense of these interpolations he states that those scholars who regard these passages as spurious are simply "bent on destruction!" It is odd to hear the language of an Old Testament prophet from a classical scholar writing in 1959.
23 Wells, G. A. (1975), 12
24 As the German theologian Harnack expressed it in 1896, "All non-Christian testimonies about Jesus and the origin of Christianity might be written on a single quarto page." *See* Eisler, R. (1931), 3.
25 Matthew 1 v 1–18
26 Luke 3 v 23–38
27 Matthew 1 v 23
28 Wilson, I. (1984), 52, 55. Wilson writes about this contradiction: "To put it bluntly, Luke has resorted to invention."
29 Stanton, G. (1995), 8
30 Wells, G. A. (1975), 144

[31] Ibid., 174

[32] Paul often refers to "Christ nailed to the cross," but in Galatians 3 v 13 relates that Christ took on the Old Testament curse of everyone "who is hanged on a gibbet."

[33] Acts never mentions crucifixion, instead Peter twice uses this description, in Acts 10 v 39 and 5 v 30. This would appear to confirm the suspicion of scholars that Acts was written in Rome where it appears suddenly toward the end of the second century in the hands of Irenaeus. To any Roman crucifixion would have suggested that Jesus had died the fate of a criminal guilty of sedition. It is significant that nowhere in the catacombs of Rome is there an image of the crucified Jesus, a depiction surprisingly not found anywhere in Christian iconography before the fifth century CE. The clever image used in Acts, familiar to any Roman who had witnessed Attis brought into Rome bound to a tree, suggests the death of a god, not that of a common criminal. Jesus was presented to his new Roman audience as fulfilling in reality a destiny carried out only mythically by the godman Attis.

[34] Matthew 27 v 5. Further inconsistencies are discussed in Wilson, op. cit., 32.

[35] Acts 1 v 18

[36] Matthew 27 v 46

[37] Mark 15 v 34

[38] Luke 23 v 46

[39] John 19 v 28–30

[40] All these variants of Jesus' last words are discussed in Doran, R. (1995), 6.

[41] Mark 15 v 44

[42] According to John, Jesus was found to be already dead but was stabbed with a spear anyway. The legs of his fellow sufferers were broken but not his, see Wells, G. A. (1975), 51.

[43] Matthew 12 v 40

[44] Mark 6 v 5

[45] Luke 24 v 4

[46] Matthew 28 v 3–4

[47] Mark 16 v 9

[48] Matthew 28 v 9

[49] Luke 24, Acts 1 v 4

[50] Brandon, S. G. F. (1969), 228. Brandon collates a mass of contradictions regarding the resurrection appearances of Jesus.

[51] Mark 9 v 40

[52] Matthew 12 v 30

[53] Matthew 18 v 22

[54] Matthew 18 v 15–17

[55] Luke 21 v 12–36. In the same spirit, the Revelation of John begins: "A revelation of Jesus Anointed, which was given him by God in order to show his slaves that which must happen very soon." Schweitzer observed that few of Jesus' prophecies were actually fulfilled, see Wells, G. A. (1975), 73.

[56] Matthew 16 v 28

[57] Matthew 24 v 34

[58] Wells, op. cit., 74. In Mark 7 v 1–23 Jesus uses an argument based on the Greek version of the Jewish scripture, in Acts Peter does the same (Wells, 125) and in Acts 15 v 13 James does likewise (Wells, 141). Matthew 27 v 9 even mistakenly cites Jeremiah for Zechariah, see Stanton, G. (1995), 8.

[59] Lüdemann, G. (1995), 219: "The view of the Bible as the Word of God or Holy Scripture belongs to a past time. Today it hinders understanding. The Bible is the word of human beings." Lüdemann considers that this must become axiomatic if the current crisis in New Testament studies is to be healed. In this discipline there is now a "splitting apart of piety and scholarship which amounts to schizophrenia," Introduction, xiii.

[60] Wilson, I. (1984), 32

[61] Ibid. Most of these "refinements" were not introduced until the Middle Ages.

[62] At that time the first language of Galilee was Greek, as it had been for over three centuries. 2 Maccabees 15 v 29, itself written in Greek c. 150 BCE, considers it a significant moment when the Jewish revolutionaries of Palestine, after a minor victory, praised God "in their native language." Obviously it was a rare occurrence and worthy of mention. In Alexandria the Jews had entirely abandoned their own language and adopted Greek by the middle of the third century BCE. Rome, unlike Jerusalem, was never Hellenized by force but by gradual assimilation. Nevertheless the Roman aristocracy all spoke Greek in the middle to late republic.

[63] Stanton, op. cit., 35

64 Ibid.
65 Quoted ibid.
66 Ibid., 34
67 Ibid., 43. In between the original version and that with the "long ending" we have several early manuscripts that add the verse that the women relayed their story to Peter. This was done for obvious political reasons and at the expense of the previous verse, which clearly states that the women said "nothing to anyone."
68 Luther demanded that ordinary people be allowed to read the Bible for themselves, a challenge to the Vatican that helped spark the Reformation.
69 The Professor of New Testament Studies at the University of Göttingen tells us this is still the case at German theological colleges today, see Lüdemann, G. (1995), 4
70 Wilson, I. (1984), 33. These scholarly endeavors required great courage, for they were confronting a deeply entrenched belief in the accuracy, indeed the divinity, of the gospels. In the eighteenth century, Hermann Samuel Reimarus, Professor of Oriental Languages at Hamburg University, wrote a work disputing the reliability of the gospel narratives but instructed that it should be published only after his death. D. F. Strauss, 1808–74, a lecturer at Tübingen University, was dismissed from his post when he repudiated the miracle stories as spurious and supernatural. It is of note that the phrase "gospel truth" dates back only to the nineteenth century, when these doubts about the gospels became widely known, see Stanton, G. (1995), 7.
71 Wilson, op. cit., 37
72 Ibid., 35. Irenaeus maintains that the author is Jesus' favorite disciple John. It is unlikely though that this simple fisherman from Galilee was trained in either philosophy or Greek, unlike the writer of John's gospel. Campbell, J. (1955), 170, notes that scholars are agreed that the Gospel of John and the first epistle are probably by the same author, but that this is not the disciple John. The second epistle is by another author and the third by still another. The Book of Revelation, also said to be by John, is a Christian recension of a late Jewish apocalypse written under a pseudonym.
73 Wilson, op. cit., 36. "The most universally accepted theological discovery of the age," according to Wilson.
74 Wells, G. A. (1975), 78ff. It is impossible to be more precise than this. For sightings of the first gospels we are dependent on the testimony of the early Apostolic fathers, men like Polycarp, Papias, and Ignatius. As well as being used disingenuously by second-century writers such as Irenaeus and Tertullian, their letters were also interpolated and added to in the fourth and fifth centuries. Picking through this mess leaves us with the generally held view that sometime between 70 and 135 might be correct.
75 Stanton, G. (1995), 102. In the second century doubts were expressed about Mark, Luke, and John—Mark because he was simply a secretary of Peter, Luke because he was said to have been an assistant of Paul (who had himself not seen Jesus), and John because that gospel was widely known to be the work of the Gnostic Cerinthus. Only Matthew was above suspicion. Our Matthew, however, is not the one that was known to Papias of Hierapolis, who is said to have been active post 70 CE in Asia Minor. He collected information about the Messiah from refugees pouring out of Judea, but refers to his Matthew as a book of "oracles." This suggests a book of proof texts based on the Old Testament, used as prophecies or "oracles" to support the Jesus story. Papias was also defensive of criticism against Mark because he was not an eyewitness of the events he recounts.
76 Wilson, op. cit., 36
77 Ibid.
78 Ibid., 33
79 See ibid., 191, note to 88. An example of this is the miraculous feeding, which appears twice in Mark, once to 4,000 and once to 5,000. As pointed out by Dr. Taylor, it seems unlikely that these were two separate incidents, particularly since in the second the disciples ask, "Where could anyone get bread to feed these people in a deserted place like this?", thus being apparently ignorant of the first occasion, which they are reported to have witnessed.
80 Mack, B. L. (1993), 24
81 Wilson, I. (1984), 37, and see Wells, G. A. (1975), 72
82 Wilson, op. cit., 39
83 Quoted ibid.
84 Chapter 21 of John does mention "the sons of Zebedee," but does not name them as James and John, as the other gospels do. Moreover it is now widely agreed that this chapter was a later addition and that the original gospel ended at Chapter 20.

[85] Wells, op. cit., 125

[86] Ibid., 122

[87] Ibid., 125

[88] Ibid., 141. The 12 are mentioned in the opening chapters. In Chapter 9 we hear they are the leaders of the Jerusalem Church. By Chapter 15 they are sharing this leadership with the "elders," and from Chapter 16 onward we hear no more of them and the Jerusalem Church is run by "James and the elders."

[89] The inconsistencies of the accounts of the apostles are clearly laid out in Wells, op. cit., Chapter 5: "The Twelve."

[90] Gaus, A. (1991), 217

[91] Ibid., 235

[92] Ibid., 243

[93] Acts 21

[94] Acts 10 v 9–16

[95] Acts 16 v 4, 6, 10, and 11. The narration of Chapters 27 and 28 also lurches violently from third to first person.

[96] Acts 9 v 7

[97] Acts 21 v 7

[98] Acts 9 v 10

[99] Acts 9 v 27

[100] Acts 22 v 17–21

[101] Galatians 1 v 15–17

[102] Acts 15 v 13–41

[103] Wells, G. A. (1975), 125

[104] Mead, G. R. S. (1906), 164. Justin also makes little use of the Gospel of John, probably because at this time it was highly regarded by the Gnostics, see Stanton, G. (1995), 103.

[105] Lüdemann, G. (1995), 196

[106] See Barnstone, W. (1984), xi, *The Apocryphal Acts of the Apostles, The Acts of John, The Acts of Peter, The Acts of Paul, The Acts of Andrew, The Acts of Thomas,* and see Robinson, J. M. (1978), 287, *The Acts of Peter and the Twelve Apostles*

[107] Barnstone, op. cit., 411

[108] Gaus, A. (1991), 224–5

[109] Wilson, I. (1984), 154. The First and Second Letters of Peter were forged in Peter's name in the third century to give an appearance of amity between Peter and Paul, even though they were at odds during their lifetimes. "Peter" writes unctuously and unconvincingly of "our brother Paul ... so dear to us" (2 Peter 3 v 15). Eusebius regarded the epistles of James, Jude, 2 Peter and 2 and 3 John as disputed books, see Metzger, B. M. (1987), 202, and Didymus in 398 CE declared 2 Peter a forgery.

[110] Wells, op. cit., 40

[111] Lüdemann, op. cit., 135: "In terms of the history of the canon, they are attested only relatively late, but always as a unity. Irenaeus (190 CE) is the first to know and use them. Indeed the very title of his work against heretics, *Unmasking and Refutation of the Gnosis, Falsely So-Called,* leans explicitly on 1 Timothy 6 v 20." Acts and the Pastorals were rejected by the Gnostic Marcion, see Lüdemann, 196. These texts are now believed to have been unknown before the end of the second century.

[112] Lüdemann writes of the current state of research (1995): "The consensus among scholars today is that the historical Paul cannot be the author of the Pastorals, either directly or indirectly," 288.

[113] Galatians 1 v 12

[114] 1 Corinthians 2 v 8

[115] Paul only says that Jesus was killed by the Judeans (1 Thessalonians 2). This is apart from a mention of Pilate in his letter to Timothy, which is one of the discredited Pastoral letters, see Wells, G. A. (1975), 18.

[116] Wells, op. cit., 157

[117] Ibid., 152

[118] Ibid., 20. The "scantiness of Paul's Jesus tradition" is regarded by several New Testament professors as "surprising," "shocking," and a "matter of serious concern." Stanton, G. (1995), 131, remarks: "Paul's failure to refer more frequently and at greater length to the actions and teaching of Jesus is baffling." As Wells observes, Paul's complete silence on the historical Jesus "remains a problem only for those who insist that there was a historical Jesus to be silent about," Wells, 21.

[119] Romans 8 v 26

[120] 1 Corinthians 11 v 24–5. Paul refers to (but does not quote) several sayings of Jesus in 1 Corinthians. But, as Stanton notes, he quite freely modifies these teachings. This scholar also observes that: "Paul fails to refer to a saying of Jesus at the very point where he might well have clinched his argument by doing so." *See* Stanton, G. (1995), 130.

[121] Matthew 19 v 12

[122] Wells, G. A. (1975), 25

[123] Mark 12 v 25

[124] Matthew 28 v 10

[125] John 20 v 17

[126] Quoted in Robinson, J. M. (1978), 260

[127] Metzger, B. M. (1987), 181, refers to "the curious differentiation of Cephas and Peter," in this text.

[128] Galatians 2 v 11

[129] Ibid.

[130] Mark 2 v 15–17

[131] Galatians 2 v 13

[132] Wells, G. A. (1975), 125

[133] Mark 8 v 33

[134] 1 Corinthians 15 v 5

[135] Galatians 3 v 1–3

[136] Wells, G. A. (1975), 206, writes in exasperation: "The realization that Paul came first has hardly yet sunk in."

[137] 2 John v 7

[138] Campbell, J. (1955), 342. In Germany the similarities between the Mysteries and Christianity have been known for a long time. For several centuries scholars at German theological colleges have received a classical education and so in tandem with their discoveries about the origins of Christianity they also gained a better understanding of the Greco-Roman world into which it had been born. Odo Casel and the monks of Maria Laach advanced this particular theory to account for the evidence they uncovered.

CHAPTER 8: WAS PAUL A GNOSTIC?

[1] Pagels, E. (1975), 9–10

[2] Ibid., 2

[3] Pagels, E. (1979), 62. Clement, *Stromata* 7.17, records the Gnostic claim that Theudas had received secret teachings from Paul—the "Deeper Mysteries" that Paul reserved from his public teaching and taught only to a few disciples in secret, *see* Pagels, E. (1988), 61.

[4] Kingsland, W. (1937), 35

[5] Metzger, B. M. (1987), 90ff. Modern research has been carried out on the earliest collections of Paul's letters, which all contain prologues. Seven of these are so similar as to suggest a common origin, and as they hold Paul to be the "true apostle" and are strongly anti-Jewish, they are now considered to be the work of Marcionites. These seven prologues are attached to the same Pauline letters that are also now accepted as genuine and the churches to which these are addressed are known to have been Marcionite strongholds in the middle of the second century. All of this suggests that Marcion, as he claimed, was indeed the true heir of Paul. By the time Paul's letters had swelled to 13, other prologues needed writing. These "clumsy works" have been dated to the fourth and fifth centuries.

[6] Hollroyd, S. (1994), 39

[7] Robinson, J. M. (1978), 256. *The Apocalypse of Paul* gives the apostle's visions in 10 heavens—a lower seven and a supernal three—not just the third that he describes in Corinthians. Another text, *The Hypostasis of the Archons*, calls Paul "the Great Apostle" and explains his teaching in Colossians 1 v 13 on the "authorities of darkness," *see* Robinson, 163. These, the text explains, are the planets and stars that control fate and destiny—just as they are for Paul.

[8] Barnstone, W. (1984), 652. The Literalist fourth-century heresy-hunter Epiphanius complains: "They fabricate another little book in the name of Paul the Apostle, full of things unspeakable, which the so-called Gnostics use, which they call the *Ascent of Paul*; the pretext (for so calling it) they find in the fact that the Apostle says he ascended into the third heaven and heard ineffable words, which it is not permissible for a man to speak. And these, they say, are the ineffable words."

9   Ibid., 445
10 Lüdemann, G. (1995), 198–9, calls these fakes "foolhardy," as they only succeeded in putting "a spotlight on the struggles" between the Gnostics and the orthodox Church to claim the powerful figure of Paul. The author of 2 Thessalonians, in a pathetic attempt to suggest authenticity, writes, "Greetings to you in my own handwriting, which is a mark of all my letters: this is what my writing looks like." This is one of the numerous addenda to Paul's letters made by scribes, usually to issue threats against dissenters. *See* 1 Corinthians 16 v 21–4, where the writer reassures the reader "This greeting is in my own hand—Paul." The most ridiculous of these is in Galatians 6 v 11–18, where a scribe launches out into a polemic against the Jews but introduces it with Paul's supposed words: "Look how big the letters are, now that I am writing to you in my own hand."

11 Lüdemann, op. cit., 61. Regarding the Pauline letters, Lüdemann writes, "Scholars generally agree that of the thirteen extant letters, seven are authentic (Romans, 1 and 2 Corinthians, Galatians, Philippians, 1 Thessalonians, and Philemon), whereas the rest have been composed by later disciples in the apostle's name." *See* Wells, G. A. (1975), 17, which refers to Schmithal's evidence that all the principal Pauline letters, apart from Galatians, are likewise composite. In the early Church, opponents of Paul were not averse to tampering with his letters. Both Irenaeus and Tertullian, for example, quote from Galatians but omit the word *not* in a key passage, thus turning Paul's meaning from the negative into the positive, *see* Pagels, E. (1975), 104.

12 Wilson, I. (1984), 154. Computer tests have confirmed the suspicions long held by theological scholars that whoever wrote Paul's letters to Timothy and Titus, it wasn't Paul, *see* Lüdemann, op. cit., 288.

13 Pagels, E. (1975), 5. Valentinian Gnostics cite only Romans, 1 and 2 Corinthians, Galatians, Ephesians, Philippians, Colossians, 1 Thessalonians, and Hebrews. This list corresponds exactly to the earliest known Pauline collection attested from Alexandria.

14 Lüdemann, op. cit., 135

15 Metzger, B. M. (1987), 202, says of Eusebius' attempt to delineate an accepted canon: "The most that Eusebius can register is uncertainty so great that he seems to get confused when making a statement about it." Nonetheless he admits that the authenticity of the epistles of James and Jude is doubted, *see* Eusebius, (1965), 61, *also* 2 Peter and 2 and 3 John. Revelation he regards as spurious. After picking our way through his well-guarded statements we end up with a canon of the four gospels, Paul's epistles minus the Pastorals, and 1 Peter and 1 John.

16 Pagels notes that Irenaeus strikingly opens his treatise *Against Heresies*, claiming "the apostle's authority to oppose the Gnostics—by citing both Timothy and Titus," *see* Pagels, op. cit., 5. He also records Tertullian's defensiveness on the issue and regards it as instructive. He notes that the heretics have dared to impugn the validity of the Pastorals, but insists that the "same Paul" who wrote Galatians also wrote Titus.

17 Pagels, op. cit., 163. The Pastorals received their name because of their major concern with how the Church is to be organized. As Pagels notes, the authentic letters like "Ephesians, Colossians, and Hebrews, on the other hand virtually ignore Paul's role as an organizer of ecclesiastical congregations."

18 1 Timothy 4 v 7
19 1 Timothy 1 v 3–4
20 1 Timothy 6 v 20
21 1 Timothy 5 v 20
22 2 Timothy 2 v 17–18. The text calls this particular doctrine "gangrene."
23 Barnstone, W. (1984), 445. The tradition of Paul's companion Thecla who baptized and preached was part of a well-established oral tradition in Syria.
24 1 Timothy 2 v 8–15
25 Pagels, E. (1975), 8–10
26 Lüdemann notes other examples of second-century hostility to Paul in addition to Clement's vigorous polemic. Acts contains veiled criticism of Paul. By the criteria of Acts 1 v 21ff Paul does not qualify as an apostle as he was not with Jesus during his lifetime and had not seen the risen Jesus, *see* Lüdemann, G. (1995), 54, 57, 199. Pagels suggests that ecclesiastical Christians might have preferred to exclude Paul's letters "but it was too late, he was already a chief apostle and stood in high regard," *see* Pagels, op. cit., 161. Toward the end of the second century the Literalists therefore took another tack. The Pastoral letters, 2 Thessalonians, 3 Corinthians, and other documents were forged to refute specific Gnostic/Pauline doctrines in the apostle's own name, *see* Lüdemann, op. cit., 201.
27 *Homily,* 17.15.2, quoted in Lüdemann, op. cit., 57. As noted above, a similar argument had already been used in Acts.

28 Ibid,. 19.1–7, quoted in Lüdemann, 58

29 Ibid., 2.17.4, quoted in Lüdemann, 59

30 Pagels, op. cit., 9–10, and see p.161: "Ecclesiastical sources that do refer to Paul often express hostility; the Pseudo-Clementines suggest that he, like Simon Magus, is a satanically inspired divider of the Roman community that is properly headed by Peter."

31 Doran, R. (1995), 5, which describes Paul as a "flash point" in the growing Christian tradition. Brandon, S. G. F. (1969), 310ff, calls him the "problem figure of primitive Christianity;" Lüdemann, op. cit., 61ff, calls him the "only heretic of the earliest period."

32 Lüdemann, op. cit., 65. Paul's mother tongue was Greek, and he uses only the Septuagint version of the Old Testament. *See* Brandon, S. G. F. (1969), 313, which notes that in Galatians 1 Paul states that his teaching was specially designed to be intelligible to those who were not Jews. Lüdemann observes that whereas the gospels are "third person accounts," "often contradictory," and "do not come from eyewitnesses," in Paul "we hear his own voice in his mother tongue, free from all background noise, accessible to all who do not shrink from the trouble of reading him." *See* Lüdemann, op. cit., 61.

33 Wells, G. A. (1975), 183

34 Ulansey, D. (1989), 68ff. Strabo writes: "The people of Tarsus have devoted themselves so eagerly, not only to philosophy, but also to the whole round of education in general, that they have surpassed Athens, Alexandria, or any other place that can be named where have been schools and lectures of philosophers." Athenodorus of Tarsus even became a tutor to Emperor Augustus. Athenodorus was in turn a disciple of Posidonius, arguably the greatest philosopher of the first century BCE. Pompey twice turned aside from campaigns in Asia Minor to visit Posidonius and Cicero describes him as a friend. He is one of the first astronomers to make an orrery, which Cicero says "shows in its revolutions the movements of the sun and stars and planets, by day and night, just as they appear in the sky," *see* Cicero, *The Nature of the Gods*, 159. In his travels to Britain he made the discovery that the moon governs the tides. This he must have considered certain proof of astrology's first axiom, that the heavenly bodies have a direct effect on the physical world. All of the astronomical and astrological knowledge acquired by the Tarsian intellectuals, particularly the discovery of the precession of the equinoxes by Hipparchus, who worked at nearby Rhodes, made a major contribution to the doctrines of Mithraism. It was into this city that Paul was born, at a time when Tarsus was at the height of its power and influence.

35 Ulansey, op. cit., 68. Tarsus was the capital of Cilicia, where, according to Plutarch, the Mithraic Mysteries were being practiced as early as 67 BCE. Ulansey considers it significant that the appearance of Mithraism coincides almost exactly with the lifetime of Posidonius and is in the same part of the Mediterranean. Hipparchus' discovery of the precession of the equinoxes had revealed that in the cycle known as the "Great Year" the sun was passing from Aries into Pisces at the spring equinox. Mithraic iconography portrays Mithras as the god who turns the wheel of the Great Year and thereby ushers in the New Age. Paul shows himself aware of "the passing age" in 2 Corinthians 4 v 4.

36 Happold, F. C. (1963), 186; *see also St Paul and the Mystery Religions* by H. Kennedy. All Paul's terms for *mature* or *perfect* Christians are variations on the Greek *telete*—"initiation." "Mature" is *teleion*, "to the level of maturity" is *ten teleioteta*, "the perfect man" is *andra teleion*, "the imperfect man" is *ateles. See also* Pagels, E. (1975), 148, 149, 123.

37 1 Corinthians 12 v 28–31

38 Burkert, W. (1992), 93, writes: "One of the main characteristics of the mysteries is the *makarismos*, the praise of the 'blessed' status of those who have 'seen' the mysteries." Charismatic Christians might be interested to know the ancient root of their name.

39 1 Corinthians 4 v 1

40 Wells, G. A. (1975), 23. The Alexandrian cult of Serapis and his consort Isis was widespread in the Greco-Roman world at this time. That Paul might have been a "Steward of the Mysteries" of Serapis is entirely possible. Emperor Hadrian writes of the citizens of Alexandria, "Here you see Christians worshiping Serapis, and worshipers of Serapis who call themselves bishops of Christ," *see* D'Alviella, G. (1981), 103. Perhaps this throws light on a passage in the New Testament, which has left scholars confused. At Cenchreae, near Corinth, waiting to board a ship bound for Ephesus, Paul "cut his hair for he had made a vow." This is a curious report and not in accordance with Jewish Law, which states that hair is only to be shorn at Jerusalem. Near Cenchreae, however, was a temple of Isis where Greek sailors cut their hair and dedicated it to the goddess as "Stella Maris" in hope of a safe crossing.

41 Acts 17 v 28

42 In 1 Corinthians 15 v 37 Paul uses the most ubiquitous of images from the Mysteries, the reaping and sowing of the crops as a symbol of mystical death and resurrection of an initiate. He speaks of the sprouting of a grain of wheat as an image of the resurrection and writes: "The seed you sow does not come to life unless it has first died."

43 Plato, *Apology*, 23b: "He is the wisest who, like Socrates, knows that his wisdom is worth nothing."

44 1 Corinthians 8 v 2

45 Plato, *Phaedrus*, 250b: "For there is no light of the higher ideas which are precious to souls in the earthly copies of them, they are seen through a glass dimly."

46 1 Corinthians 13 v 12

47 The Phillips translation, quoted in Happold, F. C. (1963), 194

48 Plato, *The Republic*, Book 7

49 Euripides, *The Bacchae*, 207, line 501

50 Quoted in Angus, S. (1925), 61

51 Justin Martyr, *Dialogue with Trypho*, 2.3, quoted in Dodds, E. R. (1951), 249

52 Plato, *Phaedo*, 111c. The Gnostic Valentinus also wrote of the Logos "who spoke of realities face to face," *see* Mead, G. R. S. (1906), 299.

53 1 Timothy 6 v 13

54 Romans 8 v 3: "God sent his own Son in the likeness of sinful flesh" and Philippians 2 v 7: "bearing the human likeness."

55 It was obvious to Celsus that Christianity and Mithraism were teaching the same doctrine, *see* Hoffmann, R. J. (1987), 95. As Ulansey notes, Christianity and Mithraism were "sister religions, arising at the same time and in the same geographical area," *see* Ulansey (1989), 4. Brandon writes: "Paul's many references to the archontes, the stoicheia, and the pleroma all indicate his easy familiarity with esoteric concepts of a Gnostic hierarchy of supernatural powers," *see* Brandon, S. G. F. (1969), 44.

56 Romans 14 v 1–5: "One man observes certain days, another considers every day the same ... I know that nothing is unclean in itself, but if anyone considers it unclean for him it is unclean." Philippians 3 v 3: "... we whose worship is spiritual, whose pride is in Christ Jesus, and who put no confidence in anything external." Colossians 2 v 20–2: "Why let people dictate to you 'Do not handle this, do not taste that, do not touch the other'— referring to things that must all perish as they are used? That is to follow human rules and regulations." As noted, the Gnostics preached the same freedom from human legislation— especially religious laws. Simon of Samaria quoted Paul in defense of his own freedom, saying, "Men are saved by grace, and not on account of their own righteous works." The followers of Carpocrates declared themselves saved "by faith and love" and considered all things "not good or evil in themselves, but only by convention," *see* Pagels, E. (1975), 44–5.

57 2 Corinthians 3 v 12–18. Paul's imagery here is uncannily similar to the initiation rites in the Greek Mysteries. Novices wore veils, hence their appellation as "brides." At this stage they were known as *mystae*—those with "closed eyes." Only at the highest stage of initiation was the veil removed and the *mystae* became *epoptae*—those who had "seen." This is the stage that Paul insists that the Corinthians should have reached.

58 Romans 1 v 9–14, quoted in Pagels, op. cit., 15

59 Romans 1 v 13

60 Pagels, op. cit., 15

61 1 Corinthians 2 v 9

62 Quoted in Pagels, op. cit., 58. Hippolytus records this as the oath of secrecy in Justinus' Gnostic group. It also occurs in *The Gospel of Thomas*, Saying 17, and in the first epistle of Clement, *see* Louth, A. (1968), 37.

63 1 Corinthians 2 v 6–9

64 1 Corinthians 2 v 6–8

65 Brandon, S. G. F. (1969), 327

66 Inge, W. R. (1899), 81. Inge notes Paul's use of other Gnostic terms like *pleroma*.

67 Philippians 1 v 9. In 1 Corinthians Paul seems to diminish the importance of Gnosis, claiming, "Gnosis puffs up." But Clement explains that this is not to be understood as "swollen up," but means in fact "to entertain great and true sentiments," *see* Stromata, 68. To the Gnostics, including Clement, the Gnosis was the Pneumatic initiation of the holy breath or spirit.

68 Colossians 2 v 3

69 Ephesians 3 v 3

70 2 Corinthians 12 v 4

71 2 Corinthians 3 v 6

72 Galatians 4 v 24
73 1 Corinthians 10 v 6
74 *See* Lüdemann, G. (1995), 26. The Literalists Irenaeus and Tertullian both preached the resurrection of the flesh. They did this by a devious exegesis of 1 Corinthians 15, which nonetheless failed to overcome the problem of Paul's categorical denial of this doctrine in 1 Corinthians 15 v 50.
75 1 Corinthians 15 v 50. Irenaeus was evidently frustrated about this verse and complained, "All heretics always introduce this passage," *see* Pagels, E. (1975), 85. To counter the Gnostic disciples of Paul, someone in the second century wrote 3 Corinthians to cast doubt on 1 Corinthians, *see* Cross, F. L. (1958), 1031. This states: "As for those who tell you that there is no resurrection of the flesh, for them there will be no resurrection." 3 Corinthians v 24, *see* Lüdemann, op. cit., 224. The triumph of the Literalists in the fourth century rendered 3 Corinthians unnecessary and the forged text was excluded from the canon.
76 Quoted in Pagels, op. cit., 5, 14
77 2 Corinthians 6 v 2
78 Ephesians 2 v 4–7
79 Romans 6 v 4 and 8 v 11, quoted in Inge, W. R. (1899), 64. Inge notes: "Paul's mystical language about death and resurrection has given rise to much controversy."
80 Philippians 3 v 10–11
81 Galatians 2 v 20
82 Romans 6 v 3–7. *See* Campbell, J. (1955), 238: "It lies in the nature of the mystery cult that the *mystae* undergo the same experience as their god, that, as St. Paul says, they die with him, are buried with him, are reborn with him, and are resurrected with him."
83 Colossians 1 v 25–8
84 Galatians 1 v 15
85 1 Corinthians 12 v 12; *see also* Romans 12 v 4
86 Ephesians 4 v 25
87 Quoted in Inge, W. R. (1899), 69. Inge notes that the heretics claimed this as a "distinct admission that the worship of 'the man Christ Jesus' is a stage to be passed through and then left behind."
88 Quoted in Pagels, E. (1975), 7
89 Ibid., 5
90 1 Corinthians 2 v 2
91 Romans 1 v 3 and 1 Corinthians 2 v 2, quoted in Pagels, op. cit., 5
92 1 Corinthians 2 v 14–15
93 Pagels, op. cit., 7
94 Paul calls himself "apostle to the Gentiles" in Romans 1 v 5 because he is a Pneumatic teacher of the Inner Mysteries. Yet he comes to teach Christians of all levels, both "the wise [Pneumatics] and to the foolish [Psychics]," *see* Romans 1 v 14.
95 Pagels, op. cit., 7
96 Quoted ibid., 59. Likewise in his Letter to the Hebrews 5 v 11–14, Paul is impatient that his followers are still not ready to move on from elementary teachings. He writes, "Concerning this we have much teaching which is hard to interpret, since you have become deaf in your hearing. For indeed, you should be teachers by now, but again you need someone to teach you the elementary things of the beginning of the words of God: you need milk, not meat. Everyone who takes milk is inexperienced in the word of righteousness; he is still immature. Meat is for the mature who have disciplined their receptive powers to discriminate good from evil." *See* Pagels, op. cit., 148–9.
97 Quoted in Pagels, op. cit., 148–9, slightly adapted
98 In Galatians 3 v 2–3 Paul asks: "Was it through performing the Law that the spirit came to you or through hearing and believing? Can you be so senseless as to finish on the physical level what you started on the spiritual level?"
99 In Philippians 3 v 5–6 Paul gives a full account of his justification according to Jewish Law— circumcised on the eighth day, Israelite by race, of the tribe of Benjamin, and a zealous Pharisee—"by the law's standard righteous without fault." Startlingly, he says in verse 8 that he counts all this as "so much rubbish."
100 Hebrews 8 v 13
101 2 Corinthians 3 v 14
102 Romans 14 v 1–15
103 1 Corinthians 6 v 12
104 Galatians 3 v 6–11

[105] Galatians 3 v 13–14
[106] Romans 7 v 6
[107] Galatians 3 v 19–20; *see also* Pagels, E. (1975), 107–8
[108] 2 Corinthians 4 v 4
[109] 2 Corinthians 11 v 4
[110] Philippians 3 v 2
[111] Galatians 5 v 2
[112] Galatians 5 v 12
[113] Philippians 3 v 3
[114] Quoted in Robinson, J. M. (1978), 132, Saying 53
[115] Brandon, S. G. F. (1969), 268
[116] Lüdemann, G. (1995), 31. Apparently this group of apostates was all that was left of the Jerusalem Church that God had so carefully preserved from destruction in 70 CE. Irenaeus leaves us in no doubt that the Ebionites were Gnostics, *see* Lüdemann, 247, note 111. Epiphanius tells us that the Ebionites were vegetarians, *see* Barnstone, W. (1984), 203, a practice almost universally associated with Pythagoreanism in the ancient world.
[117] Barnstone, op. cit., 333
[118] Mead, G. R. S. (1906), 129
[119] It should be remembered that these Nazarenes knew nothing of the Nazareth legend, which was subsequently developed by the "in order that it might be fulfilled" school of historicizers, *see* ibid., 128–9.
[120] Ibid., 126. The Nazarenes were still found scattered throughout Syria and the Decapolis in the late fourth century.

CHAPTER 9: THE JEWISH MYSTERIES

[1] Tacitus, *The Histories*, Book 5.5, 274. Tacitus refers to Dionysus by his Roman name of Liber.
[2] In *Jews, Greeks and Barbarians*, Martin Hengel, Professor of Early Judaism at Tübingen University, presents an astonishing picture of the full extent of Hellenization in Judea in the first two centuries BCE.
[3] Stanton, G. (1995), 113. Stanton quotes the New Testament scholar J. Murphy O'Connor, who writes about the newly excavated theater found in Sepphoris, "The most natural explanation of Jesus' use of *hypokrites* ('stage actor') in criticism of the religious leaders of his day (Mark 7 v 6) is that he went to this theater, the nearest one to Nazareth. The word, which has no Semitic equivalent, would not have been part of the vocabulary of a village artisan." *The Jesus Mysteries* suggests that "the most natural explanation" of this is that the words were put into Jesus' mouth by a thoroughly Hellenized Jew. Inventing new biographical details for Jesus, including trips to his local theater, is not good history.
[4] Hengel, M. (1980), 117. Gadara in the two centuries BCE was "a seedbed of Greek culture." The historian Strabo mentions four famous writers and philosophers who came from this city, including the poet Meleager and his master Menippus the satirist. Strabo also mentions Philodemus of Gadara, whose papyrus library has been discovered in Herculaneum in Italy, *see* Hengel, 118. Gadara was razed to the ground by the Jerusalem King Alexander Jannaeus as part of the forced Judaization of surrounding territory. Most of the Hellenized Jewish poets and philosophers emigrated to the West, especially to Italy. This is perhaps how Diodorus of Sicily came to know the Jewish mystery name of Iao, which he publishes in his *History* in 50 BCE, and how Virgil came to incorporate Jewish imagery from the Book of Isaiah into his "Messianic" poem written in 40 BCE.
[5] Macchioro, V. D. (1930), 188ff: "Judea was surrounded by Dionysiac religion. Phoenician coins of Sidon, Berytus, and Orthosia show a divine figure like the Phoenician god Esmum represented as Dionysus. The Nabataeans, whose dominion stretched from Arabia to Damascus, worshiped a god named Dusares who seems to have been the Orphic Dionysus. In the age of Jesus, Asia Minor was filled with Orphic brotherhoods named *speirai*. Tarsus was very well acquainted with Orphic myths and creeds, and worshiped Sandan, a dying and resurrected god who bore some resemblance to the Orphic Dionysus. On the whole, Judea was surrounded, in the last century before Christ, by a Dionysiac and Orphic girdle." Excavations of early Palestinian graves have produced numerous talismans bearing Jewish names along with figures of the gods of Egypt, Syria, and Babylon, *see* Campbell, J. (1964), 274.

[6] Hengel, op. cit., 26

[7] Ibid., 118. Larissa and Ascalon were less than 40 miles from Jerusalem. Philo of Larissa fled to Rome in 88 BCE and taught philosophy to the Roman statesmen Lucullus and Cicero, *see* Lemprière, J. (1949), 53. His pupil Antiochus of Ascalon became a friend and advisor to the Roman politician Brutus. As early as the second century BCE nearby Phoenicia had famous schools of philosophy and produced Boethus, Zeno, and the Cynic philosopher/poet Meleager. In all these cities the acquisition of civil rights was dependent on an education in the city *gymnasia*. Here the youth of ambitious local aristocracy were taught by professional philosophers, rhetoricians, and grammarians. The head of the *gymnasium*, the *gymnasiarch*, was in effect the mayor of the city.

[8] Momigliano, A. (1971), 106

[9] *2 Maccabees* 4 v 7ff

[10] The Jewish state ceased to exist until 1948.

[11] In 588 BCE, when Babylon crushed Judea, many Jews fled to Egypt, where a temple to Jehovah and an unknown god and goddess was still operating in Elephantine in 450 BCE. In 538 BCE Cyrus the Persian allowed the Israelites enslaved by the Babylonians to return to their homeland. Most, however, stayed in Babylonia, where a thriving community was still present centuries later. A tombstone from Athens records the burial of a Jewess, possibly a freed slave, in 400 BCE, the earliest reference to a Jew in Europe, *see* Hengel, op. cit., 88. During the campaign of Alexander 30,000 Jews were sold as slaves, *see* ibid., 5. In the destruction of Jerusalem in 70 CE, 100,000 Jews were enslaved. By the end of the first century Jewish slaves and mercenaries formed the basis of the Jewish Diaspora in wide areas of the Mediterranean world.

[12] Dunlap, S. F. (1866), 158; Josephus, *Antiquities of the Jews*, 1.4; Philo, *On Abraham*, 18

[13] Hengel, op. cit., 167, note 52. Hermippus, an Alexandrian Jew and pupil of the great Alexandrian poet Callimachus, claimed in 220 BCE to possess astrological books of the "most remarkable Abraham." Later Jewish scholars like Aristobulus, Philo, and Josephus repeat the claim that Abraham the Chaldaean was the inventor of astrology.

[14] By the New Kingdom period, *c.*1550 BCE, the Babylonian Tammuz had syncretized in Phoenicia with the Osiris cult to produce Adonis. In the Old Testament it is repeatedly related how the Phoenicians (the Canaanites) seduced the Jews away from their proper worship of Jehovah.

[15] Ezekiel 8.14: "Next he brought me to the entrance of the north-gate of the House of the Lord; and there sat the women bewailing Tammuz." One emendation of this text reveals that at the north gate there was in fact an altar to Tammuz, *see* Jaroslav, P., *The Tanakh*, 902. The Old Testament is full of references to Israel defecting to the Pagan cults of her neighbors: Num. 25.3.5 (in which the Lord tells Moses to have the ringleaders of the cult publicly crucified); Deut. 23.18; I Kings 15.12; Psalms 28, 105, 106; Jer. 16.5; Hos. 4.14; Amos 7.9; Wisdom 12.3, 14.5. Portrayed as an offense to Jehovah, these defections were more likely an offense to the Jerusalem authorities—the destruction of the cults of the "High Places" was part of the attempt to install a centralized cult in Jerusalem, for obvious political and taxation reasons.

[16] Frazer, J. (1922), 346

[17] Martin, L. H. (1987), 110: "The striking appearance of Dionysian-Orphic symbols in the third century CE wall paintings of the Dura-Europas synagogue in eastern Syria confirms that Philo's references to Bacchic symbols and images in a Jewish context (the Therapeutae) were not anomalies of some Egyptian-Jewish fringe group. Indeed, the Jewish god was identified by some with Sabazius, an ancient Thraco-Phrygian deity who most often was identified with Dionysus."

[18] Wells, G. A. (1975), 194. In Asia Minor the cult of Sabazius merged with the Syrian Jewish cult of Jehovah Sabaoth, the Lord of Hosts, *see* Campbell, J. (1964), 273.

[19] Turcan, R. (1992), 316. Valerius Maximus, *Memorable Words and Deeds*, 1.3.3, tells us that they were expelled along with Chaldaean astrologers.

[20] Mead, G. R. S. (1906), 534. When the Jews prepared the Greek version of the Old Testament they translated the unpronounceable name YHVH into Yahaveh (Jehovah) by adding to it the vowels from Adoni. At first this vowel name was probably a secret, but by the first century BCE it was obviously widely known. Diodorus of Sicily in 50 BCE writes: "Among the Jews Moyses [sic] referred his laws to the god who is invoked as Iao," *see* Book 1.94. The archaic Mystery name of Dionysus in Greece and Italy was "Iacho," from which derive "Iakkos" in Greece and "Bacchus" in Italy. Iacho, Dunlap suggests, was pronounced with silent "ch" as in "loch." Whether Iao and Iacho really are related by some distant ancestry is still an underresearched subject, but no doubt such an equation furnished the Diaspora Jews with

another opportunity to prove the antiquity of their religion and to suggest that the Greek Mysteries were derived from them.

[21] Macchioro, V. D. (1930), 189

[22] Hengel, M. (1980), 102. Lane-Fox also records the widely held opinion that the Jews were worshipers of Dionysus under another name, *see* Lane-Fox, R. (1986), 487.

[23] Hengel, op. cit., 71

[24] Ibid., 17. The Jewish high priest Hezekiah and many of his friends emigrated to Alexandria in 270 BCE because of the favorable status accorded to Jews.

[25] Vonge, C. D. (1993), Preface, 1

[26] Mead, op. cit., 102. Ptolemy I brought the philosopher Demetrius Phalerion from Athens to establish the library and museum and Timotheus, a priest of Eleusis, to establish the Mysteries.

[27] During the invasion by Julius Caesar the library caught fire. The damage was later made good by Mark Anthony, who donated 200,000 scrolls from the libraries of Asia Minor and Greece.

[28] Kerenyi, C. (1967), 116. Clement of Alexandria calls the spectacular drama at Alexandria a "drama *mystikon*." Its many levels represented the heavens, the Earth, and the Underworld.

[29] Ibid., 118. Hence the knowledge of them displayed by many Christian fathers.

[30] Angus, S. (1925), 19–20: "Religious syncretism, on a stupendous scale, was an immediate outcome of Alexander's intermingling of races. Every Mystery Religion was syncretistic. Religious syncretism was abetted by the almost complete absence of intolerance, by the universal demand for Savior-gods, by the medium of a common tongue, and by that mixture of races such as could be found today only in the United States. This syncretistic tendency increased in intensity under the Roman Empire. It prepared the way for the long sway of Oriental cults over the West and for the success of Christianity itself."

[31] Ibid., 22ff. This also led to anti-Semitism among the Greeks, who regarded such exclusivity as offensive. Anti-Semitism began in the third century BCE but had become endemic by the Roman period.

[32] Referring to the few Jewish inscriptions in Aramaic or Hebrew in Egypt, compared with hundreds in Greek, Hengel writes, "It is amazing how quickly the Jews in Ptolemaic Egypt gave up their familiar Aramaic and adopted Greek." The Septuagint Bible is evidence of this fundamental shift. Only the names on tombstones from the late Ptolemaic and early Roman period in Alexandria reveal that their owners were Jews. Otherwise they speak of completely Pagan concepts of the afterlife, death-bringing Moira, Hades with its everlasting darkness, and the gloomy descent to Lethe. *See* Hengel, M. (1980), 101.

[33] Angus, op. cit., 30: "The Jews of the Diaspora read Greek literature, spoke Greek, used Greek in the services of the synagogue and in family worship, while the inquisitive Greeks were not averse to studying a new cult. These two spiritual forces, the religion of Israel and the thought of Greece, confronted each other in Alexandria, the capital of the Western Diaspora and of Hellenism."

[34] Hengel, op. cit., 98. Hengel believes that this play may have been performed in the large courtyard of a synagogue. The synagogues of the Diaspora were very different from anything in Jerusalem. Known as *proseuchai*, they celebrated no rituals or sacrifice but were entirely made up of prayers and readings from the Septuagint. They could be, and sometimes were, mistaken for the meeting houses of philosophers. The Jews in nearby Cyrenaica even had an amphitheater at their disposal.

[35] The allegorical interpretation of Homer, Hesiod, and the myths of gods and goddesses was a feature of the Hellenistic scholarly tradition. Beginning with Aristobulus, *c.*150 BCE, the Jews also began to allegorize their sacred texts. This technique was then used by all his successors, especially Philo. Philo's work was in turn taken over by Clement and Origen and became indispensable to early Christianity, which found its prophecies of Jesus by an allegorical interpretation of the Old Testament.

[36] Hengel, op. cit., 96. The Septuagint provides the best evidence of this. By translating the obscure name of God in the Old Testament (Exodus 3 v 14), as "I am that I am," the translators of the Septuagint, in the words of Bickerman, "Platonized the Lord himself." At the same time numerous other changes were made to bring the work into line with Greek thought.

[37] Mead, G. R. S. (1906), 116

[38] Josephus, *The Life and Contra Apion*, 359. By the first century CE such identification was a commonplace of Jewish apologetic. Josephus writes of Moses' teachings about Jehovah, 'He represented Him as One, uncreated and immutable to all eternity, in beauty surpassing all mortal thought." It is hard to reconcile this Platonic God with the jealous, partisan, and cruel Jehovah of the Old Testament, but as the Septuagint was now presented as a gigantic

allegory, its violence was thereby neutralized. Josephus also repeats the opinion, which by now had become formulaic among Jewish scholars, that "the wisest of the Greeks (all the philosophers including Plato, Pythagoras, Anaxagoras, and the Stoics) learned to adopt these conceptions of God from principles with which Moses supplied them," *see Against Apion*, 2.163–8.

39   Hengel, M., op. cit., 100. Hermippus, in 220 BCE, was the first to connect Pythagoras with the Jews.

40   Ibid., 99

41   Ibid., 97–9. Philo is part of this long line of Jewish Pythagoreans. He repeats the claims of his predecessors and even quotes from a forged *Testament of Orpheus* to prove the charge of the "theft" of the Greeks! Eventually this propaganda became unquestioned dogma. Constantine in his speech at Nicaea repeats the charge that the Greek philosophers had plagiarized Moses, *see* Lane-Fox, R. (1986), 646.

42   Hengel, op. cit., 96. The legend that Ptolemy I and Demetrius Phalerion sponsored the translation of the Septuagint is a fiction created in the middle of the second century in a letter by Pseudo-Aristeas. Marlowe calls it a "picturesque legend," *see* Marlowe, J. (1971), 83. Also legendary is that 72 separate Jewish scribes turned out 72 versions that were unanimous in their faithful translation of the sacred texts. In fact the translation was made in parts over two centuries: the Pentateuch over the course of the third century, Isaiah and Jeremiah during the first half of the second century, and Psalms and the rest of the prophets during the second half, *see* Marlowe, 83. The Greek translation, which we have inherited as the Christian Old Testament, updated and reinterpreted Jewish scripture in line with Greek culture. It modernized its geographical picture of the world, adapted some passages to appeal to the prevailing political climate in Alexandria, and changed details of the Law of Moses to fit the current legal practices of Egypt. It removed offensive anthropomorphisms, elucidated words that are obscure in the original in the light of Greek concepts, added allusions to Greek mythology, and made its philosophy harmonious with Platonic doctrines.

43   Hengel writes of the material composed between the Old and New Testaments, "Almost all the Jewish literature from this period that has come down to us is essentially religious and political propaganda." Written mostly in Greek, using Greek rhetorical flourishes, it presents a Judaism that is often indistinguishable from Paganism. *See* Hengel, M. (1980), 51.

44   Barnstone, W. (1984), 243. *The Letter of Aristeas* was written *c*.130 BCE by an Alexandrian Jew but attributed to an Aristeas who had lived over a century earlier.

45   Ibid., 154. *4 Maccabees* was written in 40 CE as a Jewish apologetic. It later served as a model for Christian martyrdom stories. Unlike *1* and *2 Maccabees*, it was excluded from the New Testament Apocrypha. *1 Maccabees*, Chapter 12, reproduces a letter from "Jonathan the High Priest and the Senate of the Jews" to "our brothers of Sparta." It relates that: "A document has come to light which shows that Spartans and Jews are kinsmen, both being descended from Abraham." Written in the middle of the second century BCE, it is testimony to the strange alliances forged in this turbulent time.

46   Barnstone, op. cit., 485. *1 Enoch*, written in the second century BCE, reinvents the Old Testament figure as an image of the Greco-Egyptian Hermes, a divine scribe, astronomer, and messenger of God. Just as Hermes wrote 365 books, so Enoch is said to have written 366 books and lived 365 years. Barnstone describes *1 Enoch* as representing "the development of that side of Judaism to which historically Christianity in large measure owes its existence." In the middle of the first century an Alexandrian Jew wrote *2 Enoch*, which presents Enoch as a Messiah of the "invisible God." *See* Barnstone, op. cit., 3.

47   Ibid.

48   Written in the first few centuries BCE, these works include Ecclesiastes, Ecclesiasticus, Odes of Solomon, and Psalms of Solomon. Wisdom is often personified as a female aspect of the Lord, and there are numerous references to the "Son of Man," who also appears in the second-century Book of Daniel.

49   Barnstone, op. cit., 501ff. The Jewish *Sibylline Oracles* circulated widely throughout the Roman Empire.

50   Marlowe, J. (1971), 243. Another scholar explains, "The personification of this Hellenistic cosmos and feminine counterpart to, or consort of, Jehovah generally drew upon the characteristic traits of the Hellenistic goddesses and especially upon the imagery of the wisest of the goddesses, Isis. Even as the Hellenistic goddess of the cosmos opposed and was opposed by chaotic Tyche/Fortuna, so the Jewish Sophia, the cosmic principle of order, was opposed by the figure of 'the foolish woman' or Folly, the cosmic principle of disorder. This antithetical structure is recounted in the biblical book of Proverbs concerning two sisters, Folly and Wisdom." *See* Martin, L. H. (1987), 108.

51 Martin, op. cit., 108–9, quoting Proverbs 3 v 19
52 Inge, W. R. (1899), 84
53 Marlowe, op. cit., 241: "The last and greatest representative of the Alexandrian-Jewish tradition of Hellenistic Judaism." Following violent riots in Alexandria between Jews and Greeks in 38 CE, Philo was chosen as an ambassador to Rome by the Jewish community. He only visited Jerusalem once in his life, contrary to Jewish Law, which demanded thrice-yearly attendance. From the evidence of his writings he did not know Hebrew.
54 Quoted in Kingsland, W. (1937), 106
55 Willoughby, H. R. (1929), 228; see also Vonge, C. D. (1993), Preface. "Either Plato Philonises, or Philo Platonises" was an oft-repeated saying in the first few centuries CE.
56 Clement of Alexandria, Stromata, 1.15.72 and 2.19.100. Clement twice calls Philo "the Pythagorean" even though he knows that he is "Judaeus."
57 Marlowe, op. cit., 243: "Philo had undoubted faith that a study of mathematics and astronomy would lead to a perception of spiritual realities."
58 Boardman, Griffin, and Murray (1986), 703: "Ironically the clearest and most copious of witnesses to middle-Platonism is the Jewish writer Philo."
59 Inge, op. cit., 355
60 Ibid., 84. Philo, like his Pagan counterparts, is unconcerned with the name given to the Logos: "And many names belong to the Logos, for he is called the Name of God, and the Man after his image," see Wallis, R. T. (1992), 244.
61 Gregory, J. (1987), 26. There are many resemblances between the thoughts of Philo and Plotinus, including the view that the goal of human life is the vision of God. All of these ideas were inherited from the Pagan Mysteries to which, as one modern scholar remarks, "Philo's works prove a notable indebtedness."
62 Willoughby, op. cit., Chapter 9: "The Mysticism of Philo": "Philo acknowledged that he had been initiated into the sacred mysteries by Moses. He did not shrink from speaking of himself as a hierophant and he urged others to serve in a similar capacity for the uninitiated."
63 Ibid., 255ff. Philo "followed mystery practice by laying upon his disciples the charge of secrecy. Those who were adepts in the lore of his cult were regarded as an esoteric group, and he addressed them with formulas that were familiar to mystery initiates." Philo laid down the rule that none of "Moses' Disciples" might be initiated into Pagan cults as there were Mysteries in their own religion to which they ought to aspire.
64 Ibid., 256. In Life of Moses, 2.71, Philo says that God initiated Moses on the mountain. In The Giants, 54, he says that Moses thereafter became a hierophant.
65 Philo, On the Cherubim, 42–8, quoted in Burkert, W. (1992), 80. Burkert observes that this passage of Philo's is "saturated with mystery metaphor."
66 Quoted in Willoughby, H. R. (1929), 257
67 Ibid., 248. See also Marlowe, J. (1971), 249, where Marlowe regards Philo as "the precursor of Gnosticism, of NeoPlatonism, and of Christian mysticism."
68 Quoted in Willoughby, op. cit., 247–8
69 Eusebius, History of the Church (1965), 2.17ff. Eusebius is defensive about his theory from the outset. As to why Philo calls his community the Therapeutae, he writes, "Because the title Christian was not yet in general use," and ends lamely that this "need not be discussed now."
70 Philo of Alexandria, Book IX, 107
71 Eusebius, op. cit., 2.17. The editor of this edition states quite categorically that this theory is wrong, see 406. See also Philo of Alexandria, op. cit., 107, where the Loeb editor states: "Nowadays it seems needless to argue that the theory has no foundation whatever."
72 Philo of Alexandria, op. cit., see Loeb Introduction
73 Mead, G. R. S. (1906), 64, quotes Conybeare's opinion that "The Contemplative Life is one of Philo's earliest works." If it were written in his thirties that would be between 5 and 15 CE.
74 Ibid., 62. When Protestant scholars first realized that Eusebius' "Christians" predated Christ, some argued that the tract was the work of a fourth-century monk. This theory has won no supporters and the paradox of Christians before Christ remains to be explained.
75 Philo of Alexandria, op. cit., 131, 30–1
76 Ibid., 121, 13, 66
77 Ibid., 131, 32
78 Kirk and Raven, (1957), 264. In the fifth century BCE Parmenides the philosopher was "converted to the contemplative life by a fellow Pythagorean." Albinus the Platonist writes: "There are two ways of life, the contemplative and the active," but adds, "The contemplative life holds the place of honor," see Reedy, J. (1991), 21. Seneca the Roman Pythagorean writes of the two paths in On Duty, 5.1.

[79] Philo of Alexandria, op. cit., 125
[80] The Pythagoreans called seven "the virgin." Of the first 10 numbers it is the only one that will not divide the 360 degrees of a circle into equal parts.
[81] Philo of Alexandria, *Book IX*, 153, 65. Philo is cryptically referring to the *tetraktys*, the most important Pythagorean symbol.
[82] Ibid., 115ff, 3–9
[83] Philo of Alexandria, *On the Contemplative Life*, 28
[84] Philo of Alexandria, *Book IX*, 129ff, 28–9. The Therapeutaes' obsession with allegory places them securely in the Pythagorean tradition. Traditionally the Stoic philosophers are considered to have pioneered the allegorical treatment of mythology, however Delatte, supported by M. Détienne, has pointed out that the Pythagoreans practiced it long before the Stoics began to use this method systematically, *see* De Vogel, C. J. (1966), 109. Theagenes of Rhegium was the first to apply allegorical interpretation to Homer and is held to have also been a Pythagorean, *see* Burkert, W. (1972), 291, note 67.
[85] Philo of Alexandria, op. cit., 119, 11–12
[86] Ibid., 165, 83–5
[87] Ibid., 125, 21–3
[88] Herodotus, *The Histories*, Book 2, 63
[89] Philo of Alexandria, op. cit., 127, 25
[90] Ibid., 115, 2–3

CHAPTER 10: THE JESUS MYTH

[1] Campbell, J. (1988), 76
[2] Kahn, C. H. (1979), 219: "Since the basic axiom of traditional Greek piety is that the gods are immortal, to speak of their death is the gravest sort of blasphemy." Herodotus is extremely careful in his account of the death of Osiris-Dionysus: "Who it is they mourn on this occasion it is not pious for me to say."
[3] Guthrie, W. K. C. (1952), 110, referring to the Orphics, writes, "Few who had a message to preach in Greece would think of doing so by inventing new myths or new rites, and thus alienating at the outset the conservative minds of those whom they wished to influence. The change was accomplished by the infusion of new meaning into the myths and rites that were ready to hand."
[4] Wells, G. A. (1975), 111–13
[5] Campbell, J. (1964), 269. The literature of the Jews, *1* and *2 Enoch, Testaments of the Twelve Patriarchs, The Apocalypse of Baruch, The Assumption of Moses,* etc., provided the material later used in Christian apocalypses.
[6] Wells, op. cit., 112. The failure of numerous human Messiahs translated the expectation from the human to the cosmic plane.
[7] Mark 8 v 27–33
[8] Wells, op. cit., 69, note 28. The Joshua who led the Israelites into the promised land was the model for several Messiahs recorded by Josephus. A Jewish Sibylline oracle of the period predicts the coming of a man from the sky who will cause the sun to stand still, as Joshua had done, and *The Epistle of Barnabas* 12.8 also links Jesus with Joshua.
[9] Origen, *On first principles*, 4.2.9, quoted in Doran, R. (1995), 76
[10] *See* Matthew 22 v 41–6
[11] John 18 v 36–7
[12] Mark 8 v 27–33
[13] Deuteronomy 21 v 23
[14] Peter uses this description twice, in Acts 10 v 39 and 5 v 30.
[15] Hippolytus, *Elenchos*, 5.8.4ff. Hippolytus refers to the three churches of the Gnostics, the "angelic, the psychic, and the earthly, and their names are the Chosen, the Called, and the Captive."
[16] Matthew 2 v 15
[17] Matthew 3 v 17 and Luke 3 v 21 both record the words of God that were heard at the baptism of Jesus: "This is my beloved son with whom I am well pleased." The first utterance of the Pyramid Texts, written two millennia earlier, records the words of God at the coronation ceremony of the Pharaoh: "The king is my eldest son who split open my womb, he is my beloved son with whom I am well pleased."
[18] Deuteronomy 31 v 14–30
[19] Wells, G. A. (1975), 52. The name means "In Jehovah is salvation."

20 Joshua 3 v 12
21 Zechariah 9 v 9
22 The Psalms derive from Egyptian religious poetry of the Nineteenth and Twentieth Dynasties (c.1000–750 BCE), see Murray, M. A. (1949), 50. Proverbs is based on the Egyptian instructions of Amenhotep, and Moses, the writer of the first five books, was born in Egypt and brought up as an Egyptian priest. Many of his miracles are also found in Egyptian texts, see Harrington, D. J. (1996), 9. The Alexandrian Jews and later the Christians were keen to stress Moses' Egyptian origins in a Greco-Roman world overtaken with Egyptomania. Acts 7 v 22 declares: "Moses was trained in all the wisdom of the Egyptians."
23 Metzger, B. M. (1987), 172. One of the earliest "gospels" was probably just such a collection of proof texts drawn from the Old Testament. This would be a narrative, almost recognizable as the Jesus story, but composed entirely of "prophecies" from Psalms, Proverbs, and the Pentateuch. The Alexandrian Jewish scholars were systematic in their attempts to prove that the philosophy of the Greeks and the Mysteries was plagiarized from the Jews. A collection of proof texts that the story of Dionysus was derived from the Jewish scriptures might explain why so many Greek and Roman scholars were convinced that the god worshiped by the Jews was Dionysus.
24 Isaiah 7 v 14. The Greek Septuagint translated the Aramaic almah as parthenos.
25 Mark 15 v 34; see Mayor, Fowler, and Conway, (1907), 53
26 Psalm 22 v 16
27 Psalm 22 v 18
28 Barnstone, W. (1984), 202: "Since much [sic] of the inter-testamental writings were apocalyptic and messianic, the appearance of a figure such as Jesus Christ was not unexpected. Indeed, because of the messianic nature of Jewish pseudepigrapha, many of them were altered and 'Christianized' to make them reveal Christian truths."
29 Ibid., 501–3
30 As well as influencing the Jesus story, complete passages of these inter-testamental texts were transformed into Christian documents. A whole section from The First Book of Enoch appears in the New Testament Letter of Jude v 5–18.
31 Barnstone, op. cit., 485. The same imagery is found in the description of Empedocles' apotheosis.
32 Wells, G. A. (1975), 116
33 The Son of Man is a term used repeatedly in the inter-testamental literature written in the second century BCE, in Daniel, 1 and 2 Enoch, 4 Ezra and The Psalms of Solomon. See Gaus, A. (1991), 506.
34 Barnstone, op. cit., 485ff, and see 3ff
35 Wells, op. cit., 55
36 Ibid., 211, quoting The Wisdom of Solomon 2 v 13, 16–18, 20 and Mark 15 v 29, 32; and 14 v 58, 61ff
37 Ibid., quoting The Wisdom of Solomon 4 v 16 and Mark 15 v 37
38 Ibid., quoting The Wisdom of Solomon 5 v 5 and Mark 15 v 39
39 Perkins, P. (1993), 26–8, discusses several Gnostic texts that were later Christianized and comments, "Adding Christ to the heavenly eons required little modification of the basic narrative in many Gnostic texts." Perkins writes of several systems she examines, "It is possible to conceive of a saving revelation and cult without Christianity." In The Gospel of the Egyptians Christ has been inserted into a prior account of a heavenly redeemer called Seth, see 104.
40 Robinson, J. M. (1978), 220ff. The title as given in the Nag Hammadi, Eugnostos the Blessed, does not make clear the full meaning of this name.
41 Ibid., and see Introduction, 8: "The Christianizing process taking place almost before one's eyes."
42 According to a tradition recorded by Mead, Simon Magus traced his teachings back to a sage called Dositheus in 100 BCE. See Mead, G. R. S. (1906), 162ff.
43 Wilson, I. (1984), 37, and Wells, G. A. (1975), 102. Which is ironic since it is Jesus' death that marks him as definitely not the Messiah!
44 Fidler, D. (1993), 169. Saturn and Jupiter came into conjunction three times during the year 7 BCE: May 27, October 6, and December 1 in the sign of Pisces. That the New Age of Pisces had begun had been known to a few philosophers over a century earlier, but by the beginning of the first century had been widely disseminated. This astronomical event, combined with the deep crisis of the time, must have seemed like an important sign that the last days had arrived—Pisces is the last sign of the zodiac.
45 Wilson, I. (1984), 77: "Acutely conscious of his own unpopularity, Herod systematically liquidated all whom he considered potentially dangerous to him, including his own wife and

two of his sons, and surrounded himself with a network of informers and secret police as clandestine and ruthless as the KGB."

46 Brandon, S. G. F. (1969), 292. Pilate was prefect for 10 years from 26 to 36 CE, when he was sent back to Rome to answer for a massacre. He was so hated that he is the only prefect from 6 to 41 to be mentioned by name by Josephus and Philo.

47 Josephus, *The Jewish War*, 126: "Pilate, during the night, secretly and undercover, conveyed to Jerusalem the images of Caesar known as sigma. When day dawned this caused great excitement among the Jews: for those who were near were amazed at the sight, which meant that their laws had been trampled on—they do not permit any graven image to be set up in the city."

48 Mack, B. L. (1993), 51ff, 68. Galilee was known as *Gelil ha goim*, "the land of the *goim*," or Gentiles.

49 Josephus, op. cit., Chapter 10. Josephus records how most of the cities of Galilee closed their gates to him but welcomed in the Romans. After the Jewish war Rome made the loyal city of Sepphoris the capital and treasury of Galilee.

50 Wells, op. cit., 144, 71ff

51 Mark 1 v 16

52 "And passing along *by the sea of Galilee* he saw Simon and Andrew." The verb *passing along* is not used with the preposition *by* in Greek. If the section in italics is removed, the passage flows on normally and is seen as what it originally was—a teaching story set in no particular time or place.

53 Wells, op. cit., 71–2. Wells quotes Professor Nineham's view that the details of time and place are "entirely St Mark's doing."

54 Josephus, op. cit., 337. Josephus' figures are usually exaggerated, but Gibbon considers 580,000 deaths from violence, famine, and disease over a six-year period as probable, *see* Gibbon, E. (1796), 516.

55 Josephus, op. cit., 340, Chapter 22: "Jerusalem Destroyed"

56 Barnstone, W. (1984), 508, quoting *The Apocalypse of Baruch*

57 Josephus, op. cit., 135

58 Brandon, S. G. F. (1969), 294. Josephus uses the term *goetes* for all these messianic pretenders. This pejorative word describing miracle mongerers has a long history in Roman political rhetoric.

59 Mark 12 v 13–17

60 Brandon, op. cit., 287. Josephus describes Judas as the founder of one of the four schools of "philosophy," but although he outlines the differing beliefs of the Pharisees, Sadducees, and Essenes he is silent on Judas' Zealotry. As his work is a Jewish apologetic written for Roman readers, he plays down the extent to which zealotry was religiously inspired. Judas was a rabbi and the zealot war was effectively a *jihad* in which martyrs were guaranteed instant apotheosis. This tradition derived from the Maccabean revolt (173–164 BC), whose heroes were idealized as martyrs present in heaven before the throne of God. The second and fourth books of Maccabees hint at this belief, the latter stating that "those who die for God live unto God," *see* Lane-Fox, R. (1986), 436.

61 The Book of Esdras paints a graphic picture of the suffering of the Jews at this time: "Our priests burnt alive, and the Levites taken into captivity; our virgins have been ravished and our wives violated, our god fearing men carried off, and our children abandoned; our young men have been enslaved, and our strong warriors reduced to impotence," *see* 2 Esdras 10 v 22. These are the same scenes that Eusebius will later recount with undisguised relish, *see* Eusebius, *History of the Church* (1965), 65ff.

62 Macchioro, V. D. (1930), 202, referring to Acts 13 v 45ff, 14 v 1ff, 17 v 1ff, 4, 18 v 4ff, 19 v 19

63 Ibid., 203

64 The Preface to Irenaeus, *Against Heresies*, quoted in Lüdemann, G. (1995), 16. Irenaeus refers to the Valentinian Gnostics as "wolves in sheep's clothing." Over a century later, the Bishop of Odessa was still complaining about followers of Valentinus "stealing sheep from the Christian flock," *see* Lieu, S. N. C. (1985), 50.

CHAPTER 11: AN IMITATION CHURCH

1 Quoted in Robinson, J. M. (1978), 374, 376

2 Quoted in Hoffmann, R. J. (1987), 91

3 Ibid., 70

4 Wells, G. A. (1975), 61. The formula becomes dogmatic in 1 Timothy, which as noted, was forged specifically to refute Gnosticism and advance Literalism. Its repetition soon became

"almost routine" and is found in Ignatius, Justin, Irenaeus, and Tertullian. Wells quotes Canon Kelly's belief that all these authors may be echoing a baptismal creed created at this time to assure candidates "that these events did not happen anywhere at any time, and that the gospel is not simply a system of ideas."

5   2 Peter 1 v 16
6   Quoted in Wells, op. cit., 58. Ignatius, c.110 CE, is emphatic that Jesus suffered under Pilate and presses this view in three of the letters written to Christian communities. Ignatius' testimony provides clear evidence that there is "another doctrine" presenting a different story from his.
7   Ibid.
8   1 John 4 v 2
9   2 John 7–11
10   Wells, op. cit., 58
11   Luke 24 v 28–43. See Hoffmann, R. J. (1987), 130, note 25, also Wells, G. A. (1975), 159, note 7. The birth story and these concluding verses were added to Luke's gospel to refute the docetism of the Gnostics.
12   John 20 v 17
13   John 20 v 24–9
14   Fidler, D. (1993), 17. Irenaeus claims that bread and wine are literally transformed into the body and blood of Jesus and that by feeding on this substance our physical bodies are miraculously transformed into an immortal state. See D'Alviella, G. (1981), 117, which records that by the third century the holy sacrament, which for Clement was a mystical symbol, was being presented as a magical potion, a *pharmakos athansias*.
15   Hoffmann, op. cit., 70
16   2 Peter 3 v 3–10
17   Lane-Fox, R. (1986), 267. Justin was replying to the confused exclamations of his contemporaries, "We have heard these things even in the days of our fathers, and look, we have grown old and none of them has happened to us."
18   Campbell, J. (1955), 169. This muddled legend about John, of whom the other disciples whispered, "This disciple shall not die," is found in John 21 v 23.
19   Lane-Fox, op. cit., 266ff. If Hippolytus were writing today his work would doubtless be called *The Bible Code*.
20   Ibid., 266. When Irenaeus' tract against heresy was translated into Latin in the early fifth century the millennium was omitted.
21   Pagels, E. (1979), 36. Tertullian admits that his opponents find the literal interpretation "extremely revolting, repugnant, and impossible."
22   Tertullian, *The Body of Christ*, 5
23   In the latter half of the second century the argument was conducted on both sides by claiming descent from an apostolic figure, the Gnostics from Paul and the Literalists from John and Peter via various Asia Minor bishops. To prove his position in the line of apostolic succession Irenaeus was forced to fabricate a rather unusual interpretation of the length of Jesus' ministry. He shrinks the number of generations necessary to link Jesus' time to his own by extending the age of Christ as well as that of the apostles. To do this he combines the Synoptic tradition that Jesus was 30 when baptized with John's reference to multiple visits to Jerusalem and his claim that Jesus was not yet 50 (John 8 v 56–7). He concludes that Jesus must have preached until he had passed his fortieth birthday. As Perkins notes, "Irenaeus then appeals to the testimony of apostolic tradition to confirm this extraordinary claim." See Perkins, P. (1993), 180. Irenaeus thus proves that elders in the Asia Minor churches of the early second century were still able to learn the truth directly from apostles (i.e., Polycarp, who learned directly from the apostle John). The Gnostic teacher Ptolemy, Irenaeus quips, has not even seen an apostle in his dreams! (Adv. Haer. 2.22.6.) The liberties that Irenaeus then took with the length of John's life eventually gave birth to the bizarre legend that he in fact never died, but still lived on in Patmos or Ephesus, see Campbell, J. (1955), 169.
24   Pagels, op. cit., 41
25   Ibid., 61. As Pagels notes, the chief advocates of this theory were, not surprisingly, the bishops.
26   1 Clement 1. See 44, where Clement asserts that sadly this was all foreknown: "Our Apostles knew, through our Lord Jesus Christ, that there would be dissensions over the title of bishop."
27   1 Clement 63
28   1 Clement 41.3

29 Quoted in Pagels, E. (1979), 61
30 Quoted ibid.
31 Ibid., 117
32 Ibid., 61
33 Ibid., 66
34 Ibid., 67
35 Ibid., 66
36 Tertullian, *Prescription against the Heretics*, 41
37 Pagels, op. cit., 83
38 Quoted ibid., 81
39 Tertullian, *On the Dress of Women*, 1.1.2, quoted ibid., 63, and *see* Doran, R. (1995), 150
40 Pagels, E. (1979), 117, *see* 69, where Irenaeus asserts that: "The priests ... receive simultaneously with the episcopal succession the sure gift of truth."
41 Ibid., 122
42 Ibid., 117
43 Ibid., 69. Irenaeus delineates two lines of succession. One derives from God and descends through Christ and his chosen apostles, especially Peter. The other comes from Simon Magus who "put forth indeed the name of Jesus Christ as a kind of lure" but whose teaching is in fact "the malignant poison of the great serpent, the great author of apostasy." Clearly responding to criticism from the Gnostics, Irenaeus writes indignantly, "They call us 'unspiritual,' 'common,' and 'ecclesiastic' ... they say we go on living in the lower regions, as if we could not lift our minds to the things on high, nor understand the things that are above." *See* ibid., 67.
44 Lane-Fox, R. (1986), 492
45 Pagels, op. cit., 100; *see also* Gibbon, E. (1796), 522
46 Jude v 3ff
47 Jude v 22
48 2 Timothy 2 v 17–18
49 Irenaeus, *Against Heresies*, 3.15.2
50 Quoted in Pagels, E. (1975), 158–9
51 Quoted in Robinson, J. M. (1978), 448ff. *The Testimony of Truth* was written in Alexandria in the second century. The arguments of its author (believed to be Valentinus) present a mirror image of those of the ecclesiastical heresiologists.
52 Quoted ibid., 362ff; *see also* Pagels, E. (1979), 115
53 *The Second Treatise of the Great Seth*, 60, 20
54 Quoted in Pagels, op. cit., 65
55 Stevenson, J. (1957), 209, Origen on "unworthy clergy"
56 1 Corinthians 2 v 4, *see* Pagels, E. (1975), 54
57 1 Corinthians 1 v 10
58 Pagels, op. cit., 45
59 Romans 14 v 2. *See* Pagels, op. cit., 45. Paul calls the Pneumatics by the code name "the strong."
60 Romans 15 v 6. *See* Pagels, op. cit., 45
61 Pagels, E. (1979), 126
62 Ibid., 68
63 Irenaeus, *Against Heresies*, 3.16.1, quoted ibid., 54
64 Ibid., 3.15.2, quoted Pagels, E. (1975), 62
65 Pagels, E. (1979), 64
66 Ibid., 126. Theodotus, the great teacher of the East, asserted that Christ's body was purely spiritual, consisting of those who had received Gnosis. Ptolemy and Heracleon, teachers of the western school, disagreed. Against Theodotus they argued that Christ's body, the Church, consisted of two distinct elements. The Valentinian text *The Interpretation of the Gnosis* admits that the Church, which was originally one, was now split into factions and attempts to reconcile both Gnostic and Literalist Christians with each other.
67 Plato's statement that "Many carry the wand, but few become Bacchoi" became proverbial in the Hellenistic period and was often shortened to "Many are called but few are chosen." It is in this form that it turns up in the early *Epistle of Barnabas*, *see* Louth, A. (1968), 163, and in Matthew 20 v 16. The Gnostics added the term *captive* for those "enslaved in Egypt."
68 Pagels, E. (1979), 126
69 Ibid.
70 Ibid., 63

71 Pagels, E. (1975), 157. As Pagels notes, the amount of effort devoted to its refutation, and then to its complete annihilation, is indirect testimony to the popularity of Gnosticism—as is its constant reappearance.
72 Gibbon, E. (1796), 458. Gibbon writes with characteristic wit: "For the most part they arose in the second century, flourished during the third, and were suppressed in the fourth or fifth by the prevalence of more fashionable controversies."
73 Doran, R. (1995), 75, warns that we must realize "how flexible the appellation Christian was in Rome in the second century."
74 Irenaeus relates that even some of his bishops and deacons had become Valentinian Gnostics (*Against Heresies*, Preface, 4.26.3, 4.41.3–4.5.31). Tertullian likewise laments that outstanding members of his community "even bishops, deacons, widows, and martyrs" sought initiation into the Valentinian circle (*Prescription against the Heretics*, 3).
75 Tertullian, *Against Valentinus*, 4
76 Quoted in Godwin, J. (1981), 85
77 Guthrie, K. S. (1987), 42, referring to Justin Martyr, *Dialogue with Trypho*, 2
78 Mead, G. R. S. (1906), 253
79 Barnstone, W. (1984), 621. Ptolemy, or Ptolemaeus, was the head of the Valentinian school in Italy c.160 CE. He is the first known exegete of John's gospel (not surprisingly perhaps, as John's gospel was widely held to be a Gnostic work). He is also one of the first Christians we know of who was executed for his beliefs, see Stevenson, J. (1957), 30. Irenaeus is clearly aware that Gnostics have died for the faith, see Pagels, E. (1979), 104, though he of course belittles their contribution. What is peculiar, however, is the way in which Irenaeus enters ecclesiastical history. As presbyter for Lyons his first job was to carry a letter to Rome pleading for clemency for the persecuted Montanists, see Cross, F. L. (1958), 701. This would suggest that the Montanists were among the famous "Martyrs of Lyons" in 170 CE, the event that Irenaeus claims led him to Christ.
80 Eusebius (1965), 109. Eusebius claims he composed a "most effective refutation of Basilides," but, as is often the case with Eusebius' sources, we have no independent evidence of Agrippa's existence, see ibid., 341.
81 Mead, G. R. S. (1906), 148. This is Mead's belief, which would seem to be supported by the failure of later heresy-hunters to pass on Hippolytus' actual work, preferring to rely on Irenaeus. Rediscovered in 1842, Hippolytus' treatise contains a large mass of new matter, including direct quotations from the "heretics" themselves.
82 Lüdemann, G., (1995), 24
83 Pagels, E. (1979), 120. See Metzger, B. M. (1987), 149, which calls Hippolytus the first anti-pope.
84 Grant, R. M. (1959), 183
85 Metzger, op. cit., 99. According to Didymus, Montanus was a priest of Cybele who fell into a trance and began speaking in tongues. Believing himself to be inspired by the Holy Spirit (the Paraclete promised in John 14 v 15–17), he traveled Asia Minor accompanied by two women prophetesses. He regarded ecstasy as the only true Christianity.
86 Quoted in Pagels, op. cit., 121–2. Unlike Hippolytus and Irenaeus, Tertullian was not beatified, presumably because he apostated to Montanism in 207 CE. See Gibbon, E. (1796), 523, where it is recorded how after his apostasy Tertullian proceeded to attack the morals of the Church, which he had previously so resolutely defended.
87 Lane-Fox, R. (1986), 409
88 Cross, F. L. (1958), 133. The Tertullianists were still surviving in the fourth century.
89 Mead, G. R. S. (1907), 162. Marcion attempted by this method to demonstrate the total incompatibility of the Gods of the Old and New Testament. His school failed to take root in the West, but in the East was taken over and reinforced by the Gnostic followers of Mani. They too composed a treatise called *Antitheses*. See Lieu, S. N. C. (1985), 39, which notes that Marcion's influence on Mani was profound and pervasive even though he did not deign to acknowledge it. In the late fourth century an orthodox bishop wrote, "Marcion had separated his sheep, Mani fell upon them and led them away," see Lieu, 44. Both Marcion and Mani saw themselves as the true followers of Paul, still trying to free their fellow Jews from the tyranny of the Law.
90 Lane-Fox, op. cit., 332
91 Godwin, J. (1981), 85. The Manichaean treatise probably gives us a good idea of the contents of Marcion's *Antitheses*. It points out that the two testaments are mutually contradictory and that by retaining the Old Testament, the Catholics had ignored the warning of Christ and put "a new piece of cloth onto an old garment." In doing so they had returned the

Church to the bondage of circumcision. The lives of the Old Testament patriarchs violated the moral precepts of the New Testament. Abraham had a mistress and gave his wife to foreign kings, Lot committed incest, David coveted the wife of one of his generals, and Solomon was polygamous. Hosea married a prostitute at the command of God, and Moses was a murderer. *See* Lieu, op. cit., 121

92 Mead, G. R. S. (1906), 243. It is widely accepted that Marcion's critique of western Christianity was the impulse for the first attempts to create a definitive canon.

93 Gibbon, E. (1796), 455

94 Tertullian, *Apology*, 19.1, 21.1, quoted in Brandon, S. G. F. (1969), 377. The worst insult that could be hurled at a cult in the Greco-Roman world was that it was new. All Christianity's competitors were identified with ancient cultures—Isis and Osiris with Egypt, Mithras with Persia, Attis and Adonis with the Asia Minor cults of the Great Mother. Even when the cult had really been created in the Hellenistic period, as in the case of Mithraism, it had by necessity to root itself in the ancient and venerable past. Christianity's earliest critic, Tacitus, attacked it partly because it was a superstition, but also because it was new. Eusebius acknowledges this criticism at the start of his *History of the Church*. Leaning heavily on the Old Testament as his witness, he writes that there is "nothing novel or strange in the religion preached by Him," *see* Eusebius (1965), 14.

95 The Jewish scriptures are arranged in the order of the Pentateuch (the five books of Moses), the Prophets (Joshua to Malachi), and the Writings (Psalms to 2 Chronicles). In the Christian Old Testament, however, the Prophets and the Writings have been switched. Now the prophecy of Malachi 3 v 25—"Lo, I will send the prophet Elijah to you, before the coming of the awesome, fearful day of the Lord"—leads into the appearance of John the Baptist, the reincarnation of Elijah.

96 Brandon, op. cit., 251. To round off this presentation of Jewish guilt, Mark describes the Jewish leaders on Golgotha as mocking the dying Jesus, while a Roman centurion is the only person present who recognizes Jesus' divinity, declaring, "Truly this man was the Son of God."

97 Matthew 27 v 24-6

98 Brandon, op. cit., 252. Brandon is writing in 1969.

99 Doran, R. (1995), 57, notes that in the second century, as more and more Gentiles became Christians, so fewer and fewer Jews did. Justin Martyr wrote a devastating attack on the Jews called *Dialogue with Trypho*. It ran to 142 chapters, the longest book thus far produced by an orthodox writer, *see* Metzger, B. M. (1987), 144. Later Bishop Melito and Tertullian wrote polemical tracts *Against the Jews*, as did St. Augustine.

100 Doran, op. cit., 58

101 Lane-Fox, R. (1986), 482

102 The developing anti-Semitic nature of Christianity perfectly reflects the hardening attitudes of the western Empire to the Jews. By the early fourth century Eusebius was describing with relish how the destruction of Jerusalem was God's punishment on the Jews for the murder of his son. At the end of the fourth century St. John Chrysostom was preaching that demons dwelt in synagogues and in the souls of Jews, and St. Augustine was writing in a treatise *Against the Jews*: "You in your parents killed Christ," *see* Doran, op. cit., 62. In 412 Cyril became Patriarch of Alexandria and one of his first acts was to incite the monks to pillage and expel from the city the wealthy Jewish community some 40,000 strong, *see* Marlowe, J. (1971), 288. During the fifth century the Emperors safeguarded the survival of the Jewish communities, but as second-class citizens, "in order that they might serve as a living testimony to the Christian interpretation of the scriptures and to the victory of the Catholic church," *see* Lieu, S. N. C. (1985), 177.

103 Justin Martyr, *Dialogue with Trypho*, 16, quoted in Doran, op. cit., 57

104 Metzger, op. cit., 75ff, gives the orthodox view of the evolution of the canon. Barnstone, W. (1984), xviii, observes, "We can say categorically that the Bible, with the absence of sacred texts from the entire inter-testamental period, with its acceptance of a small and repetitious canon for the New Testament, with the exclusion of all later Christian Apocrypha, and the total rejection of Gnostic scriptures, has given us a highly censored and distorted version of ancient religious literature. The impression is given that somehow Christianity sprang self-generated like a divine entity, with no past, into its historical setting." Mack, B. L. (1993), 228, observes about the canon that: "What is striking is the severe reduction of a large, spirited literature to a very small set of gospels and letters." When we consider that the gospels themselves are really four versions of one story, and the letters primarily by one man, the true poverty of the West's sacred scriptures becomes depressingly clear.

[105] A fact observed as long ago as 1699 by Toland, who wrote: "There is not a single book of the New Testament not refused by some of the ancient writers as being unjustly attributed to the apostles and as actually forged by their adversaries." *See* Metzger, B. M. (1987), 13.

[106] Ibid., 54. Mead, G. R. S. (1906), 254, records that a *Traditions of Matthias* was known by the Basilidean school in Alexandria. He suggests that this could have been a "Life of Jesus" intended for public circulation, designed to be interpreted later according to the inner tenets of the Gnosis. This might bear no relation to our present Gospel of Matthew, but may well have served as the foundation document for it. If the Jesus Mysteries Thesis is right, the first author of the Jesus story must have been a Gnostic as in the beginning there was only Gnosticism. *The Traditions of Matthias* might well have formed the basis of the confused reports that Papias collected from Jewish refugees streaming out of Syria into Asia Minor.

[107] Metzger, op. cit., 145. In calling the documents he knows "memoirs of the Apostles," Justin uses the same term that Xenophon had coined five centuries earlier when he wrote *The Memoirs of Socrates*.

[108] Stanton, G. (1995), 101-2. In 172 CE Tatian, Justin Martyr's pupil, responding to the attacks of critics who poked fun at the discrepancies between the various gospels, wove them all into one.

[109] Metzger, op. cit., 151ff. Irenaeus makes it clear that for him there are four gospels and the canon is closed. *See* Stevenson, J. (1957), 117, where he gives his reasons: "It is not possible that the Gospels can be either more or fewer in number than they are, for there are four zones of the world and four principle [sic] winds." Such logic makes us realize how far away we really are from the thought world in which these men moved. As Lüdemann notes, Irenaeus' "artificial arguments" at least demonstrate that the idea was a relative novelty, which needed defending. *See* Lüdemann, G. (1995), 196.

[110] Lane-Fox, R. (1986), 381ff, calls this a "jewel of the non-canonical writings." It is thought that it was written *c.* 90 CE near Cumae in Italy, possibly by a Jew enslaved in the recent Roman campaign. It is easy to see why it was excluded from the canon, as it makes no definite quotation from either the Old or New Testament and presents a bizarre amalgam of Hermetic and Sibylline wisdom set in the form of a Jewish/Christian apocalypse. Its title and much of its imagery has distinct resonances with *The Shepherd of Hermes*, a Pagan text attributed to the Egyptian sage Hermes Trismegistus.

[111] Lane-Fox, op. cit., 381

[112] Barnstone, W. (1984), 333

[113] Kerenyi, C. (1976), 106, and *see* Barnstone, op. cit., 335, and Metzger, op. cit., 170

[114] R. A. Lipsius, 1860, quoted in Mead, G. R. S. (1906), 417

[115] Lüdemann, G., op. cit., 196. Irenaeus traces all heresies from Simon Magus and quotes Acts to show that the heretic had been amply repudiated by Peter. Justin repeatedly mentions Simon Magus but strangely does not make any reference to Acts. Lüdemann notes that the reason for Acts' sudden appearance between Justin and Irenaeus is "self-evident." The German theologian Campenhausen states, "We do not find testimony to the Acts of the Apostles before Irenaeus," *see* Lüdemann, op. cit., 315. Harnack's view offers some insights: "Acts is the key to the understanding of the Catholic canon and at the same time shows its 'novelty.'" Tertullian himself admits that Acts was rejected by the "heretics."

[116] Tertullian, *On the Proscription of the Heretics*, 23, despite, or perhaps in reply to, the censuring of Peter by Paul in Galatians 2 v 11ff

[117] Lüdemann, G., op. cit., 196. The Marcionites pointed out the incompatibility of the Paul of the letters and the person portrayed in Acts. As Wells notes, "Almost everything Acts says about Paul is tendentious." *See* Wells, G. A. (1975), 17.

[118] Quoted in Lane-Fox, R. (1986), 439

[119] Ibid., 436, 420, for the analogy between early Christians and the Islamic martyrs of Iran: "Gassing and chemical burns are the modern heirs of the fires and wild beasts."

[120] Pagels, E. (1979), 106, quoting *The Testimony of Truth*

[121] Tertullian, *Apology*, 50

[122] Metzger, B. M. (1987), 153, notes charitably that "Irenaeus had presumably been away during the crisis." *See* Gibbon, E. (1796), 548, note 100, where Gibbon dryly observes that "It is somewhat remarkable that Tertullian did not suffer martyrdom himself." Lane-Fox asks a similar question as to what Eusebius had been doing to avoid arrest during the so-called Great Persecution—especially as some 30 or more volumes continued to appear in his name during this period. He concludes that like Lactantius, Eusebius had probably "avoided excessive heroics." *See* Lane-Fox, op. cit., 606.

[123] Lieu, S. N. C. (1985), 93

[124] Pagels, op. cit., 106

[125] *The Apocalypse of Peter*, 79, 11–21

[126] Ibid., 78, 1–2

[127] Clement of Alexandria (www), 38

[128] Quoted in Pagels, op. cit., 99. Tertullian traces the rise of heresy directly to the outbreak of persecution, and although not chronologically correct this does contain a measure of truth. The violence opened up a deep division in the Christian community. Gnostics and Literalists who had previously assembled together were driven apart by their respective beliefs, as Ignatius' plaintive statement makes clear.

[129] Ibid., 103

[130] Lane-Fox, R. (1986), 439, observes, "This type of theology repels most modern readers," but notes that it was challenged by Gnostics at the time. Death for the Name was simply a hideous waste, besides, did not Jesus himself approve of flight during persecution? In Matthew 10 v 23 Jesus advises "When you are persecuted in one town, take refuge in another."

[131] MacMullen, R. (1966), 132. Philosophers (a catch-all term including astrologers, magi, Chaldaeans, and other undesirables) were repeatedly swept out of Rome, at least 10 times in the period 33 BCE to 93 CE. Tacitus regarded this as "harsh and useless," as they inevitably crept back in again. As MacMullen observes, philosophy and subversion invariably went together, it was an honorable Greek tradition that had found its purest expression in Socrates, *see* MacMullen, 53.

[132] Livy (1976), 401. Livy, Book 39, is our only source for the repression of the Bacchanalia. His account is tainted by hostile polemic and the standard Augustan political rhetoric. Fortunately the Senatus Consultum issued against the cult is still preserved and confirms that extreme measures were taken against it. Livy's account became a blueprint in the Imperial period for procedures to be followed by Roman officials when dealing with oriental cults. Gibbon, E. (1796), 502, records Tacitus' view of the Christians and notes the similarity in style to that employed by Livy, even down to identical turns of phrase. The image of "another people" who would arise and oust the *populus Romani* was a constant source of terror at Rome. The fortunate were a small minority in a great sea of the enslaved and the dispossessed. Slaves and economic refugees brought their mystical cults with them to Rome and found in them fellowship and familiarity in a strange and hostile world. No wonder that in the eyes of the nobility it seemed as if religious fanaticism and political subversion went hand in hand.

[133] Burkert, W. (1987), 52, observes, "There is nothing comparable in religious history before the persecutions of the Christians." The proscription of the Mysteries of Dionysus remained in force until it was explicitly lifted by Julius Caesar, *see* Kerenyi, C. (1976), 363. Caesar's generosity was no doubt just another cynical appeal to the plebs, among whom the cult of Bacchus had spread widely, despite, or perhaps because of, its official proscription. As the Villa of the Mysteries in Pompeii and the Villa Farnesina in Rome evidence, the cult had even penetrated to the highest level of Roman society by the end of the Republican period. Marc Antony portrayed himself as Dionysus and even the sober Augustus had himself initiated at Eleusis after the battle of Actium. A similar trajectory from persecuted minority cult to Imperial patronage, and over a similar time scale, would later be followed by the cults of Mithras and Jesus.

[134] MacMullen, op. cit., 57

[135] Ibid., 84–90

[136] Ibid., 136

[137] Lane-Fox, op. cit., 423; Trajan's famous reply to the questions of Pliny

[138] *See* de Sainte-Croix, G. E., "Why were the early Christians persecuted?," *Past and Present* 1963, no. 26, 6ff. This text is used by Lane-Fox and regarded as "still basic," *see* Lane-Fox, op. cit., 773, note 1, and *see* T. D. Barnes, *Constantine and Eusebius* (1981), 150, for survey.

[139] Gibbon, op. cit., 579. Gibbon's calculation was 2,000 persons. In the view of Lane-Fox, the persecution "has been exaggerated in Christian tradition to an extent which even Gibbon did not fully appreciate," *see* Lane-Fox, op. cit., 596, 733, note 1. Gibbon, however, was well aware of the conflict of his sources with the accounts of Christian propagandists, as note 182, Chapter 16, demonstrates. Here he picks his way carefully through Eusebius' account— "the artful management of the historian," "artfully selects," "ambiguous words," "having thus provided a secure evasion," etc. He notes that finally even Eusebius only offers nine bishops punished with death and 92 martyrs in Palestine.

[140] Lane-Fox, R. (1986), 434

[141] Gibbon, op. cit., 541

[142] Lane-Fox, op. cit., 421, records several attempts by Roman governors to deal with the enthusiasts.

[143] Ibid., 442

[144] Marcus Aurelius, *Meditations*, 11.3. In Epictetus' opinion the Christians were driven to martyrdom in imitation of their master by blind fanaticism, *see Dissertations*, 4.6.7.

[145] *Historia Augusta* (Alexander Severus, 29.2) relates that Abraham, Apollo, Orpheus, Apollonius of Tyana, and Christ all rubbed shoulders in Alexander's private chapel. *See* Angus, S. (1925), 192, and Gibbon, E. (1796), 553.

[146] Stevenson, J. (1957), 195. Interest in religion at the court of the Severi was intense. Mammaea invited Origen to visit the court and also sponsored Philostratus to compose *The Life of Apollonius of Tyana*.

[147] Lane-Fox, op. cit., 441

[148] Tertullian, *Apology*, 37.4–8, quoted in Stevenson, op. cit., 162. *See also* Lane-Fox, op. cit., 273, which says of his claim that Christians could be found among "all" German tribes and even in Britain, "Tertullian can hardly be trusted." Tertullian was also instrumental in fabricating legends about the numbers of martyrs. *See* de Sainte-Croix, 23, which quotes Tertullian's account of the visit of the proconsul Antoninus to an assize in 185 CE. Apparently all the Christians of the town approached him and demanded the privilege of martyrdom. As de Sainte-Croix notes, "We must allow for his customary exaggeration." Gibbon was one of the earliest historians to point out the absurd multiplication of the martyrs by Christian propagandists. As he records, "As a specimen of these legends we may be satisfied with 10,000 Christian soldiers crucified in one day, either by Trajan or Hadrian on Mount Ararat," Gibbon, 540, note 74. This process was aided by the similarity between the Latin for "soldier" and for "thousand," and by the misinterpretation of the word "martyr," which simply means "witness." Christian apologists willfully perpetuated such "misunderstandings."

[149] Lane-Fox, op. cit., 587: "The burden of proof lies with theories of a great Christian advance. If there was such a change in this period, where can we see it? Evidence of any sort is not abundant, but evidence for the Christians' growing presence is very tenuous indeed."

[150] Ibid., 269

[151] Ibid.

[152] Eusebius, *History of the Church*, 6.43.11

[153] Lane-Fox, R. (1986), 317

[154] Ibid., 592

[155] Ibid., 588

[156] Gibbon, E. (1796), 56

[157] Kerenyi, C. (1967), 74. The second century marks the apogee of the Roman Empire. Under a succession of adoptive Emperors from Hadrian in 117 CE there began a sustained period of peace, prosperity, and relatively benign government. All of these Emperors were more or less obsessed with Greek culture and philosophy. The "philosophic way of life" became identified as the superior life. The second century was hailed in retrospect (by Philostratus in 225 CE) as "the Second Sophistic," in honor of the first, which took place in Classical Athens seven centuries earlier. During this period all manner of cults and philosophies spread widely. Gibbon, along with other historians, begins his narration of *The Decline and Fall* with the death of the philosopher/Emperor Marcus Aurelius in 180 CE.

[158] Hoffmann, R. J. (1987), 24, observes, "They reflect the common Roman distaste for what is new and unapproved."

[159] Quoted ibid., 115

[160] Quoted ibid., 29. Galen was also critical of Literalist Christianity for teaching its adherents to accept everything on faith. He was willing to tolerate them, however, for, as he lamented, "Most people are unable to follow any demonstrative argument consecutively and need parables. Christians draw faith from parables and miracles, and yet sometimes act in the same way as those who practice philosophy."

[161] Quoted ibid., 57

[162] Lucian, *Peregrinus Proteus*, 13–15

[163] Origen, *Homilies on the Exodus*, 13.3, quoted in Doran, R. (1995), 11

[164] Ibid. *See also* Stevenson, J. (1957), 209: "The spread of Christianity leads to ambition in the Church."

[165] Gibbon, E. (1796), 556, note 127. As Gibbon notes about the Christian triumph, "Prosperity was far more dangerous to their virtue than the severest trial of persecution."

[166] Ibid., 556

[167] Wallis, R. T. (1992), 122

[168] Lane-Fox, R. (1986), 258

[169] *See* Wallis, op. cit., 111ff, which reconstructs parts of Porphyry's argument from the internal evidence found in the many Christian works written to attack it. Christian authors, including Methodius of Tyre, Apollinaris of Laodicea, Eusebius of Caesaria, and Philostorgius, wrote many volumes in response, a clear testimony to the alarm created by Porphyry's book. It was banned and burned when the Empire became Christian, but was still being censored in the 440s. *See* Wallis, 126, and Lane-Fox, op. cit., 586.

[170] Cumont, F. (1903), 82

[171] *See* Ulansey, D. (1989), 4, which repeats the oft-cited claim that "If Christianity had been stopped at its birth by some mortal illness, the world would have become Mithraic."

[172] Cumont, op. cit., 83. The monuments frequently mention slaves and freedmen alongside each other, with slaves often on a higher grade of initiation than their erstwhile masters.

[173] Ibid. Cumont observes, "If this literature were not irrevocably lost to us, we should doubtless read there the story of entire Roman squadrons passing over to the faith, and of great lords converted by the slaves of their own establishments."

[174] Scarre, C. (1995), 151

[175] Marlowe, J. (1971), 262: "There is no doubt that Constantine's conversion to Christianity was a political one. His objects were, first to gain the support of Christianity in his struggle against his rivals, and later to use Christianity which seemed to be the largest and most unified organization in the Empire, as a means of exercising his authority throughout the precariously united dominions." (Prior to Constantine there had been six rival Emperors fighting each other for supreme power.) But, as Marlowe notes, "The unity of Christianity was more apparent than real. Almost as soon as it had been released from the pressures of persecution, almost as soon as its leaders were able to contemplate the prospect of power, its latent dissensions, exacerbated by personal, regional, and racial rivalries, nearly tore it asunder and, in the process, engulfed the whole Mediterranean world in controversy and bloodshed."

[176] Lane-Fox, R. (1986), 616. Lane-Fox asks, "Did the emperor's advisors suggest this clever abbreviation for Christ (Chrestos)? Like other symbols in the years after the conversion, it had a double meaning, one for Pagans, one for Christians."

[177] Ibid., 613

[178] Ibid., 621. The arch erected to celebrate his triumph can still be seen in Rome. It shows only Pagan imagery. Even Lietzmann is forced to concede that Lactantius' story about the events leading up to Constantine's victory are "contradicted by the plain facts," *see* Lietzmann, H. (1961), 142.

[179] Godwin, J. (1981), 58

[180] Doran, R. (1995), 20. The Emperor Gratian, under the influence of Bishop Ambrose, was the first to refuse the office of Pontifex Maximus. The title had been held by every Emperor since Julius Caesar and its refusal symbolically marks the end of the Roman Empire and the beginning of the "Holy" version.

[181] Campbell, J. (1964), 388

[182] Lietzmann, H. (1961), Book 3, 160. Fausta and Crispus' murders were followed by a long list of nameless persons "and many friends." This orthodox Church history records these assassinations and asks, "Is it possible for a Christian to act like this?" A paragraph later it finds to its own satisfaction, but perhaps not to ours, that "the logical inference, however reluctantly drawn, is that he was a genuinely religious person."

[183] On May 22, 337 CE Constantine was baptized, clad in the white robes of the "newly-born," and died shortly after.

[184] Constantine had to make do with being "the Great."

[185] Lane-Fox, R. (1986), 674, observes that the finding of caves of the nativity, Holy Sepulchres and even holy oak trees mentioned in the Book of Genesis "owed much to the 'discoveries' of Imperial females."

[186] Cross, F. L. (1958), 619

[187] Wilson, I. (1984), 172. As noted, below the Vatican is actually a demolished temple of Mithras.

[188] Lane-Fox, op. cit., 664. The Emperor had them all burned.

[189] Ibid., 644, 646. *See also* Lietzmann, op. cit., 160. Even Lietzmann describes Constantine's theology repeatedly as "amateurish." Lane-Fox notes that his speech at the Council of Nicaea has been criticized as "incoherent," *see* Lane-Fox, 643.

[190] Ibid., 656

[191] Wilson, op. cit., 168, records Constantine's skillful use of the stick and the carrot, which attracted the signature of men like Eusebius. Lane-Fox, op. cit., 654, accords Constantine the

honor of being "the first to master the art of holding, and corrupting, an international conference."

[192] Quoted in Wilson, op. cit., 168

[193] Cross, op. cit., 752

[194] Fidler, D. (1993), 383

[195] Doran, R. (1995), 62. Christian legend records how God himself frustrated the attempt. Fire rained down from heaven, earthquakes abounded, a great cross was seen in the sky, etc., etc. A more likely explanation is the brief duration of Julian's 20-month reign, slain by a Christian in his own ranks while campaigning against the Persians—according to one dubious legend.

[196] Quoted in Gibbon, E. (1796), 785

[197] Doran, op. cit., 14–15; an honor that Hilary, Bishop of Poitiers, accorded to the Emperor Constantius. Lüdemann, G., (1995), 209, quotes Alfred Loisy's lament: "Jesus proclaimed the kingdom of God, and it was the church that came."

[198] Ibid., 277, note 349

[199] Metzger, B. M. (1987), 183ff

[200] Ibid., 184

[201] Ibid., 201–7; see also Eusebius (1965), 61

[202] For works forged in the name of Justin Martyr, late second and early third century, see Cross, F. L. (1958), 757. Six spurious letters were written in the fourth century and attributed to Ignatius of Antioch, see 44. Eusebius admits that letters attributed to Clement have "appeared recently," see Eusebius (1965), 101.

[203] Stevenson, J. (1957), 201. Rufinus altered the Latin text in order to defend Origen's orthodoxy.

[204] Lane-Fox, R. (1986), 678. Pagan hero cults were replaced by "men with fictitious biographies."

[205] Hollroyd, S. (1994), 67

[206] Potter, D. (1994), 85, 90. Constantine cited over 100 verses of Sibylline oracles in his speech at Nicaea in 325. Potter notes that these cannot be found in Lactantius' compendious collection made in 308 and suspects that they were forged sometime between these two dates. Later both Constantine and Lactantius argued that the oracles were not forgeries—it was simply that the verses had not been previously recognized for what they were, see MacMullen, R. (1966), 151.

[207] Guthrie, W. K. C. (1952), 255. Orpheus is led to deny his former teaching on polytheism in a text later used by St. Cyril.

[208] Philo of Alexandria, Book IX, 447, "On Providence," contains Christian interpolations "worked over by a clumsy hand" according to the Loeb editor.

[209] Runia, D. T. (1993), 4–5. Eusebius, 2.17.1, gives us this "fact," to which Jerome adds the material about John. In time Philo was almost completely Christianized. Fortunately this ensured the survival of nearly all his works.

[210] Eisler, R. (1931), 72–3

[211] Gibbon, E. (1796), 529, footnote 36. Gibbon regarded the "vulgar forgery" to have taken place "between the time of Origen and that of Eusebius," i.e., between 240 and 300 CE. Eusebius quotes Josephus' affirmation that Jesus is the Christ without flinching, see Eusebius (1965), 29.

[212] Eisler, op. cit., 72–3. This fact was known to the ninth-century Byzantine scholar Photius.

[213] Lüdemann, G., (1995), 112–13. Lüdemann considers it "grotesque that 2 Thessalonians draws attention to itself as a counter-forgery!"

[214] Ibid., 114–15, assesses the evidence for attributing the forgery of 2 Thessalonians to Hippolytus. Eisler considers the Christian whitewashing of Josephus to be attributable to the schismatic bishop.

[215] Tertullian, Apology, 21.24, quoted in Brandon, S. G. F. (1969), 266

[216] Gibbon, op. cit., 550–1, treats Tertullian's account with utter contempt.

[217] Ibid.

[218] Bernstein, A. E. (1993), 275. See also Gibbon, op. cit., 550, note 105, where Gibbon also details the "successive improvements" to this fiction.

[219] The Gospel of Nicodemus, excerpted in Barnstone, W. (1984), 359ff

[220] Cross, F. L. (1958), 1,072

[221] Brandon, op. cit., 267, demonstrates that a major theme of the gospels is the turning of blame for Jesus' death from the Romans to the Jews. Wells (1975), 64, states, "Scholars do not dispute that one of the motives underlying the gospel stories is the desire to set Christianity in the right light in the eyes of the governing class and Roman officialdom generally."

[222] Eusebius (1965), xi. Eusebius arrived at the Council of Nicaea as a condemned heretic, a supporter of Arius who had recently been condemned at the Council of Antioch. He left as Constantine's official biographer, having signed the creed and condemned Arius.

[223] Doran, R. (1995), 13. To celebrate the thirtieth anniversary of Constantine's reign in 336 his sons were appointed as Caesars. Eusebius praises this as the fulfillment of the biblical prophecy "The saints of the most high God shall receive the kingdom." He naturally enough fails to mention the execution of several other sons along the way.

[224] Andrew Louth describes Eusebius' works of flattery as "tasteless," see Eusebius, op. cit., xi.

[225] Eusebius lists his five-point program at the outset of his history: a) Establish succession lines from the apostles to himself; b) Attack the followers "of Knowledge, falsely so called"; c) Detail how the "conspiracy against our savior overwhelmed the entire Jewish race"; d) Relate the campaigns of the persecutors; and e) the heroism of the martyrs. His second point testifies to the menace the Gnostics were still seen to pose to the organization of the Church. His first and last points have been shown to be bogus by numerous authorities, and his third point has legitimized centuries of persecution of the Jews. His History is still an invaluable record of the period, although not perhaps for the reasons Eusebius intended.

[226] Lane-Fox, R. (1986), 605

[227] Lietzmann, H. (1961), Book 3, 163, quoting Burckhardt's Life of Constantine. Burckhardt repeats the charge, see Burckhardt, J. (1949), 283

[228] Kingsland, W. (1937), 39. One of Eusebius' tasks was to make the history of nations fit in with his biblical chronology. Armed with this, St. Augustine is able to prove, for example, that Plato was initiated into Jewish wisdom by the prophet Jeremiah.

[229] Ibid., 39, Bunsen quoting Syncellus

[230] Gibbon, E. (1796), 577. Gibbon notes that Eusebius thus "openly violated one of the fundamental laws of history."

[231] Eusebius (1965), xi

[232] Kingsland, W. (1937), 39

[233] Eusebius' History of the Church is the only surviving account of the Church during the first three centuries. As Andrew Louth notes (Eusebius, xii), "No one ever attempted to do Eusebius' work over again. Later Greek Church historians all pick up the story where Eusebius left off."

[234] Ibid., xxi

[235] Ibid., xxii–xxiii. Eusebius' bishop lists for Jerusalem and Rome are treated here with the suspicion they deserve. "When reading Eusebius one gets an impression of the whole host of men and women who constitute the Christian Church throughout the ages. If we inquire more deeply, it seems however that the picture is much more partial than this might suggest."

[236] Ibid., xxiii

[237] MacMullen, R. (1966), 92, records how The Acts of the Pagan Martyrs was rewritten as Jewish stories of resistance before finally being pressed into service as Christian martyrologies. He writes of Eusebius' martyr stories: "Here in Eusebius can be seen, sometimes obvious, sometimes a little more deftly hidden, almost the full range of perfectly alien motifs imported into martyrologies from Pagan writings."

[238] Eusebius, op. cit., xxv. Origen established the first Christian academy in Caesaria. Here his student Pamphilius continued his master's work and was later joined by Eusebius. Despite his earlier devotion to both Pamphilius and Origen, Eusebius never mentions any of the doctrines that Origen actually taught.

[239] Ibid., 68ff

[240] Brandon, S. G. F. (1969), 268. The Literalists Eusebius and Epiphanius are our only source for what happened to the supposed "Jerusalem Church" after Jesus' "death." Brandon states: "The present writer has submitted each of these accounts to a detailed analysis and he is convinced thereby of their unhistorical character." Later he calls them "valueless." Eusebius says that the Jerusalem Christians moved safely back to Jerusalem in 130. How this could happen when it had been rebuilt as a Pagan city called Aelia Capitolina, from which Jews were excluded on pain of death, is left unexplained.

[241] Eusebius, op. cit., 31

[242] As A. N. Whitehead put it, "When the Western world accepted Christianity, Caesar conquered and the received text of Western theology was edited by his lawyers."

[243] Quoted in Pagels, E. (1979), 103

[244] Quoted in Gibbon, E. (1796), 471. Gibbon cuts short the rest of this description "which the zealous African pursues in a long variety of affected and unfeeling witticisms."

245 Lane-Fox, R. (1986), 671, 672
246 Cumont, F. (1903), 204, records the chained skeletons discovered in Mithraic sanctuaries. The intention, he suspects, was to pollute the site and render it unusable.
247 Lindsay, J. (1970), 367ff, relates the murder of Hypatia and others in Alexandria. He records in full the distressing account of one particular incident, which "may be taken as a realistic version of what happened again and again. Christians forced their way into a temple, were resisted, called up the monks, and proceeded to smash the temples and murder the Pagans."
248 Lane-Fox, op. cit., 671. At Didyma a prophet of Apollo was seized by Christians and tortured. The same thing happened at Antioch, where under torture the poor prophet eventually confessed himself a fraud. At Aigai, in Cilicia, they razed the healing shrine of Asclepius to the ground. In 389 a riot broke out between Christians and Pagans in Alexandria after an imperial decree was posted authorizing the conversion of an ancient temple of Bacchus into a Christian church. The Pagans fled to the temple of Serapis, which was taken with considerable violence and then demolished. See Marlowe, J. (1971), 283–5.
249 Quoted in MacMullen, R. (1966), 136
250 Lane-Fox, op. cit., 326. Paganism was reclassified as a demonic system.
251 Wallis, R. T. (1992), 50: "The transformation of the gods into demons had significant psychological consequences. Life became a battleground in which men must fight for God against the enemy... Christianity filled the world with evil spirits." As this author notes, this view will pave the way for Augustine's depressing view of humanity as "the plaything of demons" and "the Devil's fruit tree, his own property, from which he may pick his fruit."
252 Firmicus Maternus, *The Error of Pagan Religions*, 29.1–2, quoted in Doran, R. (1995), 18
253 Quoted ibid., 20. Symmachus's appeal was answered by Bishop Ambrose: "What you do not know, we know by God's voice; what you seek by guesses, we have found from the very wisdom and truth of God. Your ways do not agree with ours."
254 Libanius, *Oration*, 33.8–9, quoted ibid., 21–2
255 Quoted in MacMullen, op. cit., 151
256 Doran, op. cit., 22: "Let no one go around the temples, let no one honor the shrines." Paganism did not disappear immediately, of course. Up until 691 wine-makers in Greece still wore Mystery masks and cried out, "Dionysus!" as they trod the grapes, but this was eventually forbidden, see Kerenyi, C. (1976), 67. At the end of the seventh century the third Ecumenical Council of Constantinople was still considering how to suppress those practicing the Mysteries of Dionysus in the Balkans, see Stoyanov, Y. (1994), 117. As late as the tenth century Emperor Leo VI had to lead a crusade against Pagans still practicing their faith in the Peloponnesus, see Stoyanov, 118. Throughout the Middle Ages hundreds of thousands of women were persecuted as witches for their Pagan practices. Astrology represents the clearest survival of the Pagan gods throughout the history of the West.
257 Marlowe, J. (1971), 283–5
258 Quoted in Eisler, R. (1931), 594
259 Eunapius, *Lives of the Sophists*, quoted in Turcan, R. (1992), 126
260 Marlowe, op. cit., 288
261 See ibid., 263. In 400 CE a body of priests and monks known as the *parabolani* was formed in Alexandria. They acted as a bodyguard and corps of bully-boys generally for successive patriarchs of Alexandria in their persecutions of Jews, Pagans, and heretics. See Marlowe, J. (1971), 263. In 412, when Cyril succeeded to the Patriarch, one of his first acts was to incite the monks to pillage and expel from the city the wealthy Jewish community some 40,000 strong.
262 Lieu, S. N. C. (1985), 112. In the mind of Theodosius, Christianity and citizenship were coterminous and anyone who denied Christ automatically made himself an outlaw of Roman society. As Campbell observes, "In the reign of Constantine Christianity was accorded equal status with the Pagan religion of the Empire, but half a century later in the reign of Theodosius (379–395) it was declared to be the only religion allowed, and with that the period that has since been known as the Dark Ages was inaugurated by imperial decree." See Campbell, J. (1964), 389.
263 Campbell, op. cit., 393
264 Lieu, op. cit., 39
265 Ibid., 146, and see Lane-Fox, R. (1986), 602
266 Wallis, R. T. (1992), 91–2. Synesius of Cyrene (365–414?) makes clear his Gnostic views, writing of the divine inspiration of scripture, "For one spirit inspired the prophet and the apostle, and after the fine ancient painters, he drew in outline and then subsequently portrayed in exact detail, the features of the gnosis." He studied Neoplatonism with Hypatia in Alexandria, then later married a Christian and finally became a bishop in 410.

[267] Wallis, 86–7, describes Synesius as "a fourth-century Pagan pluralist" with the "conviction that the only true religion is philosophical religion, and that the stories and practices of non-philosophical religion are, at the best, no more than helpful popular expressions of philosophic truth for non-philosophers."

[268] Ibid., 85: "an expression of his intention to tell a Christian story to the congregation and reserve the right to understand the nature of things according to Platonic dogma"

[269] Ibid., 93. Bregman writes of Synesius' Easter sermon, "The language, metaphor, and sense here are closer to the Orphic, Platonic, and Hermetic than to the Christian." He virtually "transforms the Easter ceremony into a NeoPlatonically or Hermetically interpreted mystery initiation."

[270] Pagels, E. (1988), 62

[271] Quoted in Wilson, I. (1984), 172

[272] Quoted in Pagels, E. (1979), 93. But because heretical circles continued to copy and hide this text, the second Nicene Council, 300 years later, had to repeat the judgment.

[273] Quoted in MacMullen, R. (1966), 210. Heretics are the subject of over 100 new laws in the Theodosian Code.

[274] Robinson, J. M. (1978), 20, quoting Cyril as evidence of the political situation in Egypt, which led to the burying of the Nag Hammadi library.

[275] Pagels, E. (1988), 124. Augustine "wrote the only full justification in the history of the early Church of the right of the state to suppress non-Catholics." His enemies were the Donatist Christians who denounced the "unholy alliance" between Catholic Christians and the Roman state. They vainly argued that the Church should employ spiritual sanctions, not force.

[276] Quoted in Lane-Fox, R. (1986), 265

[277] Gnosticism continued to survive throughout the Christian period, always on the fringes of society and often vigorously persecuted. Gnostic gospels continued to be copied and circulated, and were still being banned and burned in the eighth century, see Hollroyd, S. (1994), 68. Gnostic followers of Paul called the Paulicians flourished despite persistent persecution from the Orthodox Church until the end of the tenth century, see Kingsland, W. (1937), 35. The fact that Paulician came to be used as a generic name for Gnosticism suggests that the tradition of Paul's secret teachings was kept alive in these sects. In 1211 CE the Bogomils were accused of performing "unholy mysteries like the Hellenic pagan rites" in Anatolia and Constantinople, see Stoyanov, Y. (1994), 184. The Gnosticism of the Cathars, who were in contact with the Bogomils in the East, became the dominant form of Christianity in areas of southern France during the twelfth century. The infamous Inquisition was set up specifically to eradicate the heresy. The Mandaeans, a Gnostic baptist sect, still survive in the marshes of southern Iraq to this day, see Lieu, S. N. C. (1985), 30, and Barnstone, W. (1984), 123.

[278] Matthew 20 v 16

[279] As Lane-Fox notes, "Intolerance had never been rooted in the long history of Pagan philosophy and religious thought. After Constantine, many Pagans could still extend to the new worship a tolerance which its exclusivity refused to extend to them." See Lane-Fox, R. (1986), 673. The usually apologetic Angus observes, "Simultaneously with its political triumph, it turned persecutor against Pagan, Jew, and heretic. Catholic Christianity tried to exterminate heresy not merely by argument but by sword and flame." He records the view of another scholar: "There has never existed a community which displayed more clearly the intolerance that would necessarily follow its triumph." See Angus, S. (1925), 282.

[280] Doran, R. (1995), 13. In addition, Constantine had to legislate twice against Pagans falsely claiming to be clerics in order to avoid civic duties, see Lane-Fox, op. cit., 667.

[281] Quoted in Fidler, D. (1993), 180. St Augustine likewise stated, "I would not believe the Gospel if the authority of the Catholic church did not compel me," Fidler, 320.

[282] Cicero (1972), 159

[283] Metzger, B. M. (1987), 233. This was the view of Philaster, the Bishop of Brescia (died c. 397 CE). Philaster also composed a treatise to attack 28 Jewish heresies and no less than 128 Christian heresies, see Potter, D. (1994), 105. W. Hyde, *Paganism to Christianity in the Roman Empire*, 1946, presents a depressing picture of the anti-intellectual nature of the early Church, the destruction of books and temples, the closing of schools, and the killing of adherents of other faiths.

[284] The classical scholar Frank has reconstructed the main stages of Greek astronomy, in an apparently necessary order: development of the understanding of space, of solid geometry and perspective by Anaxagoras and Democritus, discovery of the sphericity of the Earth and the "movements of the planets in the form of geometrically perfect orbits" by the Pythagoreans

of Archytas' circle, first mathematical explanation of the movement of the planets by Eudoxus, discovery of the rotation of the Earth on its axis, and finally the "Copernican view of the world" in the system of Philolaus. *See* Burkert, W. (1972), 302. The earliest mention of a spherical Earth in extant literature is in Plato's *Phaedo*, 110b, *see* Guthrie, W. K. C. (1962), 295, but Bion of Abdera, the follower of Democritus, was acquainted in 400 BCE with the mathematical consequences of the spherical shape of the Earth, and in 430 Hippocrates of Chios had projected the celestial circles onto the Earth, obviously presupposing its sphericity, *see* Burkert, 305. All of these advances took place in the Classical period. The Hellenistic period saw equally momentous discoveries. Eratosthenes calculated the obliquity of the ecliptic and the diameter of the Earth with an error of less than 1 percent, *see* Marlowe, J. (1971), 71. Hipparchus, his successor at the Alexandrian library, determined the precession of the equinoxes, the size of the sun and the plane of its apogee, the mean motion of the moon, its nadir, its apogee and the inclination of its orbit and also calculated lunar eclipses, *see* Marlowe, 75. Then suddenly with the triumph of Christianity St. Augustine declared, on the basis of his own limited knowledge of Manichaean astrology, that the Earth was flat. As unchallengeable Christian dogma this belief persisted throughout the Dark Ages. As Draper observes, "No one did more than this Father to bring science and religion into antagonism," *see* Cranston, S. (1977), 149.

CHAPTER 12: THE GREATEST STORY EVER TOLD

[1] Quoted in Inge, W. R. (1899), 87

[2] Quoted in Happold, F. C. (1963), 115. With apologies to Toynbee we have changed the "Minoan" god Zagreus to Dionysus. Although there is possibly an archaic Cretan background for the name Zagreus, he was known from Classical times as the Orphic Dionysus. We have also omitted "for a Shi'i World as Husayn."

[3] Sallustius (1926), 1

[4] *The Gospel of Thomas*, 108, quoted in Robinson, J. M. (1978), 137

Bibliography

Allegro, J., *The Dead Sea Scrolls*, Penguin, 1956

Anderson, G., *The Second Sophistic*, Routledge, 1993

——, *Sage, Saint and Sophist*, Routledge, 1994

Angus, S., *Mystery Religions*, Dover, 1925

Apollonius of Rhodes, *The Voyage of Argo*, Penguin Classics, 1959

Aristophanes, *The Frogs*, Penguin Classics, 1964

Aristotle, *Politics*, Loeb Classical Library, 1935

Athanaissakis, A. P., *The Homeric Hymns*, Johns Hopkins University Press, 1976

Austin, R. G., *Aeneidos Liber Sextus*, Clarendon Press, 1977

Baigent and Leigh, *The Dead Sea Scrolls Deception*, Jonathan Cape, 1991

Balsdon, J. P. V. D., *Romans and Aliens*, Duckworth and Co., 1979

Barnstone, W., *The Other Bible*, HarperCollins, 1984

Beard and North, *Pagan Priests*, Duckworth Press, 1990

Benac and Oto, *Bogomil Sculpture*, Braun et Cie, 1975

Bernal, M., *Black Athena*, Free Association Books, 1987

Bernstein, A. E., *The Formation of Hell*, UCL Press, 1993

Birks and Gilbert, *The Treasure of Montségur*, Crucible, 1987

Boardman, Griffin and Murray, *The Oxford History of the Classical World*, Oxford University Press, 1986

Boethius, *The Consolation of Philosophy*, Penguin Classics, 1969

Bowman, J. S., *Treasures of Ancient Greece*, Crescent Books, 1986

Brandon, S. G. F., *Religion in Ancient History*, George Allen and Unwin, 1969

Burckhardt, J., *The Life of Constantine*, Deutsche Verlags-anstalt, 1929

——, *The Age of Constantine the Great*, Dorset Press, 1949

Burkert, W., *Lore and Science in Ancient Pythagoreanism*, Harvard University Press, 1972

——, *Greek Religion: Archaic and Classical*, Blackwell Publishers, 1985

——, *Ancient Mystery Cults*, Harvard University Press, 1987

——, *The Orientalizing Revolution*, Harvard University Press, 1992

Cahn, S. M., *Classics of Western Philosophy*, Hackett Publishing Company, 1977

Campbell, J., *The Hero with a Thousand Faces*, Paladin, 1949

——, *Papers from the Eranos Yearbooks*, Routledge & Kegan Paul, 1955

——, *Occidental Mythology*, Arkana, 1964

——, *An Open Life*, Larson Publications, 1988

Carpenter and Faraone, *Masks of Dionysus*, Cornell University Press, 1993

Cartledge, P., *The Greeks: A Portrait of Self and Others*, Oxford University Press, 1993

Cherniss, H., *Selected Papers*, E. J. Brill, 1977

Churton, T., *The Gnostics*, Weidenfeld and Nicolson, 1987

Cicero, *On the Good Life*, Penguin Classics, 1971

——, "The Dream of Scipio" in *On the Good Life*, Penguin Classics, 1971

——, *The Nature of the Gods*, Penguin Classics, 1972

——, *De Legibus*, Bristol Classical Press, 1987

Clark, R. J., *Catabasis Vergil and the Wisdom-Tradition*, B. R. Grüner Publishing Company, 1979

Clement of Alexandria, *Clement of Alexandria*, Loeb Editions no. 92, 1919

Copenhaver, B. P., *Hermetica*, Cambridge University Press, 1992

Cornford, F. M., *The Unwritten Philosophy*, Cambridge University Press, 1950

Cowell, F. R., *Cicero and the Roman Republic*, Pelican Books, 1948

Cranston, S., *Reincarnation: Phoenix Fire Mysteries*, Theosophical University Press, 1977

Cross, F. L., *The Oxford Dictionary of the Christian Church*, Oxford University Press, 1958

Cumont, F., *The Mysteries of Mithras*, Dover Books, 1903

——, *After Life in Roman Paganism*, Yale University Press, 1922

D'Alviella, G., *The Mysteries of Eleusis*, The Aquarian Press, 1981

De Vogel, C. J., *Pythagoras and Early Pythagoreanism*, Royal Van Corcum, 1966

Diodorus of Sicily, *Books 1–2*, Loeb Classical Library no. 279, 1933

Dodds, E. R., *The Greeks and the Irrational*, University of California Press, 1951

Doran, R., *Birth of a Worldview*, Westview Press, 1995

Dunlap, S. F., *The Mysteries of Adoni*, Williams and Norgate, 1866

Ehrenberg, V., *From Solon to Socrates*, Methuen and Co., 1968

Eisler, R., *Orpheus the Fisher*, Kessinger Publishing, 1920

——, *The Messiah Jesus and John the Baptist*, The Dial Press, 1931

Eliade, M., *The Myth of the Eternal Return*, Arkana, 1954

——, *Essential Sacred Writings Around the World*, HarperSanFrancisco, 1967

Ellis, N., *Awakening Osiris*, Phanes Press, 1988

Epictetus, *The Teachings of Epictetus*, Walter Scott Library, n.d.

Erskine, A., *The Hellenistic Stoa: Political Thought and Action*, Cornell University Press, 1990

Euripides, *The Bacchae*, Penguin Classics, 1954

Eusebius, *History of the Church*, Penguin Classics, 1965

Farrington, B., *Greek Science*, Pelican Books, 1944

Faulkner, R. O., *The Book of the Dead*, British Museum Press, 1972

Feeney, D. C., *The Gods in Epic*, Clarendon Press, 1991

Fidler, D., *Jesus Christ, Sun of God*, Quest Books, 1993

Flacelière, R., *Greek Oracles*, Elek Books, 1965

Frank, T., *Vergil: A Biography*, Henry Holt, 1922

Frazer, J., *The Golden Bough*, Wordsworth Reference Books, 1922

Freke and Gandy, *The Complete Guide to World Mysticism*, Piatkus Books, 1997

——, *The Hermetica*, Piatkus Books, 1997

——, *Wisdom of the Pagan Philosophers*, Journey Editions, 1998

Freke, T., *The Illustrated Book of World Scripture*, Thorsons, 1997

Friedman, R. E., *Who Wrote the Bible?*, Jonathan Cape, 1988

Garin, E., *Astrology in the Renaissance*, Routledge & Kegan Paul, 1976

Gaus, A., *The Unvarnished New Testament*, Phanes Press, 1991

Gibbon, E., *The Decline and Fall of the Roman Empire*, Penguin Classics, 1796

Godwin, J., *Mystery Religions in the Ancient World*, Thames & Hudson, 1981

Grant, R. M., *Gnosticism and Early Christianity*, Columbia University Press, 1959

Graves, R., *Greek Myths*, Pelican Books, 1955

——, *The White Goddess*, Faber & Faber, 1961

Gregory, J., *The Neoplatonists*, Kylie Cathie, 1987

Grüber and Kersten, *The Original Jesus*, Element Books, 1985

Guthrie, K. S., *The Pythagorean Sourcebook*, Phanes Press, 1987

Guthrie, W. K. C., *Orpheus and Greek Religion*, Princeton University Press, 1952

——, *History of Greek Philosophy*, Cambridge University Press, 1962

Hall, E., *Inventing the Barbarian*, Clarendon Press, 1989

Hall, M. P., *Mystics and Mysteries in Alexandria*, Philosophical Research Society, 1981

——, *The Adepts in the Classical Tradition*, Philosophical Research Society, 1981

Happold, F. C., *Mysticism*, Penguin Books, 1963

Harrington, D. J., *Wisdom Texts from Qumran*, Routledge, 1996

Harrison, J., *Prologemena to the Study of Greek Religion*, Princeton University Press, 1922

——, *Themis*, Merlin Press, 1963

Heidenreich, A., *The Catacombs*, Christian Community Press, 1931

Hengel, M., *Jews, Greeks, and Barbarians*, SCM Press, 1980

Herodotus, *The Histories*, Penguin Classics, 1954

Hesiod, *Theogony and Works and Days*, World's Classics, 1988

Highbarger, E. L., *The Gate of Dreams*, Johns Hopkins University Press, 1940

Hoffmann, R. J., *Celsus on the True Doctrine*, Oxford University Press, 1987

Hollroyd, S., *Gnosticism*, Element Books, 1994

Horace, *The Satires of Horace and Perseus*, Penguin Classics, 1973

Inge, W. R., *Christian Mysticism*, Methuen, 1899

Jaroslav, P., *The Tanakh*, The Jewish Publication Company, 1985

Jay, P., *The Greek Anthology*, Penguin Classics, 1973

Josephus, *The Life and Contra Apion*, Harvard University Press, 1926

——, *The Jewish War*, Penguin Classics, 1959

Jung, C., *Psychology and Alchemy*, Routledge, 1953

——, *Mysterium Coniunctionis*, Routledge & Kegan Paul, 1957

——, *Aion*, Routledge, 1959

Kahn, C. H., *The Art and Thought of Heraclitus*, Cambridge University Press, 1979

Kennedy, H. A. A., *St. Paul and the Mystery Religions*, Hodder & Stoughton, 1969

Kerenyi, C., *Heroes of the Greeks*, Thames & Hudson, 1959

——, *Eleusis*, Bollingen Press, 1967

——, *Dionysos*, Bollingen Press, 1976

King, C. W., *Gnostics and their Remains*, David Nutt, 1887

Kingsland, W., *The Gnosis*, Phanes Press, 1937

Kingsley, P., *Ancient Philosophy, Mystery, and Magic*, Oxford University Press, 1995

Kirk and Raven, *The Presocratic Philosophers*, Cambridge University Press, 1957

Lamy, L., *Egyptian Mysteries*, Thames & Hudson, 1981

Lane, E. N., *Cybele, Attis, and Related Cults*, E. J. Brill, 1996

Lane-Fox, R., *Pagans and Christians*, Penguin Books, 1986

Lemprière, J., *A Classical Dictionary*, Routledge Kegan Paul, 1949

Levene, D. S., *Religion in Livy*, E. J. Brill, 1993

Lietzmann, H., *The History of the Early Church*, 4 vols., Lutterworth Press, 1961

Lieu, S. N. C., *Manichaeism*, Manchester University Press, 1985

Lindsay, J., *Origins of Alchemy in Greco Roman Egypt*, Frederick Müller, 1970

Linforth, I. M., *The Arts of Orpheus*, University of California Press, 1941

Livy, *The War with Hannibal*, Penguin Classics, 1965

——, *Rome and the Mediterranean*, Penguin Classics, 1976

Louth, A., *Early Christian Writings*, Penguin Classics, 1968

Lucian, *Satirical Sketches*, Indiana University Press, 1961

Lucius Apuleius, *The Golden Ass*, Penguin Classics, 1950

Lucretius, *The Nature of the Universe*, Penguin Classics, 1951

Lüdemann, G., *Heretics*, SCM Press, 1995

Macchioro, V. D., *From Orpheus to Paul*, Constable and Company, 1930

Mack, B. L., *The Lost Gospel*, Element Books, 1993

MacMullen, R., *Enemies of the Roman Order*, Oxford University Press, 1966

Magnien, V., *Les Mystères d'Eleusus*, Payot, 1938

Marcus Aurelius, *Meditations*, New University Library, n.d.

Marlowe, J., *The Golden Age of Alexandria*, Victor Gollancz, 1971

Martin, L. H., *The Hellenistic Religions*, Oxford University Press, 1987

Matthews, C., *Sophia: Goddess of Wisdom*, The Aquarian Press, 1992

Mayor, Fowler, and Conway, *Virgil's Messianic Ecologue*, John Murray Publishers, 1907

McEvedy, C., *The Penguin Atlas of Ancient History*, Penguin Books, 1967

Mead, G. R. S., *Fragments of a Faith Forgotten*, Theosophical Publishing Society, 2nd edition, 1906

——, *Echoes of the Gnosis: The Mysteries of Mithra*, Vol. 5, The Theosophical Society, 1907

——, *Echoes of the Gnosis: The Chaldaean Oracles*, Vol. 8, The Theosophical Society, 1908

Mendels, D., *Rise and Fall of Jewish Nationalism*, Doubleday, 1992

Metzger, B. M., *The Canon of the New Testament*, Oxford University Press, 1987

Meyer, M. W., *The Ancient Mysteries Sourcebook*, HarperCollins, 1987

Momigliano, A., *Alien Wisdom*, Cambridge University Press, 1971

Murray, M. A., *Egyptian Religious Poetry*, John Murray, 1949

Mylonas, G. E., *Eleusis and the Eleusinian Mysteries*, Princeton University Press, 1961

Ogilvie, R. M., *Commentary on Livy: Books 1–5*, Clarendon Press, 1965

Otto, W. F., *Dionysos Myth and Cult*, Spring Publications, 1965

Ouvaroff, M., *Essay on the Eleusinian Mysteries*, Rodwell and Martin, 1817

Ovid, *Heroides and Arts of Love*, G. Bell and Sons, 1919

——, *Metamorphoses*, Penguin Classics, 1955

Owen-Lee, M., *Virgil As Orpheus*, State University of New York Press, 1996

Pagels, E., *The Gnostic Paul*, Trinity Press International, 1975

——, *The Gnostic Gospels*, Penguin Books, 1979

——, *Adam, Eve, and the Serpent*, Random House, 1988

Palmer, M., *Living Christianity*, Element Books, 1993

Perkins, P., *Gnosticism and the New Testament*, Fortress Press, 1993

Philip, J. A., *Pythagoras and Early Pythagoreanism*, University of Toronto Press, 1966

Philo of Alexandria, "On the Contemplative Life" in *Book IX*, Loeb Classical Library no. 363, 1941

Pindar, *The Odes*, Penguin Classics, 1969

Plato, *Collected Dialogues*, Princeton University Press, 1961

——, *Timaeus and Critias*, Penguin Classics, 1965

——, *Phaedrus and Letters vii and viii*, Penguin Classics, 1973

Plutarch, *The Fall of the Roman Republic*, Penguin Classics, 1958

——, *The Rise and Fall of Athens*, Penguin Classics, 1960

——, *Makers of Rome*, Penguin Classics, 1965

——, *The Moral Essays*, Penguin Classics, 1971

——, *De Iside et Osiride*, Oxford University Press, 1993

Pollitt, J. J., *Art and Experience in Classical Greece*, Cambridge University Press, 1972

Polybius, *The Rise of the Roman Empire*, Penguin Classics, 1979

Porphyry, *On the Cave of the Nymphs*, Phanes Press, 1991

Potter, D., *Prophets and Emperors*, Harvard University Press, 1994

Powell, A., *Poetry & Propaganda in the Age of Augustus*, Bristol Classical Press, 1992

Price, S. R. F., *Rituals and Power*, Cambridge University Press, 1984

Proclus, *The Elements of Theology*, Oxford University Press, 1963

Reedy, J., *The Platonic Doctrines of Albinus*, Phanes Press, 1991

Robinson, J. M., *The Nag Hammadi Library*, HarperCollins, 1978

Runia, D. T., *Philo in Early Christian Literature*, Fortress Press, 1993

Sallustius, *Concerning the Gods and the Universe*, Cambridge University Press, 1926

Scarre, C., *Chronicle of the Roman Emperors*, Thames & Hudson, 1995

Scullard, H. H., *From the Gracchi to Nero*, Methuen and Co., 1959

Segal, R. A., *The Gnostic Jung*, Routledge, 1992

Seneca, *Letters from a Stoic*, Penguin Classics, 1969

Shanks, H., *Understanding the Dead Sea Scrolls*, SPCK, 1992

Sophocles, *The Theban Plays*, Penguin Classics, 1947

St. Augustine, *Confessions, City of God, Christian Doctrine*, William Benton, 1952

Stanton, G., *Gospel Truth?*, HarperCollins, 1995

Stevenson, J., *A New Eusebius*, SPCK, 1957

——, *The Catacombs*, Thames & Hudson, 1978

Stoyanov, Y., *The Hidden Tradition in Europe*, Penguin Arkana, 1994

Suetonius, *The Twelve Caesars*, Penguin Classics, 1957

Syme, R., *The Roman Revolution*, Oxford University Press, 1948

Tacitus, *The Annals of Imperial Rome*, Penguin Classics, 1956

——, *The Histories*, Penguin Classics, 1968

Taylor, L. R., *The Divinity of the Roman Emperor*, American Philological Association, 1931

Taylor, T., *The Eleusinian and Bacchic Mysteries*, J. W. Bouton, 1891

Taylour, L. W., *The Mycenaeans*, Thames & Hudson, 1964

Temple, R. K. G., *Conversations with Eternity*, Rider, 1984

Thompson and Griffith, *The Leyden Papyrus*, Dover Books, 1974

Thucydides, *The Peloponnesian War*, Penguin Classics, 1954

Turcan, R., *Cults of the Roman Empire*, Blackwell Publishers, 1992

Ulansey, D., *Origin of the Mithraic Mysteries*, Oxford University Press, 1989

Usher, S., *The Historians of Greece and Rome*, Bristol Classical Press, 1969

Virgil, *The Pastoral Poems*, Penguin Classics, 1949

——, *The Aeneid*, Penguin Classics, 1956

——, *Georgics*, Penguin Classics, 1982

Vitruvius, *De Architectura*, Harvard Heinemann, 1931

Vonge, C. D., *The Works of Philo*, Hendrickson Publishers, 1993

Walbank, F. W., *The Hellenistic World*, Fontana Press, 1981

Walker and Bierrier, *Ancient Faces*, British Museum Press, 1997

Walker, D. P., *The Ancient Theology*, Duckworth, 1972

Wallace-Hadrill, A., *Augustan Rome*, Bristol Classical Press, 1993

Wallis Budge, E. A., *Egyptian Magic*, Arkana, 1899

——, *Egyptian Religion*, Arkana, 1899

Wallis, R. T., *Neoplatonism and Gnosticism*, State University of New York Press, 1992

Wells, G. A., *Did Jesus Exist?*, Pemberton Publishing Company, 1975

Willoughby, H. R., *Pagan Regeneration*, University of Chicago Press, 1929

Wilson, I., *Jesus: The Evidence*, Weidenfeld and Nicolson, 1984

Wright, M. R., *The Presocratics*, Bristol Classical Press, 1985

Zanker, P., *Power of Images in the Age of Augustus*, Michigan University Press, 1988

WEBSITES

The Internet contains a vast amount of information on all the subjects covered in *The Jesus Mysteries*. These are a few of the most useful sites:

CLASSICS

http://www.perseus.tufts.edu/Texts/chunk_TOC.html
English translations of hundreds of classical texts from Aeschines and Aeschylus to Xenophon.
http://www.usask.ca/classics/Resources/biblios.html#tocsin
Classics resources on the Internet. Numerous sites listed containing bibliographical, study, and teaching aids for the classics.

GNOSIS

http://www.webcom.com/~gnosis/search_form.html
The Gnosis Archive with Archive Index Search. You may search the entire contents of the huge Gnosis Archive for keywords or subjects of interest. All Nag Hammadi and many other Gnostic texts are available.

THE CHURCH FATHERS

http://www.knight.org/advent/fathers/
http://ccel.wheaton.edu/fathers
English translations of the Nicene and Post-Nicene fathers drawn from the 38-volume Schaff edition, made available to the Internet through the efforts of the Electronic Bible Society. Hundreds of texts from Alexander of Alexandria *Epistles on the Arian Heresy and the Deposition of Arius* to Zephyrinus (Pope) *First Epistle and Second Epistle*.
http://www.webcom.com/~gnosis/library/polem.htm
The Gnostic Society Library has a large collection of the Patristic polemical works against the Gnostics. The principal Patristic texts of interest to Gnostic studies are listed, including the writings of Augustine against the Manichaeans.

For further information about lectures and seminars by Timothy Freke and Peter Gandy contact:
   http://www.jesusmysteries.demon.co.uk
   P.O. Box 2638, Gastenbury, BA6 9WF, UK

Who's Who

Alexander the Great 355–323 BCE. Macedonian general and conqueror of Persia, India, and Egypt. Instigator of the Hellenistic age.

Ambrose 339–397 CE. Roman lawyer and Literalist Christian appointed Bishop of Milan *c.* 370.

Ammonius Saccus *fl. c.* 200 CE. Pagan philosopher of Alexandria. Teacher of Origen *(qv)* and Plotinus *(qv)*. Little is known about him, and he wrote no books.

Anaxagoras 503–428 BCE. Greek philosopher from Asia Minor who moved to Athens and became tutor and advisor of its leading politician Pericles.

Anthony 251–356 CE. Ascetic recluse of Egypt who organized the first community of Christian monks *c.* 305. Traditionally regarded as an orthodox Christian, he was an ardent Pythagorean and almost certainly a Gnostic.

Apollonius of Tyana First-century Pythagorean philosopher and miracle-worker. Traveled the Roman Empire confronting tyrants, working miracles, and raising the dead. His official biography was written *c.* 225 CE.

Apuleius 125–190 CE. Pagan author and initiate. Born in Africa and studied philosophy in Carthage, Athens, and Rome. Famous for *The Golden Ass*, an allegorical tale of his initiation into the Mysteries.

Aristophanes 445–385 BCE. Greek initiate of the Mysteries and writer of comedies. He was indicted for revealing too much of the Mystery school doctrines in his plays.

Arnobius *fl.* 290 CE. Converted to Christianity after being steeped in Hermetic and Neoplatonic philosophy. His works stress the compatibility of Christianity with Pagan philosophy. His pupil was Lactantius *(qv)*.

Augustine 354–430 CE. Follower of the Manichaean Gnostics for eight years. In 386 CE he became a Neoplatonist and four years later a Literalist Christian. In 395 he was appointed the Bishop of Hippo in Africa.

Augustus 63 BCE–14 CE. Founder of the Roman Empire, Emperor from 27 BCE until his death.

Barnabas *c.* 100 CE. *The Epistle of Barnabas* was one of the best known texts of the early Church, attributed to the co-worker of Paul *(qv)*. Because of its peculiar mix of Pagan and Christian ideas it was barred from the New Testament.

Basilides *c.* 117 CE. Gnostic teacher of Alexandria. Wrote a gospel and a commentary on it in 24 books, and a collection of psalms and odes. All are lost. Accounts of his teaching in Irenaeus *(qv)*, Clement *(qv)*, and Hippolytus *(qv)* do not agree.

Carpocrates *c.* 110 CE. Alexandrian Platonist who founded a sect of Gnostic Christians using *The Secret Gospel of Mark* as its initiatory document.

Celsus Wrote *The True Doctrine* in *c.* 170 CE, a critique of emerging Christianity, of which 70 percent survives in quotation in the work of Origen *(qv)*.

Cicero 106–43 BCE. Roman lawyer and politician of the late Republic. Initiated at Eleusis in 80 BCE, he was instrumental in making Greek philosophy and education fashionable in Rome.

Claudius Roman Emperor 41–54 CE.

Clement of Alexandria 150–215 CE. Born in Athens, became the pupil of Pantaenus of Alexandria in 180 and head of the Catechetical school in 190. Traditionally regarded as a Literalist Christian and even beatified by the Roman Church, his works actually have far more in common with Gnosticism.

Clement of Rome Said by Eusebius *(qv)* to have been the fourth Bishop of Rome *c.* 90 CE. Numerous letters attributed to Clement were forged in the fourth and fifth centuries.

Constantine 272–337 CE. Roman Emperor from 307 until his death. First Emperor to become a Christian.

Diagoras *fl.* 416 BCE. Athenian philosopher famous for his satirical condemnation of superstitious religion.

Dio Cassius *fl.* 225 CE. Born in Asia Minor. Roman historian.

Diodorus 80–20 BCE. Greek historian of Sicily. Writer of a *Universal History* in 40 volumes.

Diogenes 420–324 BCE. Follower of Antisthenes the disciple of Socrates *(qv)*. Founder of the Cynic school of philosophy.

Empedocles 490–430 BCE. Disciple of Pythagoras *(qv)*, priest, and miracle-worker. Wrote an initiatory poem in which he proclaimed himself an "immortal god."

Epictetus 50–130 CE. A crippled Phrygian slave brought up in the household of Nero *(qv)*. When freed he became the first century's greatest exponent of Cynic philosophy. Driven out of Rome by Domitian in 90 CE along with all other philosophers.

Epiphanius 315–403 CE. Literalist Christian who became Bishop of Salamis in Greece although he was born in Judea. His most important work is the *Medicine Chest against all Heresies*. Joined forces with Jerome *(qv)* in Rome to attack Origen *(qv)*.

Eratosthenes 275–194 BCE. Keeper of the Alexandrian library, writer on mathematics, geography, philosophy, and astronomy.

Euripides 484–406 BCE. Athenian tragedian and author of *The Bacchae*.

Eusebius 260–340 CE. Trained at the school in Caesaria established by Origen *(qv)*. Became Bishop of Caesaria in 311. Arrived at the Council of Nicaea in 325 a convicted Arian heretic, left it as the official historian and biographer of Constantine *(qv)*. Known as "the father of Church history," his work is profoundly unreliable and is widely held to be little more than propaganda for Literalist Christianity.

Firmicus Maternus died *c.* 360 CE. Wrote a compendium of astrology while still a Pagan, converted to Literalist Christianity late in life, and appealed to the Roman Emperors to destroy Pagan idols by force.

Heliodorus *fl. c.* 230 CE. Priest of Helios in Syria and author of *An Ethiopian Romance*, which encoded teachings on the Mysteries.

Heraclitus *fl. c.* 500 BCE. Mystic philosopher of Ephesus in Asia Minor who wrote about the Word of God (*Logos*). Diogenes Laertius records a saying of the third-century BCE philosopher Cleanthes, that his cryptic works can only be understood by an initiate of the Mysteries.

Hermas *The Shepherd of Hermas* was one of the most widely known early Christian texts, said to have been written *c.* 90 CE in Italy. It is a curious mixture of Hermetic, Sibylline, and Jewish/Christian apocalypse that contains no definite quotation from either of the Testaments. Not surprisingly it never made it into the New Testament.

Hermes Trismegistus Patron deity of the Hermetic literature written in Egypt in the second and third centuries CE. A fusion of the Greek "Guide of Souls" Hermes and the Egyptian god Thoth, the legendary sage and inventor of writing.

Herodotus 484–430 BCE. Greek historian known as "the father of history." He traveled in Egypt and recorded that the Mysteries of Dionysus at Eleusis were modeled on those of Osiris in Egypt.

Hesiod Greek poet of the late eighth century BCE. His *Theogeny* describes the origin of the gods of Greek mythology.

Hippocrates 460–360 BCE. Doctor and medical writer from the Greek island of Cos. Originator of the Hippocratic oath taken by all doctors at graduation.

Hippolytus 170–236 CE. Literalist Christian and heresy-hunter who called the Gnostic Bishop of Rome Callistus a heretic and set himself up as an anti-Pope. His

Refutation of All Heresies, published *c.* 210, seeks to prove that all heresies derive from Greek schools of philosophy.

Homer Greek poet of the eighth century BCE, author of *The Odyssey* and *The Iliad*.

Iamblichus 250–325 CE. Syrian philosopher who became a student of Porphyry *(qv)*. Wrote 10 volumes on Pythagorean philosophy and *The Life of Pythagoras*.

Ignatius of Antioch, said to have been active *c.*120 CE. Supposedly an early Literalist Christian, but interpolations of his letters in later centuries make it almost impossible to know what is or isn't genuine.

Irenaeus 130–202 CE. Literalist Christian and vehement opponent of Gnosticism. Born in Asia Minor, became Bishop of Lyons in Gaul in 178. Author of the massive work *Against Heresies*, a polemic against Gnosticism. Known to have forged a "Christian" work attributed to the Jewish historian Josephus *(qv)*, and probably many other pro-Literalist treatises and letters.

Jerome 342–420 CE. Biblical scholar and translator of the Bible into Latin. A Literalist Christian who attacked Origen's *(qv)* doctrines of reincarnation and the ultimate salvation of all.

Josephus 38–107 CE. Jewish historian who visited Rome in 64, aged 26. During the campaign in Galilee in 67 he defected to the Romans. His *Jewish War* was published in Rome *c.* 95. His books were later interpolated to include glowing references to Jesus.

Julian 332–363 CE. Roman Emperor who attempted to revive Paganism after the reign of Constantine *(qv)*. A humane and pious Emperor, he is unfairly known to history as "the apostate."

Julius Caesar 100–44 BCE. Roman general and last of the leaders of the Roman Republic.

Justin Martyr 100–165 CE. Born in Samaria, came to Rome *c.*140. Rejected by Platonic and Pythagorean schools, he later converted to Literalist Christianity. Wrote the first defense of Literalist Christianity and violently attacked Gnostics and Jews.

Lactantius 240–320 CE. After spending his youth immersed in Hermetic philosophy, he converted in 300 to Literalist Christianity. Later appointed by Constantine *(qv)* as tutor to his son Crispus.

Lucian 117–180 CE. Pagan philosopher. Born in Syria, educated at Tarsus, became a teacher of literature in France. Specialized in satire about religious and philosophical frauds. Friend of Celsus *(qv)*.

Mani Born in Babylon in 216 CE. Modeling himself and his teachings on St. Paul *(qv)*, he founded a Gnostic religion, which soon spread across the Roman Empire. St. Augustine *(qv)* was a Manichaean "hearer" for eight years. In the Great Persecution of 303 CE it was Manichaean Christianity that was made the first victim of the purge, followed a year later by all forms of Christianity.

Marc Antony 86–30 BCE. Roman general and lover of Cleopatra. Succeeded Julius Caesar *(qv)*, defeated by Augustus *(qv)*, committed suicide in Egypt.

Marcion Influential Gnostic teacher born in Pontus in Asia Minor, active in Rome *c.*144 CE. He rejected the Old Testament and parts of the gospels that he regarded as falsified. Acknowledged Paul *(qv)* as the "Great Apostle."

Marcus Aurelius Roman Emperor 161–180 CE. Stoic philosopher and author of *Meditations*, his rule marks the high point of the Roman Empire.

Nero 37–68 CE. Roman Emperor from 54 until his death by suicide. His reign began well under the influence of Seneca *(qv)* but then degenerated into tyranny.

Origen 185–254 CE. Born in Alexandria, studied Pagan philosophy with Plotinus *(qv)* under Ammonius Saccus. Became a pupil of Clement *(qv)* and castrated himself in accordance with Matthew 19 v 12. Established a school in Caesaria in 231. Traditionally regarded as a Literalist Christian, his works have far more in common with Gnosticism. Posthumously condemned as a heretic by the Roman Church in the fifth century.

Pachomius 290–346 CE. Egyptian founder of the first Christian monastery near Nag Hammadi in Upper Egypt. The Gnostic gospels were found buried close by. Traditionally regarded as an orthodox Literalist Christian, he was in fact investigated during his lifetime for heresy. He had visions of angels and wrote in a mystical language that has yet to be deciphered. Almost certainly a Gnostic.

Papias We know nothing of him apart from the unreliable accounts of Eusebius and Irenaeus, who tell us he lived in Asia Minor 70–140 CE, where he allegedly heard the apostle John.

Paul Greek-speaking Roman citizen of Tarsus in Asia Minor. Many of his letters are either forged or doctored and his dates are uncertain. It is believed that his mission to Greece lasted from 48 to 53 CE. Traditionally pictured as a Literalist, but claimed by the Gnostics as the great inspiration of Gnosticism.

Pausanias *fl.* 170 CE. Greek travel writer who cryptically records some of the Mystery rites practiced in the temples he visited.

Philo Judaeus 25 BCE–50 CE. An Alexandrian Jew who synthesized the Old Testament with Greek and Pythagorean philosophy. He styled himself as a hierophant of the Jewish Mysteries.

Pindar 518–438 BCE. Greek lyric poet whose work contains some of the earliest references to the doctrines of the Mystery schools.

Plato 429–348 BCE. Disciple of Socrates *(qv)*, founder of the philosophical school in Athens known as the Academy. His philosophy was inspired by the doctrines of the Mysteries, the mysticism of Pythagoras *(qv)*, and the poetry of Orpheus.

Plotinus 204–270 CE. The most influential mystic philosopher after Plato *(qv)*. After 11 years of study in Alexandria with Ammonius Saccus he came to Rome, where his lectures were attended by the Emperor and several senators.

Plutarch 46–125 CE. Philosopher and prolific author of Chaerona in Greece. Priest of Apollo at Delphi for the last 30 years of his life.

Polycarp An early Christian martyr claimed by Irenaeus *(qv)* to have been appointed Bishop of Smyrna by Peter. The story of his martyrdom is clearly legendary, deriving many features from the Jesus story. He rides on an ass to the trial, from an "upper room" where he has been praying, etc. The account given of his execution is simply absurd.

Porphyry 232–303 CE. Pagan philosopher. Born in Tyre, studied philosophy at Athens, converted to Neoplatonism after meeting Plotinus *(qv)* in Rome in 263. Wrote against the Christians in 15 volumes.

Proclus 412–485 CE. Pagan philosopher. Born in Constantinople, studied in Athens. One of the last heads of the Platonic Academy in Athens before its abolition by Justinian in 529 CE.

Protagoras 480–410 CE. First professional philosopher in Athens. Indicted for heresy and put on trial. Escaped and perished at sea.

Pythagoras 581–497 BCE. Philosopher of the Greek island of Samos. Traveled widely in Egypt, Phoenicia, and Babylon, and later founded communities of mystics in the Greek colonies of southern Italy. A hierophant of the Mysteries of Demeter and Dionysus, a poet who wrote works ascribed to Orpheus, a social reformer and scientist. His influence on Plato *(qv)* and the whole Greek philosophical tradition was profound.

Sallustius *fl.* 360 CE. Neoplatonic philosopher and friend of the Emperor Julian *(qv)*. Advised Julian on his attempts to bring about a Pagan revival.

Seneca 4 BCE–65 CE. Roman philosopher and politician. Became a vegetarian follower of Pythagoras *(qv)* in his youth. Later became tutor to Nero *(qv)*.

Sextus Pythagorean philosopher of the second century CE. A collection of his sayings were found among the Nag Hammadi library.

Socrates 469?–399 BCE. The most famous philosopher of antiquity. Executed for heresy in 399 BCE by the council of "Thirty Tyrants" then ruling Athens.

Sophocles 497–406 BCE. Greek tragedian and author of over 100 plays, of which only seven survive.

Suetonius 69–140 CE. Roman historian and author of *The Twelve Caesars*. Friend of Pliny.

Tacitus 55–117 BCE. Roman historian and author of *The Annals of Imperial Rome* and *The Histories*.

Tertullian 160–220 CE. Born in Carthage, became a lawyer in Rome, converted to Literalist Christianity *c.* 195, became a Gnostic in 207.

Timotheus Priest of Eleusis invited to Alexandria by Ptolemy I *c.* 300 BCE to establish the Mysteries.

Valentinus 100–180 CE. Alexandrian Gnostic poet, author of *The Gospel of Truth* found at Nag Hammadi. Founded a school in Rome *c.* 140.

Virgil 70–19 BCE. Roman poet who joined a philosophical community in southern Italy as a youth. His work contains many allusions to the doctrines of the Mysteries, astrology, and the birth of the New Age.

Vitruvius Roman author of 10 books on city planning and architecture dedicated to Augustus *(qv)* *c.* 27 BCE.

Xenophanes 535–435 BCE. Greek philosopher who ridiculed superstitious religion and founded a sect of philosophers in Elea in southern Italy.

Picture credits

The publishers would like to thank the following for the use of pictures:

1   Department of Antiquities, Cyprus
2   (Isis and Horus) Museo Gregoriano Egizio/SCALA
2   (Demeter and Dionysus) Museo della Terme/SCALA
2   (Madonna and Child) Museo Benaki/SCALA
3   The Walters Art Gallery, Baltimore
4   The Art Museum, Princeton University. Museum purchase, John Maclean Magie and Gertrude Magie Fund. Photo: Bruce M. White
5   Museo Nazionale Napoli/SCALA
5   Soprintendenza Archeologica per la Toscana
6   Staatliche Museen zu Berlin, Preußischer Kulturbesitz, Museum für Spätantike und Byzantinische Kunst
7   Antiquarium del Palatino/SCALA
8a) Sammlung Antiker Kleinkunst Friedrich Schiller, Universität Jena
8b) Ipogeo di Via Latina/SCALA

Index

miracles 37–42, 60
Mithras 4, 9, 23, 33, 34, 54, 77, 115
Mithras, Mysteries of 28, 35, 36, 42, 49, 51, 56, 67, 73, 75, 77, 231, 233, 237
Monoimos 103, 115
monotheism 77–82, 87, 233–4
Montanus 221
moon 34
moral purity 65–7, 86
morality, natural 107–8, 110, 170
Moses 181, 182, 187
Moses, Mysteries of 183
Mother of God 57–8
Müller, Prof Max 85
Musaeus 181
myrrh 33, 55, 60, 61
Mystery religions 3–6, 16–26, 203–4, 206, 228
  rites of 16–17
  for specific Mysteries *see* the name of the god
mystical understanding 128–30, 131
mythical understanding 128–30, 131
mythology, Pagan 92–5, 109, 131–2

Naassenes 93
Nag Hammadi texts 7, 90, 91, 197
naked young man (*Mark*) 99
name:
  of God 79
  of Jesus 116–17, 130, 132, 192, 195, 199, 206
nativity 31–4, 60, 192–3, 199, 205
nature worship 16, 79
neighbors, love of 67, 87
Nero 30, 66, 134–5, 333
New Age 75–7, 87
New Testament 72, 85–6, 87, 139–58, 209, 222, 224–5, 238, 248, 254
Nicaea, Council of 236–7,

239, 241
Nicene creed 11, 248

Old Testament 71, 152, 192, 193, 194, 195–6, 199, 222, 224
Olympiodorus 17
one God 77–82, 87, 214
one Truth 86, 100, 111, 255–6
Oneness 18, 24, 83–4, 94, 109, 180, 192, 222
only true faith 253–5
Origen 38, 56, 73, 74, 82, 83, 84, 85, 90, 92, 105, 113–14, 129–30, 137, 205, 217, 229, 230, 232, 238, 242, 333
original sin 54, 61
Orion 33
Orpheus 47, 52, 57, 83
Orpheus, Mysteries of 69, 72
orthodoxy 219–21
Osiris 4, 9, 23, 24–5, 29, 32, 35, 37–8, 44, 48, 56, 93
Osiris, Mysteries of 59, 78, 179–80, 184, 187, 188, 191
Osiris, Passion of 22
Osiris-Dionysus 4, 10, 13, 42, 52, 76, 92–3, 123, 125–6, 131
  Jewish 178–9, 184, 187, 188, 191, 193–4, 195–6, 199, 200, 203, 205, 206, 207
Outer Mysteries 3–4, 14, 21, 25, 93, 128–9
  in Literalist Christianity 90, 97–9, 109, 131, 156, 168, 170, 174, 206, 207, 217–19, 248

Pachomius 333
Paganism 1–6, 15–18
  and Christianity 231–2
  destruction 243–6, 250–1
  in Gnosticism 91–5, 109
  Jewish attitude to 177–88
  and Paul 162–3, 173
Pagels, Elaine 11

palingenesis 59
Pan 32, 93
Papias 224, 333
parables 112
passion plays 54–55
Passover 194
Paul 333
  and Gnosticism 10, 73, 85, 159–74, 225, 248, 256
  and Jesus Mysteries 148–9, 202–3, 217–18
  letters 149, 150–6, 157, 159–60, 164–72, 173, 174, 198, 238, 239
Paul of Samosata 232
Pausanias 85, 333
penitence 66
Peter (Simon Peter) 116, 121, 148–9, 150, 153–4, 162, 225, 236, 238
  letters 210, 212, 216
Phampsinitus 57
pharmakos 53, 152
Phideus 79
Philip 72
Philo Judaeus 66, 112, 132, 136, 178, 182–7, 188, 191, 194, 199, 239, 333
philosophy:
  Pagan 91–2, 109
  in Rome 228
  universal 109, 232, 247
Philostratus 29–30
Pilate, Pontius 45, 46, 133, 135, 136, 142, 200, 206, 223, 239–41
Pindar 17, 333
Plato 17, 29, 49, 51–2, 54, 64, 68, 70–1, 73, 99–100, 104–5, 126, 163, 180–1, 192, 333
Platonism 63–4
Pliny 38, 134, 135, 231
Plotinus 18, 92, 334
plurality 249
Plutarch 20, 44, 56, 59, 72, 73, 85, 104, 116, 125, 179, 230, 334
Pneumatic level 127–8, 164, 168–70, 172, 174, 194, 217
Polycarp 334

Valerian 229
Vatican 1, 12, 236
vegetarianism 69, 246
vengeance 46, 68, 86
Venus 33
Vespasian 137, 233
Virgil 30, 76, 335
virgin birth 5, 6, 29–31,
  60, 76, 141, 196
Vitruvius 83, 335

wandering wonder-
  workers 38–41, 60

water 35, 60, 93, 194
water to wine miracles 38,
  60, 124
water-calming miracles
  39, 60
wine, *see* bread and wine
women:
  as equals 185, 186, 215
  in Gnosticism 106–7,
    110, 161
  subordination 254
  see also Divine
    Feminine

women followers, three
  58, 61
Word, *see* Logos
Wrede, Wilhelm 147

Xenophanes 4, 78, 80,
  335

Zamolix 57
zealots 201–2, 206
Zeus 92, 181
zodiac 42, 92, 95
Zosimos 16

Does the mystical power of the Gnostics really have the power to elucidate the meaning of life and reveal Gnosis?

Timothy Freke and Peter Gandy are now offering lectures and seminars exploring the mystical Inner Mysteries of the ancient Pagans and the original Christians. To find out about forthcoming events or to invite them to your venue:

MAIL: PO Box 2638, Glastonbury, Somerset, BA6 9WF, England
E-MAIL: info@jesusmysteries.demon.co.uk
WEBSITE: www.jesusmysteries.demon.co.uk